Books by MELVILLE J. HERSKOVITS

The Human Factor in Changing Africa (1962)

Cultural Anthropology (1955)

Man and His Works (1948)

Economic Anthropology (1940, 1952)

Life in a Haitian Valley (1937)

The American Negro (1928)

Trinidad Village (WITH FRANCES S. HERSKOVITS, 1947)

These are Borzoi Books

published by

ALFRED A. KNOPF in New York

Books by MELVILLE J. HERSKOVITS

The Human Factor in Changing Africa (1962)

Cultural Anthropology (1955)

Man and His Works (1948)

Economic Anthropology (1940, 1952)

Life In a Haitian Valley (1937)

The American Negro (1928)

Trinidad Village (WITH FRANCES S. HERSKOVITS, 1947)

These are BORZOI BOOKS

published by

ALFRED A. KNOPF *in New York*

The Human Factor in Changing AFRICA

The Human Factor in Changing AFRICA

Melville J. Herskovits

Alfred A. Knopf NEW YORK

1962

L. C. catalog card number: 62–12496

THIS IS A BORZOI BOOK,
PUBLISHED BY ALFRED A. KNOPF, INC.

Manufactured in the United States of America and distributed by Random House, Inc. Published simultaneously in Toronto, Canada by Random House of Canada, Ltd.

FIRST EDITION

You are not a country,

Africa, you are a concept, which we all

Fashion in our minds, each to each, to

Hide our separate years, to dream our separate dreams.

—ABIOSEH NICOL

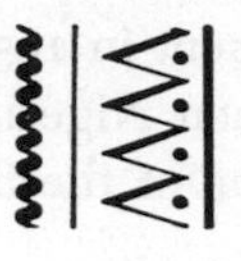 

Preface

How will the historian of the future treat of Africa when he writes of the twentieth century developments in world history that marked the ending of the colonial period? How will he relate the changing attitudes and points of view, inside and outside the continent, that characterized the emergence within a few years of so many new nations, and their projection onto the world scene? How will he balance the innovations brought into Africa against the pull of the precolonial setting?

To one who, like myself, has been privileged to follow this episode in world history from close up, as a scientific observer and, as such, a participant, the implications of these questions inform my view of immediate events, and give perspective in the face of the rapidity of developments. In 1931, when I carried on my first field research in Africa, I lived in the full colonial setting. In 1953, in Lagos, I attended the session of the Nigerian House of Representatives when the withdrawal of members from the Western and Eastern Regions broke the existing constitution and paved the way for self-government seven years later. The same year I was in Kenya during the Mau Mau rebellion and saw how violence, at the opposite pole to constitutional maneuvering, could mark African reaction. I was present in 1957 when Ghana obtained its independence, in 1960 when Nigeria became fully self-governing, in 1961 at the celebration of the first anniversary of the independence of Senegal.

Africa in 1931, in the outer manifestations of its politics, its economies, its urban centers, and in the aspirations of its peoples, was worlds apart from Africa three decades later. At the time of my first field research, not even the most fervent African nationalist—and there were few of them then—would have hazarded a guess that any African territory, much less most of Subsaharan Africa, would be fully self-governing within a little more than a quarter of a century. The path along which colonial control then moved gave few indications of the roadblocks it was soon to encounter.

As an anthropologist, my interest has centered on people. My researches in Africa brought me into the kind of relationship with Africans that revealed the underside of the colonial situation. This relationship sensitized me to the frustrations and resentments that result when any people live under a system where freedom of action, as defined by the values and ends of their culture, is denied them. These reactions occur whether the denials are enforced by those among their own people who have seized power, or are imposed by foreign peoples; but they are especially acute, as the world has found to its cost, when the factor of racial differences enters. In the case of Africa, the strength of the reaction, when it came, was surprising only because of the way in which the capabilities and determination of the Africans had been misjudged by their rulers. For those of us who had come to know Africans as people, surprise lay not in the events themselves, but in the rapidity with which they occurred.

Because my scientific orientation, without neglecting the institutions that provide the structural framework of social life, is directed toward people, this book stresses the human factor in assessing the developments that have marked Africa. In treating of these developments, my primary emphasis is on the reactions of the peoples of Africa to the situations which they have had to meet. Both similarities and differences in those reactions are examined in analyzing the forces that have molded the life of the Subsaharan continent, and this without undue regard for conventional territorial divisions or ethnic affiliation. Critical here is the study of the way in which conservatism, the retention of established custom, and change, the acceptance of innovation, have interacted. This is essential to an understanding of how these forces have functioned, and may be expected to function, in the adaptation of Africans to those who came into the continent, and to what they brought with them.

In consonance with scientific procedure, my approach holds that generalization illumines the particular; while the particular instance which puts the general principle to the test is at the same time in proper focus only when considered as a part of the whole to which it pertains. I have written out of a conviction, developed in the course of many years of concern with the study of Africans and African-derived peoples, that the resources of the science of culture must be used to the full in guiding analysis, if the vast store of information about Africa is to be mobilized to best advantage, both scientific and practical.

To mobilize these resources on a broad comparative level has presented many problems. It has been necessary to organize diffuse data; to seek objectivity in the face of varying quality of source materials, which range from meticulous scientific observation to special pleading; to establish historic depth where the documents are far fewer than in those parts of the world whose history has been intensively studied. Because my aim is analysis, the general principles I advance should be applicable irrespective of current happenings. Therefore this book is written in the past tense; my cut-off date is the end of 1960, the "Year of Africa."

Many of the illustrative materials in this book, and its generalizations, come from my own researches. The materials collected, however, could not be drawn on as freely as I should have liked, being in large part of a confidential nature, frequently with political overtones. It is my intention to arrange for their publication after a safe interval; until then, they must remain restricted.

My experience as Director of the University Interdisciplinary Program of African Studies has also helped significantly in giving me the background needed to embark on a project of this magnitude. I have had close and continuous contact with my colleagues in related disciplines at Northwestern, and have learned much from this association. It has also been my privilege to participate in building a major collection of library materials bearing on Africa. It will be evident in the pages that follow how much I have profited from the researches of the students of the Program who have worked in all parts of Subsaharan Africa, and whose studies I have been able to follow as they progressed from planning to completion.

I have, moreover, been continuously enlightened by the reports of specialists, presented before our weekly Seminar on Contemporary Africa, of which I have been chairman. To this Seminar, which has been meeting since 1948, have come scholars, administrators, missionaries, statesmen, men of affairs, to discuss the areas of their competence. Africans, Europeans, Americans have all contributed to the enlightenment of students and staff on African problems. Thus the presentations over the years of a succession of British, French, and Belgian colonial attachés gives a vivid sense of the evolution of colonial policy, while the statements of African nationalist leaders provide a complementary view of the growth of African independence movements.

The work of the Program has helped me in other ways. Those who spoke before our Seminar, or who were invited to the University for longer periods as Visiting Professors, like the Africans who studied in it, knew the long interest in African Studies at the University, and observed at first hand the intellectual position taken in discussion, and the independence of political commitment in our studies. As a result, doors in Africa were readily opened to my colleagues, our students, and myself. As I traveled about the continent, I was able to observe and hear discussed with frankness the problems of the territories I visited, and to break through reserves that were otherwise the rule on both sides of racial and administrative barriers.

All these factors have combined to make it possible for me, over the years, to approach the African scene from what has long seemed to me a most fortunate position for one engaged in the scientific study of the changing cultures of the continent. Being a national of a country without African colonial commitments was also of value, for it permitted a degree of psychological and geographical detachment which enabled me to take the broad view, projecting the insights gained from intensive research against the totality of similarities and differences that mark the realities of African life.

We have come to know that there is more than one Africa. Yet in rejecting the outworn stereotype, we must not move to the other extreme. As in any continental land mass, there are similarities that underlie the differences. I began my research, many years ago, with a question: How have the aboriginal similarities and differences in African culture been affected by the similarities and differences in the innovations to which the peoples of Africa and African descent have been exposed? I have not answered this question, but such beginnings as I have been able to make are to be found in this book.

Certain matters of usage may briefly be mentioned. One has to do with terminology. In principle, I have used the words that are common in writings about Africa, with due regard for the historical and political realities and the sensibilities of the peoples concerned. Thus I do not employ "native" because it is intensely disliked by Africans. I call a white person a European, whether he was born in Africa or not. In this I follow customary usage in Africa. Indians, Goans, and Arabs are generally grouped as Asians; I have followed this means of naming them where these subgroups have not been differentiated. There are various ways of spelling the designation of followers of Islam; I use the American form "Moslem" rather than the English "Muslim," though I know certain Nigerian Moslems prefer the English spelling.

Names of countries are those of the period under discussion. That is, when a national name has been changed, I use the one appropriate to the time referred to. Thus the Soudan is called by that name if a given event occurred during French rule, before it became Mali. Similarly, Ghana before independence is called the Gold Coast.

The use of certain terms commonly found in writings about Africa was unavoidable, even though they have not as yet become current. One of these is "Metropole," a French word meaning the country that governs a colony. "Infrastructure" is another. It means the basic human and technical resources essential to social and economic growth, such as roads, schools, telecommunication systems, hospitals, all of which need large-scale investment and are for use by society as a whole rather than by private interests alone.

I have drawn on the original French, Portuguese and German sources for data, as well as the English, and on Arabic sources in English and French translation. Except for the Arabic, I have myself translated quotations from non-English sources, with a few exceptions where adequate translations are available.

The *Bibliography* includes only those works which I have actually used. Long though the list may be, it represents but a minute portion of those books, pamphlets, manuscripts and periodical articles that might have been used. No one is more conscious than I of the works of high quality which I could also have called on, nor more regretful that considerations of space and the law of limiting returns in documenting my points prevented including all the studies I should have liked to include, and which must be present in any comprehensive bibliography of writings on Africa.

As with any research in the study of man, my foremost indebtedness is to those who have given me the basic facts for this book. From Africans, urban and rural, in all walks of life, from European officials, from European, American and Indian business and professional men, and from Christian missionaries and Islamic scholars, I have learned much of what I know about the continent. My obligation to the writers, past and present, on whose works I have drawn, is also apparent from the citations in the text.

The administrative officers of Northwestern University have consistently and generously given material and moral support for my research, and for the development of our Program of African Studies on whose resources I have drawn. Most recently, the award of the President's Fellowship gave me the release from university duties that allowed me to finish writing this book. I acknowledge with gratitude the various grants of the Carnegie Corporation of New York and of the Ford Foundation, which have so liberally aided my work through support for the Program; of the Fulbright Foundation, the American Council of Learned Societies, the Penrose Fund of the American Philosophical Society, the Social Science Research Council, and the Graduate School of Northwestern University. Their grants have literally made possible my researches. I record my gratitude as well to the two persons who, years ago when there was no interest in African studies in the United States, provided for my initial field-trip to Africa, Professor Franz Boas and Dr. Elsie Clews Parsons.

I also wish to thank those who have helped me in the actual preparation of this book. Certain chapters, or the manuscript in full, have been read by Desmond Clark, Kenneth Diké, Willard De Pree, Creighton Gabel, Thomas Hodgkins, Bruce Johnson, and Igor and Jean Kopytoff. Their suggestions have been of much value. The staff of Deering Library, especially David Jolly, Assistant Librarian, and Hans Panofsky, Curator of Africana, have been most helpful. Anne Moneypenny and Doris Paterson, my secretaries, have done a great deal, in many ways, to assist in bringing this work to completion. The manuscript has greatly benefited from the expert and benevolent surveillance of Harold Strauss and Sophie Wilkins of Alfred A. Knopf, Inc.

My deepest gratitude goes to my wife, who has participated in the fieldwork on which this book is based, and has been my collaborator in the writing of several volumes. Her extensive knowledge of Africa, and her sensitive interest in the values of African life have led to stimulating discussions as the writing proceeded; her comments on the whole manuscript, at every stage, have been invaluable.

MELVILLE J. HERSKOVITS

Evanston, Illinois
August 22, 1961

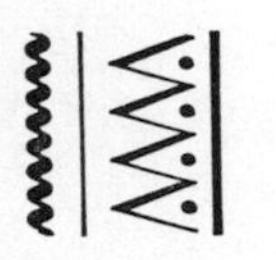

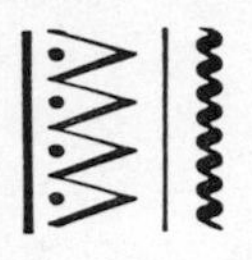

Contents

MAPS

DRAWN BY WILLIAM A. NORMAN

The Human Factor in Changing AFRICA

1

The World Setting

AFRICA, when seen in perspective, was a full partner in the development of the Old World, participating in a continual process of cultural give-and-take that began long before European occupation. Neither isolation nor stagnation tell the tale. It is as incorrect to think of Africa as having been for centuries isolated from the rest of the world as it is to regard the vast area south of the Sahara as "darkest Africa," whose peoples slumbered on until awakened by the coming of the dynamic civilizations of Europe. The only area of the world that had no contact with the others during most of the existence of man on earth was the Americas.

In this spread of culture, Africa was a donor as well as a recipient. Statements in scientific literature that "not a single animal or plant of primary economic importance was domesticated in Africa south of the Sahara,"[1] have been found to be untenable. They could not stand against the findings of agronomists who traced the origin of such economic crops as rice, sorgho, various species of millet, perhaps eleusine, two species of yams, and such oil-bearing plants as the oil-palm and the sesames to West

[1] Ralph Linton: *The Tree of Culture* (New York, 1955), p. 95.

African centers alone.[2] It has even been suggested that agriculture was independently invented in the western Sudan, "before it had diffused from Asia to the lower Nile." [3] The contributions of Africa to music and narrative, and to the graphic and plastic arts, are generally recognized. Narratives, particularly animal tales, though by no means only these, which are found in most of Europe and southern Asia as well as Africa, were diffused so long ago that the process defies dating and any attempts to ascertain direction of spread. The African contribution to world music, however, is more recent, and is well documented.

The later impact of the arts was direct; but as we shall see, music provides us with an example of how complex this relationship of Africa with the outer world could be. Europe, in what is called the epoch of discovery, brought the New World into contact with the Old, and with the passage of time caused large parts of North and South America to be peopled with Africans as well as Europeans. The Africans, singing their songs in accordance with their own musical patterns, in America altered these patterns as they were exposed to the music of the Europeans, and developed forms that are variously called jazz, or the calypso, or the rhumba or the samba. By mid-twentieth century, these forms had diffused not only to Europe and Asia, but had rediffused to Africa itself, so that in Accra and Lagos and Leopoldville and Salisbury and Johannesburg, local expressions of these New World constructs were to be heard.

The impact of the outside world on Africa has been given far more attention than has been the influence of Africa on Europe and Asia. Both currents of cultural diffusion must be borne in mind if we are to see the entire picture of the position of Africa in the world. The derivation of cattle, which play so large a role in the culture of peoples who inhabit the great stretch of eastern Africa from north of the lakes region southward, almost to the Cape, provides one example of how cultural elements from the

[2] Roland Portères: "Vieilles agricultures de l'Afrique intertropicale," *L'Agronomie Tropicale,* Nos. 9–10 (September–October 1950), *passim.*

[3] George P. Murdock: *Africa, Its Peoples and Their Culture History* (New York, 1959), pp. 64–70.

other continents of the Old World influenced Africa. While some of the cattle found in the area appear to be of indigenous ancestry, most of them are descended from Asian stock.[4] Maize, on the other hand, which most botanists agree must have come from the New World, is of recent diffusion, dating after the discovery of the Americas. But it is more than just maize that the coastal Africans received from the sixteenth century voyagers, who had got the plant from the American Indians, its domesticators. They brought over an entire agricultural complex. Maize was planted in rows, as in the Americas, rather than sown broadcast, as was the method used in planting cereals in Europe. In West Africa, the seeds were put in together with those of gourds, so that the latter could run along between the rows, and with beans, so the vines could climb on the stalks. And by the time of European expansion in Africa, maize had diffused over the entire continent, in many regions having become a major source of food, the starchy staple most abundantly produced in 1950.[5]

It would be strange indeed, when dealing with an area as vast as Africa south of the Sahara, if students of its peoples and cultures did not restrict their attention to it, or to a particular part of it. To make the point, we need but think of how varied are its indigenous languages and cultures, or how different the influences that came from the European nations that have ruled it, each with its own colonial policies, and of all this implies in the way of shaping the course of cultural change. Yet in a world where the speed of communication has constantly increased and the pursuit of scientific knowledge has provided us with ever broader generalizations for the study of human adjustment, isolationism on any level cannot be defended.

The fact that change in Africa came to command almost exclusive interest in assessing the African scene underscored this need to consider all contributory causes in studying a given problem. Even though change came to be a striking aspect of African life, the dynamic of Africa falls into place when we recog-

[4] Caesar R. Boettger: *Die Haustiere Afrikas* (Jena, 1958), pp. 56 ff.

[5] Marvin P. Miracle: "Maize in Tropical African Agriculture," *Tropical Agriculture*, Vol. XXXV (1958), p. 12.

nize that it is but a special case of a universal mechanism of cultural change; one that has probably been present ever since man has lived on earth. This mechanism is called cultural diffusion, or culture-contact, or acculturation. In essence, it means that whenever peoples having different customs come together, they modify their ways by taking over something from those with whom they newly meet. They may take over much or little, according to the nature and intensity of the contact, or the degree to which the two cultures have elements in common, or differ in basic orientations. But they never take over or ignore all; some change is inevitable.

The diffusion of culture is of course not the only concept that the sciences of man have developed that can be used to understand events in Africa. But even this single instrument of analysis proves its value in deepening our comprehension. Employing the principle of the diffusion of culture we can grasp the proper historical position of Africa as a full participant in the development of human civilization, as a continent that has contributed much of its own to other cultures, as well as one whose cultures received ideas and artifacts from outside. It thus becomes pointless to speak of Africa as moving into a wider world. Indeed, she was never out of it.

[2]

Realization of the growing importance of Africa after the Second World War caused attention to be increasingly focused on the changes taking place there. Industrialization and the growth of cities had their impact on traditional social structures. The development of schools and universities; the exploitation of newly discovered mineral resources and the utilization of hydroelectric potential; the emergence of political parties with nationalistic and culturally based ideologies expressed in concepts of *négritude* and the "African personality" all came to attract the attention of scholars and men of affairs. The interactions between missionary effort, Christian and Moslem, and the belief systems of the Africans, became an important concern of African humanists.

Investigations concentrated for the most part on the innovations in African life, and were centered on the changes brought about by contact with the cultures of Europe and, to a lesser degree, of the Americas and Asia. It is to be noted here that emphasis on change was conditioned by a complex of ideas, held in Africa no less than in Europe, which accepted it as axiomatic that the future of African development lay in the transfer to the continent of the knowledge and the techniques brought from the outside, and for an unpredictably extended future to be directed by outsiders. One result of this reasoning was that the African was too often lost sight of. The approach was focused on institutions, not on people; on social change, without taking into account current and antecedent modes of doing, behaving, and valuing, the elements that make for cultural continuity.

These human factors are, however, of primary relevance in understanding both change and continuity in culture. Accepting this premise does not imply that the institutions of a developing Africa are of secondary importance. Rather, they take on additional significance, because they are the end product of responses called forth in human beings. It is for this reason that our analyses are framed by the concepts and theories of cultural anthropology, and utilize the methods of the scientific study of culture in taking a cross-cultural point of view. Because it is a cardinal tenet of scientific method that all relevant factors must be taken into account, the cultural base from which change has come and the place of established tradition in shaping responses to innovation will therefore have to be given full consideration.

This, however, is not always easy. Changes are far more readily discernible than is the retention of old customs. To those who were focusing their attention on the whole way of life of African peoples it became clear that the older, pre-European patterns had by no means given way. On the contrary, the traditional patterns showed such vitality as to confound observers who, not grounded in the scientific analysis of the results of contact between peoples, approached the African scene emphasizing such concepts as detribalization and demoralization. Questions as different as those bearing on economic development or the future of missionary activity were too often formulated on the assumption that the traditional habits of thought and patterns of behavior were being superseded and abandoned under foreign influence.

Because the more dramatic manifestations of the movements toward African self-determination were political, these tended to receive more attention than other phases of the African scene. In part, this emphasis flowed logically from the fact that everywhere the strategy of these movements centered on the capture of the machinery of government as the prerequisite of self-determination. The nature of the strategy, too, was dictated by the fact that colonial controls, and the structure of power erected to maintain them, were essentially political, though by extension, economic and social institutions were also subjected to special pressures. Therefore, whether the struggles for self-determination were peaceful, as in the majority of cases—a fact too often overlooked when these movements were discussed—or resorted to force, the instruments of government had to be the immediate objective.

Beneath these political, social, and economic factors lay the whole range of other kinds of institutions, traditions, and beliefs that make up the total culture of a people. Each element in this complex whole—education, art, religion, music, language, the accepted scale of values—was to some degree affected by the imposition of foreign rule, and each in its own way had to readjust to changes toward autonomy. Although preconquest patterns persisted everywhere in Africa, even in the face of strong measures to change them, it was not likely that the innovations brought to peoples from overseas would be given up entirely when self-rule was obtained.

What we must understand is that the revolutions that made for African independence represent historical continuities. This holds true whatever phrases about a break with the past, heard in earlier days when the influence of colonialism was discussed, were later used to sanction African political aspirations. It must be emphasized that to give full weight to all aspects of African culture does not lessen the importance of developments in the social, economic and political fields, any more than in giving full consideration to individual responses we neglect the institutions of African societies. It is rather that these human responses, which undoubtedly sparked the drive toward self-government, are but part of a broader spectrum.

Putting this in terms of the science of culture that provides the framework for our analysis, we regard change as essentially a manifestation of a more inclusive process, to be fully grasped only when seen against a background of the retention of older ways. Both these represent adaptations which, at a given moment of history, make for a unified mode of life. Our task, then, in seeking to understand the dynamic of Subsaharan Africa will essentially be to balance the forces of conservatism and change, both as these have shaped the institutions of African society, and as they have affected African responses to the new in terms of the old.

[3]

The proposition that the place of Africa in the world of the future was to be determined by Africans began to be given serious attention in mid-twentieth century. Its implications went directly contrary to a point of view that had for some time dominated world opinion concerning Africa. This view held the Africans to be an inchoate mass, lying inert under the hand of those endowed with a wisdom which, in the final test, could be implemented by recourse to power. In this system of thought, which characterized the period of colonial control, Africans were regarded as highly malleable, a people whose destiny it was to be molded into the image their tutors delineated for them. The human resources of the continent were thought of as a supplementary resource, rather than as a force in being.

In most discussions of practical problems, policies and plans were phrased in terms of what was to be done for Africans, or to Africans, or with Africans. Decisions, even when made with patent good will, were reached unilaterally, and only rarely were Africans themselves consulted. The role of Africans, when participation was allowed, tended to be consultative; African initiative was not encouraged. The rationale of this was based on a formula which, as variously phrased, stipulated that since it had required five hundred, or seven hundred, or a thousand or two thousand years to develop European civilization, it was unrealistic to expect Africans to master the complexities of this way of life in the half century they had been exposed to it.

Underlying these expressions of policy and opinion, however, lay certain other assumptions that were contradictory to this line of thought, and thus encouraged the idea that the future of Africa must lie in the hands of Africans. The most important of these hidden premises was that, given time and opportunity—the amount of time or the degree of opportunity are beside the point here—Africans would eventually master the complexities of European ways. Another, which reinforced this first assumption, found expression in the reiterated assertion that the guardian had an obligation to prepare his ward for self-government, and for participation in a world society.

Estimates of the time needed for the Africans to achieve self-determination shrank rapidly after the Second World War. Before then, except for some Africans who urged greater responsibility be laid on their people, the question was not often given serious thought. When the doctrine of the Four Freedoms was enunciated, the formula became more precise and, as Africans became more active in government, the time span to self-determination was set at two hundred, then fifty, then twenty-five years. Toward the end of the war, the prediction was heard that the Gold Coast would be self-governing in ten years, an estimate that proved to be accurate when Ghana became independent in 1957. But for the rest of the continent, timing remained vague until about 1955, when there was a rapid change in opinion, epitomized by the statement of a high official of the Kenya Government who, in 1953, at the height of the Mau-Mau uprising, said, "the answer to our problem in Africa will be found in how well the three million Europeans can adapt to the hundred and fifty million Africans who live south of the Sahara." [6] By 1958,

[6] Melville J. Herskovits: *Notes on African Field Research, 1953–60* (manuscript), p. 53/D602.

this point of view had become so prevalent that a Southern Rhodesian journal could write of Kenya,

> There are six million Africans in Kenya to 200,000 Asians and 60,000 Whites. No dam woven of fancy franchises can hold back the pressure of that majority indefinitely in the world of today, nor can the complexities of an ingeniously balanced colonial legislature, special members and all, for long divert it.[7]

North of a line drawn along the northern borders of Angola, Southern Rhodesia and Mozambique, the principle of eventual primacy of the African in African affairs came to be accepted, albeit in some countries with more reluctance than in others. The British and French, and later, the Belgians made it a major element of policy, accepting it as an inevitability. South of the line the doctrine of earlier days continued to hold, but it rested uneasily in the thinking of the Europeans. *Apartheid*, no less than the concept of multiracial partnership, implied recognition of some degree of African control over African affairs. It soon became apparent that both these concepts were advanced as expedients for the preservation of European supremacy in the face of world opinion, and of the constantly increasing pressure by Africans for greater participation in the life of the countries where they lived. With time, it came to reflect a growing anxiety that the African would not only insist on exercising controls, but was fully capable of assuming the responsibilities he was demanding, whether the concepts were phrased, as in the Union of South Africa and in Portugal, as the need to maintain an outpost of "civilization," or as in Rhodesia, as implementing the policy of Cecil Rhodes of "equal rights for all civilized men."

This questioning of assumptions long held, even where the drive for African participation was most vigorously contested, may be seen in a statement such as was published in 1957 by the Afrikaner South African Bureau for Racial Affairs:

> It is sometimes argued that the advancement of civilization as is known in the western world is a slow process. It is pointed out that

[7] Anonymous: "Mr. Mboya Asks for More," *The Central African Examiner*, Vol. I, No. 25 (1958), p. 16.

it took Europe and America centuries to attain the standard of development of modern times, and that it will similarly take the indigenous people of Africa centuries before they can attain the same level of development. This argument is extremely vulnerable. Western techniques have to a great extent altered the time factor in nearly every direction of development. The speed at which Africa's people may acquire the same level of technical skill characteristic of western civilization should be seen in this perspective. . . . The time is fast drawing near when the non-white people in Africa will have attained the same level of technical skill characteristic of the modern industrialized world. The cultural gulf between people is slowly being bridged and the underdeveloped people of today will acquire in decades what we have slowly learned through centuries . . . Being the only indigenous white people in Africa with no other mother country, we in South Africa at least should read the signs of the times and bring about a new understanding in regard to policies and approach in our dealings with a people who is being and have been reborn.[8]

Only in Portuguese territory did a carry-over persist of the ideas of classic colonialism concerning the place of Africans in the African scheme of things, and even here a certain malaise could be detected. This malaise was evidenced by such measures as employing the legal strategy of changing the juristic position of Portuguese colonies by proclaiming them to be provinces of the Metropole, by making it more difficult for Africans, as *assimilados,* "assimilated persons," to achieve citizenship, and by establishing for them a special system of preprimary "rudimentary" education. As for Africans elsewhere, even in South Africa, they came to take it for granted that the future was theirs—and this rather sooner than later.

The fact is that whatever the theories or policies, within the space of two decades the African emerged as a factor of key importance, and in his own right. In another context, one prominent West African phrased the larger question when he asked, "Are we a part of the problem, or of the answer?"[9] In these terms,

[8] Anonymous: *SABRA Nuusbrief* (July–August, 1957), No. 25, p. 3.

[9] J. H. Ayorinde: *Nigerian Radio Times,* Vol. IV (1957), No. 5, pp. 3, 10.

Africa could be studied in full perspective, as part of a world-wide movement to re-establish the autonomy of peoples by doing away with foreign controls. So significant was this, and so far-reaching its implications, that the twentieth century may well come to be known as the Century of Self-Determination. As a writer in the London *Times* put it, "In a hundred years' time the Africans will still be in Africa. The question is, will the Europeans?" [1]

[4]

Though African movements for racial, economic and political self-determination cannot be understood unless they are projected against the broader screen of the relations of Africa with the outer world since earliest times, the particular characteristics of the African picture must not be lost sight of. Outstanding here is the factor of time, more especially the span of time during which Subsaharan Africa was under foreign control. Compared with the rest of what once was the colonial world, the experience of most of Africa in this respect has been relatively short. The expansion of Europe began during the fifteenth century, but except for the negative influence of the slave trade, Europe in reality touched but lightly on Africa until toward the end of the nineteenth century. There were European forts and factories dotted along the coast for trade in gold, ivory, or human cargo for much of the period when Africa was in contact with Europe, and Africa furnished way stations on the sea routes to the Indies. Though it would be inaccurate to underestimate the repercussions of the slave trade on the economic, political, and social life of Africa, it is well to recognize that from the point of view of later developments, what the trade took from Africa, and the attitudes to which it gave rise, left the more deep-seated and more ramified impact.

The brevity of the period of time between the onset of colonial control in Africa south of the Sahara and the end of the colonial system is one reason why the dynamic of Africa ap-

[1] Anonymous: "Blunderbuss," *The London Times* (Jan. 14, 1959), p. 9.

peared to be so striking. The six or seven decades during which the bulk of the continent existed as a series of colonial possessions stand in contrast to the time that Indonesia and other countries of the Far East existed as dependencies, or the more than three centuries during which most of the Americas were under foreign rule. Yet the difference between Subsaharan Africa and these other countries, whether we take degree of literacy, or of urbanization, or of industrialization as our criterion, is really not so great when all of them are contrasted to Europe and North America, the areas used as touchstones when comparisons of this kind are drawn.

When we ask why Africa was thus overlooked in the extension of European control, the answer is usually given in terms of geography. Certainly such physical aspects as its smooth, unindented coast line, the great interior plateau that made it impossible to penetrate the heart of the continent by ship—as was so easily done, for example, in North America—are not to be disregarded. But these do not justify the place they have been assigned in discussing the African past. This overemphasis has been largely responsible for the fiction of an Africa that for centuries lay dormant, out of contact with the rest of the world, impervious to the impulses emanating from centers of civilization—the essence of the myth epitomized by the phrase "darkest Africa."

It is quite true that for the Europeans who came by sea, contact with Africa was difficult, and conquest more so. But it should never be forgotten that for millennia the Sahara was no barrier. The caravan routes across the desert, known from medieval times,[2] indicate that the presumed isolation of Africa was, in actuality, never true as far as the trans-Saharan Arabic world was concerned, and far less true for Europe than is ordinarily stated. Moreover, the role of the Indian Ocean is usually ignored in drawing the "darkest Africa" stereotype, despite the continuous contact with the eastern world that we know came from the traffic it carried.

[2] E. W. Bovill: *Caravans of the Old Sahara, an Introduction to the History of the Western Sudan* (London, 1933), pp. 23–5.

Of equal importance in understanding the lateness of European expansion into Africa is what may be termed the historic factor. Compared to the Indies, Africa had little to offer the Europeans seeking the gold, the spices, the silks and all of the other luxuries that stimulated the movement in its early days. Africa could provide manpower in the form of slaves, but since it was simpler to arm the Africans and to stimulate the flow of slaves through intertribal warfare than to penetrate the continent and obtain them first-hand, slaves were brought to the coastal settlements by African intermediaries, to be transported to the West Indies and North and South America for work on the plantations there. Africa, too, yielded some gold and ivory, but compared with the wealth obtained from Peru or the East Indies this was not of marked importance. And while North America furnished an outlet for the growing surplus populations of Western Europe, in tropical Africa the greater numbers of Africans in comparison to the American Indians, the organized armies of native African kingdoms, as well as the deterrents of climate and disease made permanent settlement by colonists well-nigh impossible until the late nineteenth century, and then only in the eastern and southern parts of the continent.

As a result, most Africans lived their lives little touched by European influences for almost four centuries after initial contact. But it cannot be too strongly emphasized that during this time Africa was not stagnant. Currents of contact and conquest surged through the continent. The people, in short, were working out their own historical development, until the wave of European expansion swept over them and added external political pressures to internal historical drives.

The Treaty of Berlin, which sanctioned the partition of Africa among the Powers of Europe, was signed in 1885. It regularized what were in many respects existing commitments regarding territories barely known. Explorers had penetrated further and further into the western, central and eastern parts of the continent—Livingstone, Stanley, Brazza, Speke, du Chaillu, Barth, Serpa Pinto, the Landers, are only a few of the long roll that could be called.[3] Yet except for the southernmost portion, actual occupation was at that time confined to a narrow coastal belt. Islamic penetration from the north stopped at the forest, and in the east was sporadic except along the coast. In any event this was disregarded by the Europeans except where, as in the north, these rivals lay athwart the path of conquest or, as in eastern and central Africa, Arab slaving operations gave the rationale for their expulsion.

The period between effective penetration and the development of what, for want of a better phrase, may be called movements toward the re-establishment of African autonomy was, in actuality, about the same everywhere. This fact has usually been glossed over in discussing the adaptation to cultural innovations that Africans in different parts of the continent have made. Especially in the regions where there was a substantial amount of permanent European settlement, those who argued for the continuance of minority dominance over the indigenous population stressed this point. The African in eastern, central and southern Africa was undoubtedly slower in attaining the knowledge necessary for his effective participation in the post-European social, economic and political life than in West Africa. But was this because Europe was in contact so much earlier with West Africa, and for so much longer a time; or, as the phrasing usually ran, because in West Africa the African had a longer opportunity to benefit from contact with "civilization" and to learn its ways?

This argument scarcely stands when the historic facts are examined. Kumasi, the capital of the Ashanti kingdom, was taken over in 1901, about the same time as Lord Delamere established white settlement in Kenya. Abomey, the capital of the kingdom of Dahomey, and Sokoto, the center of one of the Northern Nigerian Emirates, were taken in 1894, four years after what became the territory of Southern Rhodesia was occupied. The kingdom of Kongo had for centuries been in European hands, but the Congo Free State, which brought Belgians into the interior, was only established in 1885. The beginnings of effective Portuguese

[3] Robert Cornevin: *Histoire des Peuples de l'Afrique Noire* (Paris, 1960), pp. 41–4.

occupation of the hinterland of Angola date from a decade after, about the same time the native peoples of Tanganyika were coming into sustained contact with the Germans.

Nor is the argument cogent in the light of our knowledge of the nature and processes of cultural learning. Time may indeed be a factor of significance, but of itself exposure to contact with peoples having a different way of life means little when opportunity and motivation do not enter. Meeker's comment is to the point: "There is no empirical evidence that an East African can't learn from scratch just as fast as any other sort of man."[4] There were too many East Africans who, coming from a fully indigenous background, mastered European languages and culture sufficiently to meet the rigorous standards for the higher academic and professional degrees to allow any other conclusion to be validly drawn. As one English scholar put it: "First generation literates come to Oxford and get degrees with first-class honors —and they don't just give away firsts at Oxford."

There is, moreover, little evidence that mere juxtaposition of peoples can work changes of significance in their ways of life. These do occur under contact, far more often than not, and are to be seen in Africa, for example, in the way in which guns and gunpowder supplemented bows and arrows and spears long before European occupation and control were established. But this is quite a different thing from asserting that length of contact must of itself be an effective factor in cultural change. Attempts to employ this argument in establishing a greater degree of competence on the part of West Africans to control their own affairs, in contrast to those of East and Central and South Africa, fell on scientific no less than historical grounds. The point is raised here because of the part it played in interpretations of change in Africa, especially in accounting for the differences in the reactions of the peoples of eastern and western Africa to European control. We shall later examine the extent to which these reactions were solely to be attributed to length of contact, or whether the differences in the aboriginal cultures of these two

[4] Odin Meeker: *Report on Africa* (New York, 1954), p. 305.

parts of the Subsaharan continent, and the difference in the proportion of Europeans in them, did not also play a major part.

[5]

In any discussion of African matters, it is essential that the word "Africa" be strictly defined. Too often we are confronted with works bearing the name of the continent which turn out to be concerned with only a part of it. Thus Delafosse's *The Negroes of Africa: History and Culture* dealt essentially with the history and cultures of West Africa, more particularly with French West Africa; Field Marshal Smuts' *Africa and Some World Problems* focused almost entirely on the Union of South Africa; and Chukwuemeka's *African Dependencies* limited its discussion to Nigeria.

This book deals with the subcontinent of Africa south of the Sahara, or, as we shall call it, Subsaharan Africa. This delimitation is in accord with historical, cultural, ethnic, and linguistic realities. It also corresponds to geographical realities, if we move from the accepted convention that separates Africa from the other parts of what is in actuality a single land mass, comprising Asia and Europe as well.

This is not the place to consider how and why the convention that divides this great land mass into three continents came about, but it developed at a relatively late date. "Africa is a Peninsula so large, that it comprises the third part, and this the most southerly, of our Continent," is how it appeared to the Geographer Royal of France, writing in 1656.[5] The convention, while it serves a purpose, exhibits the weakness of any arbitrary classification, in that its parts tend to have an ascribed reality not inherent in them. We need do no more than consider the boundary between Europe and Asia to recognize how arbitrary it is, with only a relatively minor mountain range separating the two, and with the political entity of the Soviet Union lying on both

[5] N. Sanson: *L'Afrique en Plusiers Cartes Novvelles, et Exactes: & en Divers Traicte's de Geographie, et d'Histoire:* . . . . (Paris, 1656), p. 1 of sig. A.

sides of it, introducing historical and cultural contradictions into the accepted geographical division. Africa as a continent is integrally a part of this larger whole. The Mediterranean, the Red Sea, are stressed when the separateness of Africa is discussed, yet not long ago, as geological time goes, the former was a series of interior lakes, while the latter is but an extension of the Great Rift Valley of East Africa.

In terms of cultural and historical understanding, the effect of separating the single Old World land mass into these three parts was to distort the relations between them. As we have already seen, this division was an important element in causing Africa to be regarded as the Dark Continent. It caused us to underscore the differences between Africa and the other two continents, and to disregard similarities of the kind we have mentioned earlier in this chapter. It obscured the ease with which the paths of cultural diffusion disregarded these artificial conventions, as in the wide spread of the complex that centers about respect for elders and ancestors found in all Africa and northern Asia; or in the world view that, in ancient Greece as in West Africa, envisages the gods as being organized into family groupings; or in forms of magic not found outside the Old World, so that the spell of the witches in "Macbeth" would be understandable to any African without further explanation, but would have to be explained to a Polynesian or to an American Indian.

When we turn to Africa itself, we find that, despite similarities arising out of particular historic developments, it is useful to distinguish Africa north of the Sahara and the parts of it that lie to the south. As a student phrased it in 1933, "Conditions in North Africa, with the early history of Carthaginian and Roman influence, and the marked differences between Egypt, Tripoli, or Morocco, and the rest of the continent, have made it seem advisable to restrict the area dealt with to the central and southern portion. . . ."[6] In doing this we do not disregard what these two regions have in common. Both, for the most part, experienced colonial control, and this brought comparable results, such as the

[6] G. St. J. Orde Browne: *The African Labourer* (London, 1933), p. 5.

introduction of European educational patterns, movements which expressed a striving for self-government, or the development of industrialization. Not to recognize the relationship between North and southerly Africa would also be to fly in the face of an important historic fact already mentioned, that the Sahara has been a highway, nor a barrier to communication, and to disregard the principles of cultural dynamics that find expression through the processes of diffusion. One need but see Touareg caravans at Niamey, or realize that much of Morocco leather comes from Kano, to understand something of the nature and duration of these trans-Saharan contacts. Nonetheless, the line drawn in this book is in accordance with these historical, linguistic, cultural and religious realities already mentioned, that reflect the basic facts of African experience; and, in addition, take into account the ethnic or racial differences which, though of minor significance in the context of any analysis of cultural differences, cannot pass without mention.

The degree of variation in the cultures of Subsaharan Africa itself likewise poses questions concerning the nature and extent of the cultural similarities and differences it displays. That considerable differences do exist there is as true as of any other major area of the world. Yet the underlying similarities in its cultures, to say nothing of the historical contacts among its peoples as revealed by these similarities, give it a unity recognized not only by scholarly observers but also reflected in the writings of the early explorers, missionaries and government officials.

There have been two sorts of reaction to the similarities and differences that are found in Subsaharan Africa. They derive from the basic orientation, training, and experience of the individual observer, as indicated in the kind of facts he emphasizes and his way of handling them. There was undoubtedly a reaction against the popular view that all of Negro Africa was far more homogeneous than it was in fact; the familiar idea of undifferentiated Africa as mostly jungle, overrun by great herds of wild animals, inhabited by human beings classed as "savages."

This idea arose at first out of the accounts given by the early explorers, who were fascinated by the exotic qualities of the

African natural and cultural landscapes, and on whose memories the great hardships they experienced were vividly impressed, so that in writing they tended to overstress them. On the human side, it was reinforced by a benevolent racism. In the spirit of nineteenth century expansionism, the early writers simply held the superiority of their own culture as beyond any question, and responded, perhaps unconsciously, to the stereotypes of the African which grew out of the abolitionist controversy. The picture they drew of Africa and the African was continued in the travel books, the motion pictures, and in many cases the reports of missionaries who, in their bush stations, knew little of the changes that were taking place in the more populous areas, and tended to portray an Africa that in time became less and less typical. All these factors contributed to a prevalent state of ignorance that caused one student of African affairs to speak of the United States as "darkest America"; a state of ignorance shared, surprisingly enough, by the general public even of those countries having possessions in Africa.

As the problems of Subsaharan Africa came to be studied more systematically, a clearer view of the cultural variations over the continent began to appear. Differentiations of the cultures on the basis of ecological setting and primary economic organization were made as early as 1880 by F. Ratzel (1896), the geographer, followed four decades later by a series of ethnographic classifications drawn as cultural areas.[7] Works dealing with a given territory, with a particular district, with a single tribal grouping, became available in increasing numbers. For those with restricted firsthand experience, the gain from analysis in depth, though paid for by a narrowing of perspective, provided a valuable corrective for a picture that had been painted on too large a scale. Such investigations, especially those carried out in line with scientific principles, laid the base for a return to more comprehensive analyses, grounded on a far firmer foundation than any earlier study could have been.

Most writings that attempted to envisage Subsaharan Africa

[7] Melville J. Herskovits: "A Preliminary Consideration of the Culture Areas of Africa," *American Anthropologist*, Vol. XXVI (1924), *passim.*

as a whole tended to take up one territory after another, discussing the salient aspects of its geography, population, native cultures, and economy, in terms of the policies under which it was ruled. This was true of most of the books written primarily to enlighten the lay public, such as those by Meeker (1954) already referred to, or by Gunther (1955). Other works, written for a more restricted audience, were a combination of the country-by-country presentation and an overall analysis of a particular field. In this category would be the geographical studies by Fitzgerald (1952), Stamp (1953), and Kimball (1960); or the anthropological works of Baumann and Westerman (1940), Olderogge and Potekhin (1954), and Murdock (1959); or the collaborative works on native African political systems, on systems of kinship and marriage, and on religion, published under the auspices of the International African Institute (Fortes and Evans-Pritchard, 1940; Radcliffe-Brown and Forde, 1950; Forde, 1954).

Still another type, not too numerous, took the synthesizing process a step further. This category was made up of the volumes that considered in broad scope, and on a comparative basis, the manifestations of a particular aspect of Subsaharan life. A pioneer work of this kind was the study by Orde Browne (1933); two decades later came the outstanding analysis of African nationalist movements by Hodgkin (1956). Unique for its coverage, though set within the territorial framework, was the Hailey *Survey* (1938, 1957).

Finally there were the literary forms, which cannot be left out of our account. Whether written by Africans, as they increasingly came to be, or by Europeans, they provide the insights that the creative artist brings to those concerned with the objective analysis of fact. Thus it would be difficult to give a clearer picture of African initial reaction to contact with European culture and subsequent adjustment to change than is provided by Camara Laye (1953, 1954) for the Malinké of French Guinea, or by Chinua Achebe for the Nigerian Ibo (1958), or by Elspeth Huxley (1939) for the Kikuyu of Kenya, or for the Cameroons by Ferdinand Oyono (1956) and Mongo Beti (1956). Amos Tutuola's *The Palm-Wine Drinkard* (1952) and the later books by this same author reveal, through their use of Yoruba mythic themes, some of the most deeply set attitudes of this people, just as, on another plane, Ezekiel Mphahlele (1960), and Harry Bloom (1955, 1956), convey the passionate outbursts of Africans reacting to the tensions they felt under the restrictions imposed on them in South Africa.

These titles give only a few examples of the treatment of Africa in scientific and literary writings. Not many realize the scope of this literature, whose items number in the thousands—surprising for a continent we have been continuously told is little known.

2

The People and Their Past

AFRICA is one of the oldest inhabited parts of the earth. Quoting Darwin's "shrewd remark" that, "It is somewhat more probable that our early progenitors lived on the African continent than elsewhere," Sonia Cole adds that East Africa "may have been both the cradle of the human race and a passageway for migrants to Europe." [1]

This point of view, however, was by no means always held. Recognition of the importance of Africa for the study of human evolution came as slowly as did an understanding of its contemporary significance, so that the attitudes of students of early man toward the African materials offer almost a case study of how scientific findings respond to the intellectual climate of their time. Just as its political, economic, and social status made events in Africa seem peripheral to major world developments in Europe and Asia, so highly significant evidence that this was the continent where human beings had first appeared suffered striking neglect for many years, because such evidence seemed so unlikely.

[1] Sonia Cole: *The Prehistory of East Africa* (London, 1954), p. 24.

For a long time, Africa was no more "open" to archaeological exploration than to any other kind. In many cases, there was nothing on which to base fruitful questions as to the nature of the early inhabitants and their place in the evolutionary process. Yet the fact remains that the Australopithecines and their associated types, on which Dart first published in 1925, were for at least two decades treated with casualness in many authoritative discussions of human evolution, and were alluded to with a degree of skepticism extraordinary even for professional skeptics.

In contrast to this, the archaeological finds being made about the same time in China and Java were replete with dramatic overtones that gave them great popular appeal. But we are concerned here with the scientists, not the interested spectators of scientific achievement. In the light of the continuing announcement of new materials, not only from South Africa but also from eastern and northern parts of the continent, the fact that "a generation of . . . repeated discoveries" passed before these fossils were "generally accepted . . . for what they were originally claimed to be—a group or family of advancing creatures midway between ape and mankind," [2] has implications worth exploring.

At the time the first finds of Australopithecines were being announced, the most prominent scholars in the field were committed to Asia as the cradle of humanity. This was in part justified by the importance of the evidence from the Far East—to say nothing of the claim of Europe, largely on the basis of what later turned out to be the manufactured fossil "finds" of the so-called Piltdown Man from England—but in part this commitment was deeply embedded in the psychological processes of identification. For Asia, unlike Africa, could be identified with cultures of historical antiquity, with recognized achievements in philosophy, literature and the arts.

Moreover, this was a time when the debate over racial aptitudes was at its height. In Germany, the legacy of Houston Stewart Chamberlain was developing into the racist ideology of the National Socialists. In England, the eugenics movement was

[2] Raymond A. Dart: "Cultural Status of the South African Man-Apes," *Annual Report,* Smithsonian Institution (publication 4240) for 1956, p. 320.

preaching the doctrine of biological salvation. And in the United States, argument about the presumed findings of the Army Intelligence Tests of the First World War centered on the question of racial superiority and inferiority of the Negro and immigrant components of its population. In all this it was taken for granted that the African was of a backward, if not an inferior race—a reflection in scientific thought of the "dark continent" stereotype—and in this configuration of ideas it was distasteful, if not inconceivable, that man could have originated in such a continent.

An examination of the precise position of these early man-ape forms in the evolutionary sequence, their relation to the forerunners of man recovered in the Far East, whether or not they used tools, and if so, what kind of implements they had, need not concern us further here. What is important is that in the world of science, no less than in those other worlds of particular orientation, the role of Africa could no longer be taken for granted in the analyses of any human problem cast in world-wide dimensions.

We must be clear, however, that to recognize Africa as a locale where mankind may have originated leaves unsolved the problem of how Africa was peopled by its later inhabitants. The evolutionary gap between the Australopithecines of perhaps a million years ago and the contemporary Africans is precisely that found between these forms and all other contemporary living human groups. It follows, naturally enough, that if man did originate in Africa, he must at some time have migrated to the other continents of the Old World, and then to the New; but it does not follow that ancient African man was Negroid in our current sense of the term. Much of this tale will turn on the nature of the palaeontological finds that will establish the relationship between those earliest southern and eastern African forms and their contemporary Far Eastern types. We will shortly review the interpretations of this aspect of African prehistory that were advanced.

In seeking to understand the racial position of the present inhabitants, it is crucial to recognize the breadth of distribution of the Negroid race. Though all the indigenous inhabitants of

Africa south of the Sahara belong to this race, it is by no means confined to the continent, but reaches eastward across the Indian Ocean to New Guinea and the Melanesian Islands beyond. It is self-evident that this distribution raises numerous problems. The scientific classification of any phenomenon depends on the criteria employed, but a substantial measure of objectively determined fact must be present in all classifications. In the case of the Negroid race, as in any other, the genetic relation between its component parts is clear, since the resemblances in physical type are too great to permit any assumption of independent lines of evolution of the various subgroupings.

[2]

In evolutionary terms, the Negroid peoples represent some of the most highly specialized human types. The fact that, for example, the Negroid race includes the tallest and shortest groups of mankind—all pygmy types, wherever found, belong to it—as well as the heaviness of pigmentation, the everted lips and the characteristic hair-forms of its members, are evidence of the specialization this race has undergone in its physical development.

What particular mechanism of genetic relation brought this about cannot be said, but some answers are suggested if we call on the phenomenon of domestication. From this point of view, man is to be regarded as the oldest domesticated animal, and the traits that mark off the members of one race, and one subtype from another, are to be thought of as resulting from the particular kind of selection that occurs under domestication. This hypothesis [3] is mentioned here only in order to place in perspective the questions arising out of the range of physical differences between the peoples of Subsaharan Africa.

We are still, however, far from having answers to our basic question of how and when present-day African types appeared. The assumption is usually made that the early migrations,

[3] Cf. Melville J. Herskovits: *Man and His Works* (New York, 1948), pp. 146–7.

which were held to be still in progress when Africa came into contact with Europe, originated outside the continent, and proceeded westward across the northern portion, southerly along the east coast, and southwesterly to populate the heart of the continent. It was not illogical that such writers as Sir Harry Johnston (1913) and C. G. Seligman (1930), accepting the intellectual currents of the period already alluded to, would assume migration along these lines.

This is clearly expressed by Haddon who, in an early work, says that "all the main races in that continent reached it from southern Asia." Noting the presence of "implements of palaeolithic type" found widely distributed south of the Sahara, he says, "We know nothing about the men who fashioned these implements, which are of great antiquity"; but concludes that they were succeeded by "pygmy folk," whose migration "was perhaps very little prior to, or contemporaneous with, the westerly drift of the primitive Negro." [4] For the writers whose works were written before the finding of the Australopithecines, the problem of the pygmies presented perplexing difficulties; but at least these could later be faced with such an alternative hypothesis of indigenous development as is evidenced in the theory of pedomorphism advanced by Drennan (1931) and placed in the larger setting by Galloway (1937) to account for the origin of the Bushmen.

There is no question that the distribution of pygmy-like types in Africa itself is wider than that of the small peoples of the Congo forest and the Bushmen of southern Africa. Such types have long been recognized in Ruanda and Urundi. They are present in the Cameroons and in Rio Muni; [5] and in the Niger Delta the Ibibio are so short of stature as to merit the designation "pygmoid." But the question whether they represent a stage in the evolution of the Negro race, an evolution that took place in Africa itself, or are the end result of a process of specialization

[4] Alfred C. Haddon: *The Wanderings of Peoples* (revised ed., Cambridge, England, 1919), p. 54.

[5] Conde de Castillo-Fiel: "Los Bayeles, una Tribu Pigmea en la Guinea Española," *Africa* (Madrid), No. 83–4, 1948, *passim*.

from a more generalized form ancestral to all Negroids, or represent the vestiges of an early migration, is far from being resolved.

Alimen, in her resumé of what is known about prehistoric man in Africa, pointed to the need to establish, first of all, the relation between the Australopithecines and similar early forms, and the North Africa types called *Atlanthropus mauritanicus*. Neanderthal man followed these earliest types, until perhaps thirty-five millennia ago, after which true *Homo sapiens* appeared in Africa, a type which, in the Maghreb resembled the European Combe-Capelle Cro-Magnon. "These men," Alimen states, "who must have been the contemporaries of the last Neanderthals, were not blacks (*ne sont pas des noirs*). They were related to the Cro-Magnon race of the upper Palaeolithic of Europe. Like them, they were buried, often in a bent position, and covered with ochre." [6]

The present type of African only appears later, perhaps some six or seven thousand years ago. The finds that represent him come from Southwest Africa, from southern Egypt and from Kenya. They are all somewhat specialized, and, particularly as regards the Asselar type, found in the southwestern Sahara, show affinities with the Grimaldi finds from the European Old Stone Age, on the one hand, and with the present-day Bushmen and Hottentots of South Africa, on the other. It was during this period, also, that evidence of the presence of the Negroid sub-types known to us began to accumulate, while the Bushmen and Hottentots continued the process of differentiation that brought them to their present specialized form.

There is a certain rationale that justifies holding to the conventional thesis of migration in more recent centuries from north to south and east to west, though there is mounting evidence which indicates that the present Negroid forms of *Homo sapiens* may have been differentiated in the general area of the bend of the west coast. The routes of migration would therefore have been west, east, and southeast. As far as the southeasterly direction is concerned, the traditions of many African peoples telling of the

[6] H. Alimen: *Préhistoire de l'Afrique* (Paris, 1955), p. 411.

movements of their ancestors support this hypothesis; and though oral history as a source of facts has its pitfalls, the degree of consensus in these accounts from many parts of the continent commands attention. In this connection, too, the emphasis laid for political reasons on the "emptiness" of the southern tip of Africa, should not be overlooked. According to this thesis, which draws from and reinforces the conventional South African view of African ethnic history, Europeans moving inland from the Cape encountered Bantu-speaking peoples migrating southward into a land populated only by sparse Hottentot and Bushman groups. Walton [7] on the basis of a survey which utilized archaeological materials, ethnographic comparison, and historical documentation, placed the early eastern Sotho tribes moving down the Caledon Valley into what is now the Orange Free State about 1600 A.D. Fuller, using early records, concluded that the facts "contradict the oft-repeated South African assertion that the Bantu entered this part of the continent after the Europeans had discovered and occupied it." [8] Contemporaneous Portuguese documents prove that the Shangan-Tonga peoples of southern Mozambique occupied their present habitat as early as the sixteenth and seventeenth centuries.[9] However, quite aside from any political implications, even if further controlled research of this type supported the thesis of relatively late migration of Bantu-speaking peoples into southernmost South Africa, this would not of necessity confirm an assumption of the origin of African Negroids outside the continent.

Another phase of this line of thought is to be found in the stress often laid on the importance of the role played by later Caucasoid-Hamitic peoples, as they were called, in changing

[7] James Walton: *African Village* (Pretoria, 1956), p. 26.

[8] Charles Edward Fuller: "Ethnohistory in the Study of Culture Change in Southwest Africa," in *Continuity and Change in African Cultures* (W. R. Bascom and M. J. Herskovits, eds., Chicago, 1959), p. 117.

[9] Henri Philippe Junod: "Os Indigenas de Moçambique no Século XVI e comêço do XVII," *Moçambique* (*Documentario Trimestral*), Nos. 17–19, *passim;* Monica Wilson; "The Early History of the Transkei and Ciskei," *African Studies*, Vol. XVIII, pp. 167–79, *passim.*

not only the physical type, but the culture of the Negroes whom they found living in the areas to which they came. The tenaciousness of this point of view is of considerable significance for the insights into the thinking about Africa it affords. Thus, for example, in Fitzgerald's standard work on Africa, the following statement has survived the numerous revisions through which this book has gone:

> We may regard the region in which the Hamito-Negroid peoples are found geographically associated with more or less pure Negroes to have been at some very early time entirely negroid in its population. From a distant period there has been a southward penetration of Hamites into East Africa and through their tendency to marriage with the sedentary agricultural Negroes has evolved the virile type to which we now refer.[1]

Here we encounter still another phenomenon that must be taken into account in any firm appraisal of currents of thought on contemporary Africa, that is to say, the confusion of physical form with cultural and linguistic usage. There is, perhaps, no word that has been more loosely used in writings on Africa than the word "race." It has been employed to designate tribal—that is, politico-cultural—groupings, as in the "Bamileke race" or the "Shona race." Its most notable misuse, perhaps, is found in the appellation "Bantu race," used to name a vast number of peoples who differ in physical type and culture, but speak languages that have certain features in common. Thus in a school textbook on the history of East Africa, we read the following: "Another group of Hamitic people drifted farther south and intermarried with the Negroes, thus producing a race often called Bantu. One link between the Bantu people is that of language. . . ."[2] We must note, however, that the more serious students, when discussing differences between African physical types, came to use the term "Bantu-speaking peoples."

[1] Walter Fitzgerald: *Africa, a Social, Economic and Political Geography of its Major Regions* (7th Ed., rev., London, 1952), p. 127.

[2] Zoë Marsh and G. W. Kingsnorth: *An Introduction to the History of East Africa* (Cambridge, England, 1957), p. 3.

Most striking in this context is the case of the so-called "Nilo-Hamitic" group, who are presumed to have developed from crosses between indigenous Negroid tribes having simple cultures, and the superior invading Caucasoid Hamites. There is no doubt that, in many instances, each of these earlier groupings had its own culture. The further probability must be dealt with that, for example, certain traditions such as those governing patterns of food consumption have had their effect on bodily build, as suggested by Hiernaux's study of the physical differences between the Tutsi and Hutu of Ruanda-Urundi.[3]

The recognition of such factors, however, differs fundamentally from the conventional approach which equates physical type with behavior in terms of implied cultural and racial superiority and inferiority, thereby placing the ruling African castes, wherever found, in a preferred category. The anthropometric investigations of Oschinsky, involving comparison of Baganda and Watutsi physical types, indicated this not to be a tenable position,[4] and led to his assertion that, except for certain facial characteristics, "the East African Hamitomorphs are to be considered as typical Negroes."

Greenberg, approaching the problem from the point of view of historical linguistics, analyzed the confusion inherent in this "Nilo-Hamitic" concept. Here, as he pointed out, "we have an extension of a term, whose original application in a linguistic sense was never made precise, to a great physical variety of populations." He went on to say:

> So all-pervading has been the loose application of the term Hamite in African racial classification that if the present linguistic analysis is accepted, the whole problem of physical variation in Africa should be approached once again independent of preconceptions based on language. It would be a rather remarkable accident if a

[3] Jean Hiernaux: "Les caractères physiques des populations du Ruanda et de l'Urundi," *Mémoires*, Institut Royal des Sciences Naturelles de Belgique, 2e sér., fasc. 52, 1954, *passim.*

[4] Lawrence Oschinsky: *The Racial Affinities of the Baganda and other Bantu Tribes of British East Africa* (Cambridge, England, 1954), pp. 128–30.

racial classification based on incorrect linguistics turned out to be valid.[5]

[3]

The physical types of Subsaharan Africa are imperfectly known because relatively little systematic research has been done to gather the basic descriptive data. On what must therefore of necessity be a tentative basis, we can distinguish five major subtypes. The first of these comprises the inhabitants of the Guinea Coast and the region inland to the North. These people are usually called the "true Negro," meaning that when the populations of the area, taken as a whole, are compared with the other groupings of Africa, their physical characteristics conform more closely than any others to the specifications of the term "Negro." That is, they are typically Negroid in such traits as hair form, facial characteristics, bodily proportions, pigmentation and the like. However, the conventional name carries an implication of genetic purity of type that is by no means valid, and some other designation, such as "Guinea-Sudanic" is preferable.

The second of these groupings is generally located in the northeastern part of our area, and constitutes the peoples generally called Nilo-Hamites. Its members range widely in stature, being the sub-race which includes some of the tallest groups of mankind. They are slender, and their faces tend to be long and narrow. Because so many of the peoples placed in this category inhabit the basin of the upper Nile, the word "Nilotic" has a certain validity. However, since the type extends across the Sudan to the Atlantic as a kind of overlay on the aboriginal Guinea-Sudanic peoples, it is suggested that the term "Nilo-Sudanic" is much more apt, especially since it avoids the cultural and political connotations of the conventional term.

The so-called Bantu-speaking peoples inhabit the heart of the continent. This name can be expected to give way to a whole series of new ones as the physical anthropologists provide us with

[5] Joseph H. Greenberg: *Studies in African Linguistic Classification* (New Haven, 1955), p. 54.

more precise descriptions of the smaller groups that go to make up this catch-all category. The peoples thus classified are Negroid to varying degrees, for this is an area where the mixture of groups having different characteristics has been going on for a long time. Even the most cursory inspection of Zulu and forest Congo tribesmen shows how much variation there is among peoples who speak Bantu languages.[6]

The term Bantu, however, could fall into disuse because of developments quite outside the scientific field. Those conversant with African reactions learned to avoid the use of the word "native"—a perfectly good descriptive word in its own right—when speaking to Africans because "native," like its French counterpart, *indigène,* came to have a pejorative connotation as indicating someone or something "primitive," "savage," "inferior," especially when applied by Europeans to Africans. With the substitution of the word "Bantu" for "native," particularly in the Union of South Africa, where it became the officially sanctioned designation for the African members of the South-African community, a parallel reaction set in. That this was justified, because of the misapplication of a linguistic term to a group set off by physical or cultural characteristics, is beside the point. Science requires that terminology be accurate, at least. When a classificatory term comes to have invidious overtones, the reactions to its use and its role in shaping the social and political scene must be noted.

The two remaining subracial stocks need only be briefly considered. The first of these, the Khoisan, includes the pygmy Bushman and the somewhat larger Hottentot of southern Africa. Both these groups deviate from the Negroid norm in such traits as skin color, which is yellowish, or hair form, which is of the so-called "peppercorn" variety. For both Hottentots and Bushmen, survival was an overriding problem. The former were largely assimilated into the mixed "Coloured" population of South Africa; the latter, after resisting attempts at extermination by both African and European neighbors, were reported in 1955 as numbering some

[6] Philip V. Tobias: "Epilogue: Some Developments in South African Physical Anthropology. 1938–1958," in Alexander Galloway: *The Skeletal Remains of Bambandyanalo* (Johannesburg, 1959), pp. 133–4.

55,000, a figure that strikingly revised earlier estimates. Of this number, about 35,000 had settled down to a stable but meager existence in the Kalahari Desert and southern Angola, leading their lives in accordance with earlier hunting and food-gathering patterns.[7]

The final group is composed of the Pygmies, or Negrillos, of the forest areas of Central Africa, for whom the generic term Twides (from the Bantu root form *twa*, "little") has been suggested.[8] They live in enclaves among types of more average human stature in the Congo Basin, the Lake Kivu area, and the Cameroons. Like the Khosian peoples, the Negrillos are "marginal," in the sense that they live in regions where a living must be wrested from a most difficult habitat. It is usually assumed that they were driven to these regions because their relatively simple technologies did not permit them to stand their ground against the larger, better equipped peoples who invaded their original, more favorable territories. The picture of the Bushman is clearer in this regard than that of the Negrillos farther to the north. Though, in 1930, Schapera indicated that "the Bushmen were preceded in the occupation of South Africa by other peoples," stating that "the Bushmen themselves came into South Africa with their culture from the north-east,[9] Tobias, in 1957, concluded that the "evidence compels us to abandon the idea that the Bushmen evolved elsewhere and migrated southwards." According to him, they are indigenous to Africa and their ancestory must be sought in the southern and central parts of the continent.[1]

As regards the relation of the Negrillos to the Bushmen, the conclusion of Schapera that this goes no further "than the fact that phylogenetically both are derived from a small variety of Negro,"[2] is reasonable. For the rest, discussions of their past lie

[7] Ibid.: "On the Survival of the Bushmen," *Africa*, Vol. XXVI (1956), *passim;* "Bushmen of the Kalahari," *Man*, Vol. LVII (1957), No. 36, p. 33.

[8] Martin Gusinde: "Pygmies and Pygmoids: Twides of Tropical Africa," *Anthropological Quarterly*, Vol. XXVIII (n.s., Vol. III), 1955, p. 7.

[9] I. Schapera: *The Khoisan Peoples of South Africa* (London, 1930), pp. 26–7.

[1] Phillip V. Tobias: op. cit. (1957), p. 37.

[2] I. Schapera: op. cit., pp. 27–8.

largely in the realm of speculation, for the essential archaeological data for a factual base are lacking. Various hypotheses have been advanced to account for a presumed earlier, wider distribution of these smaller peoples. These explanations rest on reports by the earliest voyagers along the Guinea Coast, before the beginning of the Christian Era, of small folk seen from their ships; or on the distribution over much of Africa of cave and rock paintings which resemble not only Bushman art, but also that of the Magdalenian folk who in Paleolithic times inhabited what is now northern Spain and southern France.

Those who disagreed with these hypotheses, suggested that anthropoids seen with the unaided eye from a ship lying off shore could well be mistaken for small human beings. As for the art work, aside from the fact that there is no correlation between style and the physical form of the artist, rock paintings are found not only in eastern but also in western and central Africa. Moreover, the radio-carbon analysis of the charcoal, found in association with ochre in the frescoes that fill the walls of a cave in the Windhoek region of Southwest Africa, which give a probable date of between about 1200 and 1600 B.C.,[3] indicated that whoever the painters may have been, the art tradition associated with the Bushmen was nothing very recent.

For a broad understanding of the underlying forces at work in twentieth century Africa, it is essential to realize that the Africans rank equally with other races in the range of forms classed as *Homo sapiens*. With the basic premise in mind that no causal relation can be shown to exist between physical type and learned behavior, or culture, then the description of the physical characteristics of the Negro race becomes essentially a problem in human biology. What is important for an understanding of Africa is the ideas about the significance of racial differences, as they affected the later African scene; as, for example, how they shaped race relations. To this end, we balance the established biological equivalence of races against the concept of racial superiority. But in accepting the scientific validity of the former,

[3] W. F. Libby: "Chicago Radiocarbon Dates V," *Science*, Vol. CXX (1954), p. 742.

we cannot disregard the sociological role of the latter, especially its appeal for those dominating a social structure where opportunity and reward came to be as closely associated with race as in Africa.

[4]

The broad outlines of African prehistory revealed since the first quarter of the twentieth century opened the possibility that Africa, which has come more and more to be regarded as the continent where man first appeared, might also prove to have been the cradle of human culture. This was the conclusion logically to be drawn from the existence of the so-called pebble tools [4] of the lower Pleistocene, those most ancient of implements, discovered in the Union of South Africa in 1931, which preceded the earliest known European industries, the Abbevillian and Clactonian, by perhaps five hundred thousand years.

The problem of dating African prehistoric finds proved a knotty one. There were no glaciations south of the Mediterranean such as provided a geological timetable for European archaeologists. The less precisely marked periods of heavy rainfall and dry times, called pluvial epochs, which may have resulted from the same climatic fluctuations that produced the glaciers of Europe, had to be determined by methods of geological reconstruction that were far more difficult to apply.

The culture from which the pebble tools came, existed at the time of the Australopithecines. Whether they were made or used by these creatures was a matter of much controversy, as in the question whether the parts of animal bones found associated with the pebble tools were in reality tools, as Dart argued.[5] The discovery in 1959, at Olduvai Gorge in Tanganyika, of the form

[4] The word "pebble" as used in the literature is in accordance with its English meaning of a stone up to the size of a man's fist. In the same usage, a "boulder" is anything larger than this. It is important that readers do not visualize pebble tools in accordance with the American meaning, whereby a pebble is a very small stone.

[5] J. Desmond Clark: *The Prehistory of South Africa* (London, 1959), pp. 69–73.

named *Zinjanthropus boisei,*[6] when later found to be in association with stone artifacts, seemed to show that these large Australopithecines, at least, were tool-using animals.

The dating which indicated that the pebble tools were older than the hand axe (*coup de poing*), opened the possibility that these African cultures were a source of the European stone industries. If, as seemed less and less likely, the pebble tools were thought of as having been made at the same time as the European implements, there was the alternate possibility that their proto-human makers either migrated over Europe and Africa and presumably Asia, or that the techniques of making these crude stone tools were diffused over this entire land mass at a still earlier period. Since in this latter case these implements would everywhere date from the same time, no valid assumption could be held as to the place of origin of either the tools or their makers, though the fact that the earliest types of proto-humans lived in Africa and Asia would argue against considering Europe as their source. Whatever the position taken, the early date of the pebble tools threw quite as new a light on the role of Africa in the development of human culture as the fossil finds did for its role in the evolution of man's physical form. They forced a fundamental reconsideration of the theory, derived more from the attitudes of the time than from the data, that in the history of mankind Africa had always been the recipient, never the donor.

It is certain that the development of African cultures was steady and, when considered along broad lines, showed a consistent series of changes not much different from the changes over the years that marked cultural developments elsewhere in the Old World. The correlation of materials from all parts of the continent given by Alimen led her to the conclusion that, "One cannot but be struck by the essential continuity of African prehistory."[7]

Here, once more, the question of outer influence as against inner growth arises. The prehistorians, conditioned for many

[6] L. S. B. Leakey: "A New Fossil Skull from Olduvai," *Nature,* Vol. CLXXXIV (1959), p. 491.

[7] H. Alimen: op. cit., p. 497 and Chart X.

years to the use of terms derived from European archaeology, quite naturally applied the familiar designations to African stone tools of the same types found in the same epochs. Because most of these designations took their names from the sites in Europe where a given type of implement was discovered, this unconsciously tended again to make of Africa, at least terminologically, a satellite of Europe. Yet in summarizing archaeological work in northwest Africa for 1954 and 1955, Howe stated:

> Especially in Atlantic and Southern Morocco, the western Sahara and the Constantine Department of Algeria, Lower Palaeolithic pebble tool and other typology, found in appropriate geological contexts, demonstrated that these early horizons known from East and South Africa, existed in Northwest Africa. The lithic traditions of this quarter are revealed as an integral part of the African, not European, Stone Age, at this early date.[8]

The implications of this statement become the more striking when we consider that this area is the part of the African continent closest to Europe, where European influence, if the course of diffusion in early times had actually been from north to south, would be most readily discernible. And as concerns the other side of the continent, Caton-Thompson, working in South Arabia, found little evidence of contact across the Red Sea in later Paleolithic times, even when the narrowness of the Strait of Bab-el-Mandeb is taken into account, since the stone implements from Arabia and East Africa, with a single exception, have little in common.[9]

Quite aside from the problem of the possible spread of early African Paleolithic techniques elsewhere, scientific opinion came more and more to hold for autonomy of the African prehistoric cultures. Alimen was unequivocal in her conclusions:

> One is struck . . . by the unity of this long evolution and by its independence. . . . In the 'survivals' of various epochs that are

[8] Bruce Howe (ed.): *COWA Survey, Current Work in Old World Archaeology,* Area 10—Northwest Africa. No. I, 1957. Cambridge (Mass.).

[9] G. Caton-Thompson: "The Evidence of South Arabian Palaeolithic in the Question of Pleistocene Land Connection with Africa," *Third Pan-African Congress on Prehistory, Livingstone, 1955* (J. Desmond Clark, ed., London, 1957), *passim.*

manifested here and there, we see more the mark of this remarkable continuity than any 'colonial' character. What we have here is a replica, in the human sphere, of facts already known to palaeontologists about the evolution of African fauna, and this is without doubt the influence of the geological conditions peculiar to the African continent on the free development of the human genius.[1]

The antiquity of these prehistoric African cultures, and the smoothness of their development are demonstrated in such a relatively well-studied region of the Subsaharan continent as Southern and Northern Rhodesia and Nyasaland. In discussions of the archaeological work done in those areas, presented in 1955 before the Third International Pan-African Congress on Prehistory, both Summers,[2] who described the state of archaeological knowledge in Southern Rhodesia, and Clark,[3] who treated the same topic for the other new territories, gave a picture of continuity similar to that which Alimen noted for the continent as a whole. In this region, the finds were seen to move from pebble tools through periods when the working of stone became more sophisticated, until we reach the Neolithic and later the introduction of iron-working. In one case, at least, precise dating was possible. Clark reported that in 1953 "at the Kalambo Falls . . . were found . . . camping floors in association with partially carbonized tree trunks."[4] These are the materials utilized in dating by the use of the Carbon-14 method, which supported conclusions formerly based only on the geological timetable. Later research showed that carbonized tree trunks from this camping site were to be dated at "more than 53,000 years before the present."[5] Furthermore, the same site yielded fragments of what may have been

[1] Ibid., p. 49.

[2] Roger Summers: "Archaeology in Southern Rhodesia, 1900–1955," *Third Pan-African Congress on Prehistory, Livingstone, 1955* (J. Desmond Clark, ed., London, 1957), pp. 396, 431.

[3] J. Desmond Clark: "A Review of Prehistoric Research in Northern Rhodesia and Nyasaland," *Third Pan-African Congress on Prehistory, Livingstone, 1955* (J. Desmond Clark, ed., London, 1957), pp. 412–32.

[4] Ibid., pp. 423–4.

[5] J. D. Clark: *The Prehistory of Southern Africa* (London, 1959), p. 168.

wooden implements, allowing the hope that "some of the more perishable tools of the Old Stone Age in Africa, the kind of materials that are so badly needed to round out the picture of the technological resources of these early men, might be recovered."

[5]

With the passage of time, the steady changes that marked the later prehistoric development of human civilization in other parts of the world were paralleled by those of Africa. In the later periods of the early epochs, the crudely shaped pebble tools gave way to cleavers and hand axes that were "beautifully finished," and indicated that their makers "had complete mastery over their craft. . . . for the amount of waste material and discards found at most sites shows that they were satisfied only with the best." [6] More specialized tools, found in East and West Africa, the Congo and elsewhere, included scrapers, arrowheads, lance heads, picks, burins for grooving arrow shafts, and many others. In Angola, a Later Stone Age backed blade, found in association with carbonized wood, when submitted for radio carbon analysis, was shown to have been used about eleven thousand years ago.[7]

Like prehistoric man elsewhere, African man was moving through a Mesolithic period, though here this epoch may have overlapped with the Neolithic in other parts of the Old World. In Africa, not only the earlier forms of stone tools were present, but also much smaller axes for finer work. This period may have differed in an important respect from the comparable one in Europe, for though in Europe pottery came primarily with the next epoch, the Neolithic, in East Africa pottery, well-made and decorated with incised designs, was already present in the Mesolithic. The African Mesolithic cultures were, moreover, primarily those of hunters and food-gatherers, and only with the Neolithic did they, like their European and Asian counterparts, shift to the more settled life made possible by agriculture and herding.

[6] Sonia Cole: op. cit., p. 150.

[7] W. F. Libby: "Radiocarbon Dates, II," *Science,* Vol. CXIV (1951), pp. 291–6.

The knowledge of ironworking, which wrought as impressive changes in the mode of life of Africans as it did in those of peoples living elsewhere in the Old World, was found to have come from outside the continent. In the face of discoveries that place its source in Mesopotamia, the views of those who had maintained that this technique originated in northeastern Africa, perhaps in the region of the Great Lakes, became untenable. According to conservative estimates, the beginning of the Iron Age in West Africa occurred before 500 A.D.; for North Africa, and the Sahara and the Sudan, it took place about 1000 B.C. Metalworking came to this area from the north.[8] In East Africa, dating was much more difficult, but the period about 1000 A.D. was suggested.[9] Moving southward with or ahead of the migrating Negroid, perhaps Bantu-speaking peoples, ironworking reached the southern part of the continent about the first half of the first millennium A.D.[1]

Not only iron, however, but gold, silver, copper, and tin were mined, and the combining of basic metals to make bronze was known, certainly in some parts of the continent, at a time not much later than the appearance of metal-working techniques. Though studies of this question yielded only fragmentary data on this point as far as Subsaharan Africa was concerned, the assumption was inescapable that once the requisite knowledge was at hand, the Africans did not fail to exploit their resources. Thus, along the Ashanti gold reef in Ghana there are deep pits which were used in mining operations long before the Europeans arrived. European prospectors found no gold-bearing deposits in the country where these pits were not present, indicating an assiduous search by the Africans for sources of gold.[2] The Africans worked copper in the ore-bearing belt of Katanga and Northern Rhodesia in the eighth and ninth centuries, and mined gold fur-

[8] R. Mauny: "Essai sur l'histoire des métaux en Afrique occidentale," *Bulletin* de l'Institut Français d'Afrique Noire, Vol. XIV (1952), pp. 545–95.

[9] Sonia Cole: op. cit., p. 278.

[1] J. D. Clark: op. cit., pp. 285–7.

[2] See below, Ch. VI, pp. 173–4.

ther to the south as early as the fourth century. The rich iron-ore deposits reported from so many parts of the continent provided smiths with the raw materials of their craft.

Domesticated animals were also as much a factor in the cultures of the time as in Neolithic and Metal Age societies elsewhere in the Old World. The question of what part the peoples of Subsaharan Africa played in the domestication of animals is disputed. The cat and donkey, it is agreed, were domesticated in Egypt, and perhaps certain types of dog derived from the jackal, as well as other, less widely distributed, animals.[3] In addition, Africa in these early times knew the pig, cattle, sheep and goats, which came to them from outside the continent.[4] If we assume the possibility that the domestication of a given animal might have occurred in more than one place, then the theory that cattle and goats came into Africa from elsewhere would have to be revised to allow for the crossing of certain imported types with indigenously domesticated forms.[5] Whether or not this actually occurred, the cattle of Africa, so important in the eastern and southern parts of the continent that, as we shall see, they became the focal point in the total culture of the people, undoubtedly represented a mixture of various types. According to one account, the *Bos ibericus* entered into northern Africa from across the Mediterranean, where it met and merged with the humped zebu from the east. The zebu, in turn, had already encountered the *Bos africanus*. Much of this argument is based on the study of rock paintings from northern Africa which show not only a degree of variation in these types that argues for the antiquity of their domestication, but also aids in tracing the distribution of the cattle and other domesticated animals over the continent in historic times.[6]

[3] Caesar R. Boettger: op. cit., pp. 106–27 and ff.

[4] Ibid., pp. 19–99.

[5] A. J. Arkell: *A History of the Sudan, from Earliest Times to 1821* (London, 1955), p. 11 and *passim*.

[6] G. Esperandieu: "Domestication et élevage dans le Nord de l'Afrique au Néolitique et dans le Protohistoire d'après les figurations rupestres," *Congrès Panafricaine de Préhistoire, Actes de la IIe Session, Alger 1952* (L. Balout, ed., Paris, 1955), pp. 551–62.

Although the role of Africa in the domestication of plants was similarly disputed, there was little question that some of the most widely spread staples, such as manioc, for example, and maize, were imported after the initial contacts of Africa with the world by sea.[7]

With the post-Neolithic, the settled habitat of agricultural societies gave rise to more complex political institutions than had existed previously, in this following the pattern observed elsewhere in the Old World. In West Africa, the forms of political organization that so impressed all early observers had in all probability been established, and one of the manifestations of complex, settled societies, highly developed art forms, were present. Analysis of materials associated with the Nok figurines of Northern Nigeria [8] by the radio-carbon method bracket the date of this culture as "between about 2000 B.C. and A.D. 200, with the most probable date being . . . about 900 B.C." [9] The bronze heads from Ife, deep in the coastal forested belt, are being tentatively dated as from 1000 A.D. to 1200 A.D. And the closeness of Ife to Benin suggests that the art in bronze of the latter, made known to the world when examples of it began to reach the museums of Europe after its conquest in 1897 by the British, was a further expression of a tradition of lost-wax casting that stretched from the Cameroons to the Ivory Coast and north into the Sudan. An appreciable span of time would, in any event, have been necessary to develop the technical competence essential for the production of such masterpieces.[1]

Yet for many years it was maintained that these technical re-

[7] William O. Jones: "Manioc: an Example of Innovation in African Economics," *Economic Development and Cultural Change,* Vol. V (1957), p. 98.

[8] Bernard Fagg: "A Preliminary Note on a New Series of Pottery Figures from Northern Nigeria," *Africa,* Vol. XV (1945), pp. 21–2, *passim;* and "The Nok Culture in Prehistory," *Journal of the Historical Society of Nigeria,* Vol. I (1959), pp. 288–93, *passim.*

[9] G. W. Barendsen, E. S. Deevey and L. J. Gralenski: "Yale Natural Radiocarbon Measurements III," *Science,* Vol. CXXVI (1957), p. 916.

[1] Frank Willett: "Excavations at Old Oyo and Ife," *West Africa,* No. 2153 (July 19, 1958) *passim.*

sources could never have been African, but must have been brought by the early Portuguese, whose contact with Benin, about 1500 A.D., is documented by the Benin bronze figures of helmeted soldiers, in armor and bearing crossbows. How such an argument could have been given credence can only be understood if, once more, we refer to the prevailing currents of thought in Europe and America concerning the ability and cultural resources of African peoples. Even if it were granted that these early Portuguese were long enough in contact with the Bini to have taught them the complex techniques of bronze-casting, the question of the time needed to develop the requisite technical skills for making forms of the quality of the Benin bronzes would remain to be answered. Moreover, it is hard to believe that these early explorers had brought with them artists to instruct the Bini in the intricacies of shaping molds, compounding the alloys, and casting the pieces. And even if, to this point, the conventional explanation were correct, it would not meet the difficulties posed by the Nok figurines and the Ife heads, which show that traditions of working in plastic forms were well established in West Africa centuries before any significant contact between the peoples of the Guinea Coast region and Europe. Besides, the simple question might be posed: Where in the Portugal of this epoch were the artists who wrought comparable works?

The outer influences that played on Subsaharan African societies have had perennial interest for scholars. Egypt has ranked high in the list of contributors; to the extent, indeed, that anything in Subsaharan cultures assumed or found to resemble anything in Egypt was held to be Egyptian in derivation.

The evidence, however, leaves little doubt that the influence of Egypt was minimal in prehistoric times. Mauny, for example, asserted that "in spite of certain recent work, above all that treating of Nigeria where certain authors would derive Yoruba cultures directly from Egypt (Talbot, Lucas, etc.) to say nothing of a prehellenic Mediterranean civilization (Frobenius), Egyptian influences must be spoken of with the greatest prudence." The bases of the arguments in this case, Mauny holds, are "fragile."

The few objects of Egyptian origin that had been found in West Africa—he names only three specimens that were known at the time he was writing—were, as he says, small and "eminently transportable." As regards ideas, while obviously some diffusion must have occurred, "no one can say through how many intermediaries, Berbers, Tebou, Nubians and others, these must have passed, nor at what epoch." [2] To these comments may be added those of Cole on the same point as it bears on East Africa:

> It is remarkable that Egyptian influence seems to have been so slight within the African continent. . . . Although their influence penetrated through Nubia into the Sudan, it seems to have been slight south of Khartoum, where there has been progressive desiccation for the past 6,000 years. Further progress southwards by river was barred to Egyptians and other travellers by the *sudd* block of swamps on the Nile.[3]

From post-Neolithic times onward, other cultural streams impinged on Subsaharan Africa. These were heard of less often in the writings of those who speculated on African history, perhaps in part because the influence those streams exerted proved to be so difficult to evaluate, plus the fact that they also lay outside the accepted popular formulations of the African past. Along the East Coast, from Zanzibar southward, contacts with the East antedated the beginning of the Christian era. About 80 A.D., a Greek merchant-seaman wrote a *Periplus of the Erythraean Sea,* in which he detailed the coastline from the tip of the East Horn to south of Zanzibar, naming towns of verifiable identity. He described the inhabitants as being "very great of stature," and according to Coupland, who abstracted the account, apparently of Negroid race, with separate chiefs for each place, "holding tenure under Arab suzerainty." Trade was lively, and, in the hands of the Arabs continued to be important throughout subsequent centuries. Yet though the outsiders may have ruled the coastal peoples, they rarely penetrated inland until the late days

[2] R. Mauny: op. cit., pp. 548–9.

[3] S. Cole: op. cit., p. 272.

of their slave trade, and their influence on the peoples inhabiting the interior was negligible.[4]

In the west, according to Fage, who summarized the conventional point of view, "the dominant theme" of its history "for the last 2000 years has in fact been the contact and conflict of its black peoples with white intruders . . . [and in earlier periods] . . . the white peoples of North Africa," then later the Europeans.[5] The contacts with these outsiders, he holds, were decisive in shaping the forms of later African cultural modes. Earlier the Africans seem mostly to have lived "in comparatively small descent groups, often small enough to claim descent from a common ancestor." This way of life was still to be discerned, "though usually only among peoples who for one reason or another have escaped any great degree of white influence." And while, as he points out, "it is both difficult and dangerous to generalize, it would seem that in West Africa the original impulse for the change from small descent-groups to territorial states was military conquest by white peoples from North Africa."[6]

The stress on the racial factor in this account reflects a tendency to refer almost any aspect of African history that involved conquest to racial difference, which is as irrelevant causally as it is unjustified historically. What is important is the historical fact that the tradition of empire, which can in no way be associated with any racial group, persisted in the form of stable kingdoms that weathered European conquest, particularly where policies of indirect rule permitted pre-conquest rulers to continue the forms and certain functions of their earlier power. Certainly it is difficult to sustain the proposition that Africans learned of the territorial state from invaders to the north, particularly in view of the extent to which the forms of this institution were developed in the more

[4] R. Coupland: *East Africa and its Invaders* (Oxford, 1938), pp. 14–39; see also G. Caton-Thompson: *The Zimbabwe Culture* (Oxford, 1931), pp. 260–74.

[5] J. D. Fage: *An Introduction to the History of West Africa* (Cambridge, England, 1955), p. 12.

[6] Ibid., pp. 7–9.

southerly coastal forested belt. The impressions made by Benin on early European travelers, the status attained by the kingdoms of Ashanti and Dahomey, as reflected in first-hand accounts dating from the seventeenth century, all point to a lengthy prior tradition of well-functioning, firmly established states along the Guinea Coast. Evans-Pritchard, writing of the Azande, makes the point: ". . . before even Arab or European arrived in Central Africa the Avongara-Ambonu had been moving for a century east, south and north, conquering great territories and subjugating their inhabitants." His conclusion applied far more widely than to the people of whom he is writing: "It is against this background that their institutions and culture have to be examined if they are to be well understood." [7]

The hypothesis of external influence for the political development of West Africa is anything but strengthened when we consider the similar political entities revealed in other parts of the continent on first European contact. The exploring Portuguese, in the fifteenth century, encountered the Kingdom of Kongo; further in the interior, the realms of the Bushongo, the Baluba, and of the Lunda were in process of formation or consolidation. The Baganda, the Watutsi and other kingdoms were, in the nineteenth century at least, similarly functioning, though here the difficult question of "Hamitic" influence intervenes to make any assumption of inner development hazardous.

But this was scarcely the case of the almost mythical empire of Monomotapa that figured in all the early maps of Africa, but proved to be so difficult to locate specifically in time and place. Here the argument centered about the origin of Zimbabwe and other ruins of southern Africa. Concerning this, however, Caton-Thompson, whose study is the point of reference for all students of the question, was specific: "Examination of all the existing evidence, gathered from every quarter, can still produce not one single item that is not in accordance with the claim of Bantu origin and medieval date." [8] And Wieschhoff, who did a com-

[7] E. E. Evans-Pritchard: "An Historical Introduction to a Study of Zande Society," *African Studies*, Vol. XVII (1958), p. 15.

[8] G. Caton-Thompson: *The Zimbabwe Culture* (Oxford, 1931), p. 199.

parative study of the customs of Monomotapan culture, especially as concerns the rituals of kingship, found numerous correspondences with other political entities of eastern and central Africa, combining traditions of which those of Hamitic derivation form only a part.[9]

Again, in recovering the past of Subsaharan Africa, the absence of written records necessitates reliance on the archaeological record, the spoken legend, and the comparison of cultural similarities. The history of this area has to be reconstructed. The considerable difficulties entailed are no greater than those faced in recovering the past of nonliterate peoples elsewhere—in the South Seas, for example, or in the Americas. In Africa, however, the difficulties are augmented by a mass of traditional biases. So much time had to be spent examining a postulated outside point of origin of a given cultural element that far too little attention was given to internal innovation, internal borrowing, and the contact of peoples within Africa.

Despite this handicap of preconception, the picture that emerges differs widely from the established stereotype of the African as an uninventive, ultra-conservative creature. His is a picture of consistent change over ages that reach back in time as far as anywhere in the past of mankind, and perhaps farther. Referring to the continuous population movements in Africa that made possible a wide diffusion of cultural impulses, Hailey wrote, "In present-day Africa we see the results of centuries of migration, intermarriage and conquests," where, "except in the least accessible regions . . . the geographical features of Africa have themselves facilitated the fusion of stocks rather than their segregation."[1]

It was only because the life of Africa had been known to Europe and America for so short a time that the specious portrayal of African cultures as static and unchanging attained

[9] H. A. Wieschhoff: *The Zimbabwe-Monomotapa Culture in Southeast Africa* (General Series in Anthropology, No. 8, Menasha, Wisconsin, 1941), pp. 95–7.

[1] Lord Malcolm Hailey: *An African Survey,* Revised 1956 (London, 1957), p. 28.

such currency, and the rapidity of change under industrialization occasioned such surprise. In fact, however, this dynamic of Africa was nothing new. It took on different form, and its intensity differed from that of the past. But as change, it was not different in kind. Like all other peoples, the Africans, from the earliest days of contact, took from what was brought to them, and reworked, adapted, and incorporated the new into the established ways of life.

3

The Base Line of Change:

Food-Gathering and Herding Peoples

In a work first published in 1943, giving excerpts from the writings of early travelers in Africa, there is the following passage:

> At school and subsequently, I had absorbed the idea that pre-European Africa was a place of complete and anarchic savagery. I do not know how this impression was received, but it was probably an accumulation from many sources. Now, as a student of these matters, I have come across many opinions expressed by administrators, missionaries and colonists in Africa, both living and dead, which repeat this view. "South Africa," wrote a Colonial Secretary of the last century, "beyond the reach of the White man is one scene of violence and rapine." This view still lingers, in spite of the revelations of the anthropologists, and it has important results. It helps to fix an uncritical and generalized attitude of superiority towards Africans and it acts not only as a justification of European annexation and government, for which a less gloomy view of the old Africa might suffice, but as an excuse for the less defensible activities of imperialism. How often have I heard it said in answer to some criticism of European policy of conduct, "Well,

after all, think what Africa was before the white man came!" Well, what *was* Africa? [1]

In attempting to answer this question, we may again stress the point that while the dynamics of change in Africa since the establishment of European control differed in form and in intensity from its earlier manifestations, the difference was still preponderantly one of degree. During these decades, and more especially since the end of the Second World War, the rate of acceleration was far greater, but the curve, though it became steeper, remained smooth. Because of this what seemed so impressive when viewed in short perspective and under the influence of widespread belief regarding the conservatism of African cultures, turned out to be but the latest phase in a process ages old—as old, indeed, as human culture anywhere.

It is essentially the later, steeper segment of the curve that will occupy us in this book. Yet in our thinking we must not isolate this from what has gone before, or we shall lack essential insights into the African scene. Equally important, for purposes of analysis is that the particular period which serves as our base line for plotting the course and extent of change be held firmly in mind.

For us, this will be the period just before the establishment of European control. As our point of reference we take the indigenous cultures immediately preceding the impact of those elements of European culture that have resulted in the most extensive changes—literacy, urban living, industrialization, new concepts of nature and of the supernatural, a broader outlook on the world at large, nationalism.

By taking as our base line Africa as it existed in the latter half of the nineteenth century, when the continent was being "opened," we are guided by the logic of our inquiry. It coincides with the historical reality of cumulatively directed change that followed this series of episodes in the history of Africa, and the consequences of these changes. Again, the period of effective initial contact with European ways yielded firsthand descriptions by

[1] M. Perham and J. Simmons: *African Discovery, an Anthology of Exploration* (London, 1942), p. 16.

early visitors of many fully functioning, autonomous African cultures. At the same time, the moment of penetration was recent enough so that scientifically controlled investigation could obtain much valuable information from Africans who were able to describe their precontact modes of life.

This documentation, to be sure, must be carefully scrutinized, and all scholarly safeguards must be used before we accept them as valid sources of information. A study of the writings of earlier observers, explorers, traders, missionaries, colonial officials, demonstrates that they recorded what they saw, as they saw it, even as their reports show how many questions went unanswered, and suggest the allowances that must be made for their biases. In the same way, the accounts of African elders had to be carefully checked by comparing variant versions, to determine the elaborations and deletions that mark the evocation of a regretted past, especially when recounted while experiencing the pressures of colonial rule.

What is impressive is that when the writings of untrained contemporary Europeans were checked against traditional accounts of African elders, and both tested by scientific field study, the measure of agreement was large in instance after instance, even though the two versions came from opposite sides of the acculturative experience. The description given by a member of the Dahomean royal family of the taxation system of the kingdom, as it existed some forty years earlier, before Dahomey was conquered by the French, is a case in point. One item in this account had to do with the use of tollgates to control the flow of goods along the roads and to collect customs for the central government. Duncan, writing in 1847, and Burton, in 1863, described the functioning of these tollgates in terms quite similar to those of a Dahomean speaking three or more decades after their disappearance. Such close corroboration of descriptive detail, in combination with other elements in his account that could not be checked by firsthand observation, or by recourse to written documentation, became admissible as inductive evidence.[2]

[2] Melville J. Herskovits: *Dahomey, an Ancient West African Kingdom*, Vol. I (New York, 1938), pp. 128–31.

It is apparent that the use of this technique of checking verbal against written accounts is particularly valuable in recovering those aspects of earlier cultures that were first to give way under the pressures of imposed controls. How, for example, could we otherwise recover the nature of the political structures that played so important a role in the functioning of autonomous African cultures? In some instances, the policy of indirect rule not only preserved certain earlier forms but, as we shall see in the case of Northern Nigeria, even helped to extend and reinforce them. Instances of this order were, however, far outnumbered by those where a chieftaincy that was nonexistent in the precontact political system was imposed by a European administration that took for granted the proposition that every "primitive" people must have its "chief." Where, as in the Congo under Belgian rule, for example, the *chef medaillé* was grafted onto a preexisting system of hereditary leaders, all care had to be taken to dissect out the imposed form from the earlier political pattern by the use of the ethnohistorical method. And the same precautions were called for in analyzing aboriginal economics, technology, or religion.

All over Africa, however, in areas removed from administrative or commercial centers, earlier patterns continued, and life went on much as in pre-European days. Populations might be more numerous, but established values were given new expression in changed outer forms under the impact of new influences. Consequently, the cultures, as living modes of belief and behavior, provided ample, reliable data for the mapping of areas at the time of the early, intensive European expansion.

Once our base line has been established, and something of an understanding of the cultures that preceded the imposition of European controls has been reached, we face our next methodological step. To round our picture, we must distil out of the varieties of forms that existed and have continued to exist in the Subsaharan continent, the unities that provide, so to speak, a cultural infrastructure to regional and local differences. The complexities of this problem force a balancing of similarities against differences, always in the light of the particular question that is being studied. In some regions, as in the Cameroons highlands, or in Uganda, relatively minor differences can be important. Elsewhere, unities over large areas can override conditions that were imposed either by the drawing of colonial boundaries, as along the line of division between the Congo and Northern Rhodesia, or by internal political manipulations that have made for arbitrary groupings, as in South Africa.

Even while the study, in depth, of individual cultures must be our starting point, since we must look to the results of such researches for our primary materials, it is not enough just to study one culture after another. Scientific procedure demands that description test current generalizations, or establish new ones, as a basis for eventual understanding.

It is essential, moreover, in any attempt to see African ways of life along broad lines, that the analysis focus on culture, without regard to either of the two semi-independent variables, physical type and language. The failure to separate out these variables made for the difficulties found in Seligman's early groupings of African peoples into Bushman, Hottentots and Negritos, the true Negro, the Hamites, the half-Hamites and the Bantu, where the basis of classification constantly shifted from race to language to culture.[3] On this score, the earlier classification by Ratzel [4] was more desirable, or even that of Dowd,[5] however unsatisfactory the treatment owing to inadequate command of materials and their misinterpretation. The *Ethnographic Survey of Africa*, begun in 1944 under the auspices of the International African Institute of London, follows a principle whereby "small groups of neighboring peoples are taken as units within broad geographical regions." [6] These clusters of societies are thus treated without introducing the factors of physical type or language, except as background for the social phenomena being considered. This ap-

[3] C. G. Seligman: *Races of Africa* (London, 1930; 2nd ed., 1957), *passim.*

[4] F. Ratzel: *Völkerkunde* (translated as *The History of Mankind*, Berlin, 1880).

[5] Jerome Dowd: *The Negro Races* (2 vols., New York, 1907–14).

[6] Lord Malcolm Hailey: *An African Survey*, Revised 1956 (London, 1957), p. 30.

proach has been further analyzed by Merriam in terms of its applicability to the cultures of the Congo.[7]

By basing our discussion on the concept of the culture area, which includes ecological and institutional factors, we have an approach that permits us to classify whole ways of life and to see the similarities and differences between African cultures in continental perspective. It is flexible enough to take into account all aspects of culture, and not restricted to arbitrarily selected features such as kinship structures, which have different distributions from religion or art or political organization, and which are not necessarily related to the ecological setting that provides for the satisfaction of biological needs. We must also stress the point that such culture areas are fixed in time—in this instance, just prior to the effective incursion of European influence.

At that time, the cultures of Africa south of the Sahara may be differentiated into six areas, the major outlines of which may still be discerned, despite the subsequent impact of Europe. On the accompanying map, they are, from south to north, the Khoisan Area, the East African Cattle Area, the Eastern Sudan, the Congo, the Guinea Coast, and the Western Sudan. On broader lines, they may be grouped into two categories, those that include the cultures with economies in which food-gathering and herding are primary, and those that are essentially agricultural. The first three of these will be treated in this chapter, the remainder in the chapter that follows, where the importance of this division in understanding responses to the innovations of the colonial period will also be discussed.

For purposes of scientific classification and analysis the culture area provides a time-saving device of considerable value, in that its unities give us a series of short-hand designations that permit us to group large numbers of peoples in terms of their primary orientations. Thus, when one is acquainted with the characteristics of areas, one need merely name the one in which a people live to suggest the kind of cultural forms and traditional

[7] Alan P. Merriam: "The Concept of Cultural Clusters Applied to the Belgian Congo," *Southwestern Journal of Anthropology*, Vol. XV (1959), *passim.*

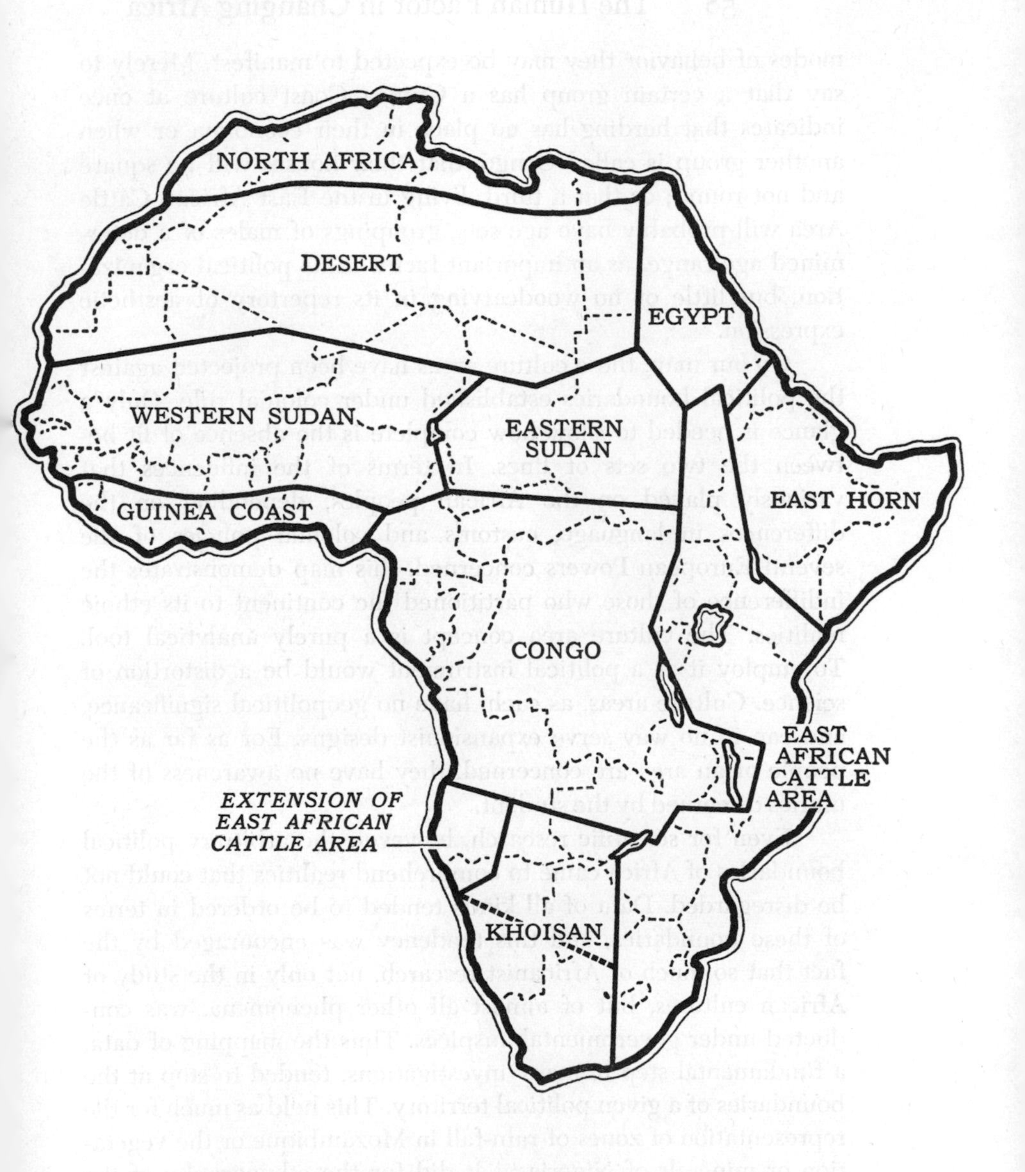

CULTURE AREAS OF AFRICA

modes of behavior they may be expected to manifest. Merely to say that a certain group has a Guinea Coast culture at once indicates that herding has no place in their economy; or when another group is called Congo, that their houses will be square and not round; or that a third, living in the East African Cattle Area will probably have age sets, groupings of males of a determined age range, as an important factor in its political organization, but little or no woodcarving in its repertory of aesthetic expression.

On our map, these culture areas have been projected against the political boundaries established under colonial rule. Only a glance is needed to show how complete is the absence of fit between the two sets of lines. In terms of the influences that variously played on the African peoples, depending on the differences in language, customs and colonial policies of the several European Powers concerned, this map demonstrates the indifference of those who partitioned the continent to its ethnic realities. The culture area concept is a purely analytical tool. To employ it as a political instrument would be a distortion of science. Culture areas, as such, have no geopolitical significance, and can in no way serve expansionist designs. For as far as the people of an area are concerned, they have no awareness of the unities discerned by the student.

Even for scientific research, however, the arbitrary political boundaries of Africa came to comprehend realities that could not be disregarded. Data of all kinds tended to be ordered in terms of these boundaries, and this tendency was encouraged by the fact that so much of Africanist research, not only in the study of African cultures, but of almost all other phenomena, was conducted under governmental auspices. Thus the mapping of data, a fundamental step in many investigations, tended to stop at the boundaries of a given political territory. This held as much for the representation of zones of rain-fall in Mozambique or the vegetation or minerals of Nigeria as it did for the ethnography of the Belgian Congo. It was recognition of this need for wider perspectives in research that in 1950 resulted in the organization of the

Commission for Technical Cooperation in Africa South of the Sahara (C.C.T.A.), and other intergovernmental bodies.

To differentiate culture areas, however, does not mean that certain traditions that mark off Subsaharan African cultures as a whole are not to be found, and in later chapters these will enter as a major factor in our analysis. Nor may we disregard the fact of intra-area variation, in accordance with which the customs of each group in an area have their own distinctive characteristics. What we do here is to draw our perspective in the middle distance.

[2]

Farthest to the south lies the *Khoisan* area, inhabited by the Bushman and Hottentot. It takes its name from a suggestion by Schultze,[8] made when he combined the first syllable of the Hottentot word for themselves, *Khoi-Khoin,* with *San,* their term for Bushmen, who give themselves no name as a people. The justification for placing the cultures of these two congeries in a single area is essentially a matter of balancing similarities and differences, for there are enough of both to justify their being treated together or separately. The balance is perhaps tipped toward grouping them under a single head when we contrast their ways of life with those of other peoples of Subsaharan Africa, and in addition recognize the special nature of their experiences with the various peoples who came into their territory.

Their past, indeed, has the quality of tragedy that everywhere characterizes the history of broken peoples such as many American Indian tribes or the aboriginal inhabitants of Tasmania. In the case of the Bushmen who, according to Tobias, "must have swarmed over the face of Africa in numbers hitherto undreamed of and unexpected," [9] the "centuries of hostility and extermina-

[8] L. Schultze: *Zur Kenntnis des Körpers der Hottentotton und Buschmänner* (in *Zoologische und Anthropologische Ergebnisse einer Forschungsreise im Westlichen und Zentralen Südafrika* (Vol. V, fasc. iii, pp. 147–227, Jena, 1928), p. 211.

[9] Phillip V. Tobias: "On the Survival of the Bushmen," *Africa,* Vol. XXVI (1956), p. 184.

tion to which they have been subjected at the hand of Europeans, Hottentots and Bantu," took a toll so great that Schapera's earlier statement stands: "There seems little doubt that the Bushmen are steadily dying out as a race,"[1] through intermarriage, if not through outside pressure.

Though the Hottentot were not, like the Bushmen, pursued by Boer and Bantu, their fate was the same. For they were absorbed by those with whom they came into contact, mixing with the Europeans who in the early days of occupation enslaved them, as well as with the Malays who were brought to South Africa, and with Bantu-speaking Africans, to form what has come to be known as the Coloured population of the Union. Their very name, in the Afrikaans form of *Hotnot,* has become a term of opprobrium. The tale of what happened to them, in scientific terms, has been told by Fischer;[2] the repercussions of their experiences on the descendants of these mixed matings has been given moving literary expression by Sarah Gertrude Millin.[3] They differ from other African peoples in three respects: Their cultures, including the languages with their "click" forms; their absorption by their neighbors; and their negligible degree of participation in influencing the course of events in the territories they inhabit.

Though Hottentot and Bushmen differ in basic subsistence patterns, they present almost classically pure forms of two kinds of economies, the Bushmen as the hunting and gathering type, the Hottentot as herders. For both, the surplus of what is produced beyond biological need is slight, though the Bushmen live closer to the subsistence level than did the Hottentot. Again, while the latter had learned to smelt iron and make metal tools, the Bushmen continued to use stone implements. Their culture has never been better described than by a Zulu who, about 1850, characterized them as follows:

[1] I. Schapera: *The Khoisan Peoples of South Africa* (London, 1930), p. 40.

[2] Eugen Fischer: *Die Rehobother Bastards* (Jena, 1913), *passim.*

[3] Sarah G. Millin: *God's Stepchildren* (New York, 1924).

> The Abatwa are very much smaller people than all small people; they go under the grass, and sleep in anthills; they go in the mist; they live in the up country in the rocks. . . . Their village is where they kill game; they consume the whole of it, and go away. . . . They are dreaded by men . . . for men do not see the man with whom they are going to fight . . . their strength is like that of the fleas, which have the mastery of the night. . . . They see them for their part, but they are not seen.[4]

The social structures of the peoples of this area reflect their economic situation. The essential Bushman grouping is the hunting band, which centers about a series of water holes recognized as belonging to it and so defining a territory within which its members move in search of game and wild vegetable foods. Monogamy is the rule, for economic rather than moral reasons; and descent is counted on both sides of the family, there being no clan structure. The political structure of Bushman life is the simplest possible. Conduct is regulated informally by the elders; there are no chiefs or courts. It is in religion, art, story-telling and the dance that they become creative and complex. The Moon, the Sun and the Stars are celestial beings that affect the affairs of men; with Mantis, the Creator, they are the subjects of an elaborate mythology. Rituals are simple, even though they are based on a well developed theology, and reflect the close relationship between religion, economic resources, and social structures.

The Hottentot have a belief system like that of the Bushmen, with similar mythic sanctions for the same supernatural beings, and similar concepts and practices centering about death and the role of the ghost. As might be anticipated because of the more secure economic base of Hottentot culture, ritual forms are more complex and more numerous, but the question why Hottentot art had nothing resembling the famed rock paintings of the Bushmen—indeed, why all the art forms of the Hottentot are so

[4] The Rev. Canon Calloway: *Nursery Tales, Traditions, and Histories of the Zulus, in their own Words, with a Translation into English, and Notes* (Memoirs of the Folk Lore Society, No. 1, Natal and London, 1868), pp. 352–5.

crude—remains unresolved. Political and social structures, on the other hand, were more complex—they had a tribal organization, headed by chiefs with authority to rule and negotiate. Hottentot groupings were made up of a series of clans, each taking the name of a legendary ancestor, with descent being counted in the male line. The clans, which have continued to exist, regulate marriage and are exogamous.

Each clan was essentially independent, and could on occasion assert this independence by leaving the tribal group with which it was affiliated. Indeed, the clan was the basic political unit, so that a tribal chief, the head of the senior clan of the tribe, was, as Schapera put it, "little more than *primus inter pares*."[5] Economically, as a cattle-raising people, the Hottentot were more secure than their neighbors. They lived in camps made up of mat-covered shelters, moving with the seasons to the places where there was the best pasturage and water for their animals. Agriculture, however, played no part in their subsistence system; like the Bushmen, they found vegetable food where they could. And when the grasses were poor and their cows gave little milk, they sought sustenance by hunting.

But these are things of the past, except in a few scattered regions of the northern Cape Province, just as they are with the Bushmen, who are found in somewhat larger identifiable numbers of bands in Bechuanaland, Southwest Africa, and southern Angola.

[3]

The *East African Cattle Area* stretches along the continent from the extreme south to the great lakes and beyond, in addition to its extension among the cattle-keeping peoples of southwestern Angola. The cattle complex, which combines elements of social and economic structure, political position and ritual, all focusing on these animals, gives the cultures their most

[5] I. Schapera, op. cit., p. 227.

distinctive feature, and the area its name.[6] Though cattle are found in many other parts of the continent—as we have seen, among the Hottentot, and as we shall see, in the Western Sudan—they rarely hold the place they do in the Cattle Area where they literally give point and meaning to the life of the people. As among the Ngoni,[7] cattle are everywhere reported as giving security, pleasure, and emotional satisfaction. When a member of the secretariat of a United Nations Trusteeship Commission Visiting Mission to Ruanda commented to an African veterinary assistant on the fact that, in vaccinating a herd of cattle, he neither branded the beasts nor otherwise marked them to ensure against duplication of effort, the answer was, "But I put down the date in my book against the name of each animal, so I don't have to mark them." On another, deeper level, this time of values, one result of an exploratory study by Marwick on public opinion polling among nonliterate peoples, carried out among the Cewa of Northern Rhodesia, is revealing. One of the questions was, "What will happen to an African who gets rich?" Of the 268 persons interviewed, 24.2%, by far the largest among the six answers recorded, responded, "He'll buy cattle." [8]

The special position of cattle gives most of these East African cultures a dual economy that derives from the functional distinction between subsistence and prestige systems, the former being based primarily on agriculture, the latter on cattle. The two are, of course, closely interrelated, which is perhaps why it has taken so much research to reveal the actual operation of the prestige

[6] Melville J. Herskovits: "The Cattle Complex in East Africa," *American Anthropologist,* Vol. XXVIII (1926), *passim.*

[7] Margaret Read: *The Ngoni of Nyasaland* (London, 1956), pp. 174–6.

[8] M. G. Marwick: "An Experiment in Public-Opinion Polling among Preliterate People," *Africa,* Vol. XXVI (1956), p. 152. A further point, not only as regards method, but as revealing interracial attitudes is found in the fact that, while only 6.7% of those queried by Marwick gave this answer, the largest group of his respondents saying, in effect, "We can't get rich, we're black," the percentages of those whom his two African assistants queried and who replied in terms of the purchase of cattle were respectively 32.0 and 29.2.

systems in integrating the social and political structures of the tribal groupings of the area. On the surface the place of cattle was so unusual as to cause early observers to highlight what to them was an exotic and dramatic aspect of the life of the people, and thus make it difficult to see the system as a whole.[9]

The subsistence economy is, in truth, sparse. The population was and has remained relatively small, and in general the unit of residence is the extended family grouping. Larger aggregates, such as towns, were unknown in pre-European days. As a result, in the countryside the traveler sees a small cluster of dwellings, often placed on or near a hilltop, and centered about a kraal into which the domesticated animals—which, in addition to cattle, include donkeys, sheep and goats—are driven for safety at night.

Because there was no pressure of population, land was a free good, certainly insofar as the individual was concerned when it came to selecting a plot for a field, to say nothing of the use of grazing land. In theory, the land was and in most instances continued to be held by the group as a whole, being vested in the king or headman, where there was one, as trustee. Once allotted to an individual or a family to be worked as a garden, however, it could not be taken back as long as it was being used, while fruit trees continued to be owned by the individual who had planted them, even after he ceased to work his plot, and by his heirs.

If we consider the subsistence economy as a whole, we are struck by its lack of complexity. Houses, generally round, are simple in construction, as is logical where shifting cultivation is practiced and habitations must be periodically moved. The hoe is the prime agricultural implement, while spear and bow and arrow were, and in some measure have continued to be instruments of the hunt. Basketry is highly developed, but pottery, where it exists, is in the main not of high quality; weaving is at best a minor craft in a land where an abundant supply of domesticated and wild animals furnishes skins for clothing and containers. There was little specialization of labor, iron workers

[9] Cf. Harold K. Schneider: "The Subsistence Role of Cattle Among the Pakot and in East Africa," *American Anthropologist*, Vol. LIX (1957), passim.

being almost the only specialists. Though canons of sex division of labor differentiated the work of men from that of women, adults were competent in all the tasks held proper for their sex.

Distribution of goods was simply a function of the extended family, so that exchange, mainly the transactions involved in obtaining hoes and spears, was on the basis of barter. Where the political structure transcended the local group, a certain redistribution of resources was achieved through the obligation of a chief to provide for his retainers and entertain visitors to his kraal; court fees and contributions in kind defrayed these expenses. There was no money, and there were no markets.

It is precisely at this point that the importance of differentiating the prestige factors in the economy from those having to do with subsistence comes into play. An early writer, Casalis,[1] put the matter cogently when, describing the Basuto, he said, "They are much more attached to their flocks than to their fields, but . . . they depend more upon their fields than on their flocks for support." Many of those who either observed these cultures or had to work with the people, concluded that since cattle were repositories of value, and were exchanged, they represented the equivalent of money. This is not the place to examine the technical point this raises.[2] It should be indicated, however, that identifying them as money equivalents led many administrative officers to adopt measures which, by trial and error, they came to recognize as mistaken and unworkable.

In eastern and southern Africa, however, though there was no currency of any kind, cattle represented wealth. And, as is implicit in the very concept of a prestige economy, cattle, being wealth, were and have continued to be primarily important as an index of social position. It is of no consequence how much land a man may cultivate, or what other goods he may possess. Without cattle he will enjoy neither position nor respect. Thus Ashton, commenting on the reluctance of the Basuto, in the southern part

[1] E. Casalis: *The Basutos; or, Twenty-three Years in South Africa* (London, 1861), p. 158.

[2] Cf. Melville J. Herskovits: *Economic Anthropology* (New York, 1952), pp. 262–8.

of our area, to alter their traditional ways of breeding and caring for cattle so as to improve the breed, in contrast to their attitudes toward other stock, said "the reason . . . is mainly that the latter . . . often produce a cash return, whereas cattle are prized as much for their social as for their economic value."[3] From far to the north, Schneider reported for the Pakot of Kenya "Cattle are more than mere economic goods. They are a subject of focal interest in the lives of the people, as is indicated by the . . . identification with and the affection for them that is felt."[4]

Nowhere has misunderstanding of the role of cattle been greater then regarding their use on the occasion of marriage. Called "bride price," this came to signify that the Africans of the area "bought" their wives, a concept that was taken over by observers of custom in other parts of Africa, where the transfer of wealth is also an essential validation of the marriage compact. So prevalent did this notion become that Africans themselves adopted it when speaking to Europeans, though on one occasion the point was turned by a French-speaking Dahomean when he remarked that he had no more "bought" his wives than a European father could be said to have "bought" a husband when he provided a dowry for his daughter.

It took years of research to reveal the actual functioning of the exchange, and to replace the earlier designation with the scientifically more valid term "bride wealth." It became apparent that cattle were a means of establishing social solidarity among kin groups, and that their transfer in marriage was an economic device for the redistribution of wealth, as exemplified by the Turkana and Jie. Among these people, social ties are cemented by the fact that the fifty or more head of cattle the bridegroom must give are obtained by him from members of his immediate family, his more distant relatives, and his friends or age mates; while these same cattle are redistributed by the father of the bride to those who have previously aided him or his son in

[3] Hugh Ashton: *The Basuto* (London, 1952), pp. 139–40.

[4] Harold K. Schneider: "Pakot Resistance to Change," in *Continuity and Change in African Cultures* (edited by W. R. Bascom and M. J. Herskovits, Chicago, 1959), p. 151.

assembling an earlier bride-wealth payment. The factor of prestige also came out clearly. For the bridegroom,

> It is a matter of genuine pride to give as large a number of animals as possible and it will bring him favourable opinion and esteem, not only in society at large but more importantly with his father-in-law and his brothers-in-law.[5]

In both the northern and southern portions of the area, the ownership of cattle was a prerogative of the rulers. Casalis observed for the Basuto, "Such is, in fact, the great social bond of these tribes; the sovereigns, instead of being supported by the community, are the chief supporters of it."[6] Among the Haya of Tanganyika:

> In former times the Chief alone disposed of cattle. From the spoils of war, from his own herds, etc., he distributed beasts among his relatives, favourites and prominent soldiers. Although for the last 50 years everyone has been allowed to own cattle, the original descendants of these recipients are still the richest cattle owners.[7]

According to the Abbé Kagamé:

> Ruanda society was based on three elements, that were of a social and political order as well as religious, and which determined the life of the country: 1st, *The king*. . . . 2nd, *The warrior*, the right arm of the king. . . . 3rd, *The cow*, wealth by and of itself, instrument of domination by the king over his subjects, determinant of social position of the various members of the hierarchy of the country.[8]

The role of cattle in providing sanctions for the stratification of Banyarwanda society has also been analyzed by Maquet;[9] among the Zulu, the social position of the individual is determined by the

[5] P. H. Gulliver: *The Family Herds* (London, 1955), pp. 228–42.
[6] Ibid., p. 155.
[7] Hans Cory and M. M. Hartnoll: *Customary Law of the Haya Tribe, Tanganyika Territory* (London, 1945), p. 167.
[8] A. Kagamé: "La Littérature Orale au Ruanda," in *Des Prêtres Noirs s'Interrogent* (by A. Abble, *et al.*, Paris, 1956), pp. 205–6.
[9] Jacques J. Maquet: "Le Système des Relations sociales dans le Ruanda ancien," *Annales* du Musée Royal du Congo Belge, Ethnologie, Vol. I (1954), *passim*.

number and origin of the herd from which the bride-wealth cattle given for his mother came.

The ritual uses of cattle also help to solidify social structures. They enter into all the "crises" in the lives of men—birth, puberty, marriage, death. Their importance is reflected semantically in a detailed and explicit terminology, as in the forty different words used by the Nuer to designate a cow or an ox of a particular color,[1] or in the convention whereby a good Ila wife is defined as one who gives herself to other men so that her husband can claim a cow in compensation from these men.[2]

Yet we must not distort the image of these cultures by a too exclusive preoccupation with this one element. For one thing, cattle enter but tangentially into the daily lives of the women, who are primarily concerned with providing and preparing food for their households, and with the care of their infants. Their association with cattle is thus passive where it is not negative, as in the rule that forbids women to milk or herd cattle. The rituals in which cattle play a significant part are in the main secular. Yet the study made by Evans-Pritchard of the relationship between men and cattle as this is conceived by the Nuer shows that cattle figure far more in religious thought than the observation of ritual alone may have led us to believe.[3]

The social structures of the East African area are based on descent counted, in most instances, on one side of the family, usually that of the father. By logical extension, those related in this line form a series of clans. Marriage is polygynous, with the wives moving to the residence of their husband. Outstanding is the system of age-grading, which cuts across kin relationships to erect a hierarchy based on residence and age. These non-kinship groupings had great political importance both for the inner structure of power and the relations of the society with its neighbors. The Zulu *impi*, the regiments of the army created by Chaka, the

[1] E. E. Evans-Pritchard: *The Nuer* (Oxford, 1940), pp. 41–5.

[2] E. A. Smith and A. M. Dale: *The Ila-Speaking Peoples of Northern Rhodesia*, Vol. I (London, 1920), p. 382.

[3] E. E. Evans-Pritchard: *Nuer Religion* (Oxford, 1956), pp. 197–230, 248–71.

great conqueror of the early nineteenth century in southern Africa, were derived from the age-grade system; in the north, as among the Masai, the age sets were the prime instruments of cattle raiding. As a set moves with time into the upper reaches of the system, its members assume more power, for in eastern Africa, as elsewhere, age is held to bring wisdom, and wisdom is the source of power.

The control of power is manifest in different degrees of explicitly institutionalized political forms. Schapera has sketched these for southern Africa; they comprise

> not only a class system headed by the chief's descent group, but also a small body of confidential advisors and senior executive officers attached to the chief, a hierarchy of subordinate local rulers with their own advisors and other assistants, public assemblies at the local level, popular participation in court cases at all levels, and the possibility of commoners obtaining promotion through personal merit.[4]

As we move toward the northern part of the area, however, political institutions tend to become simpler, at least in the sense of restricted geographical scope and numbers of people controlled. If we take the five societies of eastern Africa discussed in a work on African political structures, in terms of the concept of "state" and "stateless" groupings advanced by Fortes and Evans-Pritchard,[5] we find that the two "stateless" ones, Logoli and Nuer, are in the north, while of the three given as having "states," two, Zulu and Ngwato, are in the South.

However, there is no society in this area whose power structure is not describable; none in which well-recognized rules of conduct are not enforceable through a well-delimited judicial process. As regards government, its form, and certainly that aspect of it subsumed under the word "bureaucracy," is primarily determined by the size of the unit under control. The concept

[4] I. Schapera: *Government and Politics in Tribal Societies* (London, 1956), p. 65.

[5] M. Fortes and E. E. Evans-Pritchard: *African Political Systems* (London, 1940), p. 5.

"tribe," difficult to define, and of little utility, whether for scientific or practical purposes, will be avoided.

What is important is that in all this East African area there are self-conscious, self-identifying groups whose modes of regulating conduct are clearly understood. Everywhere there are recognized ways of settling disputes and punishing misdeeds according to rules that can be codified. When actual cases are analyzed, as Gluckman has done for the Lozi, they are found to have the logic that makes the judicial process as a whole comparable, in terms of ethical assumption and procedural regularity, to Euroamerican legal thought and procedure, however different the forms in which they are cast may be.[6]

Though here as everywhere sanctions for all aspects of life derive from world view, the theologies of East Africa has received relatively little attention from trained anthropologists. In these systems of thought, the universe is conceived as having been created by a major deity, though even here there are exceptions, as in the case of the Lovedu, who conceive of an act of creation without showing interest in its mode or instrumentality.[7] The extent to which this deity is thought to intervene in the affairs of man varies. In some cases he is considered remote, and one to be disregarded; elsewhere, as among the Banyarwanda, a being such as Imana, the Creator, is a figure constantly to be taken into account.[8] In some societies, the Creator is believed to delegate power to inferior beings, who are directly responsible for what happens to man. In this type of religion, ways and means of influencing such beings may be found by divination, so that an individual can exert some control over his own fate.

Though it is scarcely correct to state, as has so often been done, that the religion of this part of Africa is ancestor worship, there is little doubt that the ancestors figure most decisively in

[6] Max Gluckman: *The Judicial Process among the Barotse of Northern Rhodesia* (Manchester, England, 1955), pp. 327 ff.

[7] J. D. and E. J. Krige: "The Lovedu of the Transvaal," in *African Worlds* (edited by D. Forde, London, 1954), pp. 59–61.

[8] Jacques J. Maquet: "The Kingdom of Ruanda," in *African Worlds* (edited by D. Forde, London, 1954), pp. 169–70.

the world view, and that many ritual practices are directed toward them. Such worship makes explicit, or implies the belief in the soul, or rather souls of man, which retain functional roles after death. This, in turn, reflects the belief in the essential oneness of the social group; that is, of the living and ancestral generations. The ancestors are thus the intermediaries between living human beings and other forces in the Universe, who watch over their descendants and, if rightly propitiated, help to prosper and protect them. Magic, as amulet, medicine, or compelling force, also plays an important part in the belief-system, as a means for manipulating supernatural powers to insure health, increase of stock, success in mating, or harm to an enemy. Magic is specific in reference, and is often associated with knowledge of crafts. The widely prevalent rainmaker has powers of this kind.

In this area, the sparseness of the economic order would seem to be associated with paucity of art forms. This in no wise suggests a lack of aesthetic response, for many basketry and beadwork designs which embellish utensils and other objects show aesthetic excellence as well as technical skill. It may also be that in part this paucity is accounted for by the relative simplicity of the ritual observances in the area; whatever the reason, in the graphic and plastic arts, eastern and southern Africa differ strikingly from the areas that lie to the west. On the other hand, its musical resources are rich and distinctive. The drum plays an important role in validating rank, but not in accompanying song, at variance to what is ordinarily thought typical of "African" music.[9] The range of string, wind, and percussion instruments is large, however, and they are often played in solo performances. Outstanding in the musical culture of the East African area is the *timbila,* a xylophone-like instrument that has been brought to a high state of technical and artistic perfection by the Chopi of Mozambique. Especially impressive are the ensembles of instrumentalists, singers and dancers that weld the

[9] Alan P. Merriam: "African Music Re-examined in the Light of New Materials from the Belgian Congo and Ruanda-Urundi," *Zaïre,* Vol. VII (1953), *passim.*

orchestral forms with opera and ballet into a unified, well-structured production of the highest artistic quality.[1]

[4]

The third area is the *Eastern Sudan*. It reaches from the Nile to Lake Chad, lying west of the northernmost portion of the East African Cattle area. It comprehends the southern part of the Sudanese Republic, the Republic of Chad and the northern part of the Central African Republic, while its extreme westerly extension touches on Northern Nigeria. It moves from the savannah country of its southern portions to full desert; it has both quasi-agricultural and quasi-herding peoples, and full-blown nomads.

Historically no less than geographically and ethnically it is residual; indeed, in this respect it is even more pronounced than in the area of similar name that adjoins it to the west, which also manifests this trait. MacMichael, writing of Kordofan, more or less indicates the heterogeneity of the Eastern Sudan as a whole. Kordofan, he tells us, has

> three parallel latitudinal belts, viz.:—the southern mountains inhabited by sedentary autochthonous Nūba and in part by nomad Baḳḳára; the central and comparatively fertile district peopled by a mixed Arab and black race; and the rough open wastes of the north, the home of the nomad Arab.[2]

The history of the region which he gives is one of movement, of conquest, and of migration. And one gains a similar picture for the Sudan as a whole, of groupings of indigenous peoples conquered by Arabs or, toward the west, by such Mohammedanized peoples as the Bornu.[3]

To describe an area of this kind is difficult for two reasons. The first is because of its residual character. Its cultures do not

[1] Hugh Tracy: *Chopi Musicians, their Music, Poetry and Instruments* (London, 1948), *passim.*

[2] H. A. MacMichael: *The Tribes of Northern and Central Kordofán* (Cambridge, England, 1912), p. 1.

[3] Sir Richmond Palmer: *The Bornu Sahara and Sudan* (London, 1936), *passim.*

extend to neighboring areas; yet they are too heterogeneous to permit descriptive generalizations for the area as a whole, as for the Cattle Area. The characteristics of the cultures of the neighboring areas are present in attenuated form; yet none of them, even in new combinations, are sharp enough to yield distinct configurations. This brings us to the second reason for our difficulty, the fact that the cultures themselves, with a few notable exceptions, have not been adequately described. Most of the available data, found in the files of *Sudan Notes and Records,* or the *Journal de la Société des Africanistes,* are fragmentary and too often report the observations of devoted and interested amateurs, rather than the findings of trained ethnographers. For the western portion of the area particularly, aside from a few analyses of cultural details of specific traditions, little systematic research has been done at all to meet the scientific challenge of the ethnic complexities of the region about Lake Chad.

In essence, the cultures of the area are to be thought of as shading from the Congo type, as found among such a people as the Azande to the south, or the East African Cattle forms such as characterize the Nuer or Dinka to the east, to the Berber and Touareg cultures of the Desert Area to the north and northwest. Comparably, on the western side of our area the cultures partake of the traits of the Islamized peoples of the Western Sudan area, but these traits in turn become increasingly diluted as we move eastwards.

We may take the position of the principal domesticated animal in the cultures of the eastern Sudan as an example of this. As we move away from the cattle area, we find that the importance of the cow tends to give way to that of the camel. Reid, discussing the peoples of the White Nile Province, says

> As in the North it is the ambition of every Arab who has pretensions of birth and position to own one or more herds of camels, so in the south among the Baggara you are not a real gentleman until you have acquired a nice bunch of cattle.[4]

[4] J. A. Reid: "Some Notes on the Tribes of the White Nile Province," *Sudan Notes and Records,* Vol. XIII (1930), p. 172.

To the north and west, among the Kawahla, he reports that "the breeding and herding of camels has become a fine art," and gives the criteria by which, with all the attention to minutiae that characterizes the East African cattle owner's attention to his beasts, the age of camels can be reckoned.[5]

As we move to the west, in the Nuba Mountains, north of the region where the agricultural Azande live, we find that the peoples who inhabit these hills, the most carefully studied of the entire Eastern Sudan area, combine the cattle and cultivating patterns of those to the east and south of them.

> The main means of livelihood in the Nuba Mountains is agriculture. Animal husbandry and hunting, though well-organized and common everywhere, play only a secondary part. Handicrafts are of little importance; the handicrafts of the men, more especially, like blacksmith work, weaving or wood-carving, are mostly of recent origin and limited to a few individuals in tribes which adopted these crafts from their more advanced neighbours, Arabs or Daju.[6]

As might be expected in such an economy, "The Nuba people are poor herdsmen. They know next to nothing about breeding and little about keeping livestock."[7] Yet despite the emphasis on agriculture, certain of the values of the Nuba peoples recall those of the East African area. "Even more strongly than Nuba farming economy, Nuba livestock economy is characterized by that trend to display and at the same time rapidly dispose of wealth and surplus." Livestock are used to repay kinship obligations, for bride-wealth payments, and for slaughtering "at special ceremonies, by means of which individuals attain a higher status."[8]

To the north, among the Kabâbîsh, the cow is displaced as the primary prestige animal by the camel. The Seligmans differentiate the life of this people, primarily a pastoral folk like the nomadic Beja Arabs to the east, on the basis of "the severity of the dry season" they must cope with, "and the organized effort

[5] Ibid., pp. 165–7.
[6] S. F. Nadel: *The Nuba* (Oxford, 1947), p. 15.
[7] Ibid., p. 60. [8] Ibid., p. 67.

that is required to meet it."[9] We see the social importance of the camel, for instance, where payment of blood money is the accepted way to avoid "those long-drawn feuds recorded in Arabian history," unknown among the Kabâbîsh. "Theoretically," they report, "the blood fine should consist of 100 she-camels." Again, prestige marriage payments are made in terms of camels, not cattle. "Soon after the marriage agreement has been drawn up, the bridegroom's father sends one or more she-camels" for the marriage feast. "A poor man would send sheep instead of camels." During the wedding ceremonies, while "a wealthy man might give his son as many as a hundred she-camels, the least gift of a poor man would be ten or fifteen sheep, though few would give less than five or six she-camels."[1]

To the west, in Darfur, other Baggara peoples, such as the Habbania and the Beni Helba, have horses. Cultivation among these groups is rudimentary, and "all count on buying from other tribes for a large part of their supply." Their attitude toward cattle is not unlike that encountered in the East African area, since,

> It is impossible to have any understanding of these tribes without taking into account their dependence on the love of their herds. . . . Their horses are to them of infinitely less value than their cattle, and they are regarded chiefly as a luxurious means of conveyance for which ready money or cattle can be obtained easily.

Yet the presence and use of the horse, the importance of hunting in the economy, and the rudimentary nature of the agricultural effort place these groups outside the category of the peoples in the Cattle Area, properly speaking.[2]

Still further to the west, in the region of Lake Chad, cattle take on exchange, as against prestige values. Says Landeroin, the interpreter of the Tilho Niger-Chad mission of 1906–1909, of the Kanem, an agricultural and herding people, "Cattle herds are

[9] C. G. and B. Z. Seligman: *The Kabâbîsh, a Sudan Arab Tribe* (Harvard African Studies, Vol. II, pp. 105–85) (Cambridge, Massachusetts, 1918), p. 116.

[1] Ibid., pp. 121, 133–4.

[2] G. D. Lampen: "The Baggara Tribes of Darfur," *Sudan Notes and Records*, Vol. XVI (1933), p. 99.

numerous; the oxen are exported to Bornu, while the cows supply milk, which the Kanembu drink in large quantity."[3] They also, we learn, export camels. This is similarly the case with the Buduma, a fishing, herding people who sell their cattle to the Nigerian Hausa. They have some horses, and a few goats.

Other aspects of these economies and their material culture follow the same pattern of heterogeneity. Markets are generally absent, but as we move from the southeast toward the west, we find centers of trade becoming more customary. Except under influence from the north, media of exchange are not used, nor is there much division of labor, though this begins to appear in the west, where the tribes of the Chad basin impinge on the peoples of the Western Sudan area, and where technological and economic specialization becomes noticeable.

As concerns the religions of the area, we enter into the part of Africa dominated by Islam, though not everywhere; along its southern boundary, from the Nuba hills to the Chad, we find peoples who have resisted Moslem influence. From the short description of the beliefs of the Nuba that Nadel has published, we get a picture of a religion that is not at all unlike that of the peoples to the south and east, stressing, in at least three of the Nuba tribes, the "spirit cult" centering about "individuals capable of producing a state of trance and mental dissociation which is interpreted as spirit possession."[4] The report of the Seligmans on these same peoples mentions ancestral great gods, and above all rain makers, with a "general pattern to which the rain ritual conforms." On the whole, we learn, "religion appears to become more complex and is more organized as we proceed from south to north."[5] Far away, among the Kãgu group of the Fali, in the extreme north of the French Cameroons, death ceremonies consist of "a kind of mourning, the first of the numerous ceremonies which, from generation to generation, lead the souls of the an-

[3] République Française, Ministère des Colonies: *Documents Scientifiques de la Mission Tilho* (1906–1909), Vol. II (Paris, 1911), p. 394.

[4] Op. cit., pp. 440 ff.

[5] C. G. and B. Z. Seligman: *Pagan Tribes of the Nilotic Sudan* (London, 1932), pp. 393–8.

cestors to a complete purification." This would indicate that a cult of the ancestors and of death, analogous to similar cults of the peoples to the south and west of the Fali, also exists among them.[6]

Obviously, however, the long contact of these peoples with Islamized populations must have given many opportunities to Islam, so that here, as elsewhere in Africa, the question posed as to why its penetration stopped where it did. The Arabs to the north have for centuries needed no proselytizing; to the west, where indigenous folk became Islamized, they tended to accept its forms of worship without necessarily taking over the concomitant beliefs or, indeed, often without giving up earlier forms of ritual. This relatively narrow "pagan" strip in the southern part of the area may be regarded as an extension of the line of demarcation in religion that moves in a great arc from Sierra Leone northeast to Chad, and thence easterly until it reaches the Ethiopian border. North of this line, everywhere in Africa Islam prevails; to the south of it, aboriginal religions have maintained themselves, to meet the missionary efforts of the Christian churches which came with European control.

Perhaps the marked political fragmentation of the area is an expression of its residual quality. Here we find no kingdoms such as mark eastern Africa, or the Congo, or the western Sudan. Nadel, for the Nuba hills alone, tells us of four *groups* of tribes, totaling fifteen separate entities, each group having its distinctive sociological and ritualistic structure. "The total population of the Nuba tribes," he states, "appears to be in the vicinity of 300,000; it is sub-divided in over fifty different ethnic groups—tribes and tribal sections—each hill almost possessing a people conscious of its separateness and ethnic individuality." The linguistic fragmentation is as striking as the ethnic differentiation. "It has been said that there are as many Nuba languages as there are hills. This is but a slight exaggeration." And though these languages are related in families, their large number in such a small geographical compass is accounted for by "the isolation in which

[6] Jean-Paul Lebeuf: "Les Rites Funéraires chez les Fali," *Journal de la Société des Africanistes,* Vol. VIII (1938), p. 105.

most of the hill communities have lived perhaps for centuries, and the absence of any large-scale political unification."[7]

When we move to the north, in Kordofan, among the Arab Kabâbîsh, the tale of fragmentation is the same. According to MacMichael, the separate entities have little tradition of unity, and recognize no common ancestor. The various groups of Arabs who migrated to the region where they live never merged to form a political unit, and whatever unities they manifest have been imposed from without. Kordofan, that is, "formed the only break in the chain of dynastic kingdoms stretching across Central Africa from east to west. . . ."[8] In Darfur the same condition prevails. The Seligmans name many such divided groups: the people of Jebel Midob, "semi-nomadic herders," and Berti, "divided into innumerable sections," such as the Fur, comprising three groups which in the seventeenth century were welded into a single political entity under Arab influence.[9] And toward the far west, one need only consult a tribal map of the Chad region to sense how many groupings there are.

Social institutions do have certain elements in common. All peoples who have been reported count descent unilaterally, that is to say on one side of the family or the other, with the familiar Subsaharan African pattern of having rights in and obligations to the families of both parents, without regard to the fact that one is legally descended, so to speak, on one or the other side, with incest lines being most closely drawn in the recognized line of descent. Polygyny is everywhere practiced. In Kordofan, the Kabâbîsh are divided into sections and subsections, called by a term which, translated, means "mouth of the house," each headed by an elder. Descent is on the father's side, but the most favored type of marriage is that between the children of two brothers, which is unusual for this type of system. The Seligmans point out that these people feel they are following orthodox Moslem prohibitions, "yet the marriage between a man and his brother's

[7] Op. cit., pp. 1–3. [8] Op. cit., p. 4.

[9] C. G. and B. Z. Seligman: *Pagan Tribes of the Nilotic Sudan* (London, 1932), Ch. XIII.

daughter is not looked upon unfavourably, and there seems to be no feeling against the union of a man and his father's sister."[1] Age grades, strong in East Africa, are present in the Nuba hills,[2] but have not been reported elsewhere.

As contacts of Subsaharan Africa with Europe intensified pressures toward change, and new integrations increased, the peoples of the Eastern Sudan continued much on their accustomed way. It remained an area in which a European anthropologist, as late as 1938, was unable to find an interpreter.[3] With the number of development projects of all kinds being constantly augmented elsewhere, here the Gezira cotton-growing scheme of the Sudan stood alone.

In part, this was undoubtedly due to the kind of country which the people inhabit, ranging from subdesert to desert, difficult to farm or graze, slight of yield, which makes understandable the sparseness of the population, and explains why here little or no problem of urbanization or industrialization obtained. One may only conclude that the Eastern Sudan is not only residual as a cultural area seen at the moment of European colonial impact; it has remained so in the face of European contact. Hence most of the questions of cultural continuity and change with which we are concerned have only minor relevance for its peoples, who will consequently be touched on but lightly in the pages of this work.

[1] C. G. and B. Z. Seligman: *The Kabâbîsh, a Sudan Arab Tribe* (Harvard African Studies, Vol. II, pp. 105–85) (Cambridge, Massachusetts, 1918), pp. 137–8.

[2] S. F. Nadel: *The Nuba* (Oxford, 1947), pp. 134 ff., 230 ff., 298 ff., 341 ff.

[3] S. F. Nadel: personal communication.

4

The Base Line of Change: Agricultural Peoples

Before we proceed to a discussion of the three remaining areas of Subsaharan Africa, we may examine some of the implications of our broad twofold division of these areas—the pastoral east and the agricultural west—for adjustment to the post-European scene. This is important, because it is seldom realized to what extent the differences between the cultures of the pastoralists and the agriculturalists were critical in influencing the kind of adaptation they had to make to European contact and control. Thus the relative ease with which, in the agricultural western part of the continent, Africans took over the growing of cash crops may be contrasted with the difficulty that colonial officials experienced in eastern Africa and the eastern Sudan in inducing the cattle-keeping peoples to accept "economic" as against subsistence farming, or to adopt methods of breeding and care calculated to improve the quality of their livestock.

From this point of view, what can be thought of as the negative aspects of the East African Cattle and Eastern Sudanese cultures—those of the Khoisan area need not concern us here, inasmuch as their role in post-European Africa was not significant—takes on added relevance, especially when juxtaposed against the positive manifestations of their counterparts in western Africa and the Congo. The peoples whose cultures we have discussed in the preceding chapter, while self-sufficient in their subsistence economies, had minimal specialization of labor. There was little or no trade, and no tradition of the market. Their exchanges were not cast in terms of a least common denominator of value, for in their type of economy, money was superfluous. The pattern of settlement did not include towns or cities; even permanent village sites do not accord with pastoralism.

In contrast, as we shall see, in the societies described in this chapter arts and crafts were highly developed. With specialization went trade, and with trade there developed a series of monetary systems which facilitated exchange. The basis of settlement everywhere was, and has continued to be, the village. In some cases, as in western Africa, a pattern of towns and even cities of sizable proportions developed long before the advent of European control.

When reduced to such economic and technological elements, the relevance of the African traditional culture for adjustment to the imposition of colonial controls is self-evident. The agriculturally based societies were evidently closer to European modes than were those of the pastoralists. The world economic order, especially those segments of it with which the Africans came into direct contact, has an essentially pecuniary base. The agriculturalists, who knew what money is and how to use it, were able to adjust to this important aspect of their new experience far more readily than the pastoralists, to whom money was quite foreign. This is also apparent when we consider some of the features of European commercial enterprise, such as selling for profit, or the institutions of credit and interest. To make the point, we need but contrast the ease with which Indians came to dominate trade in the eastern part of Africa with the experience of Levantine traders in such West African cities as Onitsha, Aba, Lagos, Ibadan and Accra, where the lively and effective competition of Africans had to be faced.

The influences of these differentials move in widening circles throughout the entire range of adaptation. There is a close correlation between the presence of a European and Asian settler population in eastern and southern Africa and the disproportionately meager educational funds allocated to the schooling of Africans who live there. This makes clear why, in these territories, there were so many fewer Africans who received secondary and higher education than in West Africa. But this is only a partial explanation, for among the pastoral peoples recognition of the importance of schooling as an aid to meeting the demands of their changed situation came late. Among the agriculturalists, it would not be easy to find populations of comparable size and importance as the Masai or Suk who, as late as 1950, rejected projects to build schools and provide teachers.

This brings us once more to the popularly debated relation between cultural learning and length of exposure to the new cultural experience.[1] Here we are dealing with the influence of traditional patterns of belief and behavior. Just as culture, being learned, makes cultural learning a matter of opportunity and not of generation, so learning the ways of another culture depends on motivation, and not on antecedent tradition. In saying this, we do not deny the importance of time or earlier habits. But we do insist that, in the complex of forces making for cultural readjustment, the factor of length of exposure should not be given undue importance. The drive for schooling that developed among such pastoralists as the Swazi or the Hutu or the Luo quite matched anything found among the Kongo or the Ashanti or the Bambara. The Baganda developed rapidly as traders, and the Chagga and Acholi as growers of cash crops, despite antecedent traditions of subsistence economies and rudimentary systems of exchange.

It can only be concluded that, in eastern and southern Africa, given the traditional values and the concentration of power in the hands of substantial numbers of permanently resident non-Africans, Africans had little stimulus or opportunity to acquire the training needed to meet the increasingly numerous demands of a rapidly changing order. In accepting this fact, however, we must keep clear of the trap set for those who fail to recognize the dynamics of the total situation. This is the trap into

[1] *Supra,* pp. 17–18.

which those in the Union of South Africa fell, or found it expedient to fall, when they took the scientifically indefensible and retrogressive position that the "Bantu," as the Africans were termed, should profit from something called "Bantu education," which was to be in harmony, presumably, with another entity, "Bantu culture." We must, rather, accent the comparative note, recognizing that once the recognition of a need is established, the dynamic of motivated learning enters, and earlier processes are again set in motion. We therefore turn to a description of these other cultures, so that in later chapters, we can have their traditions before us as we analyze various aspects of the newer setting in which they came to be lodged.

[2]

We begin with the *Congo* area, which is situated in the heart of the African continent, embracing the entire basin of the Congo river, and stretches from the Nile-Congo divide to the Atlantic. It includes the peoples of northern Angola, of the Congo Republic and the Gabun, of Rio Muñi and the eastern portion of the southern Cameroons as well as parts of the southern strip of the Sudanese Republic and of the Central African Republic, and it extends southeastward through the Katanga into northern Rhodesia.

Most of its peoples speak Bantu languages; culturally, linguistically and physically, the mass of its inhabitants are to be differentiated from the Pygmies, or Negrillos, who dot the northern and east-central parts of the area. The simpler life of the Pygmies stands in sharp contrast to that of the groups with whom they are often associated in a symbiotic relationship which represents a common tolerance of differing custom, based on a mutually advantageous exchange of goods. But because, like the Khoisan peoples, the Pygmies were not significantly involved in the events that followed European dominance, they will consequently not take our further attention, though we must recognize their importance for the scientific study of variation in the ways of human living.

The economies of the Congo are not only to be distinguished from those of East Africa by the fact that they are essentially agricultural, but also because of the absence of any of the larger domesticated animals. Hunting is an important complementary pursuit to agriculture, for, with fishing, it is the principal source of proteins. Shifting cultivation has been the rule, with fertilizer rarely used. The heavy rain forest which covers much of the area renders the work of preparing the fields difficult. Large trees must be felled, and heavy underbrush cut and burned off. The hoe is the primary agricultural implement. Outside the forested regions, in the savannahs, where this work is less arduous, the same agricultural patterns prevail.

The peoples of the area are skilled cultivators. De Schlippe, an agronomist, has testified to the knowledge which the Azande, in the northern part of the area, have of their environment.[2] The more than forty Pazande words he records to designate different kinds of land and the special suitability of each for the growing of particular crops, the six types of eleusine, ten varieties of maize, ten kinds of cassava they distinguish by name, all point to a semantic emphasis on agriculture comparable to that made apparent by the number of qualifying words used in East Africa to denote different kinds of cattle. Far to the west, the techniques devised by the Bakongo to utilize the vegetation of the savannah, reduced to ashes by controlled burning and the addition of humus, assures optimum yield and again attests to a high degree of agricultural skill.[3] At the extreme southeastern part of the area, the knowledge of types of soils and their potential for specific crops, though not as detailed as that of the Azande, provides requisite controls for the shifting cultivation they practice.[4]

Congo cultures are characterized by numerous craft specialties. Basketry is developed to a high point; weaving, especially

[2] Pierre de Schlippe: *Shifting Cultivation in Africa: the Zande System of Agriculture* (London, 1956), pp. 39–46, 49–77.

[3] L. de Wilde: *"De inlandse Landbouwstelsels in Belgisch-Kongo," Zaïre,* Vol. III (1949), p. 999.

[4] Audrey I. Richards: *Land, Labour and Diet in Northern Rhodesia, an Economic Study of the Bemba Tribe* (London, 1939), pp. 278–86.

with the fibre of the raffia palm, produces the prized raffia cloths of the Kasai peoples; pottery, ironworking and wood carving are widespread. Toward the east, bark cloth of fine quality is made. The degree of specialization is most marked in the southern part of the area; this has been described as "the most striking characteristic of Ba-Kuba civilization." This becomes apparent as the roll of specialists is called: sculptors in wood, weavers, cloth sewers, rope makers, blacksmiths, fishermen, hunters, canoe builders, leather workers; makers of mats, of nets, of palm oil, of salt; singers, dancers, musicians. All these were organized in guilds, which were represented in the council of the chief. And this specialization included intra-industrial differentiation of tasks. Economic value was set on time and manual work; there was labor for hire, and a well-developed commercial organization.[5]

Money, known almost everywhere in the area, took on many forms. Since it was frequently a consumption good as well as a common denominator of value, exchanges were achieved by a system technically called money barter, rather than money exchange. How complex the use of these tokens of value could be is seen in the role of raffia cloths among the Lele,[6] where they served only as a subsidiary medium of exchange in the market sense, being used to buy goods imported from foreign tribes. Internally, they were used whenever anything was to be acquired from a craftsman to whom the buyer was not closely related—a drum, or a set of bellows. Their most important function was as a repository of value, and as such, figured prominently in discharging marriage and other ritual obligations.

Soon after the turn of the century, many of the tokens of value used in the Kasai were listed—iron hoes, copper crosses (imported from the Katanga) and raffia cloths among the

[5] J. Vansina: *Les Tribus Ba-Kuba et les Peuplades Apparentées* (Annales du Musée Royal du Congo Belge, Sciences de l'Homme, Monographies Ethnographiques, Vol. I; also published in the *Ethnographic Survey of Africa,* Part I, Central Africa, Belgian Congo; Tervuren, Belgium and London, 1954), pp. 16–17.

[6] Mary Douglas: "Raffia Cloth Distribution in the Lele Economy," *Africa,* Vol. XXVIII (1958), *passim.*

Basonge; spear points, ingots of copper and rings of iron among the Batetela; iron throwing knives, spearheads and other iron objects among the Bankutu; and elsewhere cowrie shells imported by the Arabs.[7] In the upper Katanga, bars of salt were used. A detailed study of the technology of the manufacture of salt bars as well as of their economic use found that the unit was a bar weighing about six and a half pounds. One of these would purchase a hoe or an axe, a calabash of palm oil or a string of beads. A load of honey or eleusine was worth four or five bars, a gun, twenty, while slaves sold for from twenty to forty.[8]

With money went trade. Though this was in the main intertribal in character, certainly in the Kasai and adjoining regions, there was also some intratribal barter. Fixed markets seem to have been unusual, however, except where centers were traditionally established at a crossroad for the exchange of goods made by members of different tribal groupings. At the apogee of Bushongo prestige, their traders traveled unarmed in their capacity as middlemen, receiving from the Basongo Meno and the Bankutu pottery, ivory, and wood, and trading these to the Bena Lulua and the Baluba in exchange for iron, copper and salt.[9]

The societies of the southern portion of this area count descent in the maternal line. To the north, however, descent tends to be patrilineal. In the progression of nuclear family, extended family, and clan, the first two smaller lineage units are found everywhere. The clan, however, is in some instances lost, so to speak, where generations are not counted back to an ultimate ancestor.

Among the majority of societies found in what has been

[7] E. Torday and T. A. Joyce: *Notes ethnographiques sur des populations habitant les bassins du Kasai et du Kwango oriental* (Annales du Musée du Congo Belge, Ethnographie, Anthropologie—sér. III, tome II, fasc. 2, Brussels, 1922), pp. 17, 50, 281, 334.

[8] F. Grévisse: "Salines et Saliniers Indigènes du Haut-Katanga," *Bulletin du Centre d'Études des Problèmes Sociaux Indigènes,* No. 11 (1950), pp. 56–9.

[9] E. Torday and T. A. Joyce: *Notes ethnographiques sur les peuples communément appelés Bakuba, ainsi que sur les peuplades apparentées—Les Bushongo* (Annales du Musée du Congo Belge, Ethnographie, Anthropologie—sér. III, tome II, fasc. 1, Brussels, 1911), pp. 92–3.

termed the "matrilineal belt" of central Africa,[1] the man usually resides with the family of his wife, and the children belong to her family. Yet this does not mean that he is subservient to his wife's relatives. For while

> the man's control over his wife and her children can never be complete, except in the case of a union with a slave woman, . . . he can gain considerable power over his wife's labour, her property, and her child-bearing powers, as well as rights over his children's work and their marriages, by virtue of the service or payments he makes to his father- or brother-in-law.[2]

Marriage, here as everywhere in the Congo, is posited on payment of bride wealth, which takes the form of current value tokens.

The ways of life of the groups north of this belt, where descent is counted on the side of the father, have been studied far less than to the south, but enough has been done to reveal the general outlines of their social structures. The rule of residence and the patterns of family domination place more power in the hands of the husband and father; in such cases, also, the extended family plays a more important role because of its relation to the rule of residence. A study of the groupings of the Ngombe shows how complex these social structures can be.

> The Gonji Ngombe man is surrounded throughout his life by his patrilineal kin who form a series of fluid, yet fully functioning, social groups . . . bound not only by kinship but in large measure by territorial ties.

Whether or not the social grouping called *etuka,* composed of a number of extended families counting descent from a single ancestor, form a clan or not, is a matter of definition, but it does regulate marriage.[3] Among the Azande there is no question as to the existence of clans which, moreover, like the Mandja to the west in the Ubangi-Shari are totemic.

[1] Audrey I. Richards: "Some Types of Family Structure amongst the Central Bantu," in *African Systems of Kinship and Marriage* (edited by A. R. Radcliffe-Brown and D. Forde, London, 1950), pp. 207–30, 241–51.

[2] Ibid., p. 208.

[3] A. W. Wolfe: *Stability and Change in Ngombe Culture* (Ph.D. Thesis, Northwestern University, microfilmed by University Microfilms, Ann Arbor, Michigan, 1957), pp. 38–47.

Political authority varied from stable, populous kingdoms to restricted groupings, with controls vested in the hands of kinship units having a minimum of formal organization. There was little geographical coherence in the distribution of these types. Kingdoms such as Kongo in the west, Shongo in the south, Lunda in the southeast, or Zande in the north existed in the midst of smaller political units, out of which, indeed, they themselves seemed to have developed through a process of conquest and accretion. The basic social unit is the village, which, in most of the Congo, typically consists of rectangular houses, placed evenly on both sides of a central axis that is both street and plaza. Each dwelling has a series of storage houses, and farms are often a considerable distance away. The village was ruled by a chief and his council of old men. Most of its inhabitants belonged to the same kinship group except, of course, for the women who married into it and retained their own kin-group affiliation, and in earlier times the slaves.

The complexity of the organization of the larger Congo states, and their historic relationship to the village types of organization out of which they grew, is illustrated by the Kuba Kingdom, created by the Bushongo (Bushoong) and controlled by them. This was a union of eighteen tribes, whose common king constituted the central authority. These tribes differed in their cultures, and did not all speak the same language. The smallest unit was the village, administered by a council of elders; the principal political institution was the chiefdom, which varied in size from a single village to an entire tribe. The affairs of each tribe were administered by three councils, one that named or deposed the chief; the second, advisory to the chief; and a third, a kind of Privy Council, concerned with current matters of administration. All these councillors exercised judicial functions. The kingdom was divided into subunits composed of different chiefdoms, which might or might not be contiguous, chosen from the same clan by the same group of clan notables. Of the eighteen tribes, however, four had no political organization that extended outside the village.

The capital, the residence of the king who was also head of

the Bushongo chiefdom, was the center of the kingdom. Special rules governed the succession to the kingship. Unlike other chiefs, he was followed by his younger brothers, the succession then turning to the oldest of the sororal nephews of the reigning monarch. The king received an annual tribute from each of the chiefdoms, and confirmed the nomination of chiefs. On appeal he mediated between chiefdoms that had gone to war, and provided military aid to those attacked by foreign enemies. Because the kingdom was a federation, each chiefdom enjoyed internal autonomy, even to the extent of being free to wage war on other units. Only among the Bushongo themselves was the king sacred; the real stabilizing element in the complex was the Bushongo army which, situated at the center, could move expeditiously to maintain order. The farther from the center, the less direct was the control exerted by the central power. "The Kuba kingdom may be considered as an imposed (*obligatoire*) federation, a union of chiefdoms, presided over by a king."[4]

This pattern of conquest and accretion was followed in various parts of the Congo by most of the kingdoms of the area. How widely it spread may be seen if we note that in the far north, for example, it characterized the development of the Zande states. Here the central controls over the constituent units were closer than in the south, at least in intent, since each was ruled by a chief, responsible to a king, who headed an administrative corps of responsible local deputies. That the system was effective is evident from a list of peoples ruled or influenced by the Zande —twenty-three groups completely "Zandeized" and twenty "ruled and greatly influenced by the Azande," in addition to seven others, influenced by the Azande "but in general politically separate." The same type of political structure was found in the Mangbetu state to the south.[5]

The centralized state must not, however, be taken as charac-

[4] J. Vansina: "L'état Kuba dans le cadre des institutions politiques africaines," *Zaïre*, Vol. XI (1957), pp. 485–9.

[5] P. T. W. Baxter and Audrey Butt: *The Azande and Related Peoples of the Anglo-Egyptian Sudan and Belgian Congo* (Ethnographic Survey of Africa; East Central Africa, Part IX, London, 1953), pp. 26–64.

teristic of Congo political organization. Over vast stretches the effective and, indeed, the only political unit was the village, based on kin grouping, ruled by the lineage elder and his associates, with social, economic and religious functions intimately intertwined. This, indeed, could almost be held to be the typical Congo political form, were it not for the gradations from it to the larger aggregates. Certainly here, as in the areas of the Guinea Coast and the Western Sudan, the village is to be thought of as the unit out of which the larger groupings developed, and which, even in the most highly organized kingdoms, continued to retain its political identity.

Whatever the structure of power, the rule of law prevailed everywhere. The principles that govern conduct were clearly defined, and disputes were settled by the local chief and his council of elders after a case had been presented by both parties. In the larger entities, appeals went to higher courts where they could be argued before the king. Murder, theft, adultery, and the practice of black magic were punished; where fines were levied, a substantial proportion of the amount paid went to the chief who had tried the case. In these courts, when testimony was in conflict, the ordeal was used. Ordeals took on many forms, though the one most often mentioned in the literature involved swallowing poison that had been ritually prepared. Death was proof of guilt; if the poison was vomited, the accused was held to be innocent, and received heavy damages from his accusers. The art of clear argumentation and eloquent pleading was greatly developed. The earliest travelers commented on the role of court procedures in the orderly settlement of disputes as one of the striking aspects of Congo cultures.

It is far more difficult to generalize concerning the world view and the religions of the Congo peoples than to describe their social, economic and political life, owing to the fact that the beliefs which control behavior have received so much less systematic study than the outer, ritualistic forms of religion. Despite the wide acceptance of the principle that cultures are integrated, we know a good deal more about the position of lineage chiefs than their role in ordering relations between the living members of a family and the ancestral generations; we know but little of the supernatural sanctions of kinship, or the beliefs that guide the rituals surrounding agricultural activities or craft procedures. Amulets have been described, but not the activating forces in the universe that give magic the power to achieve its ends; we have some accounts of religious rites, but little knowledge of the organization of gods and spirits.

It seems clear that the religions of the Congo peoples, almost without exception, embody a first principle and ultimate source of being, sometimes explicitly named as the creator or principal deity. Over the entire western sector of the area, this first principle bears a name which is a variation on the term "Nzambe." It is possible to infer that over an even wider area Nzambe has under him subsidiary gods, or messengers, mainly nature deities who exercise control over lightning, rule the earth, the waters, the forest and the like. Names of such deities are found in the Congo-Angola cults of northern Brazil; and designations and functions of these Brazilian deities were recognized in every case by Congolese and Angolans in Africa as forming part of their own world view.[6] Among the Lele there is a belief in nocturnal spirits that inhabit the forests, control the fertility of women, and can aid or hinder the work of the hunter. These beings, known only to the diviners, haunt the sources of streams.[7] Divination and the complexities of the divining processes are important in the Congo area but we have little information about the supernatural sanctions that validate the techniques employed. That such sanctions operate continuously to validate political, social and economic institutions is clear, whatever the attributions of causality.

One reason there is little beyond conjecture, speculation, and an occasional hint of now clandestine practices is perhaps that so much of what has been written about Congo religion has come from missionary observers who tended to regard it all as "superstition," with no attempt to see the beliefs as the Congolese

[6] Melville J. Herskovits: *Notes on African Field Research, 1953–60* (manuscript), p. 53/D332.

[7] Mary Douglas: "The Lele of Kasai," in *African Worlds* (D. Forde, ed., London, 1954), pp. 9–13.

themselves conceive and value them. Yet this is obviously not the entire explanation, for not all who have written on the beliefs of these peoples have been missionaries, while it is a missionary who had given us an analysis of the philosophical basis of Congolese religion. From the pen of Father Tempels came the injunction, prefatory to his discussion of what he termed Bantu philosophy, that underscored the need for more adequate information on this aspect of the cultures in the area: "If one has not penetrated into the depths of the personality as such, if one does not know the basis of their acts, it is not possible to understand the Bantu."[8]

Only a few of the concepts which Father Tempels has drawn from his data can be indicated here. In the thought of the peoples he studied, he found, first of all, an overriding value in the concepts of power and the life force (*force, force vitale*). The Congolese, as he saw them, had a dynamic concept of existence—a concept of becoming, as against the static principle of being. Everything in the universe, animate and inanimate, for them possessed its own kind of energy. Each element, each living, growing thing was endowed with a component of energy or power that added to the vitality of the most powerful being in creation, man. From this it followed that the relation of the concepts of power, of energy, and of being was basic to this world view. And from this, too, derived the significance of the concept *muntu,* which, in Tempel's analysis, came to mean more the person (*la personne*) than its accepted significance of man (*l'homme*). The system as a whole, in its dynamism, thus not only placed man as a living force in an ever-changing world, but envisaged him as a being subject to growth and decay, and as an active, causal factor in that world.

How far this analysis applies to the belief systems of peoples in the Congo other than the Baluba, the group from whom Tempels seems to have gathered most of his data, or whether it is

[8] Père Placide Tempels: *La Philosophie Bantou* (Elizabethville, Congo, 1945) (published in English translation as *Bantu Philosophy,* Paris, 1959), 1945, p. 11; 1959, p. 17.

merely an interpretation in terms of European philosophical concepts, is not altogether clear. But of this we can be certain: the gods and spirits, magic and divination, ancestors and ancestral taboos of each people embody a view of the universe and the forces that rule it which unifies the supernatural world and makes life itself meaningful to those who live in accordance with its precepts.

Closely related to the religious life is the rich variety in the art of the area. The peoples of the Congo have produced what have come to be recognized as some of the great art forms not only of Africa, but of the world. Besides the plastic forms, the wood and ivory carving for which the area is best known, we find many kinds of musical expression, supported by a wide range of percussion, string and wind instruments; the dance is ubiquitous; as are the narrative forms of myths and tales, proverbs and riddles. Nor does this exhaust the list, for more humble kinds of aesthetic expression, such as stylized and representational paintings on the walls of houses, likewise have distinction.

Nevertheless, it is predominantly in the plastic arts that the Congo achieved its fame as a center of aesthetic production. Its ivory carvings vary from the finely wrought small masks of the Bapende to the spirally-set representations in low relief carved on elephant tusks by the Loango peoples. Olbrechts, who made the most careful analysis of Congo wood carving, distinguished five major art areas on the basis of stylistic differences—the Lower Congo, including the coastal regions of Angola, of the Republic of the Congo, and of the Congo and Gabon Republics; the Bakuba region, which comprehends the basin of the Kasai; the Baluba, to the east, that takes in the arts of the southeastern Congo basin and the northwestern part of northern Rhodesia; the northeastern Congo, which also includes the extreme south of the Sudanese Republic; and the northwest, made up of the middle Congo basin, both in the Congo and the Central African Republic.[9] Among some of the best-known forms are the ancestral portrait statues and cups of the Bakuba; the Baluba kneeling figures, chief's staffs

[9] F. M. Olbrechts: *Plastiek van Kongo* (Antwerp, 1946), pp. 25–94.

and great masks; the masks in color of the Bena Lulua and Bapende; the Bakongo statuettes; and to the north, the Mpongwe and Fang masks and the stylized representations of the Bamum in the Cameroons highlands.

As elsewhere, the arts were, and in many instances continued to be integral parts of the daily life. Incised decorations on drums, on pigment boxes, on cups, on combs, on headrests, even in the cicatrized designs on the face, shoulders, arms and torsos of men and women demonstrate how widely artistry plays over the total range of existence. Of particular note is the raffia pile-cloth of the peoples who inhabit the Kasai. Here the interplay of design and color, achieved with supreme technical proficiency, have not only combined to make them outstanding examples of the weaver's craft, but also show how, within a pattern of conventionalized design, motifs can be transferred from one medium to another—in this case, from weaving to wood carving—as expressions of unity in the aesthetic patterns of a people.

[3]

The *Guinea Coast* area follows the line of the West African littoral from the Bight of Biafra to the southern portion of the Republic of Guinea. It is long and narrow, and essentially comprehends the forested belt, giving way to the Western Sudan area as the savannah that lies between it and the desert are reached. In terms of cultural differentiation, it cuts across existing political entities as we move eastward from Sierra Leone and Liberia.

Like the Congo, it is agricultural in its basic economy, but because of the greater density of its population, the implications of the ability of societies based on agriculture to produce greater economic surpluses than pastorally oriented groups strike the observer as a pertinent factor. Here this finds expression in the greater amount, though not kind, of specialization, and in extensive markets, which are more generally present and have a more continuous distribution in the Guinea Coast than in the Congo area. On the whole, the institutions of the Guinea Coast are to be thought of as more tightly structured, and more explicitly enunciated than those of the Congo.

The degree of agricultural productivity in the area has made possible a surplus over subsistence needs outstanding not only for Africa, but for nonindustrial societies generally. On this infrastructure a complex economy was reared. Based on the use of money, it took fuller shape and richer form than the Congo systems, where there was limited intertribal trade, and where the systems of exchange, using various commodities as common denominators of value, were perforce simpler than when the tokens employed have value by and of themselves. Specialization in the Guinea Coast was thus to a far greater extent on the professional level than anywhere else in the Subsaharan continent, except perhaps in certain parts of the Western Sudan.

Not all the peoples of the area had so complex an economic order. In this aspect of culture, as in others, the greatest degree of complexity, the most tightly-knit ordering of institutions is present at the geographical center in the societies of the region that stretches from Ghana to western Nigeria. Here the population is dense, and the economic support for a complex cultural superstructure most adequate. This is not to say that the central region did not draw upon the more outlying groups to augment its political and economic resources. Why this central area developed as it did would seem to be explainable in part ecologically, in part demographically, in part historically. The fact that it was characterized by a complex economic order in pre-European times is apparent from the literature, or even on firsthand acquaintance.

Thus the accounts of early travelers in Nigeria make it clear that money was present here long before European concepts were introduced, and that the trading complex was well developed. Local currency was to be distinguished from tokens of value used in trade with Europeans. Dapper, one of the earliest writers, recorded that in the period beginning roughly in 1600, cowries were used for the internal market transactions of the Slave Coast and the western Delta of the Niger, manillas, or bracelets of grey copper, in the eastern Delta, and copper rods in the Cross River area. The peoples of these regions continued to use these tokens of value until the end of the nineteenth century, and in certain instances later.

Cowries were also used farther to the west, but as we move through the Ivory Coast toward Sierra Leone and Liberia, consumable media such as mats or salt bars begin to appear. In eastern Nigeria, the tokens were imported—thus, cowries came overland from the eastern Sudan and East Africa, while the metal bracelets, or manillas, and brass rods were imported from Europe. Moreover, "Besides these more recent native currencies, ethnography and history suggest an earlier metal currency or currencies in which the unit was of iron. . . ." [1]

Specialization of labor touched all aspects of the economy, and developed a substantial degree of technological competence. Particularly in the societies of the central parts of the Guinea Coast area, specialists were organized into guilds, which controlled both modes of production and distribution, and derived their cohesiveness from supernatural as well as social sanctions. In Dahomey, we find organized groups of iron workers, weavers, cloth sewers, calabash carvers, potters, basketry makers, brass workers, silversmiths, wood carvers, hunters, and traders. Priests and diviners are also specialists here. The degree to which members of these various callings work for their individual account varies; thus iron workers are organized into "forges," and labor collectively for each member in turn, but wood carvers work as individuals. Nor is specialization, either here or elsewhere in the area, carried on to the exclusion of a certain commitment to subsistence agriculture. In Africa, there is practically no intra-industrial specialization such as marks systems of production based on the machine. African craft specialists grow some of their own food, and in some instances build, thatch and repair their own houses. But despite this, the difference between Europe and

[1] G. I. Jones: "Native and Trade Currencies in Southern Nigeria During the Eighteenth and Nineteenth Centuries," *Africa*, Vol. XXVIII (1958), p. 48 and *passim*.

West Africa as regards broad patterns of economic activity must be considered one of degree and not of kind.[2]

Markets, which reflect this specialization, attain sizable proportions, particularly in the cities and towns of the central portion of the area. Where changes incident on the introduction of world crops and European currencies took place, the market tradition not only retained its vitality, but flourished in the new situation. In general, markets rotate with the days of the traditional week, generally at four-day intervals, and provide centers where all needs can be met. In cities such as Kumasi, or Abomey, or Ibadan, or Onitsha, they represent substantial operations in any terms. Such outstanding examples, however, are only part of a distributional network that covers the territory of a given people, and varies from these great gatherings of thousands of buyers and sellers to the small roadside stalls, where travelers can obtain cooked foods to make a meal, or local residents can supplement their purchases at the regular center of trade. Nor are wholesale operations absent, for in many regions these are an integral part of a distributional system which ties in the smaller centers to the larger ones.

The village is the integer of society, and all larger groupings, whether social or political, reflect this fact. Again, we are in the region of the rectangular house-type, but the materials of which houses are built are more permanent than in the other parts of the continent we have considered. The residential unit is the compound, and consists of a group of dwelling and storage huts, usually enclosed by a wall, where a man, his wife or wives, his children, and his younger brothers with wives and children, reside. A village is thus an aggregate of compounds rather than of individual houses, and it is easy to see how it could become part of a township with quarters or wards consisting essentially of a series of these village-like agglomerates, headed by men who are related and thus form a distinguishable kin grouping. As we shall see,[3] this tendency toward urban settlement was a phenomenon

[2] Melville J. Herskovits: *Dahomey, an Ancient West African Kingdom* (New York, 1938), Vol. I, pp. 30–62.

[3] *Infra*, Ch. IX.

of considerable importance in the transitional period following colonial controls.

In the Guinea Coast area, as in eastern and central Africa, descent is counted on one side of the family, in most cases that of the father. The Akan peoples of Ghana and the Ivory Coast are usually held to be an exception to this rule, though some students classify them as having dual descent.[4] Affiliation on the mother's side appears sporadically as we move westward. The question of double descent—that is, counting unilineal lines both on the father's and the mother's side—has been much debated by students of the social organization of western Africa, but the resolution of the problem would seem to turn on definition. Thus, among such peoples as the Ibo of southeastern Nigeria, dual descent would seem without doubt to be present, since functional relationships with both the father's and mother's lineages are explicit and institutionalized, as among the Yakö[5] and the Afikpo[6] of the Niger delta region. These, however, are extreme cases; for the Guinea Coast area in general, legal descent is on one side or the other, though relations with the family of the parent with which an individual is not institutionally affiliated are close on a personal, and at times on a religious level. Even in Dahomey, a society as strongly patrilineal as any to be found, the relation between a person and the mother's family is warm and permissive, in contrast to the harsh discipline exacted by the patrilineal kin.

As elsewhere in Africa, plural marriage is sanctioned. This does not mean that polygyny is universally practiced; the number of wives a man has largely depends on his social and economic status. Bride wealth must be paid to validate marriage, though in absolute value it is much less than in other areas. Its symbolic importance is, however, undiminished, and the passage of it, how-

[4] James B. Christensen: *Double Descent among the Fanti* (New Haven, Connecticut, 1954), *passim.*

[5] Daryll Forde: "Double Descent among the Yakö," in *African Systems of Kinship and Marriage* (edited by A. R. Radcliffe-Brown and D. Forde, London, 1950), pp. 285–332.

[6] Simon Ottenberg: *The System of Authority of the Afikpo Ibo of Southeastern Nigeria* (Ph.D. dissertation, Northwestern University, microfilmed by University Microfilms, Ann Arbor, Michigan, 1957), pp. 105–70.

ever defined, is essential to control of children by the father's kinship group. Bride wealth in this area, too, is distinguished by the fact that a part of it consists of payments in kind, added to which is a continuing duty to perform certain tasks annually for the wife's parents, and to meet specific obligations when a death occurs in her family.

Residence, with few exceptions, is patrilocal—that is, a woman on marriage goes to live in her husband's compound. If he is young and she is his first wife, they may have a separate hut in the compound of his father or elder brother, but eventually he will build one for himself. Here will be his own dwelling, and one for each wife, where she will live with her children. In general she goes to the common husband in her turn, when she cohabits with him, leaving her children in her hut. This deeply affects the emotional relationship to father and mother, and it is understandable that the strongest kinship tie is with "own-brother-own-sister," and the child is much closer to the mother than to the father.

This is evident in the distribution of inherited property. There are interminable disputes between half brothers in connection with the apportionment of a father's wealth. Yet quarrels between the children of a woman who may have left a sizable estate, something not at all rare in view of the economic position of women in the Guinea Coast area, are not often encountered. This aspect of family structure has psychological overtones, with ramifications of considerable theoretical importance for the relations between siblings, and between children and parents.[7]

There are various kinds of associations which an individual may have with members of his community who are not his kin. Many peoples of the Guinea Coast area have age groupings. In the main, these are not as tightly structured, or as important as in East Africa, though in the Niger Delta the taking of titles gives formal expression to position in the hierarchy of strata based on age or on seniority of induction. Secret societies, primary instruments for the maintenance of social stability and the traditional

[7] M. J. and F. S. Herskovits: "Sibling Rivalry, the Oedipus Complex, and Myth," *Journal of American Folklore,* Vol. LXXI (1958), *passim.*

moral order, are widely spread, being found among the Yoruba as well as at the extremities of the area. Where there were strong central authorities, as in Ashanti and Dahomey, such societies were not countenanced, because they were seen as potentially subversive. Other modes of nonkinship association are to be found in religious cult groups, co-operative work and mutual benefit societies, market affiliations, and societies based on residence.

The dynastic kingdoms of this central part of the area are well known. The names of Ashanti, Dahomey, Benin, and later of Oyo, are repeatedly found in the literature, and in some respects bear resemblance to the medieval kingdoms of Europe or the kingdoms of the Near and Middle East and India in their patterns of authority and central government controls. They had the bureaucratic apparatus of all well-administered states, complete with systems of taxation that, at least, as described for Ashanti and Dahomey, provided a constant flow of revenue to the central government, and assured adequate resources for its administrative expenditures and the support of the ruling dynasty.[8]

At the periphery of the area, the village predominates as the effective political unit—a pattern that, as we saw for the Congo kingdoms, is at the base of the larger, more integrated entities. Among the Ibo, Ijaw, Ibibio, Efik and other peoples of the Niger Delta, villages or clusters of villages were autonomous and had to be on constant guard against incursions from their neighbors. This same village autonomy is found in the western part of the Ivory Coast, in Liberia and Sierra Leone, though in these territories a sense of identity with larger groupings, perhaps deriving from the widely spread Poro men's secret societies, gave some measure of unity to such linguistic and cultural entities as the Temne, Mende, Kissi, Susu, Vai, Gola, Kru, Grebo and Gagou.

This underlying pattern gives rise to a marked characteristic of West African political life, whereby parallel with the manifestations of deference towards those in authority, the young men

[8] R. S. Rattray: *Ashanti Law and Constitution* (Oxford, 1929), *passim;* M. J. Herskovits: *Dahomey, an Ancient West African Kingdom* (New York, 1938), Vol. I, pp. 107–34.

participate in village affairs, particularly to check abuses of chiefs and elders. Nowhere in Africa is it more essential to reach beneath outer form to actual practice than in this aspect of life, if the essence of the political orientations of the societies of the area is to be grasped.

The concern of the African for the nature of the universe in which he lives finds some of its most striking manifestations in the Guinea Coast area. Because of its economic resources, specialists in the administration of religious rites could be supported without difficulty, and in consequence we here find cult leaders who are philosophers, in almost the technical sense of the term. Where these men are present it is not necessary for the student to abstract underlying principles from generalized expressions of belief and observed ritual. The mythologies that have been recorded, especially for the core region of the area, show that questions of the origin, direction and control of cosmogonic forces have been faced, and their relationships and functions described.[9]

The religions of many of these peoples are ordered in terms of a number of well-defined categories. There are, first of all, the great gods, usually headed by a creator, conceived as the parent of the associated deities, controlling the manifestations of nature—sky, earth, sea, thunder and the like. There are next a series of beings having more localized or specialized scope, such as those that function in the forest and in the rivers, or act as guardians of markets; those that are concerned with war and instruments of war; those that manifest themselves in infants who represent abnormalities of any kind, such as twins, or born deviants, as the tradition defines them. Worship of the ancestors is of major importance, and rests on a series of propositions concerning the souls or

[9] E.g., R. S. Rattray: *Ashanti* (Oxford, 1923), pp. 139–212; ibid., *Religion and Art in Ashanti* (Oxford, 1927), pp. 1–47; M. J. Herskovits: op. cit. (New York, 1938), Vol. II, pp. 101–308; M. J. and F. S. Herskovits: *Dahomean Narrative, a Cross-Cultural Analysis* (Northwestern University African Studies No. 1, Evanston, Illinois, and London, 1958); J. O. Lucas: *The Religion of the Yorubas* (Lagos, 1948); L. Frobenius: *Die Atlantische Götterlehre* (*Atlantis, Volksmärchen und Volksdichtungen Afrikas,* Bd. X, Jena, 1926); P. A. Talbot: *The Peoples of Southern Nigeria* (London, 1926), Vol. II, pp. 1–351.

powers of man, and how these function in life as each individual joins preceding generations to become a link in the continuity of social existence. The ancestral cult, indeed, is one of the most effective integrating factors in the social structure, since it is the ancestors who in the supernatural world are most immediately concerned with their living kin; to certain individual ancestors, moreover, is ascribed such a degree of power that they may be deified, or viewed as deities. Finally there are the forces we may call magical, which are manipulated by the will and knowledge of man, and give him access to powers for achieving immediate ends, be they good or evil. Intertwined with all these are divinatory systems of the most varied kind, whereby the forces that permit the attainment of desired ends and the means to enlist them for a favorable outcome can be ascertained.

These religions are as rich in ritual as in complex theology. Rites of worship may involve no more than supplication of ancestors or of a personal spirit on behalf of an individual or a family. At the other end of the spectrum are the great public ceremonies, lasting for days or even weeks, attended by hundreds of devotees and onlookers, wherein dramatic representations engage the emotions of participants and spectators through song, dance, and elaborate costumes. It is ceremonies of this kind that have inspired the masks which achieved such fame in the world of art; while the carved figurines, formerly miscalled "idols," derive from more generalized forms of worship. But while worship has its markedly aesthetic aspects, the purpose of the rites is above all to give assurance of well-being.

In the central, more complex cultures, priests and devotees are organized into congregations. Rites of initiation, varying in length of time, teach those claimed by the gods the proper modes of worship—particularly the songs and the dances ordered by the drums as they beat the rhythms that are at once accompaniment and command, and the regulations governing food and behavior which are particular to each cult. With age and demonstrated ability, and at the indication of the deity as shown by the divining seeds or other paraphernalia that reveal the will of the gods, the initiate can become priest or priestess. As such, he or she directs the rituals of worship, and receives the reverence, the services, the obedience due from initiates, and the respect of the laity.

Yet this complex structure is not found in the entire area. It correlates, indeed, with the complexity of the economic base, and with the political institutions reared on a foundation of surplus over the needs of subsistence. Where social units are smaller, the institutionalization of religion becomes simpler. In the Niger Delta, as in the Ivory Coast, Liberia and Sierra Leone, specialization in the supernatural is less marked, and worship less formalized. The creator, the ancestors, the spirits of the forest, magic and divination, are everywhere manifest. Systems of this kind are not so tightly integrated, however, and the theology must often be inferred from the attitudes of the people toward the forces of their universe. Yet whether articulated or not, whether implemented with fixed ritual or loosely structured worship, to the people the relationship between human beings and the powers that rule their destiny is close and continuous, and has a pragmatic quality that carries its own conviction. For just as man is fulfilled by the gods, so, in this view, he strengthens their powers by his worship; and this very interdependence makes plausible an harmonious universe, where the malevolent forces could be rendered ineffective by the inherent and added strength of the protective beings.

Everywhere there is evidence of aesthetic productivity. This area has given us the Benin bronzes, the Ife heads, the Dahomean brasses, the Ashanti gold weights, all outstanding examples of the metal worker's art. From it come the Poro and Sande masks of Sierra Leone, Liberia and the Ivory Coast, the figurines of the Baoule and Gouro, the Yoruba carvings, the innumerable stylizations of human and animal face and form of the Niger Delta peoples. Nor do these forms tell the entire tale. Artistry expresses itself in the intricate designs woven into the long, narrow strips that are sewed edge to edge to make great toga-like mantles, in the tie-dying of white cloths dipped in the indigo vats, in pottery forms, in carved calabashes, in woven mats and coiled basketry. Here we see most clearly the correlation between economic surplus, political complexity, and artistic production. The aesthetic drive, it is apparent, goes deep in all these traditions, and plays over all aspects of life, secular no less than religious.

[4]

The character of the *Western Sudan* area derives largely from the nature of its historic relations with the Guinea Coast to the south and the Arabized Islamic peoples to the north. It is difficult to demarcate its boundaries, though roughly it may be thought of as stretching from the forested belt along the coast, to the desert. It includes most of what was French West Africa, except for the southern portions of the Ivory Coast, Togo and Dahomey; the Northern Territories of Ghana and of Nigeria also form parts of it.

There is great variation in its cultures, variation which is compounded by the social and political stratification resulting from its long history of conquest. In many respects it resembles the Guinea Coast—in the density of its population, the degree of its craft specialization, its large and complex political entities. But there are many differences. There is the presence of larger domesticated animals; houses that are round and not rectangular; the flowing robes and turbans of the men. Some centuries earlier than our base-line decades, much, if not most of the Western Sudan would have been included in the Guinea Coast area, for when we move beneath the surface, we can perceive the many aspects of social and economic life, of the indigenous religions and arts that are akin to those of the south. But the differences are significant and, in fact, crucial as far as the recent past is concerned, so that the two cannot be considered together.

Just as in the Eastern Sudan area, there is a southern strip where the penetration of Islam is still slight. Labouret, on the basis of his study of the Lobi peoples, has termed this strip the *zone guinéenne,* taking his designation from that given the region on the basis of its vegetation. This, he observes, goes from the Bauchi Plateau in the eastern part of Northern Nigeria, to Sikasso in the Republic of Mali. It is marked by the kind of clothing worn —or, rather, its absence; by a special kind of rectangular house-type, with mud walls laid in courses; by the use of the bow and poisoned arrows; by societies based on village or regional organization; and by the rhombus as a sacred symbol.[1] But in the central and northern portions of the area, the clothing is that of the desert dwellers, houses become round, kingdoms control large regions, and Islam, at least in so far as the ruling classes and urban dwellers are concerned, is the dominant religion.

We get a glimpse of the diversity of basic economies in the area if we but look at the division of cultures made as early as 1912 by Tauxier. He distinguishes pure agriculturalists, such as the Bobo and Sankura, agriculturalists and herders, like the Nankuru, agriculturalists and traders, like the Mandé-Dyoula, and pastoralists, such as the Fulbé and the Moors. The Mossi, whom he classifies as "warriors and conquerors" are primarily agriculturalists and herders. For the region inhabited by these Mossi-Gourounsi societies, he estimated that 54% of subsistence products came from agriculture, 20% from herding, 10% from hunting, 5% from fishing, 10% from the gathering of wild plants and fruits, and the remainder from cultivated trees.[2] According to Nadel, the Nupe, of the middle region of Nigeria, who are mainly an agricultural people, earlier had large herds of cattle, owned by members of the Nupe aristocracy and "the more wealthy among the Bida people." [3] The Bambara exchange cereal crops for cattle, which they obtain from Fulani, Moorish or Touareg herders; they likewise have many sheep, goats and donkeys.[4] Among the Senufo, care of herds is entrusted by local chiefs to Mandé and Fulani herders.[5] Fulani and Tuareg herders live with their animals

[1] Henri Labouret: *Les Tribus du Rameau Lobi* (Travaux et Mémoires de l'Institut d'Ethnologie, Vol. XV, Paris, 1931), pp. 13–14.

[2] Louis Tauxier: *Le Noir du Soudan, Pays Mossi et Gourounsi* (Paris, 1912), pp. 23–6.

[3] S. F. Nadel: *A Black Byzantium, the Kingdom of Nupe in Nigeria* (London, 1942), p. 201.

[4] Viviana Paques: *Les Bambara* (Paris, 1954), pp. 27–37.

[5] B. Holas: *Les Senoufo* (Paris, 1957), p. 66.

among the Songhai, who, however, themselves raise some cattle, and are also known for their horses.[6] What is important for an understanding of the economy of the Western Sudan is that, unlike East Africa, and except for the so-called Cattle Fulani, cattle are no more symbols of prestige than any other economic good in societies where rank and social position are correlated with wealth. Like all the other domesticated animals, in which this area abounds, cattle are kept to be consumed and traded, not to receive adulation and respect.

Here an economy of specialization and trade has been erected that even surpasses the one found in the central portion of the Guinea Coast area. The markets of Kano, of Sokoto, of Ségou, or of Timbuktu were singled out for their size and importance by all the earlier travelers. These urban centers are still termini of the Saharan caravan routes, which bring them into commercial contact with the Arab north, and many of them have become railheads and important centers of air traffic. All sorts of crafts are found in such towns—metal working of all kinds, weaving, pottery making, basketry, and leather working, to name only a few of those included in the impressive list that has been given for the Hausa.[7] Much of the red leather long known in Europe as "Morocco leather" was imported from the western Sudan into Morocco and from there was exported to Europe. Noncraft specialists also abound—learned men and teachers, singers, drummers and dancers, and the members of the bureaucratic hierarchy. There is reason to believe that the craft guilds described in detail by Nadel for Nupe[8] are similarly present in most of the centers of this area.

The social organization is predominantly patrilineal; whatever earlier tradition may have been, the influence of Islam undoubtedly discouraged any tendency to count descent in the mother's line. The position of women, in general, contrasts with what we have seen in the Guinea Coast; a larger proportion of

[6] Jean Rouch: *Les Songhay* (Paris, 1954), p. 21.

[7] M. G. Smith: "Introduction," to *Baba of Karo* (by Mary Smith, London, 1954), pp. 17–18.

[8] Ibid., pp. 257–94.

men, certainly in the urban centers, trade in the market. Yet their position differs from that found among the Islamized peoples of North Africa, as is illustrated by an autobiography of an elderly Hausa woman, which takes us well back into the period before the imposition of European control.[9]

Here, as elsewhere in Africa, the village is the basic unit of residence, and is clearly linked to kin affiliation. This holds for the non-Moslem peoples of the area. Yet, as has been shown for the Dogon of the French Sudan, the village system of this area has its particular character. Among this people there is a community of blood and a community of land, this double aspect of affiliation and loyalty being at the same time economic and religious.[1] The towns, however, unlike those of the Guinea Coast, are in no sense large entities made up of village-like groupings. The town dweller of the Western Sudan is distinctly an urbanite, a permanent resident of his community, despite any lines of filiation that lead to an ancestral village.

The immediate family, composed of a man, his wife or wives and their children, is the core of the social structure here as in human societies everywhere. The rule of residence, for the most part, is that wives live in the compounds or villages of their husbands. The typical progression of kin structures is, to phrase it in nontechnical terms, immediate family, extended family and clan. A principal function of the larger groupings is to regulate marriage by drawing the lines of incest. Clans are not a prominent feature of the social structures of peoples who have come under the influence of Islam; where they do exist in Islamized societies, they tend to relinquish the function of regulating marriage. It seems valid to assume that in earlier times the clan was found everywhere in the area, as for example among the Wolof, where "the presence of totemism and group self-consciousness seems to suggest that the sib . . . once functioned

[9] Mary F. Smith: *Baba of Karo, a Woman of the Muslim Hausa* (New York, 1954), *passim.*

[1] Denis Paulme: *Organisation Sociale des Dogon* (*Soudan Française*) (Études Sociologiques et d'Ethnologie Juridiques, Vol. XXXII, Paris, 1940), p. 49 ff.

in controlling the marriages of its members." [2] Among the Dogon, not only clans, but totemism associated with clan structures are found; [3] among the Tallensi there is a complex system of totemic clans and subclans.[4] The same kind of complexity is reported for the Dagomba, where many functions of the "minor lineage" [5] once more underscore the intricacy of the social arrangements in these societies, even where, as among the Senufo, the extended family is the largest unit in the system of kinship.[6]

In addition to the kin-groups, social entities based on free association range from institutionalized friendships between individuals to co-operative agricultural work societies and craft guilds. Age classes, however, are not structured in this area. Here slavery was an integral part of the social organization north of the non-Moslem belt, and played an important economic role. The children of slaves could become members of the master's "group of descendants"; and though the nature of their descent was not forgotten, these descendants had a well-recognized place in the community, often rising to positions of power.[7]

Essential to an understanding of the political systems is a recognition of the fact that stratification of class and rank was founded on ethnic—but not racial—lines, thus reflecting a long history of contact through trade, war and conquest. What has been written for the Wolof in the extreme western part may stand as a kind of a summary of the organization of all the kingdoms—"an elaborate system of government in which a 'noble' class dominated the country, and elected rulers whose functions were to ensure the power of the state by leadership in war and to bring

[2] David W. Ames: *Plural Marriage among the Wolof in the Gambia* (Ph.D. dissertation, Northwestern University, microfilmed by University Microfilms, Ann Arbor, Michigan, 1953), p. 22.

[3] M. Griaule: *Masques Dogon* (Travaux et Mémoires de l'Institut d'Ethnologie, Vol. XXXIII, Paris, 1938), pp. 28–33.

[4] M. Fortes: *The Dynamics of Clanship among the Tellensi* (London, 1945), pp. 39–146.

[5] David Tait: "The Family, Household, and Minor Lineage of the Konkomba," *Africa*, Vol. XXVI (1956), *passim.*

[6] B. Holas: *Les Senoufo* (Paris, 1957), pp. 84–6.

[7] M. G. Smith: *Government in Zazzau* (London, 1960), pp. 42–8, 253–5.

prosperity through the exercise of magical powers."[8] The names of the conquering peoples and the empires they founded recur again and again in the history and the ethnography of the area—Mali, Songhai, Mossi, Bornu, Fula. So deep is the tradition of power and prestige associated with such kingdoms that the name of one of them, Ghana, was chosen as its designation by the first West African state in the twentieth century to attain independence.

These states were administered with all the panoply of wealth and control that went with the status of their rulers. Under the system of indirect rule, as established by the British, the Emirs of the Fulani states of Northern Nigeria retained or adapted many features of the earlier forms of government. Among the descendants of the royal families of Macina and other centers of pre-European domination in what was French West Africa, these states had well-organized fighting forces, with companies of skilled horsemen. The indigenous population was controlled through a hierarchy of officials who, with a degree of effectiveness that varied with distance from the center of power, collected taxes, dispensed justice and otherwise functioned as do local administrators in any conquered territory. With time, the conquerors became a part of the total population, but the lines of stratification in no wise became lost, and descent continued to be of prime importance in determining social position. Even where the conquerors did not, or could not enforce the maintenance of the institutions they imposed, their presence, however manifested, left its impression. Among the Senufo, who indigenously had no social classes, there developed, "two quite different principles [of political organization], the one represented by the early gerontocracy . . . and one authority reminiscent of feudalism, borrowed from Mandé culture."[9]

Where the conquerors did not penetrate, or where their direct impact was slight, the indigenous forms persisted with no

[8] D. P. Gamble: *The Wolof of Senegambia* (International African Institute, Ethnographic Survey of Africa: Western Africa, Part XIV, London, 1957), p. 55.

[9] B. Holas: *Les Senoufo* (Paris, 1957), p. 83.

more change than would be anticipated under the normal processes of the inner dynamic of culture. Everywhere there is a fundamental relationship between kinship and, if one may use the term, citizenship. The Konkomba of the Northern Territories of Ghana, for example, base their political structure on the principles of seniority and filiation, plus attachment to the land. Divided into four tribes, each is a composite of units of lesser size; why the four never fused to make a single people is a question that cannot be answered.[1] The association of local rule, especially with the land, is marked, as has been demonstrated by an intensive analysis of the mythical and religious sanctions behind the structure of the Dogon village.[2]

The religious patterns of the area, as can be readily deduced, are overlaid by Islamic beliefs and rituals. Students of these cultures generally recognize that the influence of the Koranic tradition has been largely that of adding to earlier belief or, in certain cases, of reinterpreting earlier beliefs in terms of the Koran. They seem rarely to have been abandoned for the orthodox Moslem faith, as in the more Arabized countries of the Islamic world. Greenberg's study of the influence of Islam on the religion of the Hausa showed clearly the vitality of beliefs in the *'iskoki,* the local spirits of aboriginal Hausa religion. These beings which, as even the pagans hold, perform their work only with the permission of Allah, are equated by the Hausa malams, or Islamic teachers, with the black, or pagan jinn of Moslem belief.[3] Far to the west, we find the well-Islamized Wolof retaining, without any apparent reinterpretation, beliefs in the mischievous "little people" of the forest.[4] Many forms of reinterpretation appear in the

[1] David Tait: "The Political System of the Konkomba," *Africa,* Vol. XXIII (1953), *passim.*

[2] G. Dieterlein: "Parenté et mariage chez les Dogon (Soudan Français)," *Africa,* Vol. XXVI (1956), *passim.*

[3] Joseph H. Greenberg: *The Influence of Islam on a Sudanese Religion* (Monographs of the American Ethnological Society, Vol. X, New York, 1946), pp. 21–43, 67–8.

[4] David W. Ames: "The Dual Function of the 'Little People' of the Forest in the Lives of the Wolof," *Journal of American Folklore,* Vol. LXXI (1958), *passim.*

account by Nadel of Nupe religion, even though his descriptions are focused on aboriginal belief.[5]

As suggested above, these aboriginal religions have much in common with the Guinea Coast systems, both in respect to their theology and their ritual. Hence we find the great god, the Creator, and nature deities, who may or may not stand in the relationship of descent to one another; local spirits; spirits of twins and other types of abnormal births. Here, also, we see the important role ascribed to the ancestors, the ubiquitousness of magic, the place of divination. The complexity of these systems varies from one society to another, but if we take two of those whose aboriginal beliefs have been most fully studied, the Dogon and the Nupe, we are impressed with the logical organization of ideas and philosophical insight they disclose. Rituals also follow Guinea Coast patterns; indeed, were it not for the historic incursion of Islam and its influence over the centuries it has maintained itself there, these religions might well have been grouped as variants of a single tradition.

As with religion, so with the arts, though here the marginal character of the Western Sudan again manifests itself strongly. Among the non-Islamized peoples to the south, and among those whose Islamization has been superficial, the mask and the figurine exhibit the same high artistic quality as among the peoples of the forest. In Bambara villages, we can see ritual masks in the shadow of the local mosque.[6] This does not occur, in public view at least, where Islam has taken greater hold. Here, however, the question may well be raised whether the degree to which wood carving becomes less important as we move northward is a matter of Islamic influence or of the ecological setting, with its scarcity of wood suitable for carving. Certainly we see the same close relation between the pre-Islamic belief-systems and the regional art as before; the analysis by Griaule of the place of the mask in the religion of the Dogon, and how its making and use are at each

[5] S. F. Nadel: *Nupe Religion* (London, 1954), pp. 12–13, 26, 66, 83, *inter alia.*

[6] Melville J. Herskovits: *Notes on African Field Research, 1953–60* (manuscript), p. 57/D66.

moment guided by specific rituals, leaves the point beyond dispute.[7]

Yet the aesthetics of these cultures must not be thought of as confined to expression only in wood carving, here any more than elsewhere. The same multiplicity of crafts that marks the Congo and the Guinea Coast areas is present, and the same tradition of aesthetically embellishing utilitarian objects. The patterns incised on trays and other brass objects, the designs on sandals, hassocks, bags, saddles and bridles, to name only some of the work done by the leather workers; the fine camel's hair blankets and rugs from Timbuktu, and the Bida cloths, with their intricate embroidered designs; the decorated pottery, the motifs woven into mats and baskets, all demonstrate this. The musical arts are similarly rich, both as regards wealth of song and the instruments used. And here, again, we see the factor of marginality, as we move from the emphasis on percussion and rhythm in the southern parts of our area to the predominance of stringed instruments and Arabized singing style to the north.

[7] M. Griaule: *Masques Dogon* (Travaux et Mémoires de l'Institut d'Ethnologie, Vol. XXXIII, Paris, 1938), *passim.*

5

The Incomers

AFRICA, like Asia and the Americas, was an objective of the European expansionist movement that began in the fifteenth century, but the experience of Subsaharan Africa during the period of European expansion differed from that of the New World and Asia in two important respects. In the first place, incursion into Africa came not only from Europe but continued to come also from Asia and the Arabized north. Just as the Portuguese and British and French, the Hollanders and Danes established themselves on the western and southern coasts, so from the east came Arabs and Indians, while in addition the impact of Islam was continuously felt in the north. The fringe of forts established by European powers on the Guinea Coast, the Portuguese depots in Angola and along the eastern coast, the Dutch possession of Table Bay were paralleled by the trading centers of Arabs and others that by the fourteenth century reached almost to the mouth of the Limpopo, as far south as Sofala, in what became Mozambique, and sent cargoes of precious stones, gold, amber, ivory, rare woods, and slaves to the ports of the Persian Gulf and the Indian Ocean.[1]

[1] R. Roolvink: *Historical Atlas of the Muslim Peoples* (Amsterdam, 1957), pp. 17, 18.

This last item, slaves, brings us to a second way in which the contacts of Africans with the peoples of other continents differed from those of the inhabitants of Asia and the Americas. The peoples of the three continents experienced cultural shock, so extreme in some cases as to bring about serious or even complete social disintegration. In North America the brutalities of conquest were also accompanied by exposure to epidemic diseases hitherto unknown, against which no immunities had been developed, resulting in almost unprecedented depopulation. But in Africa one of the prime elements in the contact, from its earliest days, was the slave trade, toward the east and the north as well as to the New World, a trade that was intensified with the passage of time.

Both the Americas and Asia knew the institution of domestic slavery, as did Europe and aboriginal Africa. In the New World, the foreign masters impressed American Indians as slaves; but they died in large numbers, and were replaced by Africans. Asian slaving operations were largely internal and comparatively local, though the presence of Indonesian slaves in the Cape, soon after its occupancy by the Dutch, demonstrates that the Far East did not entirely escape the eternal trade.

The history of African slaving has been treated almost exclusively from the point of view of those who were engaged in its European–New World operations. The modes of acquiring, handling, transporting and disposing of slaves in the trade to the New World, and the later movement to abolish this trade, dominate the literature. Arab slaving has usually been discussed from the perspective of the Europeans who suppressed the Arab trade in the eastern portion of the continent.[2] The African reaction, it is assumed, is lost; or it is suggested that Africans accepted slave raiding as a normal circumstance of life. Where its impact on African societies is recognized, it is viewed in general terms of demoralization or, as Coupland saw it, a factor that inhibited development out of a "primitive" state by preventing

> the growth of any relationship between the people of the three neighbouring continents other than the nexus between the European

[2] E.g., John Kells Ingram: *A History of Slavery and Serfdom* (London, 1895), *passim*.

and Asiatic slave-buyers and slave-hunters, together with the native agents they employed, and the Africans they hunted and bought.[3]

Works such as that of Diké, which analyzed the impact of European operations on the societies of the Niger Delta,[4] or of Hamet, in which the effect of Moslem expansion on the peoples of the French Sudan was discussed,[5] are exceptions.

A humanistic approach cannot fail to recognize the African reaction to this historical tragedy as a continuing influence in shaping attitudes toward non-Africans, and between African groups. The questions to bring out these attitudes have but rarely been asked even by the most competent investigators. The sociologically oriented students were little concerned with the historical dimension, while the historians were not prepared to deal with oral tradition. From the African point of view, reticence before a stranger and the circumspectness that so strongly marks the African in his human relations blocked his volunteering the requisite information when historical traditions were being discussed with him.

Yet certain glimpses can be caught behind the curtain of reserve. Many tales in West Africa point the moral that children should not stray from their own compounds, or answer when addressed by a stranger, a legacy from the time of child snatching by slavers. When a bullock is sacrificed for the souls of the royal ancestors in Dahomey, a goat is also given for those sold into slavery. The priests chant:

> Oh, ancestors, do all in your power that princes and nobles who today rule never be sent away from here as slaves . . . Punish the people who bought our kinsmen, whom we shall never see again. Send their vessels to Whydah harbor, . . . drown their crews, and make all the wealth of their ships come back to Dahomey.[6]

[3] Ibid., p. 4.

[4] Kenneth Onwuka Diké: *Trade and Politics in the Niger Delta, 1830–1885* (Oxford, 1956), *passim.*

[5] Ismael Hamet: *Chroniques de la Mauretanie Sénégalaise—Nacer Eddine* (Paris, 1911), pp. 27–80.

[6] Melville J. Herskovits: *Dahomey, an Ancient West African Kingdom* (New York, 1938), Vol. II, pp. 64–5.

Memories of slavery are so living that, in 1953, on the lower Congo, it was possible for Baseronga villagers to point to an island to show where, on a sandy spit at its western end, the Portuguese had conducted a *marché des hommes.*[7] Or, among the Bena Lulua, in a village near Luluabourg, one could hear in 1957 how the Portuguese and Arab slavers competed for allies, and how from east and west they each supplied their agents with guns and gunpowder, to raid for slaves and to fight off rival traders.[8]

However, our conclusions need not rest solely on evidence of this kind. Later events also testify to the influence of traditions of slaving on the attitudes and behavior of Africans. Thus the uprisings in the southern part of the Sudanese Republic, on the establishment of its independence, were directly attributable to the suspicion of the peoples of the south that the slave raids which preceded British occupation would be resumed, or new forms of dominance over them established. Nor had the tale of active slaving from Africa been told by 1955, as was shown by testimony regarding the illicit trade across the Red Sea given before the Economic and Social Council of the United Nations in 1955–6.[9]

This is not to say that the fears bred by the slave trade or the other acts of conquest and occupation of Subsaharan Africa, such as marked the quest for rubber in the Congo Free State, or the *corvée* and other forms of forced labor imposed elsewhere, continued unabated. The reactions of colonial powers to a changing world opinion on colonialism, particularly after the Second World War, and the changes set in motion under African pressures looking toward self-government tended to focus on problems and attitudes of the moment. Yet if one but read the signs, it was not difficult to perceive that the historic past was neither entirely forgotten nor forgiven. The slogan of anticolonialism continued to retain its full power to mobilize opinion and release hostility. If we consider that in the United States and Latin America the

[7] Ibid., *Notes on African Field Research, 1953–1960* (manuscript, 1953–60), p. 53/D352.

[8] Ibid., p. 57/D328.

[9] United Nations: *Economic and Social Council, Official Records,* 21 Session (New York, April 17–May 4, 1956), *passim.*

tradition of revolutionary action against overseas governments survived as a living force in molding policy in international relations for more than a century, it would be unrealistic in analysis and folly in practice to expect anything very different in Africa. The African past, too, remained an effective force in the African present. "We may pass the sponge over that long period during which the paternalism of certain powerful forces trod underfoot the real interests of the autochthonous peoples," wrote a Congolese editor from the Kasai, in 1958. "Yet the faithfulness of our memory will long tell us of those forces. . . ."[1]

[2]

The roster of non-African peoples represented in the population of Africa is literally world-wide. There are the nationals of European colonial Powers who went out to the African overseas possessions of their countries, to work, to trade, to administer, to evangelize, to teach, to settle as permanent residents. Those who know eastern and southern Africa add to these the large numbers who migrated from India, or in the western part of the continent, the Lebanese traders. But this only begins the list —Germans, Hollanders, Swedes, Irish, Russians, Poles, Swiss, Czechs, Italians and Greeks; Australians and New Zealanders; Chinese, Goans, Pakistani, Turks and Israeli; citizens of Canada and of the United States. Some of these were found in appreciable numbers, some were only slightly represented; this varied with time and territory. There was a substantial population of Greeks in Tanganyika; Goans dominated the clerical ranks of the public services in Kenya and Uganda; Portuguese were active in trade in the Congo; Liberia had an appreciable proportion of Germans and Swiss and Swedes in its small foreign colony that continued to count United States citizens as its principal component.

The tale of the Incomers, however, is even more complex than this roster would indicate. Neither in terms of historical

[1] *La Lumière:* "À Monsieur Petillon, Ministre des Colonies," Vol. 2, No. 24 (August 1, 1958), p. 1.

significance nor of acculturative impact can we overlook those of African origin or descent who, particularly in West Africa, returned or were brought back to Africa from the Americas and the West Indies. They represented a wide sampling of aboriginal African peoples. According to Koelle, the missionary who in 1852 recorded the languages of Africans brought to Freetown after having been released from ships illicitly engaged in the slave trade, their sources of origin reached from the Gambia to the Congo.[2] For many years the most influential segment of the population of the Colony of Sierra Leone, the so-called Creoles, consisted of the descendants of those and others brought from the New World who had been strongly influenced by association with European ways of life. As the first "educated" group in British West Africa, they played a distinctive and important role in its history, especially in Ghana and Nigeria.

Through the efforts of the American Colonization Society, Liberia was founded and in 1822, Monrovia was peopled by released slaves from the United States. They were later joined by American Negroes, who were seeking a degree of freedom denied them in the country of their birth. As the history of Liberia shows, these settlers, like the Creoles of Sierra Leone, identified themselves but slightly with the indigenous peoples. Psychologically, if not biologically, they held themselves apart from the Africans among whom they lived. The role of the Brazilian Negroes who returned to Africa must likewise not be overlooked. In Ghana a "Brazilian colony," established about 1825, became a permanent segment of the Accra population; in Dahomey the Brazilians acted as intermediaries between the Dahomean monarchs and European traders and slavers along the coast; in Nigeria the returned Brazilians were skilled artisans, who introduced Brazilian colonial architecture to Lagos, Benin and other centers.

Yet all these incomers, taken together, numbered but a small fraction of the total population of Subsaharan Africa. Only in the Union of South Africa did the non-African population rise to as much as twenty-five per cent of the total inhabitants. Here, according to the Census of 1951, out of 12,667,759 inhabitants,

[2] S. W. Koelle: *Polyglotta Africana* (London, 1854), *passim.*

there were 8,560,390 listed as Bantu, 2,641,689 as White, 1,103,016 as "Coloured"—defined as "persons not of pure European, Bantu or Asiatic stock, including *inter alia* Hottentots, Cape Malays, Cape Coloureds, Bushmen, Griquas, Namaquas, Korannas, and St. Helena Islanders"—and 366,664 as "Asiatics." At the other end of the scale, Ghana (then the Gold Coast) in 1948 reported, out of a total of 3,735,682 inhabitants, 3,728,963 as African, with 4,190 British, 1,370 Lebanese and Syrians, 796 "Europeans," 120 from the United States, and 243 "others."[3] The indigenous population of the Union of South Africa was thus 76%, of Ghana 99.36% of the total. Between these lay Spanish Guinea, with 80% of its people Africans, Southern Rhodesia, with 92%, and Kenya with 97%. With trifling exceptions, all other countries counted their indigenous population as being above 98% of the total, including the Belgian Congo (12,317,000, or more than 99% as against 89,000 non-Africans), Angola and Mozambique, Uganda (with 4,917,555 Africans, 33,767 Indians, 3,448 Europeans, 1,475 Arabs, 1,448 Goans, 643 persons of color, and 184 others) and the territories administered under the Trusteeship agreements of the United Nations.[4]

Figures of this kind, long commonplace among students of Africa, bear repetition because they lay the groundwork for an understanding of some of the varied approaches to what is characterized as adjustment in Subsaharan territories. The very word "African," for example, has come to require clarification since the end of the Second World War. Before that time, the usage was simple and the meaning clear—it denoted any person whose ancestry was indigenous to the continent, and carried a strong connotation of membership in the Negroid race. In the face of the challenge of African nationalism, however, the permanent European and Asian settlers gave a new meaning to the word African—that of any person, irrespective of race, who had been born in Africa.

[3] United Nations: *Demographic Yearbook,* Eighth Issue (New York, 1956), pp. 258–9.

[4] Ibid., loc. cit., and W. Goldschmidt: *The United States and Africa* (report of the American Assembly on Africa, New York, 1958), pp. 232–3.

The degree to which this new emphasis on an African identity was an outgrowth of South African custom, where *Afrikaner* supplanted "Boer" as the name for the long-established settlers of Dutch-Huguenot descent, cannot be said. But much of the argument for the primacy there of the white segment in the population came to turn on the point that those whose ancestors settled there before the eighteenth and nineteenth centuries had as much right to be considered Africans as the Bantu-speaking majority. By extension, this came to include all permanently settled Europeans in South Africa regardless of where they, or their forebears, had been born.

The concept of the "white African," however, was by no means restricted to the Union. "We teach our children to take pride in the fact that they are native Africans in the correct sense of the word 'native,'" wrote a Kenya settler, "and they do take pride in that fact." [5] Nor was this postwar shift in meaning confined to Europeans. Second and third generation descendants of Asian settlers in Kenya, Uganda and the Rhodesias, as well as in the Union, also came to assert their right to the name African. Their claims were couched in the same terms, their arguments moved along the same lines as those of Europeans in these same countries, or in the Belgian and Portuguese territories.

[3]

If, for simplicity of phrasing, we return to earlier usage, whereby the word "African" means those of autochthonous stock, we find that the non-Africans themselves, even those derived from the same continent, by no means formed a single community. There was, first of all, the division between Europeans and Asians. Under the influence of the "racial" thinking that was a major factor in setting patterns of personal attitude and social and political action everywhere in the Subsaharan continent, this division ordered a hierarchy of groups in accordance with degree of pigmentation. In this system, the most lightly pigmented were

[5] J. F. Lipscomb: *White Africans* (London, 1955), p. 18.

at the top, the intermediate groups between, and the darkest—the Africans—at the bottom. In many parts of the continent, therefore, there were three communities—African, European and Asian. These, when looked at in the mass, could be ranged in accordance with a descending scale set on the basis of pigmentation, in all aspects of their lives, whether of privilege or of opportunity, or education, or standard of living. Just as where, in a twofold division, non-African housing was in sharp contrast to that of Africans, so in the tripartite centers, the housing of this middle group, except in individual cases, was much less favorably situated, or well-built, or supplied with amenities than that of the Europeans, but in all these respects almost always superior to that of the Africans.

In the smaller centers Asians, usually the local traders, formed a homogeneous social unit. But where they were concentrated in larger numbers, they by no means had a monolithic social structure. The Sikh, with his turban, did not identify himself with the Bengali; Moslem Indians distinguished themselves from the Buddhists, and among the Moslems those who followed the Agha Khan were set off from others of the same faith. Pakistani and Goans, again, were grouped separately; and though the Arabs, in Kenya and Tanganyika, were also socially classed between Europeans and Africans, they were differentiated from other Asians both officially and unofficially, and by their own preference. Not only was this middle group split along ethnic, religious, social and linguistic lines, but the economic position of its members varied widely. Thus in the Union of South Africa, the Moslems of Durban were on the whole prosperous and conservative, but the Hindu heritors of the tradition of Mahatma Gandhi, with the exception of those in the professions, were for the most part small shopkeepers or poverty-stricken workers. In Uganda, there was as much of a social, economic and ideological gap between the Asian estate owner and the small Indian merchant in Kampala as ever existed in the earlier days of colonial rule in British Africa between the University "blue" in the political service and the English employee of a trading company.

There were certain centripetal forces in these tripartite societies of eastern and southern Africa which brought on a measure of unity to this middle range. Though the differences between the subgroups of Asians may have seemed large when viewed from within, they were slight in contrast with the differences between them and Europeans and Africans. Asians were the most minor of the minority groups, and in all countries except Uganda had to face pressures from Africans and Europeans alike. In these multiracial societies, Asians suffered the disabilities of the racially underprivileged without having the compensating inner security and long-range certainties that enabled the members of the African majority to face the future with confidence.

This uncertainty, arising out of a fundamental conviction that there was no basic security for them in the continent, dominated their thinking. Its most acute and most frequent expression came from communities large enough to be set apart as an identifiable unit, but it was by no means absent where, as in West Africa, the numbers of Indians, who with Lebanese and Syrians comprised the middle groups, were smaller. Particularly in eastern and southern Africa, the threat of being ground between the upper and the nether stones of the multiracial mill was too great, where the reality itself was not being experienced, to permit any relaxation of vigilance.

Historically, Indians were brought as laborers—into Kenya to work on the railway, into Natal as plantation hands on the sugar estates. Because they worked hard, lived parsimoniously, and saved their earnings, they were able to go into trade. Their standard of living, low as it was, was higher than in India, and they brought their families, their relatives, their fellow townsmen. The vast majority of Indians came to look upon Africa, not India, as their home. Despite all disabilities, they did what they could o maintain what they felt was their rightful place.

From every point of view, their position could not have been more exposed. Politically powerless, they had little means of redress against the enforced rules of racial segregation, especially in South Africa and Southern Rhodesia. From Europeans and from educated Africans one repeatedly heard—and read—the charge that the Asian, as it was phrased in Kenya, never gave his whole allegiance to East Africa, and this was held to be especially true of the Hindu. A further cause of the European attitude—by no means restricted to British territories—was the suspicion that some day there might be a shift of control from Europe to India. This reasoning, which certain Indians felt had in fact somewhat improved their tactical position, was based on the rise of India as a world power. At the same time, Indians in Africa stressed the fact that the Government of India, though taking a strong anti-colonial position, also insisted that Indians living outside India should think of themselves as citizens of the country in which they resided, and not as citizens of India.

This middle group of the multiracial communities increasingly came to associate itself politically as much as possible with the Africans, and in other ways sought to gain favor with the racial majority, whose members they regarded as fellow sufferers from discriminatory practices, though they did not consider them as equals. In this, their acceptance, however reluctant, of the proposition that the future of the countries in which they lived—even in the Union of South Africa—must come more and more to lie in the hands of the numerically predominant African sector of society, was evident by implication where it was not made explicit. And since their future was held to rest in the hands of the Africans, it was they whose good will must be secured by such political support as the Asians could muster; by such gifts as schools and school equipment, recreational facilities and other contributions to African communities; by training African staff in business procedures; and even by permitting Africans a modicum of association in commercial ventures.

Just because so much of the success of the Indians was in the field of retail trade, they became an immediate object of African hostility. Again and again, Africans fixed on the Indians as the nearest target for releasing their frustrations, even those the Indians had no part in causing. There was little question that the practices of the majority of Indian shopkeepers, especially in the smaller towns and the countryside, were not such as to win them friends among the Africans. Indians, being above Africans in the social scale, were wont to treat them in much the same way as they themselves were treated by Europeans. The resentments that gave rise to the Durban riots of 1949, where Indians were attacked by Africans in the city, revealed the depth of these feelings. With the stresses that arose out of their continuous contact, under circumstances which gave rise to sharp competition with and exploitation of the Africans, with whom the Indians knew they must above all be friends, their situation was, in truth, precarious.

The middle group of non-Europeans was of minor importance in territories controlled by Portugal and Belgium. Some Goans were to be found in the former, mainly as minor functionaries, or as waiters, barbers, and the like. Under Belgian control, except for the Trust territory of Ruanda-Urundi, into which Asians moved in appreciable numbers, this middle group was in effect nonexistent. In British West Africa, in the large cities of Ibadan and Lagos, Accra and Kumasi, Indian-owned shops were frequently encountered. Certain larger retail concerns, with branches in the towns of Sierra Leone, Nigeria and Ghana, belonged to those of the middle group, but as we have seen, commercial operations by smaller merchants were rendered difficult in centers of Eastern Nigeria such as Onitsha and Aba because of the competition of the Ibo traders.

In the former British West African territories, at least, and to some extent in what was French West and Equatorial Africa, and the Cameroons, the effective element in this middle group was not Indian but Lebanese, or Syrian. The migration of these Levantine merchants to Africa dated from about 1880, and seems to have been an offshoot of the Lebanese exodus of that period, which was principally directed toward the United States. The experience of the Lebanese, except for the fact that initially they came to trade, and that they came individually rather than as members of work gangs, was not unlike that of the Indians elsewhere. It unfolded a tale of hard work, privation, parsimony, willingness to defer immediate well-being for future advantage, and eventual accumulation of savings that in specific instances made for an impressive economic position.

Unlike the Indians in eastern and southern Africa, however,

who came to regard the countries where they settled as their home, the Lebanese, certainly until the countries where they lived attained independence, continued to identify themselves with the land from which they had emigrated. As a general rule, they deposited their savings there, and returned upon retirement. Though in many cases themselves without schooling, they were eager for education for their children, often sending them to Lebanon, or England, or France, for training. The prevailing opinion, however, was that those Lebanese who received professional training rarely returned to Africa with the skills they had acquired.[6]

The value of Lebanese enterprise for the countries to which they migrated has been variously appraised. Analyzing their contributions in economic terms, Bauer argued that by their commercial activities they made available to Africans goods that could otherwise not have been obtained, and were thus responsible for raising the general standard of living. Stressing the fact that the Levantine immigrants were "resourceful, industrious, enterprising," and independent of existing commercial interests, he underscored the importance of the functions they performed in promoting internal trade, and the fact that they constituted the only challenge to the large monopolistic trading companies.[7]

Others held, however, that the activities of Lebanese traders inhibited the development of an African class of small merchants. Continuously in contact with the Africans whom they supplied, they were for some time objects of animosity and, as in the case of Indians in East Africa, charges of sharp dealing were often lodged against them by Africans and Europeans. After about 1950, Levantine immigration into British West Africa became subject to very strict controls. In Liberia, efforts were made in 1945 to restrict their trading activities to the coast. Though socially less aloof than other non-Africans, like other trading Incomers they conducted their business in a manner that corroborated the African view that they came to profit and return

[6] Marwan Hanna: "The Lebanese in West Africa," *West Africa*, No. 2142 (1958), pp. 415–17.

[7] P. T. Bauer: *West African Trade* (Cambridge, England, 1954), p. 164.

home, rather than to build their future into the structure of their adopted country.

Regardless of the merits of either argument, there is little question that the Lebanese shared much of the malaise of middle group communities everywhere in Africa. Hanna, himself a member of this group, has given us explicit documentation on this point. "One of the sore points that is always causing anxiety to the Lebanese immigrants is their feeling of insecurity and isolation." He noted their fear that they might come to be thought of as "white settlers," and stressed the good reputation they had gained in other parts of the world for lack of bias.[8]

Hailey has stated that to represent the Levantine community "as the West African counterpart of the Asians in Southern and Eastern Africa" would be to draw an analogy that "is not actually close." Yet as concerns the stratification of society there is little doubt that the situation of the Levantines of West Africa differed only in degree from that of the Asians in the eastern and southern parts. Though there was no permanent European settlement in the west, and there had been no mass importations of non-Africans as laborers there, both Europeans and the middle group, however small in proportion to the total population, had since the Second World War become increasingly more conscious that the control of affairs by the African majority was imminent. The total situation of the middle group thus proved to be no more assured than it was on the other side of the continent. Looked on with suspicion by the African majority, barely tolerated by the Europeans, they were in both regions deprived of certainty as to their future, except for the certainty that any future they might have in Africa would be at the pleasure of a racial majority with which they would not be permitted to identify themselves, and at whose suffrance they could continue only as a minority under scrutiny.

[4]

From every point of view, the nationals of the colonial powers made up the most important segment of the non-African

[8] Op. cit., p. 487.

population of the continent since its partition brought European controls. Inasmuch as our concern is with the repercussions of these controls on the African scene, it is unnecessary to review here the tale of how they were established. This is the most thoroughly explored and documented aspect of African history. Its importance for our discussion here lies in the fact that it was the Europeans in Africa who, in constantly increasing measure brought about the reshaping of the traditional ways of life we are seeking to understand. Consequently, we need to assess the position and contribution of this European group of Incomers in the same way as we have examined the position and role of other kinds of Incomers in Subsaharan Africa from mid-nineteenth century onwards.

At this point, we should note that the Africans were not alone in experiencing cultural shock as a result of their contacts with Europeans. This was a mutual experience. If the power of those from overseas seemed awesome to the peoples to whom they came, if their behavior seemed inscrutable, their rules incomprehensible or inconsistent, their desires unpredictable, the Europeans complained that the Africans were difficult to fathom, evasive in face to face encounter, unable to understand instructions, their traditions seemingly without reason.

The difference was that the European was in control. It was his system of values that framed the rules and ordinances which were established. The "natural justice" so often referred to in earlier British statements on colonial policy, and the *mission civilisatrice* of the French, like the Belgian and Portuguese counterparts of these concepts, were implemented by legal and other conventions that from the point of view of European culture were self-evident, essential, and right beyond doubt for human societies everywhere. The White Man's Burden was therefore a discipline for the African which would bring him eventually to what was firmly and sometimes fervently believed to be the better ways of life of what were considered more advanced societies.

The ideology of any great historical movement, on analysis, proves to be the result of the interplay between a complicated and often conflicting set of factors. European expansion in Africa was no exception. The ideology that underlay such concepts as that of the White Man's Burden combined a set of rationalizations that justified a ruthless struggle for material gain and political position with the rationale for an idealism that aimed at saving souls, educating untutored minds, and healing the sick. The comment of Captain William Snelgrave on the African slave trade is apropos, when we consider it in the light of the currents of thought which underlay subsequent events that marked European occupation: "And, let the worst that can, be said of it, it will be found, like all other earthly Advantages, tempered with a mixture of Good and Evil." [9]

Williams has shown how the wealth of English owners of New World sugar estates, invested in cotton mills, became a force in the abolitionist movement; [1] in similar fashion, the same European society that was enslaving Africans was also establishing refuges for freed slaves in Sierra Leone and in Liberia. It is difficult, except from this point of view, to contemplate without cynicism the name given the Congo Free State. The Congo was "free" indeed—but only from domination by a major European power. There was no freedom for the indigenous people. One aftereffect of the Congo Free State was the legacy it left Belgium, of guilt over earlier excesses. This feeling, and a pragmatic economic policy of conserving the work force of a sparsely populated colony, thus opened a way for later developments in the evolution of Belgian policy and the eventual disappearance of Belgium as a colonial power.

In a world where shifts in the structure of power forced a reconsideration of judgments based on concepts of cultural superiority and inferiority, it is difficult to appreciate the force of the assumptions held by Europeans who came to Africa in various capacities. Deep-rooted convictions, for example, on the ways of life and capabilities of "civilized" versus "savage" peoples pro-

[9] Captain William Snelgrave: *A New Account of Some Parts of Guinea, and the Slave Trade* (London, 1734), p. 161.

[1] Eric Williams: *Capitalism and Slavery* (Chapel Hill, North Carolina, 1944), *passim.*

vided ample ideological justification for any measures they might take to establish their controls. If the cultural shock to Africans resulted from an attack on the sanctions and values that had made for social stability and personal adjustment, for the Europeans it derived from a kind of bewilderment that the presumably self-evident propositions of a superior civilization were not always self-evident to the recipients and potential beneficiaries of their application. A later parallel was the bewilderment of the technicians and other specialists who came to Africa from eastern Europe at the end of colonial times and, without any background of African experience, attempted to fit their Marxian model to the actualities of the newly independent African states.

That African peoples have traditions and values to be understood and taken seriously was an idea that, if ever advanced, elicited little response during the colonial period. The racial as well as the cultural inferiority of the Africans was taken for granted in most of the Euroamerican world. And this point of view, which gave way in the matter of inherent racial inferiority, continued to hold concerning African cultures, so that, as late as 1957, the President of the Council of Portugal, in an address setting forth basic policy, could say of the indigenous inhabitants of its African overseas territories,

> We believe that there are races, decadent or backward, as one wishes, in relation to whom we must discharge a duty to summon them to civilization—a task of human training to be discharged humanely.[2]

The ethnocentrism in this statement makes clear the lines of historic continuity that guided official and unofficial thinking about Africa and the Africans under the colonial system.

After the end of the Second World War, when the fallacies of the racist doctrine had been laid bare, it was the assumption of *cultural* superiority—what may be termed "culturism" rather than racism—that served to justify policies maintaining the differences in opportunity and reward between Africans and non-

[2] Antonio de Oliveira Salazar: Radio Address on Portuguese Policy, *Notícias de Portugal,* Supplement to No. 548 (November 2, 1957), p. 4.

Africans that characterized the African colonial scene. In historical terms, culturism furnished the rationale for the color bar, a phrase too often used for what actually, in most instances, was what Lord Hailey called the culture bar. It underlay the reasoning that called forth the concept of senior and junior partnership in a multiracial state. First advanced in the Rhodesias, this concept postulated that culturally more advanced Europeans, though in the minority, must have the direction of affairs, because the Africans could not then or in the foreseeable future be expected to attain a requisite level of knowledge and experience.

Culturism was behind the various projects advanced in East and Central Africa for a differential franchise, for the slowness of political change in the Congo, for the brutality of the controls to which Africans were being subjected in Portuguese Africa. Many of the reservations encountered in European capitals to the idea of self-government for Africans, except in the indefinite future—reservations expressed even by those who were in principle hospitable to the idea—turned on the belief that cultural inferiority made questionable the readiness of Africans to emerge from the status of tutelage and dependency, to determine their own destiny. Any European as such was thought to have an advantage that no African could overcome, because of the heritage of the "thousand years of history" to which we have earlier referred.[3] And in postcolonial Africa, culturism became manifest in the assumption of the Marxists that it was their mission to hasten the inevitable arrival of African societies at the higher stage of civilization which the Communist countries had reached.

[5]

The Europeans of any African territory, and indeed, of any single community except that of the isolated outlying stations, were no more homogeneous than the middle group. For one thing, the habit of thinking in terms of color established social differentials within European groups, as well as between them

[3] *Supra*, pp. 9–14.

and other sections of a given population. These subtle distinctions were further complicated by concepts of national worth, by the fact of economic position, and by the degree of deviation from the behavior and values of the dominant element in a given territory.

Put in its simplest terms, those of the European ("white") communities of Africa who came from countries whose populations are more lightly pigmented enjoyed higher social status than the swarthier types. Of course the nationals of the governing country had the most advantageous place in any dependency, if only because of the relation of social position to the structure of power. But even in Portuguese territory, the Swiss, the German, the Britisher found ready acceptance and frequently ranked socially higher than many Portuguese. On the other hand, the Portuguese in Belgian territory showed all the marks of middle group status, much like the Lebanese in British and French West Africa.

No sociological study of the differentials within European communities was ever made during colonial times, despite the importance of those communities in determining the direction of change in Africa. One wonders why no analysis was attempted of the play of these evaluative patterns, considering how useful it might have been in defining the forces at work and their consequences. For example, the Hailey *Survey,* which included a chapter on "The Non-European Immigrant Communities"—those termed the middle group in our discussion—ignored the organization, functioning and basic values of the much more numerous, and more important European societies in Africa.

The differentiation of subgroups within a dominant European community was carried farthest in South Africa, where it was given juridical as well as social sanction. It is also unique, for Africa, in that it derived historically from actual armed conflict between two European groups. The scars left by the Anglo-Boer War were continuously irritated in the years that followed it by the conventions of social superiority and the forces of economic dominance which compounded the resentments felt against the British by the Afrikaners after their military defeat. This is not the place to discuss the complexities introduced into this situation by the cultural, linguistic and religious sanctions for Afrikaner nationalism. What is relevant here, however, is that the acceptance of the principle of racial segregation, basic to the thinking of the vast majority of the Europeans in the country, English as well as Afrikaner, made for a situation best illustrated by the fact that, after about 1950, the phrase "race problem" was popularly applied more often to differences between English- and Afrikaner-speaking sections of the European population than it was to tensions between Europeans and non-Europeans. Beneath this, however, lay the relations of both major groups with more recent European immigrants—East Europeans, Jews, Italians, Germans, and others. As in the Rhodesias, the question of what constituted a desirable immigrant continued to be much debated, and it is revealing to note the extent to which the discussion turned on the desirability of having a "homogeneous"—that is, a north European, white, Protestant—population.

In one sense, the European community as a whole of any given territory was set off from the other groups in economic opportunity, with all this implies. As a group, it was far better paid, better housed, better fed, with more ready access to educational facilities and other social amenities. Thus, in Port Elizabeth, in the Union of South Africa, as late as 1957, even Europeans living in "sub-economic" low-rent municipal housing were observed to have African servants.[4]

Elsewhere, however, there were exceptions to this state of affairs. In French territories and in British West Africa were to be found Africans whose standard of living was equivalent to that of many Europeans, and higher than that of many Levantines. This was true particularly of those Africans who came to hold positions of importance in government or business. In the Belgian Congo, where segregation was officially sanctioned until 1954, the gap between the racial communities continued to be striking until the end of Belgian rule. It was even more striking in the multiracial societies of the eastern and southern parts of the con-

[4] Melville J. Herskovits: *Notes on African Field Research, 1953–1960* (manuscript), p. 57/D499.

tinent. In Kenya, for example, when traveling by car, one could tell at once by the condition of the road when one passed from an area inhabited by European settlers into one where Africans lived. An exception, perhaps, was the block of apartments in Salisbury provided for the African members of the Parliament of the Central African Federation. Physically, this was of a standard that would be acceptable to any European, though it rose austerely from a treeless clearing. Because of racial housing regulations, however, it was situated on the periphery of the African township. There it stood, separated from the European-occupied city and a little removed by its bleak setting from the modest housing of the African community.

Overlapping between racial groups at the lower end of the scale also occurred, as in French Africa, where the *petit blanc* competed with Africans for jobs. In consequence, one might be waited on in a shop in Abidjan by either an African or a European; a taxi-driver in Brazzaville might be a Frenchman or a Mukongo. One could hear from an African worker in Douala how he sheltered a destitute French immigrant in his own home, until the newcomer could find work, with the comment, "Poverty knows no color line." Standards of living also varied widely among Europeans, though no situation existed comparable to that of the poor whites in the Union of South Africa in the period between the two world wars.

But the blurring of differences between whites and Africans was atypical. Differentials in pay between African and European for the same work, for many years the rule everywhere, gave way only slowly, mainly because of the increasing political pressure brought to bear by Africans. Bauer stated that

> In 1949 the then managing director of the United Africa Company in a public address estimated the cost to his company of employing and maintaining the most junior European employee in West Africa at over £1,400 a year.

He added, "The cost of employing . . . a Levantine, is much lower, and is at most certainly less than half this figure"; [5] and

[5] P. T. Bauer: *West African Trade* (Cambridge, England, 1954), p. 65.

though he did not mention Africans, we can be quite certain that they would have received no more than a Levantine, if at that time Africans had attained a comparable position.

Earnings of European mine workers in Northern Rhodesia averaged £2,295 in the peak year of 1956; of Africans, £160 per annum. This did not include fringe benefits, which had a comparable differential. Between 1950 and 1956, wages of Europeans increased 115%, from £1,068 to £2,295; of Africans, 162%, from £61 to £160.[6] In 1959, earnings of Europeans on the mines averaged £1,868, those of Africans £218.[7] For the three territories, according to the 1959 Economic Report of the Federation, the average cash earnings of Europeans and Africans in 1958, a poor year for farming and copper, were for Southern Rhodesia £995 and £80, respectively; for Northern Rhodesia £1,273 and £99; and for Nyasaland £889 and £46.[8] In 1953, one Leopoldville owner of a garage estimated that it cost 50,000 Belgian francs, or about $1,000 a month to bring, employ and maintain a European mechanic and his family. The minimum monthly wage for Europeans recruited outside the Congo was FB.10,000, or FB.8,100 for those recruited locally ($200 and $160).[9] In absolute terms, this was somewhat, though not strikingly, higher than that of an African clerical worker who, after ten years' experience, was receiving FB.7,000 ($140) as his basic salary.

Though the gap in rates of pay tended to narrow with time, especially where government posts were involved, change came slowly even here. In Kenya, the principle of parity for equivalent work was introduced in 1954, though Africans continued to complain that, as in other parts of East Africa, parity in principle could be defeated by devices for classifying workers in certain grades, the highest restricted to Europeans. In British West Africa parity came much earlier and was a cardinal point in the

[6] *East Africa and Rhodesia:* "Survey of the Copperbelt," Vol. 34, No. 1733 (December 26, 1957), p. 563.

[7] Northern Rhodesia Chamber of Mines: *Year Book, 1959* (Kitwe, Northern Rhodesia, 1960), pp. 33, 40.

[8] Shirley Williams: *Central Africa: the Economics of Inequality* (Research Series 215, Fabian Commonwealth Bureau, London, 1960), p. 12.

[9] Melville J. Herskovits: op. cit., p. 53/D341.

drive for Africanization not only of the civil service, but of the educational system and of the managerial ranks of business. Here it was observed so rigorously that African staff members of institutions of higher learning received "summer home leave" with travel expenses to England, for themselves and their families, just as did their European colleagues.

Parity in pay for the same work was also accepted in principle in French, Belgian and Portuguese territories, but the gap between principle and practice was considerable, particularly in Portuguese Africa, due largely to the play of opportunity against the discriminatory classification of jobs. In French and Belgian territories, the upgrading of Africans in government and in business enterprises of all sorts was consistently followed after the end of the Second World War. There was, however, another side to this picture. Serious questions were raised, often by those who had no stake in the matter, as to whether the scale of pay necessary to import administrators, teachers, technicians and others from overseas should not be higher than that paid to Africans. As explained by the Finance Minister of one territory, the problem was to pay for development and capital improvements, such as roads, schools, and the like, and at the same time to finance out of current revenue the greater going costs of government that parity would entail.

It was argued that a growing country which needed specialists would profit in many ways if it could, for example, have three African doctors for the cost of two European ones. Racial wage differentials were held to represent inducement costs essential to attract expatriates. But these were arguments drawn from the broad background of public finance. Africans recognized their logic in the abstract. However, to the African teacher who received markedly lower pay than the European teaching a class in the room next to his, yet who was reproached for not maintaining a higher standard of living, these arguments were not too persuasive.

Socially, the European community was self-contained. Except officially, even in British and, to a certain extent, in French West Africa, there was limited contact between its members and those of other groups. Interracial clubs were rare enough to be a cause for comment—indeed, in many parts of the continent, not only Europeans but middle-group populations each had its own club. During most of the colonial period, Africans and non-European immigrants were present at official functions, except in South Africa, but the unselfconscious give and take that arises from personal acceptance and a common interest was quite lacking.

The state of race relations at any period and in any African territory could be gauged by the extent to which it was possible for a European or American interested in a given local situation to find Africans who would discuss such matters, and by how long it took before they would speak frankly. The proportion of non-African settlers in a given territory, which was directly related to the willingness of Africans to discuss issues, gave another index of the degree of racial tension in a given country. Thus it was possible, at mid-twentieth century, to plot a curve of racial tension, with Ghana at the point of least stress, and South Africa at the opposite end.

Within a given European community, almost without exception, save in independent countries like Ghana and in a more limited way in Liberia, life was lived as much as possible in terms of homeland patterns. Europeans strove unceasingly to recreate the middle- and upper-class life of their homeland. This does not mean that Europeans shut themselves off completely from local influences, for here and there in vocabulary, in food, in household devices, African cultural elements had been taken over.

Even in a changing Africa, few buildings of any kind showed the influence of an African tradition. Significantly enough, the exceptions were to be found in West Africa. The hospital in Kumasi, with the decorations on its many-storied walls taken from the bas-reliefs of the Ashanti house, or the grille of the Bank of Ghana in the same city, with its gilded enlarged reproductions of Ashanti gold weights, were notable exceptions, as were some of the buildings of the Ethnographic Museum in Abidjan or the Centre Artisanal in Bamako. The architecture of none of the institutions of higher learning, however, showed any African influence; this was equally true of the curriculum.

Europeans, even in small communities such as Yaounde, Usumbura, Lobito, or Lusaka, lived their lives without, in the sociological sense, "seeing" an African. They assumed that the African must adapt himself to their own norms, and judged Africans by these norms alone. When the sociology of the European community in Africa is studied, not the least significant part of it will be the folklore about African culture and behavior as told by Europeans among themselves—a folklore that Africans matched almost point for point when talking among themselves of the Europeans.

Herein lay one of the dangers in the African scene. In time, less was heard about Europeans "knowing" the Africans; pleas for a better understanding, more communication, between the two groups, were heard more often. Such knowledge as existed was chiefly the Africans' knowledge of the Europeans. It was the knowledge those who serve always have of those in power, gained in ways that often brought more bitterness than understanding. The African household servant in the European community, coming more and more to know the language of his employers, registered what he heard and saw. Being ubiquitous, he learned much that was scarcely conducive to creating an image commanding trust or respect.

In this way, and in analogous situations in places of work, a picture of the "other" group came to be built. If, to the European, the African was a shirker, dull and lazy, the European in the eyes of the African was lazy and not competent to perform the simplest tasks. Each, with full documentation that satisfied teller and listener, could recount instances of untrustworthiness, of disregard for facts, of inability to be truthful, of cruelty, of generally irrational behavior. Being in the position of power, the European made no secret of his attitudes; the African aired his resentments to other Africans. We can but speculate on the degree to which the apprehensions of Europeans as to their future in Africa, with African control of government coming closer, can be equated with an increasing awareness of the strength of these resentments once the pressures that hold them in check were released, resentments that, for example, were one of the prime causes of the outbreaks in Leopoldville in January, 1959, and that led to the later incidents of the early days of Congo independence.[1]

Thus the past shaped the present. Both groups were aware of the consequences of earlier excesses. The Europeans expressed this awareness in their protests against change that were to be heard and read. It was implicit in the frequency and urgency with which the contribution made by the European to the African was emphasized, the need of the African for the European asserted, the silence of the African on the positive benefits conferred by the colonial Powers deplored. Significantly, too Africans seldom said anything in answer.

Disparities in economic opportunity and social position, the existence of institutional discrimination and patterned misunderstanding between groups, are not only found in African societies. They are ubiquitous, certainly in all industrial communities. In Africa, however, the disparities were associated with, and in practice did characterize, racial groups. For though underprivileged elements in society where relatively homogenous physical types may be similarly segmented, and resentments may be lively, the organizing principle is social or economic, not racial. Differences are not emphasized by the high degree of "social visibility" which exists when class and race are coterminous as in Subsaharan Africa. The binding of race to social position and economic role exacerbates the tensions that arise whenever aspiration and opportunity are out of line.

Yet despite discontent and frustrations, Africans rarely resorted to physical force to redress grievances. This is one of the more striking aspects of the history of contacts between the races in Africa. The predictions, freely heard from Europeans in Ghana on the eve of independence, that there would be incidents of aggression against whites during the celebrations not only were unfulfilled, but the attitude of the Africans toward individual Euro-

[1] Chambre des Représentants: *Rapport* (on events in Leopoldville in January, 1959; Brussels, March 28, 1959), p. 9.

peans and Americans on the street reflected a pattern that made this transfer of power certainly one of the most peaceful revolutions in human experience. Even in South Africa, with its almost unsurpassed restrictions on the Africans, its grossly submarginal urban living conditions for Africans there was a minimum of violence against Europeans as such.

Without doubt it beclouds perspective to emphasize situations of crisis at the expense of the less dramatic daily routines of most people, wherever they may live. For an undistorted view, we must recognize ambivalences, as well. Many Europeans, even while denying the ability of Africans to govern themselves, or to exercise managerial responsibility, or to handle complex machinery, identified themselves with the achievements of a tribal group they had come to know well. A parallel on the other side was the case of the Congolese man in Leopoldville arguing for political responsibilities such as were being accorded by the French to the Africans in Brazzaville just across the river, while criticizing African ways of living on the French side in a manner reminiscent of a Belgian burgher finding fault with the habits of the Parisians.

The past in Africa cannot be ignored. Since the present at any given moment is incorporated into the past, the more clearheaded the analysis of the present, the more realistic will be judgments of the future. For though the past may be with us, it is not to be recaptured in its original form. It is fantasy to think in terms of nativism, whether it is a chosen or an enforced tribalism, or, on the European side, to insist on the unchallenged privileges of earlier days. Of this we can be sure: the African future will be shaped by the contributions of all those who have been participants in its past, Africans and non-Africans alike.

6

The Land

In 1913, Solomon Tshekisho Plaatje, who described himself as a "South African Native," wrote to protest against what he considered a particularly irksome act of discrimination against his fellow Africans. His photograph, the reference given him by the Duke of Connaught, whose interpreter he had been, and a story about him in the Pretoria *News,* were included as his credentials. He was, in the words of the newspaper account,

> no agitator or firebrand, no stirrer-up of bad feelings between black and white. He accepts the position which the Natives occupy today in the body politic as the natural result of their lack of education and civilization.[1]

What was it, then, that had stirred this moderate man to protest? It was "The Natives' Land Act, 1913," which according to Plaatje prohibited "Natives . . . from investing their earnings in land whereon they could end their days in peace." [2]

It is not chance that it was a question of land tenure that provoked Plaatje to write his polemic and his plea. Nothing has been

[1] Sol T. Plaatje: *Native Life in South Africa, Before and Since the European War and the Boer Rebellion* (fifth edition, London, n.d.), p. 10.

[2] Ibid., p. 45.

of greater importance in Africa. Its special place in the thought of Africans was rooted in values that go beyond immediate economic considerations. "At the heart of all the new Commissioner's problems" in Nyasaland of the 1890's, we read, "lay the one question still in the centre of that triangle of troubles among native Africans, European settlers and administrators in modern Africa: ownership of the land." [3]

Actual pressure of population on the land has figured only in a few areas of Africa. This differentiates Subsaharan Africa from overpopulated nonindustrial parts of the world such as China, India, the Nile valley, or the valley of Mexico. But in terms of the most widespread and deepest African values, the land not only provides subsistence, but enters into religious belief. The rituals having to do with land touch many aspects of African culture. It is difficult indeed to write of any phase of aboriginal custom and induced innovation without taking the land into account. Emotional responses called forth by traditional claims to the land go far to explain why the persistence of earlier patterns of occupancy and use presented those concerned with "developing" Africa with some of their knottiest problems. Even with the changes brought about by the onset of urbanization and industrialization, the land problem remained paramount.

A mere sampling of the literature, whether written by Africans or by Europeans, will document the importance of the land in aboriginal ways of life. The comments of Jomo Kenyatta on its role in Kikuyu culture take on added significance in view of the Mau Mau revolt of 1952–4 which erupted because of the growing land hunger. Land tenure, wrote Kenyatta, is "the most important factor in the social, political, religious, and economic life of the tribe." He expands on its importance:

> As agriculturalists, the Gikuyu people depend entirely on the land. It supplies them with the material needs of life, through which spiritual and mental contentment is achieved. Communion with the

[3] George Shepperson and Thomas Price: *Independent African: John Chilembwe and the Origins, Setting and Significance of the Nyasaland Native Rising of 1915* (Edinburgh, 1958), p. 14.

ancestral spirits is perpetuated through contact with the soil in which the ancestors of the tribe lie buried. The Gikuyu consider the earth as the "mother" of the tribe, . . . it is the soil that feeds the child through lifetime; and again after death it is the soil that nurses the spirits of the dead for eternity. Thus the earth is the most sacred thing above all that dwell in or on it. Among the Gikuyu the soil is especially honoured, and an everlasting oath is to swear by the earth (*koirugo*).[4]

Ethnographic accounts of other peoples bear unanimous testimony to the symbolic value of the land. Though concerned with social structure and legal procedure rather than with attitudes, studies of aboriginal land law such as that of Schapera for Bechuanaland show indirectly the reflection in institutional procedures of the feeling the people have for their ancestral lands.[5] In Swaziland, when the land was partitioned,

the natives were aghast. . . . They won their subsistence from the soil, their major rituals were directed to increase its yield; the land was ritually identified with the king, with prosperity, health and power; . . . To lose the land struck at the roots of their economic and political system.[6]

Similar feelings about the land, to take another example from the vast array of materials bearing on this point, are found in the western part of Subsaharan Africa. Among the Susu of Guinea, a principle of ownership long recognized in the study of African property concepts remains in full vigor; that only those things made by an individual belong to him, and therefore land must lie in a different category.

No man, no human group made it, even at the beginning of things. It should not pass as being the product of any human labor. It belongs to itself and, in consequence, does not belong to anyone. . . . In the same way no individual, even though he may be the

[4] Jomo Kenyatta: *Facing Mount Kenya, the Tribal Life of the Gikuyu* (London, 1938), p. 21.

[5] I. Schapera: *Native Land Tenure in the Bechuanaland Protectorate* (Lovedale [C.P.], South Africa, 1943), pp. 35 ff.

[6] Hilda Kuper: *An African Aristocracy: Rank among the Swazi* (London, 1947), p. 30.

greatest king in the world, no group, can manipulate or acquire any real property rights in land.[7]

A primary crop can call forth the same depth of feeling as the land that produces it. For the rice-growing Kissi, also of Guinea, "All life, not only material but emotional, is here dominated by solicitude for the rice. . . . Mālo, rice, is certainly by far the word most often heard spoken."[8] Reciprocally, this feeling goes beyond the crop to the land itself. Thus, for example, Kissi dead are buried within the village, but a stranger never, since to dig his grave there "would correspond to admitting the dead [stranger] into the community."[9]

Some of the most widespread patterns of aboriginal culture in Subsaharan Africa, and thus perhaps among the oldest traditions of its present inhabitants, are found in the complex of beliefs and behavior involving the relationship between man and the land that nourishes him. Here we find general principles that transcend the boundaries of areas, that cut across our dual classification of African societies into those that live by agriculture and those in which herding and food-gathering are of primary importance. These general principles of land tenure are well-known. We recall them here, because they are so fundamental for an understanding of some of the forces of culture contact whose interplay is our principal concern. Merely to name them will indicate some of the points of tension that have arisen out of the imposition of controls based on foreign concepts.

Most important is the fact that the relationship between man and the earth is what many writers call "mystical," but which can be more fruitfully regarded as a relationship which lies at the very core of their world view. Where the ancestral cult plays the primary role, the ancestors are the connecting link between man and the earth; where polytheistic beliefs explain the nature and functioning of the universe, the deity who controls the earth in-

[7] Roger Doublier: *La Propriété Foncière en A. O. F., Régime en Droit Privé* (Saint-Louis, Sénégal, 1952), p. 6.

[8] Denise Paulme: *Les Gens du Riz, Kissi de Haut-Guinée Française* (Paris, 1954), p. 23.

[9] Ibid., p. 128.

variably is one of the most powerful gods. In much of the continent, the bond between the land and its inhabitants, once established, is so enduring that a people who migrate to a new territory will give offerings not only to whatever supernatural beings may control its new habitat, but to the spirits of the former human inhabitants. This tradition was so strong that in the African religions which have persisted in the New World, offerings are made to the land and the rivers in the name of the autochthonous American Indians, known or unknown, who "owned the land."

A second set of principles which must always be considered in treating of African land has to do with its tenure and use. Tenure is customarily recognized as "communal" rather than individual. Invariably in theory, and often in practice, the ultimate word in the allocation of land was that of the head of a given group—the ruler where the political system was of the order of an organized state, a territorial chief or the head of the kinship unit where the state, as defined, did not exist. The sanction for this was religious, going back to ancestors or deities; the controls in a given society followed well-recognized rules. Those controls, and their underlying sanctions were, however, more complex than such a statement implies. Thus, while in Dahomey a cloth was given the king in payment for the earth in which a Dahomean was buried, each king during the rituals of enstoolment which marked his accession as ruler, distributed cowrie shells to the people, whereby he symbolically "bought" the land from them.[1]

The abundance of land simplified making and receiving allocations, especially where its use was confined to agriculture. In the case of grazing land, the communal character of ownership was pronounced. No individual, as such, would think of laying claim to such land. It is easy to understand how, in the light of this tradition, the Africans who lived in the areas where herding is important came to detest nothing more than fencing.

The communal tradition did not, however, negate the fact of

[1] Melville J. Herskovits: *Dahomey, an Ancient West African Kingdom* (New York, 1938), Vol. I, p. 80.

individual tenure. Here a complementary principle concerning private property comes into play. An individual owns the utensil or other object on which he has expended effort, whether it be a mortar, a canoe, or the harvest of a field he has worked. The land he farms, though theoretically it "belongs" to the chief as representative of the community, is his for use; and as long as he uses it, it cannot be used by another. Regulations regarding trespass are clearly indicated in analyses of African land law.[2] Among herding peoples, one of the tasks of the herd-boys is to see that the animals they watch do not stray into cultivated fields.

A corollary to the principle of ownership provided the sanctions needed to accomplish the transfer from a communal to a more personal form of landholding, when tree crops became important. We have noted the traditional code, whereby the individual has a personal, inalienable claim to those things for whose existence he has been responsible. Included in this category are the trees he plants in the field or fields he cultivates. The principle holds everywhere, for the fruit trees or bamboo in East Africa as it does for palm trees in the Congo and the Guinea Coast. Hence one who has planted a tree must be granted access to it after he has ceased farming the plot in which he planted it, while a person who later cultivates this plot must protect such a tree from damage by fire when he burns over the field at the end of the dry season.

All this does not mean that the ownership of land by social groups, or the allocation of rights over it for use did not respond to the stresses arising out of the dynamic nature of the African experience before European control. Thus in large parts of Subsaharan Africa, where, as in the Sudan and along the Guinea Coast there was a continuous history of dynastic expansion, the spiritual controls over land were often consciously held in check by rulers who had come from outside. Since the earth deity is generally conceived as favoring the people who originally occupied the land, it was obviously politically expedient for their

[2] E.g., T. Olawale Elias: *Nigerian Land Law and Custom* (London, 1951), pp. 201–2, 209.

successors to play down the importance of such a deity or deny his existence. Where cattle-keeping invaders imposed their rule on the agricultural population, as in East Africa, land was pre-empted for their needs. But in no case was the basic pre-existing system discarded; it might be modified, and the controlling agents be different, but fear of supernatural beings, especially the autochthonous ancestors or gods, prevented too radical a change.

The traditional stress laid by Africans on the importance of the land, as evidenced by the many regulations concerning its use, and by the symbolic values attached to it, highlight a situation that continued under European control. The wealth of Africa derives largely from the land—primarily from subsistence and export crops. Thus, if we consider the principal commodities exported from Subsaharan African territories in 1957, we find only four countries, Sierra Leone, the Federation of Rhodesia and Nyasaland, the Belgian Congo and South Africa, where agricultural products did not predominate. In Sierra Leone, iron ore and diamonds accounted for 48.1%; in the Federation, copper yielded 47.3%, and in the Congo, 32.1% of the total; while in South Africa gold and other minerals made up 57.3%.[3]

According to an exhaustive analysis of the Nigerian economy,

> Field crops accounted for 44.8% of the 1952 gross domestic product, tree crops for 11.3%, livestock products for 5.1%, forest products for 4% and fish for 0.9%. Yams and cassava together constituted 40% of the total agricultural product; grains, 17%, palm produce, 8%, and cocoa and groundnuts, each 4%. Numerous other crops are produced in relatively minor quantities.[4]

In Angola, coffee beans contributed 42.7% to the commodities exported in 1957, sisal 5.7%, and raw cotton 3.7%, with diamonds furnishing 11.8%, wood 2.1%, and fish products 14.6%. Coffee and groundnuts constituted 49.9% of the exports for that year

[3] United Nations: *Economic Survey of Africa Since 1950* (No. E/CN.14/28); (New York, 1959), pp. 168–71.

[4] International Bank for Reconstruction and Development: *The Economic Development of Nigeria* (Baltimore, 1953), pp. 192–3.

from French West Africa, with cocoa beans, palm kernels and bananas totaling 16.5%. Even in the industrialized Union of South Africa where metals were the principal item of export, products from herding, such as wool, cattle and hides, and agricultural products made up about a quarter of the total.[5]

When the importance of the land in Africa, both before and after the colonial period, is stressed, it is not solely because of the place of agriculture in the total colonial system. Under precontact conditions, the forests yielded many by-products of value; in addition to wood, they furnished vines to make rope and bark for bark cloth, to name but two which since contact have continued to figure in the local and external economies. Thus in French Equatorial Africa, in the period between 1953 and 1955, the forests, especially in the Gabon, made a heavy contribution; wood in the round represented 28.4%, veneer and fibrewood 5.9% and sawn wood 1.9%.[6] The animals of these forests continue to provide a significant supplementary source of food. The rivers, too, are valued, both for their fish and as avenues of communication and transport. Forests and streams are everywhere conceived as the seat of powerful deities or supernatural forces. Those who hunt in the forests and, among some groups, those who fish in the rivers are thought to possess or have access to especially powerful magic for their own protection, and capable of being used for or against others. The ownership of forests and streams is much like that of grazing land; it is held communally, and trespass occurs when a member of one kinship group or society hunts or fishes outside its recognized territorial limits.

[2]

The changes that occurred in the approach to the question of control over land, which came with the imposition of foreign rule, can be thought of as having come in three waves. These

[5] United Nations: op. cit., pp. 170–1.

[6] W. Goldschmidt (ed.): *The United States and Africa* (report of the American Assembly on Africa, New York, 1958), p. 219.

understandably overlapped, just as the aboriginal patterns continued to persist after new orientations were introduced. In some countries all can be found operating simultaneously at a given moment; and various combinations of them also occur. They had best be treated separately, as different approaches to the question of control over land, particularly since their impact on African peoples has been different.

The initial wave of change followed the classical form of conquest or, in the case of European expansion, took the form of treaty arrangements with a native ruler. In both cases the transfer of power carried with it an assumption of sovereignty that conferred the right to reallocate land as the occupying power deemed best. This was the period of the concessions, when European private or government-controlled companies were allotted land for plantations or for mining, with minimal consideration for pre-existing rights based on traditional concepts.

With the passage of time, particularly toward the end of the Second World War, various "schemes" were introduced—the Gezira cotton-growing scheme in the Sudan, the Niger Project in what is now Mali, the ill-fated postwar Groundnut Scheme in Tanganyika, are examples. These were large-scale operations, employing African labor and, in some instances, African supervisory personnel, and were to varying degrees mechanized. They were under the supervision of the colonial governments when, as was more often the case, they were not initiated and controlled by the governments themselves. The government share of revenues went into the public treasury, and might support projects in the public interest, though, as with the schemes in Portuguese territory, this was not always the case.

Finally, there was the movement to improve agricultural output by working through the African farmers. In general, these attempts were based on two principles. The first was that improvement could only come with the application of the findings of scientific agronomy to the small holding. Associated with this was the idea that the necessary financing could be provided only if land was individually owned and farmed in plots large enough to make farming economically profitable. This appeal to science and to the principle of free enterprise stimulated various moves, principally in eastern, central and southern Africa, looking toward projects for the consolidation or utilization of land, which in turn frequently necessitated the resettlement of the populations involved.

While the actual amount of land involved in the concessions varied from region to region, their considerable aggregate obviously affected earlier usage. A map given by Hailey shows the percentages of land "alienated or reserved for European occupation" in British, French and Belgian territories, and the Union, at about mid-twentieth century, as follows: South Africa, 89%, Swaziland, 49%, Southern Rhodesia, 49%, Belgian Congo, 9%, Kenya, 7%, Bechuanaland, 6%, Nyasaland, 5%, Southwest Africa, 5%, Northern Rhodesia, 3%, Ruanda-Urundi, 2%, and Tanganyika, 0.9%.[7] Ghana had alienated 5%, but this consisted mainly of mining concessions, where land was leased by the companies who paid rentals and royalties to local and central governments, and who in any case were required to care for the land by keeping it clear of underbrush or, in some instances, making it available to the families of their workers for growing subsistence crops. In all other parts of the Subsaharan continent, the proportion of alienated land was under 5%.

No percentages were given for Portuguese or Spanish territories, nor for Liberia, since none sufficiently precise were available to the Hailey research staff, while the Sudan was not included in his study. However, land alienation presented no serious problem in the Sudan, since the country was thinly populated, had little non-African population, and had only one project for which land was taken, the Gezira Scheme. In the case of Angola, in 1933, 401,180 acres out of a total of 30,806,464 were in the hands of Africans, the remainder being state domain.[8] What proportion of this vast acreage was allotted to private concessionaries is unknown. In Portuguese Africa even the casual traveler could see that very substantial amounts of land had been granted Euro-

[7] Lord Malcolm Hailey: *An African Survey, Revised 1956* (London, 1957), p. 687.

[8] Ibid., p. 755.

pean agricultural or railway enterprises in both Angola and Mozambique.

In 1945, in Spanish Guinea, Europeans and "assimilated natives" held 154,000 acres out of a total area of 6,772,480, as against some 210,000 acres held by "nonassimilated natives," but we are told little as to the details of acquisition, and know nothing of the effect of the system of land tenure that had been established, or the results of its imposition on the African population.[9] Liberia presented a special case. From the beginning of the existence of the country, the American Negro settlers appropriated land for their own purposes, with little regard for indigenous tenure rights. Though this was later placed under a measure of control, concessions for rubber plantations, both to Liberians and foreign firms, and for growing bananas, sisal and other crops, as well as allocations to mining companies, took still more land.

Discussions of the land problem in Africa have recognized that the amount of land given over to the use of outsiders is only one factor to be taken into account in assessing the causes for social change under colonialism. Among other factors were the density of population in the particular districts where land had been expropriated, the quality of the land taken, what other land was available to those who had been dispossessed. But the extent to which changes in ownership affected social structure and invaded religious sanctions is rarely given equal consideration. From the figures, it is apparent that relative to the total amount of available land, the proportion expropriated from African control, except in southern Africa, was not extensive and in some places slight. But the importance of the question of landholding and land use has no direct correlation with these figures, for the problems associated with land have arisen again and again since the earliest days of contact. We have here an illustration of how essential it is to weigh the human, as well as the political and technical factors, in seeking to understand changing Africa.

[9] José Condere Torres: "Las Dependencias Españolas," *Enquête sur l'Anticolonialisme* (Estudos de Ciências Políticas e Sociais, Centro de Estudos Políticas e Sociais, Ministério do Ultramar, Junta de Investigações do Ultramar, Lisbon, 1957), p. 275.

[3]

During the first of the periods we have distinguished, the tale was the familiar one of one people dominated by another, of conquest leading to control. By and large, however, interference with their earlier ways was tempered. If operations involved large areas, those at the center were most immediately affected, and the peoples on the periphery were pretty much let alone as long as they paid their tribute.

This was the pattern of conquest in the Western Sudan. The objectives were man power in the form of slaves, tribute, and, not least, the destruction of the caravan trade controlled by the conquered. Control of the land passed from the indigenous head to a group of the conquerors, who in the name of Islam came to exercise spiritual as well as political controls over vassal chiefdoms. Techniques of making war were understandable to the conquered, even though the use of cavalry was new to them, and did not take on the mystical quality early attributed to the guns and gunpowder of the Europeans. Moreover, the Fulani conquerors settled among the people whom they had conquered, and gradually became part of the socio-cultural landscape. Where they remained apart, they superimposed a kind of caste-like stratum on pre-existing levels of society. Since under Moslem law children born of a concubine to a man of the faith had full rights, it is not difficult to see how a conquering minority could rapidly improve its demographic position and at the same time gain loyalties in the ranks of the conquered.

The spread of European control was different. Islam is an evangelistic religion, but its proselytizing was confined to formal aspects of the belief-system, to which conformity was enjoined while touching but lightly on the total culture. Crops were sown and harvested as before; land use was little changed. Markets continued as the direct, face-to-face mechanism of exchange they had always been; spinning, weaving, pottery making and iron working were carried on in the customary manner. Sanctions behind family affiliations persisted.

European expansion, however, especially as it consolidated

its position in Africa, brought to the indigenous peoples elements of European culture that were entirely new, such as a system of technology based on power-driven machinery, entry into a world market, and exposure to world-wide ideological and political currents. Even though the differences between new and old modes of conquest were differences of degree, they were important. The tribute imposed by Islamic conquerors was accepted in kind, or took the form of direct labor. But the Europeans, while employing forced labor, also introduced a new monetary system and imposed taxes that could be paid only in their currency; measures calculated to impose wage-labor on peoples to whom this had been hitherto unknown. Christianity was not only more militant in its proselityzing than Islam, but it differed more from the aboriginal systems of belief, and invaded all aspects of life. European science brought new medicines, new modes of transportation, urbanization of an unprecedented kind and scale. New kinds of goods appeared, new agricultural techniques were imposed, new crops introduced, to be disposed of in new ways. And pervading all these changes were the obvious physical differences between the rulers and the ruled, which became associated in the minds of all concerned not only with superiority of force and of resources, but of inherent ability.

The account given by Gamble of land tenure in two Mandingo villages in the Gambia shows how the new controls operated. Under Mandingo rule, tenure was obtained by initial settlement or by a grant from the king at Manding, while sovereignty over larger areas depended on the fortunes of dynastic conflict. In 1893, however, when British control was extended to the interior, "the Administration assumed many general rights over land." The first Traveling Commissioners stressed the point that "all unoccupied land now belonged to the Government," though they noted that "the people maintained there was no unclaimed land, and that all outlying land belonged to the villages." Later, with the establishment of native courts, the head chiefs, now named or confirmed by Government, "were given jurisdiction in all suits relating to the ownership or possession of land." Above this, however, the Government, through the Administration, was charged with construction and care of roads and wells, with forest conservation, and many other developments that impinged on land tenure and use. Both Protectorate and Crown lands were placed "under the management, control and direction of the Governor who had powers to make grants of such lands without consulting the native authorities." [1]

Allowing for variation in detail, this is the story for all of Subsaharan Africa: the assumption of overlordship through conquest or treaty, the transfer of controls over land from aboriginal to European authority, and the continuously increasing invasion of earlier sanctions by the governing power. Everywhere, too, the questions, usually interrelated, of occupied and unoccupied land, and individual as against communal ownership of land, proved to be major points at issue.

The importance of the problem of what land Africans actually occupied when the Europeans came, can be seen in the extent to which this has been of moment in such countries as Kenya, the Belgian Congo, or South Africa. In Kenya, the matter centered primarily on the area known as the White Highlands, the scene of the Mau Mau troubles in 1952–4, and the region of permanent European settlement. Much of the claim to this land, both of Europeans and Africans, rested on whether or not it was occupied at the time of settlement. The typical European point of view is to be seen in this passage:

> It was the empty spaces that were, in the main, filled by the Europeans. When they arrived they found only two thickly populated, narrow agricultural belts in the whole of the country between the coast and Uganda . . . In these two relatively small islands of cultivation set in a pastoral sea, occupying about one-eleventh of the present area of Kenya, were concentrated nearly two-thirds of the total population. If you subtracted these islands, you had an area of 205,000 square miles (nearly as large as France) supporting a population of little over one million people.[2]

[1] D. P. Gamble: *Economic Conditions in Two Mandinka Villages, Kerewan and Keneba* (Revised Version, Research Department, Colonial Office, No. RES 88/12/01, mimeographed, London, 1955), pp. 41–42.

[2] Elspeth Huxley: *White Man's Country: Lord Delamere and the Making of Kenya* (London, 1953), Vol. I, p. 73.

The Africans, on the other hand, and those who supported their position held that the sparseness of habitation was justified by the fact that herding requires a great deal of land. With respect to the Kenya Highlands, it has been established that the area was unoccupied when the Europeans arrived on the scene, because four major disasters had destroyed much of the human and bovine population—"the great smallpox epidemic, the great rinderpest outbreak, an intense drought with consequent famine, and a devastating locust invasion." In the pre-European system, the Kikuyu purchased land from the Wandorobo, whom "they could have driven out . . . by force" but for the fact that "such action . . . would have been futile, for the land so obtained would have been valueless to them for settled occupation and crop growing, since God and the spirits would not bless activities carried out under such conditions." [3] Before 1902, when land was first alienated for European occupation, "the Kikuyu were a big tribe, . . . with the whole of the Kiambu district owned by individuals and families. . . ." No historical accident has been more clearly delineated:

> There can be very little doubt that, had the start of white settlement in Kenya come at this particular time instead of later, very little (if any) land in Kiambu, Kabete, and Limuru would have been alienated to white farmers, for the land was carrying a big native population and no government would have tried to dispossess them for the sake of European farmers.[4]

In South Africa, where most of the land was pre-empted by the European minority, the question of prior occupancy was also of considerable importance. We have already encountered the argument that here land was largely unoccupied when the Europeans began their trek north and east; that, as Marquard put it, "the Xhosa and Tembu, the tribes that had come farthest south . . . were the African frontiersman." In his analysis, he noted striking similarities between Boer and Bantu. Both were "cattle

[3] L. S. B. Leakey: *Mau Mau and the Kikuyu* (London, 1952), pp. 9, 3–4.

[4] Ibid., pp. 8–9.

farmers first, and agriculturalists second," both needed more herding land, both sent out hunting parties in advance of the principal groups. Yet, "the differences were, however, more significant than the similarities, and nowhere so much as in the interrelation of land ownership." To the European, land had to be owned privately; the African could not conceive of any but communal landholding. Hence basic misunderstandings arose that were to have far-reaching consequences. "European governments made treaties by which they believed they had *acquired* land from an African chief, while the chief thought he was merely giving them the right to *use* the land." [5]

On both sides the matter involved a tangle of motivations and needs. As we have seen, the very limits of occupation by the Bantu-speaking peoples were disputed, whereas the prior presence of Hottentot and Bushmen in the Western Cape was never denied. It was assumed that the Africans came southward primarily because of population pressure, despite the established fact that the territories from which they were supposed to have migrated were anything but overpopulated. Why the Boers undertook their trek was likewise disputed. The popular explanation is couched in the romantic terms of the lure of the frontiers, the love of freedom, the drive for individual expression, escape from old associations, and a desire to be away from other people. The existence of a thriving trade in cattle in the region of the Fish River, between Boers and Africans, long before the outbreak of the First Kaffir War in 1779, indicates, however, that on both sides economic drives played an important role.[6] Of the Boers, at least, it seems clear that while migration "was pricked . . . by a deep sense of grievance," it was "stimulated by the knowledge that plenty of good land lay beyond the official boundary." [7]

In the Congo, as early as 1885, land "without an owner" was

[5] Leo Marquard: *The Story of South Africa* (London, 1955), pp. 78–9.

[6] S. Daniel Neumark: *Economic Influences on the South African Frontier, 1652–1836* (Stanford, 1957), pp. 97–106.

[7] C. W. de Kiewiet: *A History of South Africa: Social and Economic* (Oxford, 1941), p. 57.

declared to be the property of the State. By 1906, however, the right of Africans to land, whether held individually or collectively, was recognized as long as ownership was established. Moreover, the use of the word "occupied" was extended not only to land in use, but to that which had been allowed to lie fallow under a system of shifting cultivation, as well as that in which Africans hunted or gathered wild fruits. Afterward, the rule established by the colonial government was that "Occupied land is thus that land which is required to satisfy the actual need of the natives." [8] The concession system continued to be important. Thus, for example, in 1911 the Huileries du Congo Belge (Lever Brothers) received allotments that, if certain conditions were fulfilled, might amount to a maximum of 750,000 hectares and, after twenty-five years, would become their freehold property.[9]

We need not go into the development of the laws regulating land use in the Congo under Belgian rule, since this has been discussed many times from various points of view.[1] Evidently here also land and labor were the prime objectives of occupation. The early concession system, that gave rise to the excesses during the regime of the Congo Free State incident on the collecting and marketing of wild rubber is only one of the means by which the transfer of ultimate authority was achieved. We shall return later to some of the manifestations of these controls as they were exercised over African agriculture; here we need only note the historical importance of the land, and that, in the first days of the Free State, the pattern of regarding "unoccupied" land as available to European concessionaires was laid down—a pattern which, with due modifications in the light of changing conditions, persisted through the decades of Belgian colonial control.

Our second question, that of private as against public owner-

[8] Th. Heyse: "Notions Générales sur le Régime Foncier du Congo Belge et du Ruanda-Urundi et Legislation sur les Terres Indigènes," *Land Tenure Symposium, 1950* (organized by Afrika Institut Leiden, P. J. Idenburg, ed., Leiden, 1951), pp. 1, 9.

[9] Charles Wilson: *The History of Unilever, a Study in Economic Growth and Social Change* (London, 1954), Vol. I, pp. 170–2, Vol. II, p. 327.

[1] E.g., Raymond Leslie Buell: *The Native Problem in Africa* (New York, 1928), Vol. II, pp. 415 ff.

ship of land, was much discussed by those responsible for French policy in Africa, while the concession system as found in Belgian and Portuguese territory continued to be operative, particularly in the Gabon and in the Ivory Coast. Reconciliation of African patterns of common holdings, tenure during occupancy, and ownership of yield with the principles of French law presented many difficulties. In the Ivory Coast, this made for a shift in the modes of African land tenure, whereby the principle of ultimate ownership by the group was retained, but something like freehold tenure obtained in practice. According to Köbben, "If we ask an Agni of Ndenie to whom the earth belongs, he will answer that it belongs to the king. But this does not prevent the same Agni from saying, as he shows his cocoa-farm: 'This is mine, it is my land!' "[2] Many of those who came to grow cocoa were "strangers," individuals from other groups, to whom in earlier times, when land was plentiful, it was ceded for use. For the most part, however, this practice was stopped, and land no longer cultivated reverted to the control of the traditional rulers. But the earlier principles remained, so that in practice, though not in legal terms, it functioned like freehold land. Among the coffee-growing Bété in the western part of the same country, where land was scarce, forested land in 1953 brought 10,000 fr. CFA per hectare.[3]

The impact of a pecuniary economy, where production of a cash crop for export is a principal objective, on a system of agriculture in which produce is grown for local consumption, could also be seen in Nigeria and Ghana, where acquisition of land by non-Africans was not permitted. The pattern described for the Ivory Coast, when initiated in the Gold Coast, was accelerated. A detailed analysis made of the Yoruba cocoa farmers of Nigeria indicated early the difficulties of adjusting a system where group rights held under traditional forms of ownership "prevent social disintegration but to some extent also hinder economic adaptation," since "group rights impede the free grant, sale, and most

[2] A. J. F. Köbben: "Le Planteur Noir," *Études Eburnéennes*, Vol. 5 (1956), p. 147.

[3] Ibid., p. 174.

grazing of land" required under a system of free enterprise in a competitive market.[4]

In the functioning of cash-crop agriculture, where the factor of credit is important, freehold land can be offered as security for loans. The absence of freehold tenure was the reason given for refusals of banks to make loans to Africans; a point Nigerians, among others, repeatedly raised when they described the disadvantages under which they labored as colonial subjects. Of 370 Yoruba families with outstanding loans in 1951, 5.3% had mortgaged or pledged land; 3.0%, houses; 3.4% had pledged trees; 8.5%, crops. But in 78.6% of the cases, personal security had been given, either by "the borrower's simple promise to pay" or by the willingness of someone to go surety for them.[5] "The fact of the matter," said one European bank manager in Nigeria, in 1957, "is that our loans to Africans are made on the basis of my knowledge of the man's integrity. But if I were to leave and another chap take my place, it would be very difficult for him to collect the loans I have made, and he would have to be here for some time before he could know whom he could trust." [6]

The need to reconcile traditional agricultural patterns with the demands of a system which produces cash-crops for a world market is without doubt one of the most far-reaching aspects of cultural change in Africa. There is no part of the life of Africa, whether economic, political, social, or religious, which has not been involved in this, and where a concomitant re-examination of underlying values and ethical principles has not been necessary. The differences in policies of land allocation introduced in various parts of Subsaharan Africa after the establishment of European control, moreover, had their most serious repercussions in the racial tensions of those countries where the alienation of land for permanent European or Asian settlement occurred. We may, indeed, read much of the history of the subcontinent, fol-

[4] R. Galletti, K. D. S. Baldwin and I. O. Dina: *Nigerian Cocoa Farmers: an Economic Survey of Yoruba Cocoa Farming Families* (London, 1956), p. 280.

[5] Ibid., p. 535.

[6] Melville J. Herskovits: *Notes on African Field Research, 1953–1960* (manuscript), p. 57/D100.

lowing its partition, in terms of the interplay between indigenous and the induced patterns of land ownership and use.

[4]

The middle period, when "schemes" of various sorts were initiated, can be passed over briefly. Conceived and executed on a large scale, they posed requirements in the way of land, capital equipment and technical direction that were far beyond the capacity, not merely of any single African participant, but even of any group of Africans and, later, of most African governments. In the main, such schemes were remote from the daily life of the people, African and non-African alike, though on occasion they became subjects for political debate. Their functioning as agents of cultural change was thus minimal except as they may have indirectly stimulated movements to raise standards of living in the territory at large.

One of the first of these "projects," whose effect in the country in which it was sited was greatest, was the Gezira Scheme of the Sudan, for the irrigation, by means of water collected behind a dam erected north of Sennar, of a large tract of land for growing cotton. It is not our concern here to examine its financing or its technical problems. There have been criticisms of the way in which artificial social units were established, and of the intrusion of management into pre-existing custom. Whatever the validity of these criticisms, the shift from British to Sudanese control when the Sudan Republic became independent resulted in no major changes in the working of the scheme, nor in attitudes toward it. Its philosophy seemed to have made possible the achievement of its aims:

> The Gezira Scheme . . . was based on the belief that stability and permanence of economic investment will depend in the end on the contentment of the people and is unlikely to be attained merely by imposing on a country the quickest way to a higher standard of living irrespective of the political circumstances which accompany it.[7]

[7] Arthur Gaitskell: *Gezira, a Story of Development in the Sudan* (London, 1959), p. 333.

As regards the material advances it brought, the scheme was without question highly successful. In 1950, the average net income of the individual tenant was estimated at about £250 to £300 per annum, though in a good year such as 1950–1 the return went to more than twice this figure. The model of governmental plus private ownership worked out so well that its applicability elsewhere was much discussed, and the activities of its Social Development Branch have been commended for making available good educational and health facilities.

> In a part of the world which previously produced little of any value and was indeed subject to periodic famine, . . . an immense material change has been effected. For the local people famine has been banished and a standard of peasant livelihood as high as any in the Middle East or Eastern Europe created.

The Sudan Government was enabled not only to balance its budget from the revenues of the scheme, but "to increase educational and health services throughout the land and to finance new productive undertakings." Fifty years after the scheme had been initiated, its export crop had placed the Sudan in the world market, while it had trained its farmers to carry on agriculture sufficiently diversified so that millet and fodder crops were also grown, and about 250,000 head of cattle supported.[8]

Another early scheme was the *Office du Niger,* initiated about 1932 as a rice and cotton growing project. Here the object was a more effective utilization of labor power and land than had been possible under pre-existing conditions. At the outset, Africans were conscripted for the work, though recruitment was later placed on a voluntary basis. Attempts were made to reproduce, physically, the traditional setting of the workers who were brought in. But without the sanctions that underlay the life in the ancestral villages, and in view of the close relationship between the social structure and other aspects of the culture, the affiliations of the settlers continued to be primarily with their kinship group at home, rather than with members of their new place of settlement. This has been clearly shown in an analysis of

[8] Ibid., p. 7.

the life of Mossi colonists, in which both the acculturative factors of Islam, new agricultural techniques, different objectives of work and the like; and those factors which support earlier traditions—family obligations, the sense of security given by affiliation with a large relationship group, obligations imposed by the ancestral cult and the worship of earth deities—were balanced.[9]

Excepting perhaps the Gezira, most of these "schemes" were planned and executed with little understanding of the human values in the earlier social and economic structure. As a result, the Africans did not strike their roots deeply in the resettlement areas, as envisaged by the planners. Even where some material benefits accrued to participants, participation was held to so low a level, and the mode of operation was so foreign to African patterns, that no strong sense of identification could develop which might have overcome the reluctance to exchange earlier associations and values for those demanded by the new way of life.

This led to one of the major problems that had to be faced in all these developments. At the Gonja Scheme in the Northern Territories of Ghana, one of the less publicized failures, members of the administrative staff turned repeatedly to the question of cultural adaptation in discussing the problem of developing an adequate labor force. The Corporation, with Government support, operated as an experimental center to discover what new crops could be profitably grown in this semi-arid part of the country, and how better use could be made of the land by employing mechanized farming techniques and converting unused acreages to agricultural purposes. In 1953, after several years' effort, there was but one worker, a Tale, who had developed a good garden and showed signs of becoming permananetly established. Those in the managerial group agreed that the question of family obligations, in the broad sense, and especially of the ancestral cult, made it difficult to conceive of Africans settling there permanently. A section head recounted how he had worked over a period of time to convince his men of the advan-

[9] Peter Hammond: "Economic Change and Mossi Acculturation," in *Continuity and Change in African Cultures* (W. R. Bascom and M. J. Herskovits, eds., Chicago, 1959), *passim.*

tage of saving some of their wages for working capital. But one of them, who had accumulated £30, drew the entire amount to discharge his obligations at the death of a family member. "If only some of the old people would come to live and die here, and be willing to be buried in their new home, the thing would start," said another.[1]

The number of "schemes" was considerable. In British territories alone "some 31 projects were in 1953 being financed either from the funds provided under the Colonial Development and Welfare Acts or from the revenues of the Administrations concerned." [2] Their effects, however, were thought of essentially in terms of their long-range influence on the technical aspects of agricultural productivity. From the broader point of view, whatever their potentials for increasing the national incomes of the countries concerned, they proved at the very best no more than a gloss on the social, economic, and religious life of the peoples they were intended to benefit.

[5]

The third type of agricultural development was aimed at raising the level of productivity by changing the methods of farming and the allocation and utilization of land by African growers and herders. It represented a response to a very real need. Where scientific medicine and improved methods of hygiene are brought to peoples who traditionally produce little more than what is necessary for their own subsistence, the increase in population demands at least a corresponding increase in productivity. Failing this, the future would hold a progressive lowering of what, at best, was a modest standard of living. The alternative was clear. In Africa, it was argued, there were few peoples so removed from the impact and stimulus of new expectations and new wants that they would reject changes in older methods of production, especially where there was the

[1] Melville J. Herskovits: *Notes on African Field Research*, p. 1953/D153.

[2] Lord Malcolm Hailey: op. cit., p. 906.

promise that income from a cash crop would allow these expectations and wants to be satisfied.

As administrators and planners saw it, in the dilemma presented by the pressure of population on productive capacity, something had to give way. The agricultural complex, based on modes of ownership and use of land, seemed a logical place to begin, even though industrialization had been advanced by some as an alternate solution. The need for reconsideration of earlier patterns was in some countries recognized by Africans themselves. This is precisely what happened in western Africa where, as we have seen, traditional patterns of communal ownership of land were reinterpreted through the concept of individual ownership of economically valuable trees so as to reconcile the need for permanence of tenure needed when producing cash crops for the world market.

Though a policy of developing *paysannats indigènes,* "native settlement schemes" was announced for certain parts of the Belgian Congo as early as 1935, the real drive to change African agricultural patterns came after the Second World War. In this drive, the *Report* of the East African Royal Commission, issued in June, 1955, acted as a catalyst and exerted an influence far beyond the area with which it was concerned. That its influence on policy was so considerable testified to the reality of the problem and the thoroughness of the analysis. The technical recommendations of the *Report* were widely debated, but we are rather concerned here with its implications for cultural adjustment, particularly as these were revealed in the assumptions about the peoples who would have to adapt themselves to the proposed changes.

Fundamentally, the Commission held that the best and quickest way to promote the economic development of East Africa was by establishing and encouraging free enterprise. The statement, "a policy without the co-operation of the indigenous people is no policy at all," is encountered [3] toward the end of the *Report;* yet the portrayal of the indigenous system disclosed far-reaching misunderstanding of earlier ways of life, and implied no

[3] East Africa Royal Commission: *Report* (Cmd. 9475, London, 1955), p. 385, par. 10.

great faith in the ability of East African peoples to change their ways except through pressures brought by the more "advanced" or "modern" groups of the society of which they formed a part. The judgment of a Kenya governor [4] about "the extraordinary backwardness and ignorance of the African people of east and central Africa at the time when the European entered these regions . . ." was noted at length, and with approval.[5] We read that "the primitive African was part of a closely knit community," a verifiable fact, but we also find the prevalent erroneous stereotype that "almost his every action was determined by a customary obligation." [6] A contrast was continuously drawn between "static tribalism" [7] and the "dynamic problems" of transition to an exchange economy,[8] as though adjustment to new conditions was a novelty in Africa. "Training in conduct and morals is so important that nothing should be done to discourage the mission schools," in view of the "progressive dissolution of tribal society," which the Commission expressly stated was in their opinion "an inevitable and beneficial process in the African's progress, from a subsistence economy to integration in the modern world." [9]

If we accept the proposition that social policy should be based on the facts, statements such as these give us pause, if only because of the misconceptions they reveal. One need but read African history and ethnology to understand the fallacies in the assumptions of the static society, the custom-bound automatons that presumably make up its membership, and the supposed fragility of its traditions in the face of outside pressures. Nor need we turn to West Africa for facts that demonstrate the ability of the African to adjust to the requirements of a new system by his own effort. The adaptations made by the Chagga of Tanganyika, to cite an outstanding instance, show that this could be done in the eastern part of the continent as well.

In point of fact, the success which the Chagga had in adapting their traditional institutions to the production of cash crops

[4] Sir Philip Mitchell: *The Agrarian Problem in Kenya* (Nairobi, 1948), p. 2.

[5] East Africa Royal Commission: op. cit., p. 22, par. 53.

[6] Ibid., p. 23, par. 55.

[7] E.g., p. 51, par. 9.

[8] Ibid., p. 81, par. 11.

[9] Ibid., pp. 176–177.

for the wider economy deserves more attention than it has received. The Kilimanjaro Native Cooperative Union, established to market the coffee grown by its members, soon ramified into many aspects of Chagga society, and this without destroying earlier social structures or basic values. The adjustment was not reached without differences that had to be resolved, nor can the case of the Chagga, especially in its ecological aspects, be considered typical for eastern Africa. From the point of view of the people themselves, their motivation to change arose from a recognition of the benefits that would accompany change. But the case was exceptional for East Africa in that the changes owed nothing to outside pressures, whether from government or private capital. It is true that the Chagga had competent, disinterested counsel, and initial guidance was given them. But this advice was taken or rejected on the basis of their own decisions.

The technological aspect of land reform in Africa involved balancing the findings of scientific agronomy against the traditional knowledge of the nature of the soil and how it could best be used. Difficulties often arose simply because agricultural and administrative officers rejected in principle the value of this prior experience of an administered group.

> "Agriculture, as an ancient art, began in the tropics and has various special complexities there by reason of its long persistence in those areas. Agriculture as a modern science developed in the Temperate Zone. Most of our scientific understanding of agriculture comes from our experiences during the last few centuries with the relatively simple agricultural problems of northern Europe and North America. When the average scientific agriculturist goes to the tropics he has much more to unlearn than to teach, but he frequently seems to be unaware of that fact." [1]

The question was phrased most succinctly by De Schlippe who, after giving numerous examples of how the efforts of agricultural officers were wasted because of failure to take traditional knowledge into account, asked:

> Is any understanding between the two worlds possible, or is the gulf too wide? On the one side there is the curriculum of Cam-

[1] Edgar Anderson: *Plants, Man and Life* (London, 1954), p. 125.

bridge, Grignon, Wageningen, Gembloux or Bonn, with, in the background, a field of uniform golden wheat falling under the blades of a McCormick combine harvester. On the other side there is this extraordinarily intricate fabric of a traditional system of agriculture on the background of a mottled pattern of grass-bush land which a small hoe and a small axe, helped by fire, transform into a no less mottled pattern of crops, varieties and associations.[2]

This analysis of the problem arose from the experience of its author in what was the Anglo-Egyptian Sudan, among the Azande, where he was engaged in an attempt to improve their agricultural techniques. His discussion of the factors involved in introducing changes in agricultural practices arose out of this experience, and his analysis showed clearly that the induced changes, brought about through the exertion of pressure from outside the society, violated the principle that "the pattern of behavior inherent in the customary system of agriculture constitutes the force of adhesion of the group to its natural environment," and that the status of the indigenous agricultural complex as "a vital part of its culture" meant that directed change could not be achieved without taking it fully into account.[3]

The reactions of the Africans whom well-intentioned agricultural experts were trying to help, and the experience painfully gained by these experts, that techniques tested elsewhere did not necessarily apply in Africa, gradually taught them that persuasion and coercion could not change deeply ingrained habits of work and thought. Resistance to administrative edicts followed the almost universal rule of African protest—though massive, it was without overt action, and was consequently frustrating in the extreme to those charged with implementing policy. The realities of African resistance as revealed in De Schlippe's account of a typical conversation between an agricultural extension officer and a native farmer,[4] have been rarely presented more effectively than in this passage, which, though it cannot be reproduced here, has a significance far beyond the immediate problem of which it

[2] Pierre de Schlippe: *Shifting Cultivation in Africa: the Zande System of Agriculture* (London, 1956), p. xi.

[3] Ibid., p. 241. [4] Ibid., pp. ix–x.

treats. To the scientific agronomist, it long seemed unthinkable that African "folk" techniques could hold any lesson for him; to the African, the demands of the agricultural officers were unrealistic, and doomed to failure. "When they talk they seem to be young men of good sense," one Murundi remarked to a visiting ethnologist, "but nothing they tell us to do works out well." [5]

The constant pressures needed in these regions before the African farmer could be induced to do what was thought best for him often made it an endurance contest between farmer and agricultural officer. From the many instances that could be cited, the resistance of the Pakot of Kenya to new crops and new methods of animal husbandry [6] and the negative reaction to super-phosphate fertilizer on the part of the Kanuri of Bornu, in northeastern Nigeria, make the point that "the social and psychological context of innovation requires careful analysis so that variables affecting innovation may be isolated and prepared" if an experiment in directed change is to have a chance of success.[7]

Despite coercion, there were instances where projects worked out as planned, as for example coffee growing in Ruanda-Urundi, where it was decreed that each cultivator must plant sixty-four trees, eight by eight, with fines when the seedlings were not mulched and cared for as instructed. In 1953, when the project was new, the order was resisted whenever possible. However, by the time the trees began to bear, and the growers began to realize a good cash return, not only was there a steady demand for free seedlings from government nurseries, but there were those who came at night to take what would have been freely given, in order to enlarge their coffee plantings. Moreover, the African farmers began to mulch their banana groves in order to obtain a better yield from them.[8]

In many cases, the political overtones of these plans for

[5] Melville J. Herskovits: *Notes on African Field Research,* p. 57/D297.

[6] H. K. Schneider: "Pakot Resistance to Change," in *Continuity and Change in African Cultures* (W. R. Bascom and M. J. Herskovits, eds., Chicago, 1959), pp. 153–5.

[7] Ronald Cohen: "The Success that Failed: an Experiment in Culture Change in Africa," *Anthropologica,* Vol. 3, (n.s.), No. 1 (1961), *passim.*

[8] Melville J. Herskovits: *Notes on African Field Research,* p. 57/D271.

economic farming called forth various kinds of resistance. There are those instances when the feeling of administrators that, in one way or another, it was necessary to have on record an expression of African acceptance of a plan resulted in heavy pressures to obtain a vote of endorsement. Thus, in South Africa, the desire of Government to further farming schemes, even those which might profit the Africans economically, on occasion led to official pressure on chiefs who could assure a favorable vote for agricultural "reform." Where chiefs refused to comply, the support of the Department of Native Affairs was withdrawn from them, or they were removed from office. In the case of the Mamatola, the entire recalcitrant group was forcibly moved to a new site. In 1957, a high official in Southern Rhodesia described the philosophy of the Land Husbandry Scheme, wherein Africans were resettled and required to cultivate as directed, in terms not calculated to encourage voluntary compliance: "The Native will have to own land privately, like we do, if he is to come to think like us." [9]

There is little question that the principles of scientific agronomy, applied under rigid surveillance and even by force, can bring about impressive increases in yield. The case of cotton-growing in Mozambique shows this clearly. In 1931, out of some 14 million tons imported into Portugal, all but one million came from outside the Portuguese Empire. During the period 1946–50, 34 million tons were consumed by Portuguese mills, and of this amount but 4 million came from outside. Most of the increase, which went from under a million tons in 1930 and 14 million annually during 1941–5 to 24 million a year during 1946–50, came from Mozambique.

On inquiry in the field, it became apparent that the increased yield had been as much due to the controls imposed on the African farmers as to technical improvement. The essential instrument in Mozambique was the system that required Africans at all times to carry passes. Because of the exportation of labor to work in the South African mines, a period of six months was permitted Africans between contracts when they returned to their villages, during which they could be unemployed. Should

[9] Ibid., p. 57/D416.

an African exceed this period, he would, if discovered, be impressed by the police to work on the roads, or on a privately owned plantation. The pass of a farmer living in a cotton-producing region would, however, be endorsed only if a fixed portion of his land was devoted to growing cotton under supervision. That this might mean that he grew insufficient food for himself and his family was disregarded. The Africans, moreover, were required to sell their cotton at prices fixed in Portugal. The reactions of the Africans to this agricultural achievement may be guessed.[1]

African farmers are no more conservative than farmers elsewhere; they are quite ready to accept change when it is demonstrated that this is to their advantage, and when changes do not involve too radical a departure from established canons of social organization, beliefs and modes of behavior. In effect, the communal character of African society can facilitate the diffusion of new ideas. "If a new method of production, or a new product, is approved by the leaders it may be adopted by all the members of the community far more rapidly than in a highly individualistic society."[2] The greatest obstacle to acceptance of innovation, especially in eastern and southern Africa, was the long history of racial discrimination and its resulting tensions, which raised suspicions to a point that advice from Europeans, official or unofficial, became acceptable only after the most convincing demonstration of disinterest. Nor were Africans encouraged to accept innovation when, as in so much of the continent, the idea of consulting them, to say nothing of collaborating with them on these matters, continued to be foreign to the thinking of the planners. Characteristically, the question was cast in terms of European scientific knowledge, and even where the planners wished to benefit the Africans, the question was how to get them to accept with a minimum of tension and resistance what was thought best for them.

The psychological reactions of Africans to advice backed by the power to enforce it, were what might be expected. Even

[1] Ibid., pp. 53/D481–483.

[2] William O. Jones: *Manioc in Africa* (Stanford, 1959), p. 54.

where there was consultation at the early stage of a project, experience taught that acquiescence to the European in whatever was proposed was advisable. Yet what happened in Ghana, when measures had to be taken to control the swollen-shoot disease that was attacking vital cocoa plantings, is significant. Here the suspicion against measures easily misunderstood, because imposed by outsiders, was allayed when African officials explained the scientific facts, and applied the necessary correctives. As a result, the problem was not only resolved, but the continuation of the fight against the disease, with the understanding and cooperation of the growers themselves, was assured. This change was equally evident in Nigeria, when with the Africanization of government services, agricultural extension work was carried on by African officers. By the time Nigeria gained independence, this had not only resulted in acceptance of technical innovations suggested to the farmers, but farmers were pressing the research services of the Ministry of Agriculture for still more new methods to improve crops.

[6]

Land is important in Africa not only for its agricultural yield. There is vast wealth in subsoil resources and hydroelectric potential. The development of the latter gives rise to certain reflections on the ironies of history, since it is precisely that aspect of the topography, the rapid fallaway from the highlands to the coastal plain which "closed" the continent to penetration by river, that provides Subsaharan Africa its most effective means for taking its place in a world economic system. Figures concerning this hydroelectric potential vary widely, but there is agreement that it constitutes an impressive proportion of the total world supply. The implications of the conjunction of vast power and mineral resources for change in the social and political no less than in the economic structures of Subsaharan Africa, are far-reaching.

The great subsoil wealth of Africa only gradually came to be exploited. Except for the gold of Ghana and Mozambique, the early period of colonialism conceived economic return from Africa as deriving primarily from trade, particularly in such commodities as palm oil, ivory, and later, rubber. When the discovery of gold on the Rand began the dramatic transformation that marked the subsequent history of South Africa, exploitation of the mines was resisted by the Boer farmers. The realization that there were extensive major mineral resources in iron, copper, bauxite, tin, manganese, diamonds and valuable rarer minerals, plus the continuing finds of substantial oil deposits, increased the significance of this sector of the African economies.

The reaction of Africans to the exploitation of subsoil wealth understandably differed from their attitude toward the expropriation of their agricultural and grazing land, or to projects of improved land-use and ownership. Mining operations need relatively little space above ground, while they give employment to large numbers of Africans. This is perhaps why the earlier protests against the activities of outsiders rarely mentioned mining. Only with an increase in the number of university educated Africans was the point raised that African peoples were not benefiting, as they should, from these highly valuable natural resources. In 1942 Nnamde Azikiwe pointed out that "50% of certain mineral royalties" were being paid to the Niger Company, Limited, and to its successors. His "critical examination of the treaty rights," which gave rise "to this unfair burden to the Nigerian taxpayer" was, he stated, undertaken with the hope that this "might reveal lacunae for its discontinuance."[3] Since then the question of subsoil rights and the terms on which mineral resources were to be exploited, in Nigeria and elsewhere, was increasingly treated by Africans in discussing problems of colonial taxation and the allocation of revenue.

Mining came as no dramatic break in African history; Africans made use of their mineral resources long before the coming of Europeans. Extraction of iron ore was a commonplace over all the continent. The rich copper deposits of the Katanga were first mentioned in a report made in 1798 by a Portuguese

[3] Nnamde Azikiwe: *Land Tenure in Northern Nigeria* (Lagos, 1942), p. 7.

explorer. In this, he speaks of the great chief Cazembe, south of Lake Mwero, who "has mines of copper and of gold, and is at war with a chief whose territory produces some *latão* (yellow copper)."[4] The smelting of malachite, from which copper is derived, continued to be practised by the Africans. As we have seen, copper crosses, used as money in the eastern Congo area were exported far beyond the boundaries of the region where they were made. The vein that stretches from the Katanga into Northern Rhodesia, the region later known as the Copper Belt, was first discovered by Europeans who, in 1899, found Africans mining the ore.[5] It has, indeed, been said that no geologist ever uncovered a site yielding copper that had not been previously worked by Africans.

This seems also to be true of gold, certainly as far as alluvial deposits are concerned, and where underground seams are not too deep beneath the surface. From the earliest days of Arab and European contact, the presence of gold in Africa was known; in the middle of the tenth century, gold was being carried from the legendary Kingdom of Ghana overland to North Africa. The Portuguese explorers found gold when they came to Mozambique, undoubtedly traded from deposits further inland. Livingstone came upon African digging operations in 1850. He reported that only gold dust was gathered, nuggets being reburied, either because of the belief that they represented the "seed of the gold" which would jeopardize the future crop if taken out, or because these "pieces or flakes were considered the perquisites of the chiefs" and would have had to be surrendered to them.[6]

In West Africa, the term "Gold Coast" took its place in the early literature as a geographical designation, with the Slave Coast, the Ivory (Tooth) Coast, and the Grain Coast, though gold was exported from many other parts of Guinea. The English term "guinea" came from there, a gold coin of that name worth

[4] Anonymous: *Union Minière du Haut Katanga, 1906–1956* (Brussels, 1956), p. 23.

[5] Lord Malcolm Hailey: op. cit., p. 1502.

[6] David Livingstone: *Missionary Travels and Researches in South Africa* (25th edition, New York, 1859), p. 683.

twenty-one shillings, no longer minted, having been first struck in 1663. In 1701, Bosman, writing of the Denkira, an Akan group in present-day Ghana, stated: "They are possessed of vast Treasures of Gold, besides what their own Mines supply them with; either by Plunder from others, of their own Commerce; . . ." After naming other peoples, particularly the Ashanti and Akim, as those whose lands were sources of much gold, he says,

> "There is no small number of Men in *Europe* who believe that the gold Mines are in our Power; that we, like the *Spaniards* in the *West-Indies,* have no more to do but to work them by our Slaves: Though you perfectly know we have no manner of access to these Treasures; nor do I believe that any of our People have ever seen one of them: which you will easily credit, when you are informed that the *Negroes* esteem them sacred, and consequently take all possible care to keep us from them." [7]

With access to the interior of West Africa, more became known about the extent and techniques of African gold mining. Studies of the remains of gold diggings, together with an analysis of earlier accounts, revealed the scope and the importance of the industry.[8] In Ashanti, it is clear that the Africans worked underground deposits and also did placer mining. As seen, for example, on the concession of the Konongo Gold Mines, they are impressive in number and depth. The aboriginal miners had no means of pumping out water, so that the holes go only to the water level. Since the laterite does not cave in, the holes are close together, so that it is dangerous to walk through the bush where the underbrush has grown over them. In some places, the Ashanti even tunneled through the earth, and these workings provide airholes for the more recent diggings of the European gold-mining companies.

According to tradition, the actual labor was done by slaves. A man was ordered to begin at a given spot, and worked his way downward. One can see the indentations where the digger put

[7] William Bosman: *A New and Accurate Description of the Coast of Guinea* (2nd edition, London, 1721), pp. 64, 70–1.

[8] N. R. Junner: "Gold in the Gold Coast," *Gold Coast Geological Survey,* Memoir No. 4 (Accra, 1935), pp. 5–15.

his heels, bracing his back against the opposite side of the excavation, as he cleared the earth beneath him to send it up for panning. The slave stayed in the hole until the water-line was reached, sleeping there and subsisting on the food sent down to him.[9] An actual count of these holes on the Konongo compound gave an average of nine for each twelve square yards, an average that, according to the official of the company who made the count, held for its entire concession, about a mile in length and 500 feet wide. He stated, "It can be assumed that this average of holes existed over the lie of the reef wherever it existed in Ashanti. . . . They are broken by modern surface works, but I have seen large areas of them in existing deep bush as far as 9 miles from this camp, always following the lie of the known reef."[1]

In the later economy, mining presented many special problems—of financing, of technical equipment, of taxation, of labor. It has been the greatest single force making for industrialization. It was responsible for the development of railways and road systems, it contributed materially to the budgets of the territories where it is carried on, it stimulated the building of power dams. Perhaps more than any other of its natural resources, it brought Subsaharan Africa into the world economy. The experience of the Second World War showed how vital the mineral deposits of Africa were for strategic purposes, and this realization carried over and was intensified as new deposits were mapped and their contribution to the peace-time technological requirements became more and more apparent.

Repercussions of mining on the life of Africans have touched on every aspect of social change. Perhaps the most serious example of this, and the one most often cited, was the influence of the workers' compound system at the gold mines of the Witwatersrand on the structure and functioning of the African societies for hundreds of miles around. From Angola, from the Rhodesias and Nyasaland, from the High Commission Territories, from Mozambique, from all parts of the Union came

[9] Melville J. Herskovits: *Notes on African Field Research,* p. 53/D78.
[1] G. W. Carter: personal communication (1953).

African mine workers, so foreign to the industrial routine that many of them had to be taught how to use a shovel. The demoralizing effect on family life of the withdrawal of a large percentage of the men from a village was from the early period emphasized by those who saw the social dangers of this system.

In the copper-mining districts of the Katanga and Northern Rhodesia the mining companies took measures to establish a permanent labor force by furnishing family housing and, in the Congo, by providing food rations and schooling for the children. Yet labor policy, particularly on the Rand, was based on a wage scale that took no account of the needs of dependents. Workers were employed only during their productive years. No thought was given to providing any kind of security in old age. This meant that the village, or the reserve, gave an invisible subsidy to the mining corporations, since it actually underwrote the support of the workers' dependents. The superannuated worker of the Witwatersrand, or even of the Katanga, whose only home was where he had been employed for perhaps three decades, was dependent on his immediate family if he was not to be completely destitute. The continuing movement from rural areas to industrial centers, in earlier days so much encouraged, also began to show its effects. In 1957, for example, a commission of Belgian experts in the social sciences was brought to the southeastern Congo to study the problem of reducing the oversupply of workers, and to draft plans to reverse the drift to the cities. Village life was to be made attractive enough in terms of earnings and recreational facilities to bring back some of those who had gone away, and to induce those who remained not to leave.

The discovery of oil in various parts of the continent gave new resources to governments to promote projects in the fields of education, health, communication and the like, and at the same time profoundly influenced the regional ways of life where such discoveries occurred; just as, on the broader canvas, they tied those African territories the more firmly into the world economic system through international channels of investment and trade. In Sierra Leone, diamond strikes in 1955 had shattering consequences for the organization of village life in terms of accepted patterns of agricultural effort and social controls; in neighboring Liberia, its effect was felt most in the industrial sector, the rubber plantations and iron mines, when members of the labor force left their employment in large numbers to win diamonds. Mining is also responsible for the formation of strong trades unions in Africa. Some of the most effective movements to organize African workers developed in the coal mines of Enugu in Nigeria, and on the Rhodesian Copper Belt.

The impact of mineral resources on developing African economies is found in various power projects that were initiated over the continent. The Volta Scheme of Ghana may be taken as an example. With years of social, economic, and technical planning, it turned on the financing of a power dam to make it possible to exploit the extensive bauxite deposits in the country. This costly project enjoyed so high a degree of priority that it was one of the first objectives of the newly established Government of Ghana. It was otherwise in the multiracial countries. The development of the copper mines at Kasese in Uganda, which required an extension of the railway, and was one of the reasons for building the dam and power plant at Jinja, was opposed by the Baganda, who feared an influx of foreign technicians likely to form a core of permanent white settlers threatening their social structure. Similarly, extensive resettlement made necessary by the flooding of the Zambezi plain, on the completion of the Kariba dam, also designed to furnish power for mining operations, was accompanied by African protest and discontent.

7

The Book

THE KORAN and the Bible symbolize the proselytizing forces in Subsaharan Africa. The Koran was first carried by a movement that, beginning about the tenth century, brought Islam to the northern boundaries of the forested belt in the west, and in the northeast to the Great Lakes and the littoral of the Indian Ocean, where the limits of its influence were more or less stabilized. The Bible arrived some five centuries later, as the Portuguese established their stations along the African coasts while pressing for a sea route to India. However, it was not until the period of European expansion into Africa, about four centuries after this, that Christianity penetrated into the interior, and the activities of the two wings of the Christian missionary movement, Catholic and Protestant, began to exert a widening influence.

These proselytizing movements are especially significant in Subsaharan Africa, where the relation of man to the totality of forces in the universe have always been of immediate concern. In many African societies the complex of ideas and behavior bearing on these forces is focal to their cultures. Since the focal aspect of a culture holds a predominant place in the interests of a people, alternatives are subject to continuous scrutiny. In this way the members of a society are psychologically prepared to reconcile innovation with prior principles and practices,[1] with resulting complexity in their core institutions.

In our earlier discussions of the culture areas of Subsaharan Africa, we have seen something of the indigenous patterns of African belief. When we abstract certain general principles out of the many religions of Africa, we find that these religions do not differ either from Islam or Christianity to an extent that would preclude a measure of accommodation under contact. The categories in which are grouped the supernatural forces most African societies conceive, as exercising control over the universe illustrate the areas of compatibility. This fourfold division, comprises first a Great God with subsidiary beings to whom executive powers have been delegated; then the collective powers of antecedent generations, often manifested in worship of the ancestors; thirdly, destiny as it relates to problems which can be clarified by divination; and finally, magic.

None of these is foreign to Islam, while only the third is entirely absent from formal, though not popular, Christianity. The second element, having to do with the ancestral spirits, is less immediately apparent in Protestant belief than in Catholic, but it is implicit in both. The wide distribution of this fourfold division of supernatural powers, which is Old World rather than just African, probably reflects a diffusion of ideas that antedated by millennia the beginnings of the proselytizing activities with which we are concerned.

Beyond these similarities, however, lie the differences that must be kept in mind when we attempt to account for the changes to be observed in African societies that have been subjected to Islamic and Christian influence. Our clue here lies in the statement, repeatedly made by adherents of both faiths, that each is more than a religion; that each symbolizes a total way of life. These assertions but rephrase the scientific principle of cultural contact whereby the proselytizing activities touching on religious elements in Christian and Islamic cultures are to be

[1] Cf. Melville J. Herskovits: *Man and His Works* (New York, 1948), pp. 542–60.

thought of as spearheading historic movements which resulted in the introduction of innovations in all aspects of life. We are thus treating of an acculturative development in which religion is only one of the elements involved.

From this point of view, certain differences of opinion about the nature of the missionary effort in Africa become clarified. First of all, the relation between the spread of Islam and Christianity, and the imposition of political controls comes into perspective. Were missionaries moved to bring the revealed Truth to peoples still ignorant of it, or is it true, as an African critic of Christian missions said, that they were "one of several agents, each of whom played their part in the subjugation" of the inhabitants of the country where they worked? [2]

The debate over this emotionally charged issue becomes pointless considering what we know about the role of cultural learning under contact between peoples. In this light, a statement by an early South African missionary falls easily into place:

> While our missionaries . . . are everywhere scattering the seeds of civilization . . . they are extending British interests, British influence and the British Empire. . . . Whenever the missionary places his standard among a savage tribe, their prejudices against the colonial government give way, their dependence upon the colony is increased by the creation of artificial wants. . . . Industry, trade and agriculture spring up. . . .[3]

Were those who brought new religious beliefs to the Africans concerned only with bringing the Kingdom of God, or was theirs the Work of Empire? For the missionary just cited, the two were the same, and he was but stating honest convictions about his way of life as a desirable totality.

Whether propagating Islam or Christianity, missionaries act in response to cultural imperatives, which are expressed in terms of the institutional framework of the societies to which they belong. Where religious and political commitments are complementary, the relation between the conqueror, the administrator

[2] Nosipho Majeke: *The Rôle of the Missionaries in Conquest* (Johannesburg, 1952), p. 6.

[3] Ibid., p. 18.

and the missionary will be close. However, where the institutionalization of belief, as represented by church or mosque, stands in no organic relation to the instruments of political power, the interplay between the two in the conquered territory or the colonial setting will be more pragmatic, and will be influenced by the demands of the specific situations in which both function.

The Moslem conquest in the eastern and western Sudan areas brought Islam in its train as a normal and understandable consequence. In the African territories under Portuguese and Spanish control, the Catholic Church had the same vast powers it enjoyed in the metropolitan countries. That the ancillary secular activities of both Protestant and Catholic missions in the way of technical training, the development of hospitals, and secular schooling have no counterparts in territories under Islamic influence, reflects differing emphases in the total cultures of Christian and Moslem societies.

Our approach likewise clarifies the observation that the introduction of Islam was effected with far less cultural dislocation than marked the introduction of Christianity into African societies. The well-established reason for this is that acculturative shock is in direct ratio to the degree of difference between the cultures in contact. Christianity was brought to Africa by men and women whose basic cultural orientations differed much more from those of the indigenous African ways of life than did those of Islamic societies. Furthermore, the Moslems, in penetrating Subsaharan Africa, had absorbed elements of the cultures of those they sought to convert, and were usually fluent in the local language. Thus, among the Nupe, a people who remained "largely pagan," Islam became "a real means of social approach" between them and their Moslem Fulani rulers.[4]

This difference in the impact of the Christian and Islamic proselytizing movements antedates the industrial revolution. The early gains of Islam in the eastern Sudan, where it was faced by the established Coptic Church, have been ascribed to the fact that

[4] S. F. Nadel: *A Black Byzantium, the Kingdom of Nupe in Nigeria* (London, 1942), p. 142.

> The Church in the Sudan always remained exotic, and never became indigenous in the sense that Islam is today. Christianity came as a new cult, weakly grafted on to the regressive pre-Ptolemaic culture of the country, without revolutionizing the lives of either the nobles or the masses.

Some of the problems faced by Christian missions in the twentieth century seem also to have been present then:

> The cult was intimately associated with foreigners and foreign culture. All the bishops and many of the clergy were Egyptians, and there was no system of devolution of authority. Nor did any truly independent theological schools develop, their function being filled by the monasteries which were packed with Coptic monks.[5]

Another factor of importance is that in the spread of Islam in Africa, differences based on skin-color played a minor role, where they entered at all. Christianity, in contrast, was essentially brought by white non-Africans. One example from any number that could be cited, gives an African's phrasing of what he held to be,

> the central problem of Christianity in contemporary Africa, . . . its attempting at one and the same time to be a universal religion within whose folds all mankind are brothers, as well as the white man's religion whose ethical values are specifically European and whose greatest bulwark is the prestige and power of the white man, a prestige and power that apparently cannot accommodate the prestige of the African or the idea of the universal brotherhood of man.[6]

This factor of color in the proselytizing effort was one of the primary determinants of attitudes that pervaded African life in the post-European period. Wherever nationalistic movements arose among colonial peoples, the terms colonialism and imperialism invariably came to be defined as the rule of colored peoples by Europeans. Even in European and American usage, to speak of the Moslem conquest of the peoples inhabiting the

[5] J. S. Trimingham: *Islam in the Sudan* (London, 1949), p. 76.

[6] J. F. Ade Ajaye: review of C. P. Groves, "Christianity in Africa," Vol. IV, *West Africa*, No. 2160 (September 6, 1958), p. 853.

Sudanic belt as imperialism, seemed as inappropriate as the term colonialism for the conquest of Alsace in 1870 by the Germans, or the occupation of Hungary by Russia in 1956. Functionally, however, all these represent historical phenomena of the same order.

Because of the relative degree of resemblance in the physical type of the Islamic conquerors to that of the indigenous peoples, it was easier for them to superimpose themselves on existing social structures and become an integral part of the whole, than it could have been for the Christians from Europe or America, even if they had been free of color bias. E. W. Blyden wrote in 1871:

> Mohammedanism, in Africa, has left the native master of himself and of his home; but wherever Christianity has been able to establish itself, with the exception of Liberia, foreigners have taken possession of the country.[7]

The European, whether administrator or missionary—or, indeed, a student coming as a participant observer to the African scene—was effectively barred by the fact of his physical characteristics from too close an association. Given the historic circumstances of the imposition of European control, these physical differences inevitably played a major part in the identification of Christianity with racial exclusiveness and social privilege.

[2]

It is difficult to come by reliable figures on the number of adherents of the principal proselytizing faiths in Africa south of the Sahara. Such statistics as are available partake of the uncertain character of all kinds of African demographic and census data.

> The basic material in many cases is too defective to permit the drawing of final conclusions. . . . The demographer . . . is confronted by thousands of reports which submit as facts what are

[7] Cited in H. S. Wilson: "E. W. Blyden on Religion in Africa," *The Sierra Leone Bulletin of Religion,* Vol. 2 (1960), p. 59.

actually reasoned guesses. He finds over and over again a consensus of opinion without any real evidence to support this opinion.[8]

The difficulties with census counts and vital statistics are compounded when we try to ascertain the facts about religious affiliation. Let us review these problems before we examine certain tabulations that suggest the relative strength of the religious groupings found in the subcontinent.

An initial problem has to do with definitions. When can a given individual or group be regarded as being Moslem or Christian? When should they be listed among those called "pagan" or, in later terminology, given the equally meaningless designation "animist"—that is to say, those who have retained their aboriginal religions? Answers that may represent formal affiliation need not reflect the reality of belief, as in the case of an active member of a Christian church who at the same time faithfully fulfills the obligations of the ancestral cult, or of one who calls himself a Moslem and observes the forms of Islamic ritual but continues to give offerings to the tutelary deities of the locality in which he lives.

How individuals are counted can also greatly influence the figures of a given enumerator. In some instances, investigators, having interviewed the family head, assigned all members of the family to the same category of religious affiliation, on the assumption that they would follow the head of the family in religious choice; an assumption that a knowledge of Subsaharan ways of life reveals as wholly fallacious. Factors of prestige, of social pressure, or a wish to obtain places for children in a mission school, also determine statements of affiliation, without regard to religious conviction. This will be especially true where an investigator associated with a church seeks information, or takes attendance at services as evidence of religious interest.

The source of the figures must also be carefully evaluated. Statistics are essentially a Euroamerican creation, and numbers are of comparable importance in no other societies. Hence there

[8] R. R. Kuczynski: *Demographic Survey of the British Colonial Empire,* Vol. I (London, 1948), p. v.

are few Moslem sources for the numbers of adherents claimed by Islam, and none for Subsaharan Africa. Even for Euroamericans, quantitative data are far more important to the administrator, the business man, or the scientist than to the theologian, the philosopher, or the missionary. Therefore the estimates of the numbers affiliated with a given Christian church vary widely. And Christians will estimate the numbers of Moslems differently, depending on whether the commentator is impressed by what is sometimes termed the "inroads" of Islam, or by the resistance to Islamic persuasion.

Missionary statisticians have recognized the difficulties with which they are faced, as when the editors of the 1952 edition of the *World Christian Handbook* preface their tables with a scholarly caution that these tables "are derived from various sources, some good and some very indifferent and no induction from them can improve on its source."[9] We must thus use all estimates with full reservations on the grounds of faulty definition, loose methodology, and unconscious bias, as we seek to obtain an even approximate idea of the numbers of adherents claimed for Islam and the two wings of the Christian missionary effort.

Population totals for Subsaharan Africa, in the lists drawn by Comhaire,[1] reached 139,614,052 in 1953. The 1952 tabulations of the *World Christian Handbook*,[2] gave an estimate of 116,494,000, though to this the 235,200 persons listed by Comhaire for São Tome and Spanish Guinea must be added. Christians in Subsaharan Africa, according to Comhaire, totalled 24,304,510, of whom Catholics comprised 12,419,686 and Protestants 11,884,834. The *World Handbook* numbered the Catholics at 10,684,055, while Dain listed the Protestants at 9,232,000, for a Christian population of 19,926,055. Price, using materials from the 1957 edition of the *World Christian Handbook*, numbered Protestants

[9] E. J. Bingle and K. G. Grubb: *World Christian Handbook, 1952 Edition* (London, 1952), p. 119.

[1] John J. Considine: *Africa, World of New Men* (New York, 1954), pp. 352–7.

[2] A. J. Dain: *Mission Fields Today, a Brief World Survey* (2nd edition, London, 1956), pp. 102–3.

as 12,698,000 and Catholics as 17,998,000, increasing the estimates for Christians to 30,696,000.[3] The *Annuaire du Monde Musulman* in 1954 gave figures for Moslems that came to 30,427,574. Many of the components that made up this total, however, were expressly stated to be rough estimates; except for a few of the territories, the size of the non-Moslem populations, Christian or unconverted, was not given.[4] Only Comhaire attempted to assess the total picture for all of Subsaharan Africa, placing the numbers of Moslems at 38,702,579 and of "animists" at 75,456,229.

Despite the disparities in these tabulations for gross numbers of adherents to the major proselytizing faiths, they show a reasonable consistency when reduced to proportionate figures. In the listings in Considine's work, the Christians comprised 17.5% of the total population of Subsaharan Africa, in those of Dain, they made up 17.1%. According to Comhaire, 55.9% of the Christians were Catholic, 44.1% Protestants. The corresponding proportions, computed from Dain's tables and those of the *World Christian Handbook*, gave the Catholics 53.7%, the Protestants 46.3%. In Price's tabulations, 58.6% were Catholic, 41.3% Protestant. For the total picture, according to the figures gathered by Comhaire, Moslems were 27.7%, and those who had accepted neither Islam nor Christianity 53.9%. Taking these findings for the unconverted, the *Annuaire* for the Moslems, and Price for the Christians, we see that out of a total population for Subsaharan Africa of 136,579,803, some 55.3% held to their aboriginal beliefs, 22.4% were Christian, 22.2% Moslem.

Figures reduced to percentages are seductive, however, and tend to give a false sense of statistical security. It will, therefore, be wiser if we content ourselves with saying that at about mid-twentieth century, more than one-half of the population of Africa south of the Sahara retained their earlier modes of worship. Between one-fifth and one-fourth were Christian, divided between

[3] Frank W. Price: "World Christian and Missionary Statistics," *Occasional Bulletin*, Missionary Research Library, New York, Vol. 9, No. 4 (1958), p. 8.

[4] Louis Massignon: *Annuaire du Monde Musulman, Statistique, Historique, Social et Économique* (Paris, 1955), pp. 280–378 *passim*.

the two principal wings of the Christian community, of which the Catholics made up slightly more, the Protestants slightly less, than one-half. The Moslems were credited with about the same proportion of the inhabitants of the subcontinent as the Christians.

[3]

Gross estimates usually mask significant differences, and the present case is no exception. It is well recognized that the category "Protestant" encompasses a variety of denominations which diverge as widely from one another in their missionary procedures as they do in certain aspects of their theological systems. It is not so generally understood that there were also differences among the various orders, or brotherhoods, or sects of the other two categories. In the case of the Catholic missions, the centralization of authority through the hierarchical controls of the Church effectively modifies this, so that controversies are little publicized. Consequently, the kind of competition among different Protestant denominations in a given territory, which made necessary the negotiation of formal agreements limiting the activities of each to particular districts, rarely occurred in the case of the Catholic missions. However, in the field, in contact with working Catholic missionaries, it was not uncommon to hear criticisms of the activities of a rival order that were quite as pointed as any made by members of one Protestant mission about another.

Nor did the rivalry between mission groups go unnoticed by those whom they sought to convert. The problem was posed as follows by one authority:

> African tribal life, while providing a strong if narrow local cohesion, has proved very divisive over wide areas of life. The missions and Churches have had their share in disintegrating tribal life, but it is sometimes complained that they have only replaced it by tribalism in another form—denominationalism. The two have, in places, joined together in tribal denominations. Moreover Africa is increasingly aware of the keen evangelism of mission groups lack-

ing any strong church sense and in sharp denunciation of existing Churches.[5]

The same observation was tersely and more colorfully phrased by an African who was asked about the current activities of the missionaries in the district where he lived. "They keep busy fighting each other," he replied.

In the Christian missionary literature, Islam is frequently discussed as though it were a monolithic structure. But the historians of Islam, and those who have studied its influence on the Africans at first hand, have made no such error. Whether concerned with the religious developments in a single territory such as Guinea,[6] or with western Africa as a whole, the conflicts within Islam, especially the rivalries between the brotherhoods (*tarīquas*), are fully treated. The overall picture, it is true, differs from the denominational competitiveness of the Christian missions. This difference arises out of a fact already noted, that Islam came to the Africans as a movement of conquest. It is therefore understandable that preconquest internal conflicts among groups, all of which proclaim their fidelity to Islam, should have continued.

The spread of Islamic influence in the whole of the western Sudan was accompanied by strife among contending Moslem groups, wherein theological differences gave a rationale for political ambitions. The closest analogy to this in the history of Christian missions—and one that is not too close, at that—is found in the early conflicts between the "Fransa" and the "Ingleza," the native Catholics and Protestants of Uganda, where converts and missionaries joined in a struggle for power that took the form of a religious war.[7]

We may briefly consider some of the contending groups to show something of the inner strains within the African Moslem

[5] E. J. Bingle: "The World Mission of the Church—a Survey," in *World Christian Handbook, 1952 edition,* E. J. Bingle and K. G. Grubb, editors (London, 1952), p. 22.

[6] E.g., Paul Marty: *L'Islam en Guinée, Fouta-Diallon* (Paris, 1921).

[7] Margery Perham: *Lugard, the Years of Adventure, 1858–1898* (London, 1956), pp. 297 ff.

community. One, early on the ground, was the Qādiriyya, a mystical sect devoted to the practice of pietistic charity, and given to ecstatic religious possession. In the early twentieth century, in Nigeria and Dahomey, the Qādiriyya was giving way before the Tijāniyya, which was at the same time maintaining equal strength in French West Africa to the north, though yielding to its rival in the more westerly territories. This group, more democratic in its organization, holding strictly to the pronouncements of the prophet Mohammed, rapidly became an order of warriors.[8]

The brotherhood of the Sanūsiyya originated during the middle of the nineteenth century as a reform movement, whose leader conceived it as his mission to remove from Islam the impurities that had been introduced over the centuries. This brotherhood, which had as one of its principal aims the establishment of a strong state in the interior of Africa, and which was Pan-Islamic in its orientation, took advantage of the trading activities of its members as a way to further its political influence. Because of this, it came into conflict with the French in 1917, at Agadez, where its defeat caused many of its followers to defect to the Tijāniyya.[9]

Another sect that grew steadily in power over all the Islamic world was the Aḥmadiyya. This reached Africa from India, and was propagated by its Indian adherents, especially in eastern Africa, though they later brought it to western Africa, notably Nigeria, where Indian traders had been permitted to establish themselves. The Ismailia movement, headed by the Aga Khan, also became active in Africa; its pattern of proselytizing followed closely the methods of peaceful persuasion and infiltration of the Christian missionaries and was directed more toward Indians than toward Africans.

Change within Islam in Africa was continuous. As interpreted by André, "Islam in French West Africa has become 'maraboutized,' has become localized. . . ." He draws the generalization that, "the Blacks attach themselves more to persons than to ideas." He cites the statement of Governor Brevié,

[8] P.-J. André: *L'Islam Noire* (Paris, 1924), pp. 49–70.
[9] Ibid., pp. 71–8.

> For the very large majority of Moslems of the Sudan, to be Qādiriyya or Tijāniyya is to be labelled with a designation which has no precise meaning, it is to add a formula to his prayer, it is above all to follow the way which his father or the religious innovator has laid out. . . . Most often, affiliation with one sect or another is a matter of entire indifference; it is to the point that the same marabouts will admit to being members of the Qādiriyya or of the Tijāniyya order.[1]

This was in 1924; in 1953 this continuing process of "maraboutization"—the term used by the French for fission resulting from the influence of an "inspired" religious leader and teacher—could be seen in a village near Dakar, the seat of the Grand Marabout Khalifatoune Limamon-Laye, Seydina Madione Laye, head of another dissident sect whose influence, in preceding years, had spread widely throughout Senegal and Mauretania.

Within the Protestant wing, the groups engaged in converting the Africans ranged from the most fundamentalist sects to those that called for a liberal interpretation of the Bible; from the great denominations to small churches with relatively few communicants. They varied in the degree to which they accomplished their missions, and in the means they employed. Some defined their activities in terms of preaching and religious instruction, others stressed their social role as agents of cultural exchanges. The Catholic effort was more closely defined and held more rigorously to the line set by the hierarchy. It combined emphasis on conversion, conformity, and social service, with the training of Africans for the priesthood.

Christian missions in Subsaharan Africa grew to considerable proportions. According to Considine, who gave no figures for Protestants, the Catholic Church in 1952 had in its African missionary services south of the Sahara 7,468 non-African priests, 2,342 brothers and 10,533 sisters, a total of 20,343, not including the much larger number of Africans who were priests, members of various orders, and catechists. This total, it is true, contrasts with the figures presented by Price, of 9,605 Protestant missionaries in Subsaharan Africa and 11,830 for the Catholics, a differ-

[1] Ibid., pp. 96–100, *passim.*

ence not to be accounted for by scrutiny of the tables themselves. However, even if we accept these smaller figures for Catholics, we reach the substantial total of over 20,000 Europeans and Americans who had gone to Africa to further the spread of Christianity south of the Sahara.

There seems to be no way of obtaining comparable figures for the total of Islamic missionaries, due perhaps to the fact that Moslem proselytizing has only to a minor degree been a separate, identifiable aspect of penetration. This would indicate that Islam, as a way of life, was for Africans an easily integrated daily routine, whereas Christianity, which came to them as a formal, emotionally low-keyed, religious experience, was represented by specialists separated from the other Europeans or Americans who were concerned with business, or administration, or technology.

[4]

The spread of Islam presents two major problems in our examination of the forces that made for religious change in Subsaharan Africa. The first has to do with the point just touched upon, the character of its appeal. The second, more difficult by its very nature, has to do with the stabilization of the limits of its influences. Given its formula for conversion, why did not Islam move farther into Africa during the centuries when it could have pressed its proselytizing activities, unopposed either by European administrators or by Christian missionaries? There are few data to draw on, and most statements, especially those bearing on the first question, have come from persons concerned with halting any further expansion of Islam.

Logically, the essential appeal of Islam was that its belief system was based on a "Book" which recorded truths revealed to a Prophet, whose introduction entailed little cultural dislocation.[2] One commentator, directing his analysis toward the situation in East Africa, summarized it as follows:

> For the majority of tribal Africans, Islam . . . appeared as a support, and not as a challenge, to their traditional way of life. Within

[2] *Supra*, pp. 180–2.

> the framework of Islam it has been possible for the convert to retain the greater part of tribal custom without any radical change. In a true sense, no conversion is expected of the tribal African of East Africa in becoming a Muslim, for conversion means a turning away from those aspects of belief and of life which are not acceptable in the converting religion.

It was pointed out that even from a theological point of view, there was no essential conflict between Islamic and aboriginal beliefs; that polytheism is the only tenet inconsistent with being a Moslem. Therefore East Africans believing in a universe headed by a single deity needed no far-reaching reorientation.[3]

Another student, also treating of Islam in East Africa, attributed its appeal to other causes. For one thing, though Arab slave-raiders did not proselytize, the peoples who were allied to them were subject to Moslem influence, as among the Yao of Nyasaland.

> It was difficult even for eye-witnesses to assess the religious influence of these traveling Muslims, since, unlike Christian missionaries, they demand no baptismal renunciation of ancient beliefs, and their followers could express their adherence by an infinite number of gradations, from simple imitation of dress and demeanour to the stringent observance of circumcision, fasting and prayer.

Prestige attached to the Arabs and Swahili because of their military prowess, because they were skilled craftsmen and traders, and because in German territory they were "the visible instruments of the new authority," or overseers of work gangs. This, it is to be inferred, must have given the fact that they were also Moslems a significance that facilitated acceptance of their beliefs.[4]

Westermann, noting that "the spread of Islam has come about, not by organized missionary activity, but in an indirect manner through immigration, political conquest, trade and cultural assimilation" also indicated that affiliation with Islam had a certain survival value. In the "holy wars" among Africans,

[3] Lyndon P. Harries: *Islam in East Africa* (London, 1954), pp. 33–4.

[4] Roland Oliver: *The Missionary Factor in East Africa* (London, 1952), p. 202–4.

the conversion of pagans was not to the interest of the conqueror, because according to Moslem law a Mohammedan cannot be discriminated against in civil rights, and cannot be sold as a slave. But this same fact was a strong incentive to conquered Negroes to adopt Islam, and in this way even slave-raiding assisted the progress of Mohammedanism.[5]

For West Africa, Considine enumerated a series of reasons why Islam had an advantage over Christianity. One was the increasing ease of contact with the aboriginal peoples that resulted from improvement in the means of communication, which in turn brought the unconverted into contact everywhere with the Moslems, and gave them access to mosques and Koranic schools. Again, the French policy of *laïcisme,* or the "neutrality" of the British, favored Islam, since both policies were directed toward preserving aboriginal custom, which was less affected by Moslem than by Christian effort. The zeal of the brotherhoods and the marabouts, the activities of the local traders, more often than not Moslems, even the influence of the Moslem herder who hired out to the "fetishist" farmer to tend his cattle, all tended to propagate their faith. In addition, the incentive of the unconverted to join a "respected social group," the fact that mere acceptance of "easy Moslem tenets" was sufficient, and the work of newer missionary sects, especially the Aḥmadiyya, are given as reasons for Islamic successes.[6]

All these were undoubtedly contributing factors in the spread of Islam in the colonial period, especially since the various manifestations of the *pax Europaeica* inhibited the conquests that marked the earlier successes of Islam in Africa. Bovill, for the earlier periods, stressed the role of commerce, since, "The buying and selling of commodities is always accompanied by the exchange of ideas" and "the constant circulation of the population in pursuit of trade encouraged tolerance to foreigners and created an atmosphere favorable to the maintenance of commercial in-

[5] Diedrich Westermann: *Africa and Christianity* (London, 1937), pp. 114–15.

[6] John J. Considine: *Africa, World of New Men* (New York, 1954) pp. 33–5.

tercourse . . ."[7] Those who traded settled among the peoples to whom they came, and thus extended their influence.

Taken as a whole, these reasons add up substantially to the formula of culture contact discussed in preceding pages, which holds that the less the differences between the customs of peoples in contact, the less the degree of resulting cultural shock, and consequently greater receptivity to innovation. It would be a simplification, however, to think in terms of strict opposites, with Islam as unfailingly permissive, and Christianity as inflexibly exacting. Relatively speaking, a difference of this kind between the two proselytizing faiths can be discerned. As one troubled Christian missionary phrased it,

> Between those tribes that are recognized as Moslem to the North, and the pagan tribes to the South . . . there lie a thousand tribes that are more or less under the influences of this Moslem menace. This babel of tongues presents no formidable difficulty to the emissary of Mohammed. Genuflexions, reiterated prayers, clothing, and comradeship, do not depend on the reduction of a pagan language to writing, and a measure of education that shall prepare the way for the Word of God.[8]

Such advantage as enjoyed by Islam must be recognized as critical, especially when the factor of race is added.

This is illustrated by the penetration and maintenance of Islam in the Nigerian city of Ibadan. At mid-twentieth century, professing Moslems numbered less than one-sixth of the population, but this was not the limit of their influence, since perhaps half the city participated on occasion in their festival rites. The reasons for their "progress in Yoruba country" were enumerated as follows: Islam ". . . permits polygamy and many superstitions." Chiefs found it useful to belong for reasons of prestige and politics, and their subjects followed them. "The social side of Islam" had its appeal, and the support of Moslem religious leaders was no burden, since their livelihood did not depend entirely on their connection with the mosque. Moreover, the Moslem

[7] E. W. Bovill: *Caravans of the Old Sahara* (London, 1933), pp. 267–8.

[8] W. J. W. Roome: *Can Africa Be Won?* (London, 1927), p. 75.

teacher or trader came closer to the people, if only because he spoke their language. Finally,

> Islam gives the appearance of unity and universality. . . . The mosques are independent of one another and form groups of the faithful, like little communities, but outwardly their doctrine and worship is the same.[9]

Why then, despite all this, did Islam not effectively penetrate farther south than about 10° north latitude, the so-called "Moslem line"? Bovill's explanation of the earlier spread of Islam to the Sudanic belt as having resulted from commercial contacts is an attractive one, until we come on this passage:

> The only barrier to the spread of these . . . influences were the great forests of the south. In the Sudan itself a number of isolated groups of highlands, such as the Hombori Mountains and the Bauchi Plateau, or swamps, such as fringe the shores of Chad and the great lakes of the middle Niger, became islands of survival where hardy mountaineers or shy fisherfolk sturdily resisted the intrusion of new thought and learning.[1]

On examining the facts, however, it becomes clear that the question is not to be answered by simple reference to geographical factors. Trade did not always depend on the use of cavalry or the ability to deploy camel corps to attain political controls. We see this in the commercial contacts of precolonial times between the Islamic Hausa of Northern Nigeria and the Ashanti of what was then called the Gold Coast. In Kano, in 1931, aged merchants who had themselves employed slaves in pursuing it could give details of the route they took to Kumasi, a distance of some 1,800 miles. Each point they named, was located on maps of the region, thus providing a check on the validity of the information. The route went westerly and then southwards, to avoid the hostile peoples of Dahomey and the Yoruba of Western Nigeria.[2] Ashanti is in the forested belt, and the Hausa traders had so little

[9] Geoffrey Parrinder: *Religion in an African City* (London, 1953), pp. 84–5.

[1] E. W. Bovill: *loc. cit.*

[2] Melville J. Herskovits: "The Significance of West Africa for Negro Research," *Journal of Negro History*, Vol. 21 (1936), *passim.*

difficulty in penetrating there that, as we shall see, the *zongo*, the strangers' quarter, inhabited mainly by Hausa traders, became a feature of all Ashanti towns. The presence of these strangers, all Moslems, however, affected the religious beliefs of the Ashanti not at all. Those Ashanti who did not retain their aboriginal beliefs—and many who did—became Protestants and Catholics. Here, unlike the Fulani who took over Hausa territory by military conquest but never prevailed over the Yoruba of the forest or the peoples of Bornu,[3] peaceful followers of Islam did penetrate, but neither conquered nor converted.

On this point, Hardy writes that in Africa,

> Islam is not fundamentally intolerant; it permits other religions to live at its side without difficulty, it refrains from engaging in prosecution that is purely religious, and its liberalism is even more accentuated when it passes from the Arab to the Berber or Sudanic spirit. But Islam is not only a religion: it is in addition a source of political organizations, and what is called its intolerance or its fanaticism is most often no more than a desire for independence or power.[4]

Another factor entered, however, which is rarely given the place it deserves. Mission historians and others who have discussed the spread of Islam in Africa have tended to denigrate the theological insights and social sanctions of indigenous African religions, dismissing them as "primitive," or as a body of "superstitions," beliefs under no conceivable circumstances to be classed with the proselytizing faiths. A scientific approach does not dismiss belief-systems that are meaningful to more than half the population of Subsaharan Africa, but rather suggests that in the absence of conquest, the strength of aboriginal religious systems, especially those formally institutionalized, must have acted as an effective barrier not only to alien belief and ritual, but to foreign cultural values. The Dogon and other peoples of the deep Sudan, or the Baganda of East Africa, no less than the Ashanti, the Dahomeans and, to a very large degree, the Yoruba, the latter

[3] E. W. Bovill: *The Golden Trade of the Moors* (London, 1958), p. 229.

[4] Georges Hardy: *Vue générale de l'Histoire d'Afrique* (2nd edition, Paris, 1930), pp. 62–3.

three within the forested belt, had well-structured and closely organized religions with profound theological and philosophical insights having well-integrated support in myth, ritual and political organization. Among such peoples, Islamic proselytizing had minimal success. Even among a people such as the Nigerian Tiv, whose religion has been described as one whose "logic is . . . one of concordance and analogy rather than of syllogism and equation," and which, having "no heresy," has "no orthodoxy," Islam made no headway.[5]

Such being the power of aboriginal faiths, we must ask why Christianity came to be accepted by so many peoples within this same forested coastal area of western Africa? It is a matter of culturally associated prestige. The bearers of Christianity brought not only their religion, but also innovations in technology and medicine, and education in a world language, which Africans themselves came to regard as desirable. In this case, indeed, the very fact of cultural differences carried conviction, as against Islam, where cultural similarities exerted their powerful influence. But neither similarities nor differences should be thought of as more than a single item in a multifaceted structure of explanation of the complex phenomenon that engages us. Despite this complexity, the sanctions of both systems, where they were effective, were the concomitants of conquest and foreign rule.

Christianity failed to penetrate Islamic territory partly because Islam had had time to consolidate itself there, and partly because of the discouragement by the colonial governments of Christian missionary activity in the Moslem areas under their control. Islam, as a world religion, carried by peoples with a proud history of conquest, enjoying formal acceptance by the Europeans who came to govern these territories, offered few points at which it was vulnerable to Christian persuasion. More than this, Islam provided not only prestige but a sense of cultural comfort. The account of Trimingham concerning the beliefs and practices of "popular Islam" in the Sudan,[6] or the reports of

[5] Laura and Paul Bohannan: *The Tiv of Central Nigeria* (Ethnographic Survey of Africa, Western Africa, Part VIII, London, 1953), pp. 81, 93.

[6] J. S. Trimingham: *Islam in the Sudan* (London, 1949), pp. 126 ff.

Greenberg, Ames, and others already noted concerning the syncretisms between Islamic and aboriginal practices throughout the western Sudanic belt, show how cultural flexibility made for a firm attachment to a world religion that could at the same time tolerate deep-rooted pre-Islamic traditions.

[5]

It is clear that the influence of Christianity in Subsaharan Africa as a whole, after the partition of Africa among the European powers, was far greater than that of Islam. This is evident, for example, if we do no more than compare the area of that part of the subcontinent which lay north of the "Moslem line" with that to the south of it. This is not to say that the influence exerted by the Christian missions is to be judged only by the number of communicants reported. The case of the large number of Yoruba who attended Islamic feasts, cited by Parrinder to show the extent of Moslem penetration of Ibadan, has its parallels in Christian influence. If we are to make comparisons, we must take into account the number of Africans, not members of any Christian church, who attended mission schools, were treated in mission hospitals, received training in mission artisan centers, or flocked to watch religious processions, in calculating those who came under the influence of Christianity.

A major difference between Christianity and Islam in Subsaharan Africa arose from the direction each gave to cultural change. The drift of world opinion and organization during the first half of the twentieth century may be summarized as having been toward industrialization and mechanization—that is, toward economic development; toward increased ease and speed of communication, including the spread of literacy; and toward nationalism, with the countervailing drive toward integrating the peoples of the world into a world organization. Only in its support of nationalistic goals can Islam be said to have stimulated the peoples of Africa to place themselves in the stream of global developments. Even in this, the contribution of Islam began only toward the middle of the twentieth century, when it helped to accelerate a political movement that had already taken firm root in Africa on the initiative of Africans exposed to the ideologies of Western Europe and the United States.

In all this, the Christian missions were a significant propagating force, participating with the other sectors of Euroamerican culture brought to Africans by agencies of government and commerce. It is not only their strongly evangelistic religious tradition that made them effective. While European cultures were not the only ones which had the concept of the religious evangel, they were unique in extending this into a social evangel. This broadened a movement for religious conversion into one active in such fields as medicine, schooling, agriculture, health and hygiene. On a secondary level, particularly as regards the activities of certain denominational missions, it became one which promoted the values of democracy, individual initiative and those other articles of Euroamerican cultural faith which, developed in societies with a strong evangelistic bent, were kneaded as a leaven into the acculturative dough. One student, writing when there was little organized protest against the colonial presence, said, "Because the African loves what the European offers him, he also loves Christianity, which in his eyes is the religion of the white man and part of his civilization." [7]

Christian missions not only reflected the broad patterns of belief and behavior of the societies out of which they came, but were taken as representative of these societies. Hence the charge so often laid against them, that they were the agents of colonial expansion. Viewed objectively, the logic of this charge lies in the fact that, in a period when alien political controls over Africa were being extended, the missionary effort was a sympathetic, and at times a very active participant in shaping European expansion. "In the search for adequate means to develop the potential resources of land and people even the hitherto supercilious German critics of missions," it is stated concerning German colonization in Africa, "now experienced a sudden conversion, not indeed to appreciation of their Christian purpose, but to their

[7] Diedrich Westermann: *Africa and Christianity* (London, 1937), p. 33.

significant service as effective civilizers of uncouth tribes and admirable purveyors of the national culture." [8]

However this missionary role is viewed, it would be unrealistic to ignore or underestimate the humanitarian currents and the commitment of dedicated individuals to bring to the rest of the world what they accepted as a highest value—the revealed Truth which could lead all mankind to a better way of life. This, indeed, was the prime motivating force of those who went to distant lands, often at the risk of their lives, to minister to peoples who, as they saw it, lacked and needed this Truth.

This dual role of the missions—their own dual mandate—gained increasingly wide acceptance. One of the works that deeply influenced French thought about overseas possessions, had this to say:

> Perhaps too highly praised three centuries ago, too much discredited today, the religious missions have an important role to play in colonization. . . . Moral and material innovation, benevolent tutelage, continuing education of these peoples or, even more, of their tribes cannot be achieved only by our traders, our administrators, or our school-masters; this is folly. . . . Religion, notably the Christian religion, with its gentleness, its elevated principles, its love of the lowly, . . . is the only teacher that can . . . lead savages and barbarians to understand our civilization and to cooperate in developing it.

But if the missionary were to achieve this,

> . . . the European colonial powers must protect the missionaries and facilitate their work among all savage or barbarous peoples. . . . Only we must recommend to the missions that they add, as soon as possible, to their religious propagandizing certain moves looking toward the initiation of their flocks into more improved agricultural methods, and into industry.[9]

Groves, the historian of Christianity in Africa, pointing out the trials that beset the early missionaries, stated,

[8] C. P. Groves: *The Planting of Christianity in Africa* (Vol. III, London, 1955), p. 53.

[9] Paul Leroy-Beaulieu: *De la Colonisation chez les Peuples Modernes* (Vol. II, Paris, 1902), pp. 654–6.

where missionaries had been the pioneers among independent African peoples, they naturally would welcome, if some European control was inevitable, a civil government of their fellow nationals. . . . And the compliment could be returned, Governments also preferring missionaries from the homeland rather than the citizens of a foreign power.[1]

Occupation meant greater benefits—"greater security for themselves and their converts," with the missionaries being "progressively relieved of a heavy burden through the prohibition of offences against the person which were repugnant to humanity, and the presence of a police force to secure the law's observance."[2] Occupation also brought liabilities, "in relation to the Government to whose policy he must now conform, and *vis-à-vis* the African people to whom he now often stood for the first time as a member of the ruling race."[3] Aupiais was even more explicit on this point:

Colonization has profoundly modified the status of the pagan peoples of Africa, of Asia, of Oceania. The missionaries owe to it the power to pursue their evangelizing labors everywhere . . . They need no longer fear being expelled from their countries, nor to expose to violent death the natives who would have ended by following them.[4]

It was natural for Africans to conclude that the missionary was an agent of those who came to rule. The literature is replete with expressions of this opinion, which had as its basis the fact that the missionary, like the trader, was a forerunner of the imposition of political control. Maunier, a student of colonial sociology, put the matter harshly:

Under the missionaries' wing later comers were able to make peaceful contact; it was often the missions which made occupation possible. Exploitation, the opening of business and of concessions, sprang up and flourished in the shade of the mission. There were even missions which, on their own initiative, organized plantations in new countries.[5]

[1] Op. cit., Vol. III, p. 45 [2] Ibid., p. 46. [3] Ibid., pp. 49–50.

[4] F. Aupiais, *Le Missionaire* (Paris, 1938), p. 93.

[5] René Maunier: *The Sociology of Colonies*. E. O. Lorimer, editor and translator, Vol. I (London, 1949), p. 23.

In 1911, an African preacher, Charles Domingo, expressed his view in this way:

> There is too much failure among all Europeans in Nyasaland. The three combined bodies, Missionaries, Government and Companies, or gainers of money—do form the same rule to look upon the native with mockery eyes . . . If we had power enough to communicate ourselves to Europe we would advise them not to call themselves "Christendom" but "Europeandom." Therefore the life of the three combined bodies is altogether too cheaty, too thefty, too mockery. Instead of "Give" they say "Take away from." [6]

Of the many contemporaneous statements that show the early reactions of Africans to Christian missionaries, several given by Groves from southern Africa may be cited. One of those tells of a report to the Zulu ruler, Shaka, by an African interpreter, as recounted in 1836 by Gardiner:

> He assured him that a white man, assuming the character of teacher or missionary, would arrive among them, and obtain permission to build a house; that, shortly after, he would be joined by one or two more white men; and in the course of time, an army would enter his country which would subvert his government, and, eventually, the white people would rule in his stead.

Lobengula, the head of the Matabele, expressed himself to a missionary with characteristic African imagery:

> Did you ever see a chameleon catch a fly? The chameleon gets behind the fly and remains motionless for some time, then he advances very closely and gently. . . . At last, when well within reach, he darts out his tongue and the fly disappears. England is that tongue and I am that fly.[7]

That the relation between missionaries and other Europeans should have been close is understandable, even though it does not prove that the missionaries were as concerned to keep the *status quo* of colonial control as were those politically or economically interested. In some instances the semi-official position held by a

[6] George Shepperson and Thomas Price: *Independent African: John Chilembwe and the Origins, Setting and Significance of the Nyasaland Native Rising of 1915* (Edinburgh, 1958), pp. 163–4.

[7] C. P. Groves, op. cit., Vol. III, pp. 51–2.

particular wing of the Christian movement lent credence to this belief, and was reflected in African attitudes. Thus, in the earlier days of Belgian rule Protestant missions in the Congo were permitted to work on sufferance, and this continued to be the case in Portuguese territory, while they were consistently excluded from Spanish Africa.

The African reaction, where certain missions labored under a handicap of official disfavor, was often one of tenacious loyalty, whereas the church officially recognized was viewed as an arm of government. The instance of a Protestant missionary who had spent many years in Mozambique, and who, for reasons of health was transferred to Northern Rhodesia, illustrates this point.

> I made many converts in Rhodesia, and I have never been less satisfied. In Mozambique, to become a member of our church meant a real sacrifice, and a real conviction. In Rhodesia, it is a matter of paying £5 and becoming a member of a group that has prestige.

Conversely, in Uganda, after the Kabaka, the ruler of Buganda, was sent into exile in 1953, the Catholic churches were crowded, draining away the worshippers from the Church of England, which had semi-official status.

Historically, the relation of Christian missionaries to the governing administrations was what can perhaps best be described as correct. In part, this may have been the result of relations that dated back to the earliest days of penetration. In part, especially with missions from the United States, whose activity in Africa was extensive, it was perhaps the feeling, reinforced by the reservations of officials of the governing Power, that they were permitted to work in their stations more or less at the pleasure of the authorities.

There are few instances on record in Subsaharan Africa where missionaries took their stand against a major policy of a Government that was regarded by Africans as disadvantageous. A case in point was the South African Bantu Education Act. After its passage in 1956, it speedily became a focus of African apprehension because it threatened African chances to obtain the schooling they must have to cope with the requirements of the industrialized culture in which they were living. The missions were faced with two alternatives. They could adopt a policy of non-cooperation, which would entail transferring their schools to government control, unless they could themselves finance them, or close them. Or they could comply, and make available to Africans such inferior schooling as might be permitted under the Act. The Anglican missions closed their schools, the Catholics financed theirs. The other Protestant groups, in the main, took the second course.[8] Another example was the stand taken in 1959 by the Church of Scotland against the repressive policies adopted by the central government of the Federation of the Rhodesias and Nyasaland in putting down the disturbances in Nyasaland. But these are exceptions to the rule of political acquiescence or neutrality on the part of the missions.[9]

In the colonial territories, one reason for this reluctance to oppose the colonial governments may have been the declared policy of all Christian missions to prepare Africans for eventual taking over control of the religious establishments. Gradually, and for many reasons, not the least of which was the continuous disparagement of indigenous beliefs and traditions, African dissatisfaction expressed itself in growing mistrust of missions. In time, even the Christian missionaries who most clearly demonstrated their active friendship for the Africans could not achieve full acceptance because of the political identifications they had to bear and because of the mounting hostility toward racial identification.

The formula of Cetshwayo, the Zulu ruler, who is reputed to have said, "First a missionary, then a consul, and then come army,"[1] is often repeated in discussing Central and South Africa,

[8] Gwendolyn M. Carter: *The Politics of Inequality; South Africa Since 1948* (New York, 1958), pp. 106–8.

[9] Church of Scotland: *Report on Central Africa,* including Supplementary Report (Edinburgh, 1959), pp. 31–6.

[1] C. P. Groves: *The Planting of Christianity in Africa* (London, 1950), Vol. III, p. 52.

just as the names of Rhodes, the empire builder, and Livingstone, the missionary, are so often coupled. This must represent a sure, even if unconscious, sense of historic reality.

[6]

There is perhaps no aspect of the African experience that has been analyzed with less objectivity than the Christian missionary effort. Opinions on few other African topics have varied more widely, or been phrased more positively. "What was it," asked a former governor of Kenya, "that suddenly, in a few years, roused so many of these placid, incurious people to the restless energy and ambitions of today?" For him,

> it was the Bible, . . . and the brave, determined, merciful men and women who carried it and its message of hope . . . to a people who were living in a brutish lethargy induced by continuous danger, horror, and sufferings.[2]

At the other end of the spectrum, we find as an early judgment the statement of one of the almost legendary figures of European penetration into West Africa, Mary Kingsley who, in pointing out "the weak spot in nine-tenths of the mission effort," says:

> They have been trying to look after the Negro's soul and teaching him Christianity, which in the native mind is cutting at the root, not only of all their ancient customs, but actually aims at taking away their living without attempting to teach them any industrial pursuit which may help them in the struggle for life.[3]

While objective evaluations of missionary activities and achievements have been few, the self-criticism inherent in missionary psychology has produced much valuable discussion. Characteristically directed toward analyzing techniques and attainments, they rarely considered underlying assumptions or their sociological and psychological repercussions. Emotions have tended to run so strong that discussion on this level has generally

[2] Sir Philip Mitchell: "Africa and the West in Historical Perspective," in *Africa Today*, C. Grove Haines, editor (Baltimore, 1955), p. 15.

[3] Mary H. Kingsley: *West African Studies* (London, 1899), p. 56.

been verbal and undocumented, anecdotal and selective, lacking the psychic distance essential to the scientific analysis of social movements and cultural influences. The African point of view, moreover, was not easy to ascertain. As it has been put by one student, "Christianity has always been the object of invidious observation by African pagans though courtesy and concrete self-interest have often forbidden criticism to be outspoken."[4] Published critiques by Africans of the missionary effort were usually associated with political aims, and had the tendentious character of political debate.

The activities of Christian missions varied according to sect, creed, and the balance drawn between religious and secular elements in the obligations assumed. An early historian of missions attributed to the multiformity of the problem the tendency of African missions to follow "more the methods of early Christian work . . . individual rather than general, personal, rather than national." The objectives of the effort, he stated, entailed the "many particulars" which arose out of the "duty of the Church to obey the divine command." "Undoubtedly the first," we are told, "is the conversion of individual souls," since the "'passion for souls' is one of the most marked features of missionary life."[5]

The education of a native ministry and the formation of a native church were also held to be important, and the propagation of "civilizing influences" was ranked high. This was exemplified in "the gospel of the clean shirt," not more needed "even among the South Sea Islanders" than in Africa, and defined as "showing the virtues of cleanliness, illustrating the value of improved industrial appliances, demonstrating the evil results of many customs, introducing the use of better dress, house comforts, etc." The values of higher education, which had also been brought within the purview of mission activity, were held debatable: "Instruction in reading so that the people might be able

[4] M. J. Field: *Search for Security; an Ethno-psychiatric Study of Rural Ghana,* Northwestern University African Studies, No. 5 (Evanston, 1960), p. 50.

[5] Edwin Munsell Bliss: *A Concise History of Missions* (New York, 1897), p. 115.

to understand the Bible was recognized as legitimate, but what had the study of algebra to do with the conversion of souls?[5a] The fundamental aim of the missions always remained clear:

> If God has not made known his mind and purpose in Christ, the ground of Christian missions disappears. They stand or fall with the belief in a Word that is not from man but from God.[6]

Schooling was undertaken by the missions because it was essential to teach Africans to read the Bible and the catechisms, thus extending Christian influence by using them to guide their fellow-Africans:

> . . . As Livingstone always foretold, the evangelization of Africa could hardly begin until it was in the hands of native Africans as well as of foreign missionaries. The fact that is so very little realized in Europe is that it is seldom indeed the white missionary who is in direct contact with the African pagan. In the beginning he was. He had to be. There was no one else. But almost his first task was to find and train the people who could take his place in the front line of the advance; the twelve who would ultimately succeed him, the twelve who meanwhile could man a dozen stations while he himself could occupy no more than one.[7]

We have observed that the extension of Christian missionary effort to secular fields represented a system of values that included a social as well as a religious gospel; a system in which strong motivation derived from an overall evangelical tradition. Hence the missionary "passion for souls" was inseparable from "the gospel of the clean shirt." From the point of view of the science of culture, both were vehicles for the dissemination of basic Euroamerican values. Regarded as a phenomenon of cultural psychology, it becomes apparent why trousers and the Mother Hubbard dress came to connote higher moral values than the loincloth and the woman's *lapa;* why monogamy was exalted and polygamy denounced; why bride wealth was considered immoral, though the European dowry was not. As Groves says,

[5a] Ibid., pp. 231–5.

[6] J. H. Oldham and B. D. Gibson: *The Remaking of Man in Africa* (London, 1931), p. 17.

[7] Roland Oliver: *How Christian is Africa?* (London, 1956), p. 9.

. . . the ordained man for overseas was long to suffer from the limitations of a course, however admirable for the Church at home, which had little relevance in its human relations to the life and thought of the peoples whom he was called to serve. The result was almost inevitable: he reproduced overseas what he had grown up in and learned to value for himself at home, confidently regarding his social inheritance, coupled with his own ecclesiastical tradition, as the norm of all good life and sound churchmanship.[8]

Every proselytizing movement must have as its predominant drive the conviction that its world view is superior to any other, and this is as true of Islam as of Christianity. In Africa, at least, the two differed markedly in the range of secular cultural elements which called forth emotional responses because they had religious associations. In the Christian missionary effort, clothing, marriage customs and many other sociological and aesthetic phenomena became firmly tied to creed and ritual. In some measure this was also true for Islam, and where symbolic value was assigned to some item of secular behavior, the emotional charge was as strong as with Christian identifications. Thus, it is no less abhorrent to a Moslem to enter a mosque with bared head than to a Christian to go into a church with his hat on. Or, as illustrated, for example, in *The book of the difference between the governments of the Muslims and the governments of the unbelievers,* by the Fulani conqueror Shehu 'U͟thmān dan Fodio, where in speaking of beating drums by both Moslems and the unconverted, the former was held to be "for a legal purpose," the latter denounced because they do "vain things . . . without legal purpose."[9]

The implicit assumption of total cultural, if not racial, superiority that is so striking in missionary writings in general, was especially important in the history of the missionary effort in Africa. Thus Moffat, writing of the people of southern Africa in the early days of the missions, said,

[8] C. P. Groves: op. cit., Vol. III, p. 28.

[9] M. Hiskett: "*Kitāb al-farq:* a work on the Habe kingdoms attributed to 'U͟thmān dan Fodio," *Bulletin of the School of Oriental and African Studies, University of London,* Vol. 23, Part 3 (1960), p. 569.

> While Satan is obviously the author of the polytheism of other nations, he has employed his agency, with fatal success, in erasing every vestige of religious impression from the minds of the Bechuanas, Hottentots and Bushmen; leaving them without a single ray to guide them from the dark and dread futurity, or a single link to unite them with the skies.[1]

Over a century later, we read the following in a book describing mission work:

> Black with its primeval superstitions, the general picture turns to a muddy gray as Africa meets and clashes with the culture and ways of the West. . . . Still with its sparsely populated regions and wide-open areas, it has a future. Will it remain black or an unregenerate gray? Or will the light penetrate through the darkness to give life and freedom? This is the question of Africa.[2]

It must not be concluded that such quotations represent the only position taken by those propagating their Christian faith in Africa. After the end of the Second World War particularly, there was an increasing tendency in missionary circles to re-examine and re-assess some of the current assumptions about certain secular aspects of the life of the peoples among whom they worked. Much of this change was understandably due to the resistances encountered in the field. In addition, there was the questioning of Euroamerican values by educated Africans, which inflamed resentments against continued denigration of indigenous ways. These resentments, especially as manifested in anti-white attitudes, brought about a series of reappraisals of earlier points of view.

Nida, a proponent of understanding for traditional ways, wrote:

> Good missionaries have always been good "anthropologists." Not only have they been aware of human needs, whether stemming from the local way of life or from man's universal need of salvation, but they have recognized that the various ways of life of dif-

[1] Robert Moffat: *Missionary Labours and Scenes in Southern Africa* 3rd edition (New York, 1843), p. 168.

[2] Ruth Christiansen: *For the Heart of Africa* (Minneapolis, 1956), p.

ferent peoples are the channels by which their needs take form and through which the solutions to such needs pass.[3]

He showed, with many examples, how difficult it is to transfer values across cultures. "'But we are not going to have our wives dress like prostitutes,' protested an elder in the Ngbaka church in northern Congo, as he replied to the suggestion made by the missionary that the women should be required to cover their breast."[4] Though the cross-cultural approach suggested to missionary theorists that certain evaluations inherent in proselytizing should be transmuted to a more selective level, evaluation was not to be given over:

> While customs such as idol worship, caste, color ban, and child marriage must be rejected, others, such as frequent bathing, proper exercise, and good dietary practices, should be encouraged, even though they may be sanctioned by non-Christian religions.[5]

This same cross-cultural point of view, though never allowed to weaken the sense of a special mission to disseminate the Truth, was similarly to be found among Catholic writers. A French student of the missionary activity of the Church described the importance of cultural differences:

> Charged with proclaiming the evangel of Christ, the missionary in no way dreams of destroying the culture of the people to whom he comes, for he recognizes there a normal human development, even if there may be certain deviations to correct.[6]

Nonetheless, the critical exception was again indicated:

> . . . the intervention of the Church in the secular world flows directly from its mission and does not constitute a phenomenon resulting from the encounter of one culture with another. The moral principles which it re-establishes under the light of the Revelation are not restricted to any particular culture, but must inspire all of them: they are not alien to anyone, but on the contrary innate in man, though they may have become obscured.[7]

[3] Eugene A. Nida: *Customs and Cultures, Anthropology for Christian Missions* (New York, 1954), p. xi.

[4] Ibid., p. 1.

[5] Ibid., p. 262.

[6] Charles Couturier: *Mission de l'Église* (Paris, 1957), pp. 36–7.

[7] Ibid., p. 60.

We must also not lose sight of the counter-current of positive action against native practices that continued, and was even extended by "... the relative growth of missions and missionaries of strongly conservative and traditionally fundamentalist outlook," as the Editors of the 1957 *World Christian Handbook* characterized it. The "greater denominational missions" were alive to the delicacy of their position in a world of growing nationalisms. "But this," the Editors pointed out, "is of little avail if the suspicions of rulers are aroused by the rapid entry of large numbers of men and women who, although devoted, have little comprehension of the sensitivities of the world to which they have gone."[8]

[7]

When we add to the evangelistic tradition of Euroamerican society, backed by the power of a more effective technology, the process of investing secular practices with religious meaning, we have an equation that does much to explain why the introduction of Christianity in Subsaharan Africa brought about such extensive changes.

We can assume that any massive social movement such as the Christian missionary effort could not but affect the groups to which it gave its attention. The question is, to what degree, and with what results? Here it is especially difficult to find objective treatment, since this question goes to the heart of the argument over the values in missionary activity, and is laden with implicit judgments drawn from assumptions based on belief. We have seen that the missionary approach was conceived along broad lines, and was designed to replace antecedent custom, both religious and secular, with Christian practices. In terms of the dynamics of culture contact, what was involved was an attempt to transfer entire cultural systems, developed in a particular society and adapted to its requirements, to another which ordered its life quite differently.

[8] E. J. Bingle and K. G. Grubb: *World Christian Handbook, 1952 Edition* (London, 1952), pp. xix–xx.

This question was raised at a Conference on Missions, held in 1953, where scholars joined missionaries in assessing basic aims and evaluating achievements. Here Bascom gave particular attention to the interpretations of native traditions that guided missionary efforts, and the effects of these interpretations when translated into action. For example, in the area of religion itself, he pointed out how a wholesale rejection of all African belief as worthless—except, perhaps, the concept of the high god, which was interpreted, especially in Catholic writing, as an aboriginal monotheism—resulted in weakening the moral foundations on which African social structure was reared. He summarized his findings in this way:

> The use of ordeals and oaths is widespread in Africa, with the belief that the one who swears falsely will inevitably be punished. In these and other ways African religious beliefs provided important ethical sanctions which controlled and regulated individual behavior. For those who have been convinced that these beliefs are completely false and without foundation, these controls are removed; and where no substitutes have been provided, they are left with a completely individualistic and materialistic philosophy regulated only by the possibility of legal punishment.[9]

This generalization is illumined by a detailed study of religious acculturation made about the same time among the Anang, an Ibibio people of southeastern Nigeria.

> Missionaries oppose swearing oaths more than any other traditional religious practice. As a result of their influence . . . swearing on the Bible was substituted, with grave consequences, since most Christians believe that God (Ata Abassi) will forgive any lies they may tell, and they are no longer compelled to take the dreaded oath *nnɛm* into their bodies. . . . Barring oath swearers from tribunals has brought about an increase in the practice of evil magic and oath-swearing. Persons who do not gain justice through the judiciary turn to magic and the oath spirit to punish their opponents who have escaped punishment by lying in court. After destroying

[9] William R. Bascom: "African Culture and the Missionary," *Civilisations*, Vol. 3 (1953), p. 493.

the guilty party, the *nnεm* attacks others in his patrilineage and community; thus many innocent people die.[1]

Anthropological findings cite many similar instances. Bascom noted Shapera's analysis of the way in which the Kgatla of Bechuanaland continued to practice magic and sorcery; and from his own experience, described how the Christian Yoruba who had given over their traditional gods "seem to be left completely at the mercy of . . . witches" so that "the fear of witches, if anything, is stronger today than before." He ranged farther in assessing what he termed "the negative approach to African religion" of the missionaries. He showed how this had discouraged the African artists, who had produced what is recognized as one of the world's important art forms, from continuing to carve their masks and statuettes. Africans, he stated, who "have become ashamed of anything associated with African religion" had come to be "embarrassed by the traditional forms." [2]

In the rejection by missionaries of the aesthetic aspects of African cultures, Islam and Christianity have played similar roles. The disapproval of drumming and traditional dancing has been particularly strong, often accompanied by punitive measures, as where in 1953 a high official of the Protestant missionary organization in the Congo stated that when drums were heard in a Christian village the schoolmaster was withdrawn and the school closed, until a promise was given to suppress the drums.[3]

We need not labor a point which can be confirmed by even casual observation in Africa. The volume by Nida already cited provides a wealth of instances of the bewilderment that results where there is insistence that a people adopt particular forms of behavior based on values that are strange if not incomprehensible to them. There are, however, exceptional missions where drums, not church bells, call to prayer, or where, as in one station in the Cameroons, in a church built in traditional style, the altar rail was

[1] John C. Messenger, Jr.: "Religious Acculturation among the Anang Ibibio," in *Continuity and Change in African Cultures,* W. R. Bascom and M. J. Herskovits, editors (Chicago, 1959), p. 292.

[2] Ibid., pp. 495–6.

[3] Melville J. Herskovits: *Notes on African Field Research,* p. 53/D336.

carved with indigenous motifs by local artists, and the communion table was a copy of a large chief's stool.[4]

The changes that were induced in Subsaharan Africa through missionary action are nothing essentially new in human experience, nor are they considered here in order to assess praise or blame. Our concern here is to analyze the impact of proselytizing effort, and the facts can only be determined by a willingness to look at all the data. The fact that the missions were responsible for bringing literacy to Africans is no less to be praised than procedures which undermined the power of the ancestors, or the suppression of dancing, are to be condemned. Judgments of value derive from presuppositions, and with these we are concerned only insofar as they deepen our understanding of the varied processes of change operative in Subsaharan Africa.

The cultural results of the missionary activities of Christian proselytizing were, in many respects, similar to those achieved by Islam. There was the same question of the extent to which adherents, in their beliefs and ritual observances, could be regarded as true followers of the Prophet. There were the reinterpretations and syncretisms common to both. There were, finally, the same tendencies to form separatist sects which, disagreeing with the more established groups on doctrinal interpretations or matters of ritual, set up independent organizations.[5]

We know, as a result of intensive first-hand studies among peoples in contact, that it is naive to assume complete acceptance of a total range of cultural elements presented to the members of a society. In most cases, acceptance will be partial. Even where an element seems unchanged in form, we find that it has been reinterpreted to make the new accord with what preceded it, or continues to exist alongside it. Where pressure is exerted for a people to take over what is presented, whether this pressure be economic, social, political, or religious, the innovation will customarily be accepted in the spirit in which it has been proffered. An example from the West African territory of Dahomey will make the point. This dates from 1931, and has to do

[4] Ibid., p. 53/D296. [5] *Infra*, pp. 419–21.

with the consternation with which a French Huguenot missionary learned of the defection of his oldest and presumably most trusted convert. "I had thought he was living with one wife. . . . I found out that he has one wife—one in each quarter of the city." Or again, almost three decades later we find certain Anang and Ibibio students stating that they had contact with ghosts and witches, not only in Nigeria, but in the United States as well.[6]

The question was well posed by an African member of the Catholic hierarchy, writing out of his knowledge of the society to which he belonged by right of birth.

> . . . In view of the enormous success that has crowned the missionary effort in central Africa during this last half-century, it is legitimate to ask oneself the following question: Has this magnificent movement toward Christianity in Africa achieved complete success? Is the flowering we have seen rooted in the soul of the African, or is this simply an expression of the Europeanization of the Black Continent? Is our missionary method adequate? Is Christ "incorporated" in the African?

He answered his own query: "Who has never encountered cases that are truly deceptive: Someone who has been an excellent Christian for twenty, thirty years, but who, suddenly, returns to the practices of his ancestors. Hypocrisy? Perhaps!" [7]

In the Kwango area of the Belgian Congo, Baptist missionaries were called to aid the Africans in burning their indigenous religious paraphernalia—their "fetishes," to use the term in the account we follow here. Though the burning was successful, it apparently did not allay the malaise that brought it on. Later, an African deacon came to the missionary:

> Tata, you are going to run out of follower's cards. I have burned fetishes in several villages, and now the people are coming to me

[6] John C. Messenger, Jr.: "Reinterpretations of Christian and Indigenous Belief in a Nigerian Nativist Church," *American Anthropologist*, Vol. 62 (1960), p. 277.

[7] Vincent Mulago: "Nécessité de l'Adaptation Missionaire chez les Bantu du Congo," in *Des Prêtres Noirs s'Interrogent*, A. Abble, *et al.* (1956), p. 21.

asking for cards. They say they have given up their fetishes and now they want to become Christians and join the Church.[8]

We see here the mechanism of reinterpretation in the transfer of the power symbolized in the charm or image of earlier days to another object, the symbol of still greater power, the church membership card. Projected on a larger scale, this instance, which in varying forms can be multiplied indefinitely, indicates how significant the process was in effecting essential reconciliations to the new religions.

Still another type of reinterpretation of aboriginal custom in the face of missionary pressure came to take on the institutionalized form of the separatist church. These churches, found in many parts of the Subsaharan continent, were first treated in systematic fashion by Sundkler in 1948, when he described and analyzed their numerous manifestations in South Africa. In a "synoptic chart of African heritage in Zulu Zionist churches," for example, he showed how the tradition of ancestor worship continued in the face of European skepticism and the "sweeping condemnation of ancestor cult, because involving sacrifices and divination," with the "ancestral spirit" being reinterpreted as "holy spirit" or "angel." He showed how in the Roman and Anglo-Catholic mission churches the concept became an integral part of the belief in saints, while the Protestants laid emphasis "on the High-God uNkulunkulu, in place of the Ancient Spirits." [9]

One aspect of the proselytizing movement that becomes clear when seen as part of the total range of culture contact in Africa, is that the drive toward political and economic self-determination also manifested itself in the religious sphere. The long history of Islam in Africa demonstrated the capacity of Africans to accept, absorb, and ingest ideas and concepts brought to them, without yielding established beliefs held to be critical for the adjustment of men to the Universe. It became clear that Christianity in Africa was being accommodated to African ways

[8] Donald C. Niles: "Fetish Burning in the Kwango Area," *Congo Mission News*, No. 169 (1955), *passim*.

[9] Bengt G. M. Sundkler: *Bantu Prophets in South Africa* (London, 1948), pp. 262–3.

of life through similar processes. The Catholic Church came to understand this, and by bringing increasing numbers of Africans into the priesthood and the hierarchy, looked toward continuing control, and expansion of the community of believers. The Protestant sects, with their traditions of individualism, varied in their acceptance of this new horizon, but were generally more reluctant to place authority in African hands. Yet in a study of the Protestant Christian ministry in Africa, made in the years 1953–7, the problem was given full weight. This study, defining Christian theology as, "an ever-renewed re-interpretation to new generations and peoples of a given Gospel, a re-presentation of the will and the way of the one Christ in a dialogue with new thought-forms and culture patterns," made the point that, "theology in Africa has to interpret this Christ in terms that are relevant and essential to African existence."[1]

Through their separatist churches, through individual re-interpretation of the newer faith in terms of traditional beliefs, through greater control of mission activities, however, the Africans continued their adaptation to this process of cultural change. A greater familiarity with the European and his religion, and greater knowledge of accepted modes of behavior in terms of the new demands upon him, brought the African to the point of making explicit his reservations and his desires. At the Protestant All-African Conference, held in Ibadan, Nigeria, in 1958, the Chairman of the Church Council of Nigeria, Sir Francis Ibiam, in another context, put the position succinctly: "If you Europeans try to keep us out of your churches, we shall fight to get in—but when we have won the battle, do not expect to find us there."[2]

[1] Bengt G. M. Sundkler: *The Christian Ministry in Africa,* Studia Missionalia Upsaliensia II (Uppsala, 1960), p. 281.

[2] Anon.: "Prayer and Politics," *West Africa,* No. 2128, January 25, 1958, p. 75.

8

The School

The drive of the Africans for literacy and schooling was a response to two aspects of European penetration. In its earlier phase, Africans related the new power over them to the ability of Europeans to communicate in writing, and to the technological controls associated with this ability. Later, as European ways became better known, literacy and, in a broader sense, higher education opened vistas of attainable goals in the mastery of European skills and higher standards of living. It became increasingly clear that these advantages were available only to those who held the key of education to the door of this treasure trove. The resultant pressure for schools at all levels was so strong as to be a major political and budgetary factor in shaping policy, to say nothing of its broader influence in changing African everyday life.

Since all factors which bear on African acculturation must be examined in treating any phase of it, we may begin by examining non-European influences on education. The Indian contribution was negligible. Indian children learned their parental languages at home, but Africans were neither exposed to these Indian languages nor, in any formal sense, to the associated modes of life.

In the Indian schools of eastern and southern Africa, indeed, teaching was carried on in English.

Islamic influence on African education was exerted mainly through the Koranic schools. In these, however, the teaching of writing tended to be directed toward training religious practitioners. Such reading as was included in the general curriculum was confined to sacred texts, more often than not recited by rote. This does not mean that Moslem education did not reach high levels in Subsaharan Africa. During the Middle Ages, the universities south of the desert, such as Timbuktu, attained renown, and Islamic scholars of wide reputation continued to be developed in this area. Yet the impact of the Koranic schools on the total population, even in Islamized Africa, was relatively limited. In French West Africa, "the mere functioning of the French educational system alongside the Koranic school . . . revealed to the . . . Muslims the anachronistic character of the latter and . . . also caused it to decline in both popularity and quality." [1]

With respect to British Central Africa, the matter has been put in this perspective:

> . . . before the Turkish and Egyptian Revolutions, Islam had not fused itself with the economic spirit and technology of the West. . . . Western culture had obviously much more to offer in the way of technical improvements and creature comforts than the traditional ways of life of the Mohammedan countries, however attractive in other respects their religion might seem to Africans.[2]

Arabic thought, which made such impressive contributions during medieval times, remained outside the later stream.

Elsewhere in Subsaharan Africa, where Koranic schools had long existed, just as in French territory, the advantages of competence in the European world languages came increasingly to be desired. Pressures grew stronger for places in schools offering European-oriented education. Thus, despite the fact that in the

[1] Virginia Thompson and Richard Adloff: *French West Africa* (London, 1958), p. 530.

[2] George Shepperson and Thomas Price: *Independent African: John Chilembwe and the Origins, Setting and Significance of the Nyasaland Native Rising of 1915* (Edinburgh, 1958), pp. 183–4.

field of religion Islam proved its ability to withstand Christian proselytizing efforts, and the Koranic schools persisted in the face of mission teaching, the introduction of secular European education exerted a profound influence on African attitudes and aspirations in a world of change. The continuing increase in the number of pupils of both sexes in European schools testified to their effectiveness in satisfying a need.

In drawing the distinction between European and non-European influences on African schooling, and in emphasizing the European contribution as the more significant, we must recognize the differences in approach within the European component, particularly as these differences reflected policies of the colonial governments. The educational systems established in Subsaharan Africa, before developing African nationalisms forced fundamental revision of colonial policies, could perhaps be characterized as paralleling in approach the policies of the metropolitan powers to the broader field of administration in their overseas territories.

British colonial policy was one of "elasticity." It was described by Lord Hailey as being "based on the principle that the maximum of initiative and responsibility should rest with the colonial administration."[3] The educational arrangements, according to him, were characterized by the same "lack of system," partly because of

> the predominance acquired at an early period by missionary activity in education, but in part also . . . to the projection into the Colonial field of the traditional disinclination of the British to subject education or any other intellectual movement to State control.[4]

This "elasticity" meant differences in handling the problems of African schooling in British West and East and Central Africa, whether in degree of access to higher education, in curriculum, or in type of training.

For the French, with their policy of "assimilationism," it was

[3] Lord Malcolm Hailey: "British Colonial Policy," in *Colonial Administration by European Powers* (London, 1947), p. 92.

[4] Ibid., p. 122.

logical that schooling be an instrument for making Frenchmen of an African élite. How close the association of educational and political policy was conceived to be was made explicit in a 1930 statement of Governor-General Brévié, where the results of schooling to that date were held to be "living and lasting achievements," representing

> the ever more certain and more closely attainable evolution of a native educated class whose quality will rise as the process of selection becomes more severe; . . . and the establishment, as circumstances offer, of a native élite, of whose zeal for a thorough and exclusively French culture signs are already visible.[5]

Belgian "paternalism"—its *politique d'évolution*—laid stress on the practical, and paid little attention to studies not directed toward craft proficiency and economic need. The paucity of schooling for Africans in Portuguese territory and the "pseudo-assimilationist" policy of Portugal, which allowed a token number of African *assimilados* to qualify for schooling beyond the elementary level, reflected both the high rate of illiteracy in Portugal itself, and the official slogan of non-racialism.

Beneath these surface differences, however, this phase of the African acculturative movement had certain features in common. One was the steadily growing desire for schooling everywhere. Another arose from the fact that schooling was of necessity concerned with matters outside the scope of the native cultures, which meant that extensive adjustment had to be made not only by the African child in school, but also in his later life. More particularly, and less ordinarily taken into account, was another factor, whereby these extraneous, non-African elements gave rise to judgments of value in comparing indigenous and introduced cultures which became determinants of later policy. This process of cultural evaluation made it easy to confuse intelligence with proficiency in handling European culture, and raised the question of whether an African or European tongue should be the language

[5] W. Bryant Mumford and G. St. J. Orde Browne: *Africans Learn to be French, a Review of Educational Activities in the Seven Federated Colonies of French West Africa . . . in 1935* (London, n.d.), p. 89.

of primary instruction. All these, however, were but aspects of the most pervasive factor of all, the tendency to write off aboriginal beliefs, moral codes and other regulatory social devices, along with material culture and native technology, as being of a quality that deserved little or no attention in planning curricula or classroom procedures for African schools.

[2]

That "education" came to be identified with literacy and schooling in the European manner is fundamental to understanding change in Subsaharan Africa. Here the word "education" came to denote processes peculiar to literate societies, following the lead of the earliest European educators, who took it for granted that to "educate" Africans meant just this. In their day, an educational philosophy which held that there might be values in African social life and customs on which a curriculum for Africans might be built did not exist. This point of view died hard. As late as 1953, when it was suggested to a professor of philosophy in an African university college that his syllabus, which was exclusively concerned with Greek, Roman, medieval and later European philosophers, might profitably be widened to include some attention to the world view of the societies from which his African students came, his reaction was firm; there was no profit in anything outside what, for him, were the eternal verities expressed by the philosophers of the tradition to which he was committed.

Africans, during all the centuries that their societies have existed, trained their children in morals as well as in the ways of getting a living; in modes of conduct governing their relations with other members of their communities, as well as in the creative expression of their cultures—graphic and plastic arts, the dance, spoken verse, and narrative—and in the rituals that were designed to maintain in favorable balance the forces of the universe. Often the training consisted of watching a parent, then helping him perform a task until proficiency had been acquired. In other cases, a child sat quietly by, listening to his elders as they told the tales and myths that set forth and explained the workings of the universe, and the system of values by which the people lived.

Indigenous education, however, was by no means confined to these informal techniques. The apprenticeship system was widespread. Its role was vital in facilitating change, as where an automobile mechanic turned out to belong to a family of ironworkers, or a man who carved ivory curios for a tourist market was taught ivory working by his father. The moralizing and explanatory tale continued to be regarded as an educational device. The value as an important pedagogical tool of the evening story-telling sessions was well understood, not only for imparting lore and teaching the art of communication, but for memory training as well. Initiation rites carried a significant educational component. We need only consider the Venda puberty school at the extreme southern part of the continent [6] or the Bemba *chisungu* rite [7] or the formal training given Mende and Vai and Gola boys and girls in Sierra Leone and Liberia in the Poro and Sande initiations,[8] to realize how widely the pattern was spread. Nadel, writing of the Nupe, in the opening paragraph of a chapter entitled "Education for Citizenship" groups together the "formalized educational institutions" this people had—"the institution of the Koran school, . . . and the institution of age-grade associations." [9]

What the European brought to the African was *schooling* which, however important it may be, constitutes but a portion of the total process of social and cultural learning. The schooling brought to the African, moreover, was European schooling, with curricula and objectives that, drawn from the background of the Metropole, incorporated curricula and aimed at objectives which were oriented toward the experiences of children there. When

[6] H. A. Stayt: *The Bavenda* (London, 1931), pp. 10 ff.

[7] Audrey I. Richards: *Chisungu, a Girl's Initiation Ceremony among the Bemba of Northern Rhodesia* (London, 1956), pp. 125–32.

[8] M. H. Watkins: "The West African 'Bush' School," *American Journal of Sociology*, Vol. 48 (1943), *passim;* Kenneth Little: *The Mende of Sierra Leone* (London, 1951), pp. 120–2, 126–8.

[9] S. F. Nadel: *A Black Byzantium, the Kingdom of Nupe in Nigeria* (London, 1942), p. 378.

transplanted to Africa, they set up far-reaching discontinuities between the school and the rest of the African child's social and cultural environment. This, perhaps, more than anything else, accounted for the stress on rote memory which came to characterize the schooling of Africans, and which gave rise to the charge that Africans were unable to do creative or critical thinking. In terms of the transfer of culture, however, it is self-evident that the schooling of Africans under these conditions could be no more than exercise at memorizing facts.

Nonetheless, the schooling that came to the Africans, despite its built-in discontinuities—or perhaps because of them—was destined to provide resources far greater than anything that was foreseen when the system was instituted. If the school imposed psychological hardships on the African child, and exposed him to cultural stresses, it also prepared him effectively to meet on its own terms the world that was advancing into his native land. It gave him a discipline, beginning with the insistence that he command a language vastly different in its organization and symbolisms from his own, which enabled some to move, often with distinction, to the highest levels of the European academic system. And in time, as Africans began to search for and re-examine the values in their own cultures, their schooling enabled them to weigh the elements derived from both the worlds in which they had been trained.

From the point of view of the science of man, this underscores the fact that culture is acquired. It testifies to the fact that acculturative learning can be achieved under forced draught as well as by the slower customary give-and-take of cultures in contact. Above all, it gives pause to the fallacious reading of the scientific principle that educational continuity is a means to achieve cultural adjustment, a reading used to implement the policy of *apartheid* in South Africa through the Bantu Education Act. While correctly stressing the relation between experience and adjustment, this misreading introduced a mystical and rationalized combination of racism and culturism which ignored the supremely important fact that the clock of cultural change cannot be turned backward. Acculturation, once achieved, makes impossible the return to a prior mode of life, no matter how glowingly envisioned under social deprivation.

[3]

The identification of education with literacy goes to the beginnings of European schooling in Africa. In part, it arose out of the stress laid by the missionaries on the teaching of reading and writing.[1] The Africans also soon observed that in the African setting the Europeans, who could read and write, did no manual labor, but enjoyed higher status and remuneration than the Africans who could not. The obvious conclusion was that literacy was a prime factor in permitting a man to become the manager, the supervisor over those who did not know how to read and write. Moreover since many African societies are characterized by class structures based on age, or descent, or control of supernatural power, a ready mechanism was at hand for the reinterpretation of customary patterns to allow for social stratification on the basis of literacy.

In a letter written in 1952, an African teacher in Nigeria showed how the desire for literacy, as a symbol of status, dominated the thinking of the villagers who lived near the boarding school in which he was teaching:

> I am giving my spare time helping in the Adult classes in the village. Our big disease is the wrong conception of "education" which to our people is the ability only to read and write. People in this area as in most of Africa are underfed, diseased (hook-worm), [live under] unsanitary conditions (etc.). We have organized a small team of students . . . to help in showing the villagers to dig cess-pits so that they can stop going to the bushes, to stop erosion by planting trees and grasses, and [by giving] simple hygiene lessons . . . ; but strangely enough their one big desire is to read and write.

Since literacy was at first regarded as the high road to satisfying many hopes and aspirations, the discovery that it was but a

[1] *Supra*, pp. 205–6.

first step in a long process frequently brought disillusionment. Experience gradually corrected this misconception, as Africans increasingly achieved competence in trades and commerce, proficiency in the law or in administration, or attained the background needed to enter on a university career. "If we establish a technical school"—that is, a trade school—"with a capacity of two hundred students," said a high official in the Belgian Congo in 1953, "five hundred present themselves on the opening day." [2] Here, as in other parts of Africa, the realization grew that training as masons, carpenters, blacksmiths, shoemakers, tailors, and mechanics could also bring advantages in a changing world. This gradually broadened the base of an educational system too exclusively intent on literacy alone.

Until after the First World War, those concerned with African schooling seem to have sensed no need to take the cultural background of their pupils into account. The Africans, it was felt, had everything to learn, and nothing to teach, either to their own children or to the rest of the world. The prevalent point of view exemplified, in almost classical form, the conception of the African as envisaged in the nineteenth-century theory of social evolution: a straggler in the march of mankind toward civilization, whose progress was to be shaped by those who brought to him the benefits of a higher order.

An example of this is provided by the study of African education made in 1920 and 1921 by a Commission sent to Africa by the Phelps-Strokes Fund. The Commission included in its membership J. E. K. Aggrey, the African who played so important a role in founding Achimota College in the former Gold Coast, a fact of some significance as showing the degree to which the dominant point of view had come to be accepted by leading Africans of that time. The report of this Commission was widely discussed, and deeply influenced the policy of the American missions, which from the early days were active in establishing and maintaining schools in the Subsaharan continent. In the opening chapter we read,

[2] Melville J. Herskovits: *Notes on African Field Research,* p. 53/D328.

> The present distribution of the African groups through the various stages of human society, whether that stage be cannibalistic, barbaric, primitive, or civilized, is a natural condition that has been almost completely duplicated at some time with all civilized races. In the long process of evolution, it is well known that the civilization period of the most advanced races has been but brief in comparison with their long period of barbarism.

Africans, however, were not to be thought of as incapable of advancing to a higher stage: "The improvability of the African people is clearly shown by their response to the efforts of missions, governments, and commercial organizations."

Many Africans, and the descendants of Africans in the New World, the report noted, had become entirely "civilized"—that is, had accommodated themselves to European and American culture.

> Nor are the possibilities of the Africans to be judged only by the progress of those who have entered the ranks of civilization. . . . An adequate study of the tribal customs and capacities of those who are still in barbaric and primitive stages will more and more reveal the fact that the present condition of the masses of the African people is normal and comparable with other peoples at the same stage of development.

Arts and crafts were reported to be "substantial evidences of their capacity to respond to the wise approaches of civilization so that they may share in the development of the African continent. . . . There was evidence of considerable knowledge of agriculture, and, even though the results were often crude, they were definite indications of Native powers." [3]

Another work written a few years later also exerted considerable influence on African educational practice in British dependencies:

> A fact of primary importance in African education is that outside Egypt there is nowhere any indigenous history. . . . This . . . has had two effects. It has prevented the growth of a self-conscious culture, and it has lowered the status of the African in the eyes of the outside world.[4]

[3] Thomas Jesse Jones: *Education in Africa* (New York, 1922), pp. 5–7.
[4] A. Victor Murray: *The School in the Bush* (London, 1929), p. 19.

The argument here is of special interest because of the way it equates history with the presence of written records, and because of the circular reasoning it employs in ascribing European attitudes toward the Africans to this fact, rather than to the reiterated emphasis on the presumed lack of an African history as evidence of African "backwardness."

> There is no "African culture,"—as yet. There is this universal heritage waiting to be taken up by them. . . . For while the African has no history in the sense which I have held to be necessary for culture, no recorded stages of development through which we can see some mental quality persisting, he has at any rate before him history in the making.

Unfortunately, we are told, the picture of European civilization presented to the African, "in the person of the trader, the labour recruiter, the Government demand for taxes, missionaries of every sort of view, and administrators of every sort of policy" could not but bewilder him as he participated in the changing scene. Thus we come to what is stated to be "the real function of the school, . . . the rationale of African education." This is to "present this alien civilization *as it really is*."[5]

The point of view expressed in this work dominated the thinking and the orientation of policy everywhere in Africa. Ryckmans, writing at the time he became Governor-General of the Congo, summarized the reasoning underlying the Belgian *politique d'évolution:*

> The role of the colonizing power in an African country is not only to establish the reign of peace, order and justice—the essential task of every government—but it is in addition and above all to substitute for the indigenous conceptions of order and justice new conceptions that conform to an ideal of civilization that is foreign to them.

This was a policy of manipulation ". . . to promote the progress of the indigenous societies in accordance with their own nature, by avoiding the obstacles that intervene in stimulating the factors that are favorable."[6]

[5] Ibid., pp. 323–5.
[6] Pierre Ryckmans: *La Politique Coloniale* (Brussels, 1934), p. 37.

In practice, little attention was given to the African experience of the student. To such an extent was the curriculum of the Metropole imposed on the African pupil that the authors of the 1954 Memorandum on the reform of education in the Congo, in connection with a discussion of the "delicate problem" of whether Greek as well as Latin should be taught in secondary schools for Africans, were moved to comment:

> For our part, we will always prefer to see Congolese pedagogy inspired by real Congolese requirements—to which the majority of those who use it must respond—rather than to have it follow blindly an outmoded formalism after Belgian practice, already subjected to severe criticism in the metropole. If one day there is to be an effective system in the Congo, it must be specific, and abandon the idea of establishing—and eventually ending with—a regime which will be the equivalent of that in Belgium.[7]

Reservations to the convention of ignoring African culture in the curricula of schools for Africans, however, began to be heard. As early as 1925, an Advisory Committee on Native Education in the British Tropical African Dependencies, reporting to the Secretary of State for the Colonies, laid down this proposition:

> Education should be adapted to the mentality, aptitudes, occupations and traditions of the various peoples, conserving as far as possible all sound and healthy elements in the fabric of their social life; adapting them where necessary to changed circumstances and progressive ideas, as an agent of natural growth and evolution.[8]

There is no record that this suggestion was put into effect; on the contrary, the conventional position continued to hold sway. As a leading authority on African education, commenting on the sentence just quoted, observed twenty-five years later:

> These principles have as it were remained on the statute books. Remarkably few teachers in Africa, whether European or African,

[7] Congo Belge, Ministère des Colonies: *La Réforme de l'Enseignement au Congo Belge, Mission Pédagogique Coulon-Deheyn-Renson,* Conseil Supérieur de l'Enseignement, Publication No. 1 (Brussels, 1954), p. 95.

[8] Great Britain, Colonial Office: *Education Policy in British Tropical Africa,* report of Advisory Committee on Native Education in British Tropical Africa Dependencies, Cmd. 2374 (London, 1925), p. 4.

have ever heard of them. A quarter of a century after these principles were laid down, it was still possible for the editorial in *Overseas Education* . . . to answer the question "What are the best elements in African culture?" as though all that was needed was an ethical and intellectual sieve applied to the elements of African cultural tradition. It is impossible to escape from the conclusion that the authors of the 1925 memorandum believed also that some kind of sifting process could take place, and . . . all that was "best" would come through the sieve and be used in the schools, and that what was "defective" and did not get through could be conveniently and quietly thrown away.[9]

[4]

After the Second World War, and especially with the growing emphasis by Africans on the values in African culture, the position concerning the objectives of schooling began to change. In 1953, a West African teacher of long experience put his newer point of view in these terms:

> The goal at which we teachers in Africa must aim is a better and still better generation of Africans, efficient in the discharge of their professional, social, civic, religious and domestic duties, getting the most out of life, while putting the most possible into it. The teacher must lead the child to drink deep out of the fountain of Western knowledge and culture, while learning the history, customs and traditions of his own country and doing his best to preserve all that is good and of value in them.[1]

In the Congo, also, a certain recognition had developed that in some aspects of African education indigenous ways could no longer be overlooked. In the *Report* already referred to, though the curricular principles recommended were in the main in accordance with the conventions of the Belgian system, the need to shape instruction to African patterns also entered. In the section

[9] Margaret Read: *Education and Cultural Tradition,* University of London, Institute of Education, Studies in Education, No. 2 (London, 1950), p. 9.

[1] S. A. Banjo: *A West African Teacher's Handbook* (London, 1953), p. 13.

in which the schools that prepare artisans to work in the villages (*écoles artisanales*) were discussed, we read:

> Why train bricklayers when the village has only mud huts, why train auto mechanics when there are no trucks, why train wood-workers to use power machines when the village does not yet have electric current, why train printers and artistic book-binders when the villagers do not yet know how to read? [2]

The questions asked in this passage could also be raised elsewhere. Thus in a school in Tamale, in the Northern Territories of the then Gold Coast, in 1953, one could observe teachers who were training for work in village schools learning to operate the European-style wide loom, or to make pots using a complex electrically-driven potter's wheel, despite the fact that the highly developed weaving techniques of the people they would presumably teach employed the West African narrow loom, and that they make quite satisfactory pots by hand.[3] Several years later, at Bamako, in the French Sudan, Bambara boys in the *Artisanat* could be found learning all manner of trades—carpentry, gold-working, leather-working—taught them with minimal regard for the conditions of village life.[4] The authors of the Belgian *Report*, with this point in mind, urged that the teaching of art to Africans should be based on the rich artistic tradition of the Congo. Thus they noted with approval, the "real obsession with aboriginal inspiration and a phobia against European counterfeiting" which guided the teaching of art to Africans by some of the pioneers in this field.

Recognition of the need to adapt European schooling to the facts of African life, and to draw on the values of that life in shaping curricula for Africans, arose from several sources. In part, it came as a result of recognition by Africans themselves of the cultural factor in the adjustment of children to a changing situation, and of the many elements in their own cultures which, particularly in the early years of schooling, could be profitably used in

[2] Ibid., p. 121.
[3] Melville J. Herskovits: op. cit., p. 53/D158.
[4] Ibid., p. 57/D73.

achieving this end. And since Africans had risen to high administrative and policy-making levels in the school systems, especially in French and British West Africa, they were in positions to make their opinions heard and taken as the basis for action.

To European teachers and educational administrators, the growing number of scientific studies of African cultures brought a realization that these were ways of life with values to be respected. In addition, developments in the field of educational psychology that stressed relating schooling to total experience were an effective factor in altering approaches to African education. Experience, moreover, demonstrated that it meant little to African children to learn, for example, the names of the counties of England, or to read books that taught them about, "Our ancestors, the Gauls, who were tall, blue-eyed people with golden hair." In 1953, a normal school instructor in a French territory who prepared prospective teachers to pass the same examinations set for students in France, commented that she was uncertain of the educational value of teaching African students the full details and techniques of the French Revolution.

There were two exceptions to the general mid-century trend in the school curricula of Subsaharan Africa. One of these was the Portuguese educational pattern; the other, the one developed in South Africa.

As we have seen, all Subsaharan school systems were to some extent based on general government policies, and were used directly or indirectly to implement long-term political decisions. The controls, however, were relatively light, with a kind of implicit, though unambiguous agreement between administrators and educators on the ends of colonial policy, rather than active imposition of governmental aims on the schools. In the Portuguese African territories, however, and in South Africa, the implementation of political objectives through the manipulation of the curriculum and the strict control of classroom procedure and extracurricular activities was explicit, and achieved through a close integration of the schools with the machinery of government.

Other characteristics set off the educational operations of the

Portuguese and South African regimes from those elsewhere in Africa. In neither were Africans permitted any voice in the determination of educational policy or in its direction. This arose logically from the conception held by Portuguese and South Africans as to the nature of African culture, and of the role of Europeans in relation to it. In this too familiar view, African cultures were considered to lie on so low a level of development that the direction of affairs would be safe only in European hands.

Beyond these similarities in approach, agreement between the two policies ended. Portuguese professed policy was the scientifically unrealistic one of the eventual absorption of the Africans into the Portuguese way of life. In South Africa the policy was not only scientifically unrealistic but historically regressive in the sense that the Africans, the "Bantu" of the official documents, were to be forced back to their aboriginal ways. Once there, they were to be set on a new path of separate development, with a rigidly limited access to European ways of life, much less to European ideas, and more to continue under essential European control.

Portuguese educational policy, as a means to furthering political aims, was expressed consistently and clearly. In 1921, a Governor-General of Angola published a decree ordering that a mission must have his formal consent before establishing a school, and that, to obtain this, it must ". . . submit for the approval of the Governor-General the civilizing program which it proposes to institute; . . . teach in the Portuguese language; . . . not teach in any foreign tongue," so that, "the native languages should rapidly disappear from the Portuguese provinces of Africa." [5] More than two decades later, a work by an official in Mozambique, who wrote at a time when the bases of African education were coming under re-examination elsewhere, stated Portuguese educational aims as follows:

> . . . Our mission as concerns the native populations is one of civilizing and nationalizing. We have not sailed the seas, nor established our sovereignty in distant lands for dishonest gain, or for

[5] J. M. R. Norton de Matos: *África Nossa, o que queremos e o que não queremos nas nossas terras de África* (Lisbon, 1953), pp. 95–6.

material ends. We have come to the natives to make Portuguese out of them. . . . We have a life which is the emanation of a spirit and the realization of a faith, to give to the peoples whom we wish to bring along with us.[6]

The logic of this philosophy makes it understandable why all teaching had to be in Portuguese, and the textbooks used in the African schools were those written for the children of Portugal. Because of the doctrine that African culture makes for undisciplined habits of work, and that the civilizing mission of Portugal was to inculcate application, regularity and reliability, much of the curriculum was pointed to these ends. The introduction of a special curriculum of "rudimentary" education for African children was in line with these conceptions. Its execution was entrusted to the Catholic Missions, since it was "understood that by moral uplift"—another basic Portuguese objective for African schooling—"is meant the abandonment of indolence and the preparation of future rural and industrial workers who produce enough to meet their own necessities and fulfil their social obligations," as the *Estatuto Missionário* of 1941 put it.[7]

The school program of the Portuguese for Africans showed no great effectiveness. With the high rate of illiteracy in Portugal itself, neither in Lisbon nor in the African territories could administrators view African desire for schooling without distrust. This attitude is reflected in the facts. Thus in Angola, in 1950–1,

There were 13,586 pupils in primary schools, 2,277 in secondary, 1,548 in technical, and 154 in normal schools, not a very noteworthy achievement for an Administration which has in its charge a population of over 4 million people.[8]

In South Africa, on the contrary, the numbers of Africans to whom schooling was accessible, on all levels, and who attended these schools, was large. Official statements invariably stressed

[6] V. M. Braga Paixão: *Educação Política e Política da Educação, Três Anos em Moçambique* (Lisbon, 1948), pp. 104–5.

[7] Quoted in Marvin Harris: *Portugal's African "Wards,"* Africa Today Pamphlets: 2 (New York, 1958), p. 15.

[8] Lord Malcolm Hailey: *An African Survey, Revised 1956* (London, 1957), p. 1216.

that South Africa, over the years, had spent larger sums *per capita* for African education than any other country in Africa. The history of schooling for Africans there goes back to the early days of the Christian missions, and until the coming of the Nationalist Party to power in 1948 continued to be carried on in substantial proportion under mission auspices with government subvention. As we have seen, with the emphasis on implementing the policy of separate development (*apartheid*), however, earlier agreements with missions came under review, on the assumption that mission education was not designed to fit in with this doctrine.

An authoritative statement of the South African Government as regards education for Africans was given in 1954 by the then Minister of Native Affairs, in which he presented the rationale for the changes subsequently made in administration and curricula of African schools. His criticisms of the previous system were summarized in two of his three points: "(a) there was no coordination between the interests of the school with those of the community: and (b) there was no coordination between the education given in the schools and broad national policy." From this it followed that "the natural development from mission school to community school could not take place." [9]

By ignoring "the segregation or 'apartheid' policy," he continued,

> the curriculum (to a certain extent) and educational practice . . . was unable to prepare for service within the Bantu community. By blindly producing pupils trained on a European model, the vain hope was created among Natives that they could occupy posts within the European community despite the country's policy of "apartheid." This is what is meant by the creation of unhealthy "White collar ideals" and the causation of widespread frustration among the so-called educated Natives.[1]

Changes to correct these defects in the system would be instituted under the strictest supervision,

[9] H. F. Verwoerd: *Bantu Education, Policy for the Immediate Future* (Pretoria, 1954), p. 5.

[1] Ibid., p. 7.

> to ensure that Union regulations are fully complied with and that departures from them do not take place as in the past. The curriculum, therefore, envisages a system of education which is based on the circumstances of the community and aims to satisfy the needs of that community. The vehicle of instruction will be the mother tongue of the pupil.[2]

However, since

> the economic structure of our country results in large numbers of Natives having to earn their living in the service of Europeans . . . it is essential that Bantu pupils should receive instruction in both official languages from the earliest stages, so that even in the lower primary school they should develop an ability to speak and understand them.[3]

Implementation of the Bantu Education Act followed soon on its passage. Schools for Africans were taken out of the hands of Provincial Departments of Education and placed first under the national Department of Native Affairs, and later under a separate Ministry of Native Education. Greater stress was laid on training for manual labor, and the use of African languages and Afrikaans as media of instruction extended. These changes, Africans asserted, would materially handicap African students who wished to go on to a university, to which the reply was made that a number of tribal institutions of higher learning—Zulu, Xhosa, and Sotho—would be made available to Africans, a project that was in full operation by 1960. The entire plan was marked by consistent adherence to the philosophy of *apartheid.* The exposure of Africans to another way of life than their own, it was held, had created problems of personal and social adjustment. Education cast in terms of their aboriginal cultures, and a return to tribal patterns, would solve these problems, so that in areas specially reserved for them they could develop along their own lines, under European supervision, until they reached some remote future point when they could function without direction from outside.

[2] Ibid., p. 17. [3] Ibid., p. 18.

[5]

Official statistics tell a graphic tale of the response of Africans to opportunities for schooling. A sampling of figures from the Subsaharan continent may be called on to illustrate the rapidity of the process, though as with other statistical data, their level of accuracy is not high.

For the parts of West Africa then controlled by France, the report to the United Nations transmitted in 1949 by the French Government stated that 5% of the children attended school in 1948, not counting those in "the numerous Koranic schools and schools of nomadic tribes, the catechism centres of various missions, schools opened by chiefs, courses for adults, or courses in handicrafts." In 1947, children in primary schools had numbered 105,607; there were 112,000 in 1948.[4] A 1957 summary of information, however, gave a revised figure for primary school attendance for 1948 of 65,904 pupils, 41,220 boys and 24,684 girls, in public and privately controlled European type schools in the primary and secondary grades, and in teacher training. Taking the lower, revised 1948 figures as a base, we find that four years later the number of boys had more than tripled, that of girls almost doubled, the figures being 158,246 and 41,296 respectively, for a total of 199,542—a substantial increase even if the larger estimate given earlier is taken as a point of reference. In 1953, the number of boys had grown to 199,007, of girls to 53,942, for a total of 252,949; 1954 found 251,643 boys and 63,632 girls in school. This is more than five times the smaller figure of six years before, or about two and one-half times the larger earlier estimate.[5]

In Liberia, in 1958, it was estimated that there were "approximately 55,000 attending elementary classes . . . and about 2,500 students in the high schools." If the total population is

[4] United Nations: *Non-Self-Governing Territories* (Summaries and analyses of information transmitted to the Secretary-General during 1949), Vol. II (New York, 1950), p. 86.

[5] United Nations: *Non-Self-Governing Territories* (Summaries of information submitted to the Secretary-General during 1955), ST/TRI/SER. A/12 (New York, 1957), p. 218.

generously estimated at two million, this meant about 400,000 children to be educated; [6] at a perhaps more realistic estimate of about one million, the same proportion of children would be about 200,000. Under the larger estimate, 12 to 15 percent of eligible children were in school, or 24 to 30 percent for the smaller figure. The number of primary schools in Ghana rose from 1,083 in 1951 to 3,402 in 1958.[7] For Nigeria, a fairly long series of statistics for pupils in primary, secondary and teacher-training schools documents in depth the growth of schooling in that country during the years indicated: [8]

1926:	144,577
1937:	244,304
1947:	667,250
1949:	959,552
1951:	1,005,900
1953:	1,244,350
1957:	2,525,628

Equatorial Africa also showed a rapid growth in its program of schooling. Here "the percentage enrollment rose from 2.5% in 1945 to 17.75% in 1952, 18.6% in 1953 and 19.57% in 1954." The difference between the constituent territories, however, was striking—3.2% in Chad, 19.05% in Ubangi-Shari, 49.2% in Gabon, and 55.8% in Middle Congo. In terms of absolute numbers, not including enrollment in vocational schools, attendance in 1948 was given as 47,824; in 1952, 110,516; in 1953, 124,666; and in 1954, 131,734. Growth was steady in the Belgian Congo. It was estimated that in 1949 about one-third of the African population was

[6] James Johnson: "Education in Liberia: I," *West Africa,* No. 2153 (July 19, 1958), p. 681.

[7] Anonymous: "Overseas Scholars," *Ghana Today,* Vol. 2, No. 8 (1958), p. 1.

[8] United Nations: *Non-Self-Governing Territories* (Summaries and analyses of information transmitted to the Secretary-General during 1949) (New York, 1950), p. 316; *Non-Self-Governing Territories* (Summaries of information submitted to the Secretary-General during 1955), ST/TRI/SER. A/12 (New York, 1957), p. 251; *Progress of the Non-Self-Governing Territories under the Charter* (Territorial Surveys), No. ST/TRI/SER. A/15/ Vol. 5 (1960), p. 197.

able to read, and that the number of children enrolled in schools was "somewhat higher than 50% of the population of school age, . . . calculated to be 1,850,000." In 1946 a total of 913,100 children were in primary schools, in 1947, 930,170.[9] In 1952, this had increased to 984,438; the following year it crossed the one million mark; for 1954, it was given as 1,112,562; and for 1957, as 1,584,255.[1]

The slight amount of schooling provided by the Portuguese for the African population in Angola has already been indicated;[2] the results to 1950 were summarized as follows: "Unofficial estimates place literacy at 85% for the European population but at less than 5% for the African population."[3] More specifically, a Portuguese student informs us that in this same year "only 1% of the male population" of the Mozambique district of Sul do Save "was able to speak Portuguese and only 1% of these Portuguese speakers was able to read and write it. These figures drop to 0.1% for the women."[4] The statistics for Mozambique, taken from the Hailey *Report*, are also relevant:

> In 1952 there were 16 State primary schools, having an attendance of 6,669 pupils, one secondary and ten technical schools. The missions maintained about 1,000 primary schools in which about 150,000 Africans are educated, 44 technical schools, and three teacher-training institutions. . . . The Salazar *Liceu* was opened in 1919 with 44 students, a number which increased by 1953 to 941. But in this, as in other high schools, the number of Africans is

[9] United Nations: *Non-Self-Governing Territories* (Summaries and analyses of information transmitted to the Secretary-General during 1949, New York, 1950), p. 26.

[1] United Nations: *Non-Self-Governing Territories* (Summaries of information submitted to the Secretary-General during 1955), ST/TRI/SER. A/12 (New York, 1957), p. 65; *Progress of the Non-Self-Governing Territories under the Charter* (Territorial Surveys), No. ST/TRI/SER. A/15/ Vol. 5 (1960), p. 18.

[2] *Supra*, p. 233.

[3] United States Department of Commerce: "Angola (Portuguese West Africa)—Summary of Basic Economic Information," *International Reference Service*, Vol. 17, No. 129 (December, 1950), p. 2.

[4] Manoel Simões Alberto: "Populações nativas do Sul do Save, distrito de Lourenço Marques. I. Os Ronga do Maputo," abstracted in *African Abstracts*, Vol. 10, No. 420 (July, 1959), p. 134.

negligible owing to the age limit of entry being set at 13, when the African has not yet completed his elementary education.[5]

That the educational achievement in western and central Africa was sustained is apparent when the rate of increases in fifteen countries—excluding only those under Portuguese and Spanish control–in enrollments in primary and secondary school in the years 1955 to 1959, is considered. These range from 5.4% (for Ghana) to 119.6% (for the Ivory Coast) as regards primary education, and from 1.5% (for Gambia) and 2.2% (for Sierra Leone) to 141.2% (for Nigeria). These are the extremes of the distribution. Between these extremes, ten countries show increases of between 20% and 40% for their primary school enrollments, and for secondary education, eight show increases of from 30% to 60%.[6]

The presence of a substantial European population appreciably influenced educational policy. This was particularly true in Kenya or the Federation of Rhodesia and Nyasaland; it was somewhat less a factor in Ruanda-Urundi, with its relatively small European and Indian permanent population; South Africa, as we have seen, presented a special case. We may approach the question of access to educational facilities and the numbers of Africans who have benefited from their use by taking this as an index of the educational effort for Africans in the eastern and southern parts of the continent.

As has been pointed out in considering the aboriginal cultural base, the gap between African and European economies was greater in the eastern and southern parts of the Subsaharan continent than in the western. European schooling, therefore, was a concept more readily understood in the sedentary agricultural societies of the west than by the herding peoples of the eastern and southern regions. However, as in the case of economic change, this does not imply that the herding peoples were in-

[5] Lord Malcolm Hailey: *An African Survey, Revised 1956*, p. 1216.

[6] United Nations Educational, Social and Cultural Organization (UNESCO): *Report on the Needs of Tropical Africa in the Matter of Primary, General Secondary and Technical Education* (General Conference, 11th Session), No. 11/C/PRG/1, Annex I (1960), p. 4.

herently less able to participate in the experience of formal schooling. Once convinced that literacy and schooling were desirable, they sought these benefits as did their fellow Africans in other parts of the continent. A typical herding society, the Swazi, despite the usual reluctance of cattle-keeping peoples to fence in their grazing land, came to the conclusion that they must put up fences so that more herd-boys could be freed for school attendance.

In eastern and southern Africa, the permanent European residents did not have to adjust their educational patterns. These they established in the lands where they settled after the manner of immigrant European groups elsewhere. With schooling high on the list of their values, it seemed obvious that the education of their children should be a charge on the resources of the country where they came to live. In outlining plans for education in Kenya, for example, their point of view is clearly put: "Very roughly, the European educational problem is one of maintaining standards, the Asian problem is one of raising standards, and the African problem is one of creating standards and building up a system." [7]

Schooling was nowhere free. One of the most difficult problems in public finance in economically underdeveloped countries arises from the need to provide revenue that will not only pay the recurrent costs of government, but provide capital for long-term projects. European parents paid school fees that were high, even if not as high in proportion to their income as the fees paid by Africans. If we compare this to West Africa, where little or no part of revenue had to be allocated to schools for Europeans, we find that there were many more Africans at any given period in all categories of schools than in East and Central Africa. African backwardness in schooling could be ascribed in large measure to the fact that in the countries with appreciable European populations so much of the available revenue went for the support of schools for European children.

We can see how this differential allocation of funds worked

[7] Colony and Protectorate of Kenya: *The Development Programme, 1957/60*, Sessional Paper No. 77 of 1956/57 (Nairobi, 1957), p. 65, par. 230.

out by taking as an example the 1957 educational proposals for Kenya. Plans were projected against the figures for the total population of each of the three groups. In 1956, the year after the end of the decade used as a base, roughly 96% of the 6,144,-600 people in Kenya, or 5,902,000, were Africans, 184,900, or about 3% were Asians (that is, Indians, Arabs and Goans), and 57,700, or something less than 1% were Europeans.[8] In 1946 there were 29 European schools having 3,219 pupils, 90 Asian schools with an enrollment of 17,705, and 2,291 African schools with an attendance of 209,318. These were respectively 12.9%, 15.9% and 4.1% of the total of each racial group at that time. At the end of the decade, in 1955, 57 European schools had 9,045 in attendance, there were 140 institutions for Asians with 38,755 pupils, and 398,398 Africans attended 3,488 schools. All showed an increase in the proportion of the total population they represented, 21.4%, 24.2% and 7.0%, respectively.

Scrutiny of the differences in percentage increases further enlightens us as to the factors in play. For Europeans and Asians these were 8.5% and 8.3%, while for Africans, the increase was 2.9%.[9] In a sense, the differences reflect a change in demographic balance between the racial components. Between 1946 and 1955 the Europeans, through immigration and natural growth, became 110% more numerous, and the Asians, who also added to their numbers by immigrants from abroad, 61%. On the other hand, the African population "by virtue of natural increase of the rate of 1½% per annum" grew about 15% during the decade.[1] Yet this is obviously not the entire explanation, since in proportion to their numbers, many more European and Asian children than African were in school in 1955 than in 1946. Hence even granting that a higher standard of living, better infant care, more adequate medical facilities and better diet of non-Africans would make their

[8] Colony and Protectorate of Kenya: *Report on Asian and European Education in Kenya, 1958* (Nairobi, 1958), p. 1, par. 2.

[9] Colony and Protectorate of Kenya: *The Development Programme, 1957/60*, Sessional Paper No. 77 of 1956/57 (Nairobi, 1957), p. 65, Table 21.

[1] Ibid., p. 13.

school-age potential greater than that of the Africans, this would yield only a partial answer.

For a further explanation of the disproportionate growth in school attendance, we may recall the statement we have quoted which presents the philosophy underlying the approach to the problems of European, Asian, and African education. Thus we learn that while in 1956 education was "compulsory for all European children between the ages of seven and fifteen, and, in the three main towns, for Asian boys of the same age. . . .[2] the general introduction of compulsory education for Africans" was "ruled out as a practical possibility" because of capital needs and recurrent commitments.[3] This meant that governmental sanction confirmed earlier patterns to enforce schooling for European children; for the Asians, partial aid was given, to strengthen a tradition not unfamiliar to them, despite its formal difference from their own. African school attendance, however, was stimulated by no pronounced expansion of governmental facilities to encourage training African children in schools. Given the aboriginal forms of education, the increase in absolute numbers of Africans in school reflected the drive for schooling in the face of strong negative factors.

There is also the factor of opportunity. "In the last resort," it was stated in discussing plans for the development of educational facilities in Kenya, "the total size of the educational programme depends on what the country can afford, not only in respect of the initial cost of building and equipping new schools, but also of subsequently maintaining them."[4] It was estimated that Kenya could afford £2,055,006 annually for education during the quadrennium 1957–60. Of this, about 19%, or £379,100, was to go for European education, some 28%, or £581,831, for that of the "Asians" and "Arabs," and £1,094,075, or about 53%,

[2] United Nations: *Non-Self-Governing Territories* (Summaries of information submitted to the Secretary-General during 1955), ST/TRI/SER. A/12 (New York, 1957), p. 120.

[3] Ibid.

[4] Colony and Protectorate of Kenya: *The Development Programme, 1957/60*, Sessional Paper No. 77 of 1956–57 (Nairobi, 1957), pp. 66–73, pars. 231–55.

for African primary, secondary, teacher training, and trade schooling.[5] We can see in these figures how the European-centered approach to the problem in terms of the need to maintain standards for European children, raise them for Indians, and build up a system for Africans, brought it about that the larger the population group to which a child belonged, the less opportunity there was for him to obtain schooling. That is to say, the European 1% was to receive 19% of the educational budget, the Asian 3% was to have 28%, the African 96% was to be allocated 53%.

Statistics showing similar proportions could be adduced for other parts of eastern and southern Africa. The relatively smaller increase of pupils in primary and secondary schools of territories in this part of the continent, as compared to western Africa, makes the point. Thus, in Northern Rhodesia, for the years 1948 to 1953, African attendance was:

	Primary	*Secondary*
1948	156,427	130
1952	156,164	405
1953	165,324	432
1954	183,627	746

The number of children in schools for "Coloured and Asian" pupils was:

1948	72	–
1952	386	5
1953	483	9

[5] Ibid., pp. 68–72. Reporting to the United Nations, the Kenya Government gave a "breakdown of expenditures according to racial groups for education in 1954 as £2,096,000 for Africans, £762,000 for Europeans, £699,000 for Asians, £73,000 for Arabs, £31,000 for Goans, and £549,000 for mixed races" (United Nations: *Non-Self-Governing Territories* [Summaries of information submitted to the Secretary-General during 1955], ST/TRI/SER. A/12 [New York, 1957], p. 121). No explanation can be given for the disparity between these and the estimated figures for 1957–60, but for the purposes of our analysis this is unimportant, since both sets show about the same proportion of the total budget allocated to the different racial groups.

For Europeans, the figures were:

1948	3,758	337
1952	7,019	1,148
1953	8,004	1,425

As estimated at the end of 1953, the Africans in the population totaled 1,960,000, or 97.3%, Asians and Coloureds 5,000, or about .03%, and Europeans 50,000, or 2.4%. Actual expenditures for European education rose from £144,100 in 1948 to £523,700 in 1952 and £1,108,700 for the period January 1, 1953, to June 30, 1954. For African schooling, the comparable amounts were £338,000 for 1948, £702,600 for 1952 and £1,600,000 for the final eighteen months.[6] Proportionately, slightly under 30% of the total 1948 educational budget was allocated for European schools, rising to about 42% in 1952; in 1953–4, when the Europeans numbered 2.4% of the population, their schools received 41% of the funds available.

[6]

The desire of Africans for schooling followed the curve of growth of other social phenomena. In the earliest days of its introduction it often met with resistances, though these varied in intensity and duration. Because it was associated with the European conquerors, schooling was at times regarded with suspicion, as an instrument to bring about more effective denial of established custom. Often opposition was based on the conviction that schooling was a threat to traditional rights. Nor was this fear allayed when the sons of kings and chiefs, where such rulers existed, were favored in extending opportunities for schooling to Africans. It cannot be denied that the danger sensed by the chiefs was not groundless. The subsequent history of African nationalism demonstrated how strong was the challenge to their prerogatives from educated nationalist leaders.

[6] United Nations: *Non-Self-Governing Territories* (Summaries of information submitted to the Secretary-General during 1955), ST/TRI/SER. A/12 (New York, 1957), pp. 80, 88–9.

Early resistance to the development of schools was most often due to antecedent cultural orientations, or to misunderstanding. Where schools were not accepted, it was rather a matter of indifference, that characteristically with time gave way to acceptance, first by a small segment of the people, then by increasingly larger numbers.

We have seen that the nature of the base line of cultural change made for a readier acceptance of schooling in the western part of the subcontinent that in the eastern. As an instance of the cultural reasons for this, the statement of a Kenyan Somali leader makes the point:

> . . . these people (the Africans in southern Kenya) and particularly their leaders, consider that education is all-important. While not belittling the value of education, water and grazing are to us of infinitely greater importance. They are matters of life and death to us, our cattle and our camels in our thirsty country. Our people can, if they must, live without schools. They cannot live without water and grasss.[7]

Yet there were exceptions. It will be recalled that in the western Sudan Area, where Moslem influence predominated, the fact that European education was in the hands of missionaries caused schools to be avoided. It was precisely the secular character of the schools in territories controlled by France that caused their earlier acceptance there than in the British dependencies, where mission schools predominated. Or, turning to the eastern part of the continent, it would be difficult to match anywhere in Africa the readiness with which the Kikuyu of Kenya or the Chagga of Tanganyika accepted schooling.

From the earliest days, it was everywhere easier to induce parents to send their sons to school than their daughters. In this case the cultural patterns governing the position of women in society, particularly the marriage customs, were controlling factors. This does not mean that the commonly enunciated formula that women have a low status in African societies, that they are

[7] Ali Abdi: "Kenya Somalis Put Their Case," *East Africa and Rhodesia*, Vol. 37, No. 1892 (1961), p. 538.

drudges who work while the men take their leisure, is valid. Rather the traditional restrictions of women to tasks that center about the home and the rearing of children, universals in human experience, plus codes regulating the sexual behavior of young women, checked the relative mobility of girls, and thus in various ways influenced the degree of readiness to accept cultural change for the respective sexes.

Psychologically and functionally, the position of women in African society has been high. "A woman is one who bears the people (of the country). Women are very important. Women are like God, because they bear children," is how a Nsaw Cameroons man expressed it.[8] Yet male dominance in the economic and political sphere made it seem natural that boys should be schooled and girls continue in their traditional ways. Moslem doctrine reinforced responses of this kind when, as in Northern Nigeria, pressure was brought to bear on the Emirs to send girls to school. The response, according to the head of one institution, was in terms of "your daughters, not mine." As late as 1957, numerous cases were cited of pupils in schools for girls, daughters of poor Hausa families who had been forced by local chiefs to send them, often with a strikingly high incidence of truancy resulting from the reluctance of the girls, like their families, to break with accepted tradition.[9]

It is scarcely necessary to mention again the importance of the role played by Christian missions in introducing formal schooling into Subsaharan Africa. The Africans whom they brought to literacy may be said to have proved more fervent in spreading the gospel of reading and writing than in propagating the message of Christianity. The reasons for this, when mission educational activity is viewed in historical perspective, are twofold. The first has to do with what might be called the conviction carried by cultural consistency. Literacy brought its demonstra-

[8] Phyllis M. Kaberry: *Women of the Grasslands, a Study of the Economic Position of Women in Bamenda, British Cameroons,* Colonial Research Publication No. 14 (London, 1952), p. vii.

[9] Melville J. Herskovits: *Notes on African Field Research,* pp. 57/D90–91.

ble rewards in the culture to which the Africans were being introduced. These rewards were immediate in the form of well-paying employment, and the accompanying prestige that accrued to those who controlled this instrument of power. And while the advantages of being able to read and write were scarcely apparent to pupils in primary schools, they were clear to their parents, and to those who continued their educational careers into the higher grades.

The second reason is the reciprocal of the first. If the advantages enjoyed by the literate person quickly became evident to Africans, this by no means held for the religious system preached by the missionaries. Africans soon discovered that whereas Europeans were agreed on the importance of schooling, they were not at all agreed on the approach to the supernatural. As a consequence, the unquestioned place of literacy in a higher standard of living was thus in contrast to the more tenuous relation between those two and religious adherence. The persistent attempts of missions to establish a closer relationship between the two seem to have carried only wavering conviction to Africans.

Other things being equal, Africans everywhere came to prefer schooling under secular auspices. One reason for this, phrased in various ways by many Africans, was that in lay schools they were less subjected to the continuous denigration of their own cultures. In the mission schools, many aspects of African ways of life that continued to be highly esteemed, or were important for the functioning of society, particularly customs associated with sexual behavior and with marriage, fell under missionary disapprobation, and were attacked in the classroom. This was one reason often given by Congolese for their preference for lay schools over those under mission auspices after the government, in 1956, decided to take over a considerable share of the educational task, the other reason being that the instruction in French in the lay schools gave proficiency in handling the language of government and commerce. One of the most dramatic examples of reaction to the judgments passed by missions on aboriginal custom was the establishment in Kenya of separatist churches and independent schools as a result of attempts by certain missions to suppress the Kikuyu rite of clitoridectomy. According to Leakey,

> A number of the Kikuyu adherents of the various Christian missions had begun to ask themselves whether the mission insistence on monogamy and on the abandonment of certain Kikuyu customs was really essential to the status of Christianity.[1]

There have been many situations, however, in which other things were not equal. One of the surest ways to make Africans turn to the schools of a given mission was to have them come under the disapproval of government. The situation in South Africa, following on the taking over of mission schools for use in implementing the doctrine of *apartheid,* is a case in point. The direction and control of the educational system below the university level had traditionally been lodged in the governments of the various Provinces, which gave subsidies to the many schools administered by the missions, with curricula and teaching supervised by the Provincial Educational Departments. Under the Bantu Education Act, all this was changed. One important effect of this was that the contribution of the mission schools became enhanced in the thinking of the Africans. Institutions debating closure were in some cases urged to remain open, even with the revised syllabus they were required to follow under the new system. Another example is provided in Portuguese Africa. Where some choice between the officially sanctioned Catholic schools and those under Protestant control was possible, the Africans tended to prefer the latter; though here the fact that the standards in the Protestant schools were higher also entered.

The problem of the language of instruction in African schools has been much discussed. This was especially the case in the Congo, where mission schools, both Catholic and Protestant, used for their primary teaching medium "the vernacular," as African languages have frequently been termed. The decision of the Belgian government to open schools where beginning instruction would be in French—the use of Flemish, which was also urged

[1] L. S. B. Leakey: *Mau Mau and the Kikuyu* (London, 1952), pp. 89–90.

in Belgium, was not welcomed by the Congolese—was a powerful inducement for Africans to send their children to the lay schools, and brought about a general revision of teaching practices where the native tongue had been hitherto employed.

The question was particularly acute in regard to the primary grades. According to some educationists, the novelty of the classroom situation and the new discipline to which a child is subjected, require so much adjustment that to add the additional burden of learning a second language must materially handicap him. This was held especially applicable to African children, who heard nothing but their own mode of speech, once away from school. Those who took an opposite position urged that just because the situation in which the African child found himself was so new, one added element would not materially affect the rate or quality of his adjustment.

There can be little question that whichever course was favored, the psychological and pedagogical problems that presented themselves were of the first magnitude. Our concern here, however, is with motivations and reactions on the part of administrators and parents, rather than the problems of pupils. What was most striking in this respect was that the matter became a cause for general debate only where a position could be identified as a political issue. Where this was not the case, discussion remained on the technical level. Usually, it was accepted that instruction during the first three or four years of schooling should be in the child's native tongue, with the European language taught as a "subject"; after this, the new language would become the vehicle of instruction. In South Africa, however, or to a degree in the Belgian Congo, where Africans were convinced that a policy of using their own languages in the schools meant the continued denial to their children of opportunities open to Europeans, the negative reaction was strong and often bitter.

What Africans over all the subcontinent came to realize was that literacy was not enough. Command of a world language was essential if they were to function to best advantage in the new setting of their lives, whether locally or in the wider scene. Above all, as higher education came within reach, they found that it was essential to have gained command of a world language as early as possible. This was one reason for the resistance of Africans to Flemish in Congo schools, and to Afrikaans in those of South Africa. The conviction as to the value of a world language as against a local tongue was registered in the choices of their language of instruction by non-European students in the University of South Africa. During 1956, of the 1,200 or more Africans studying in this degree-granting, extra-mural institution, only two were taking their work in Afrikaans, the rest in English.[2]

The question often raised with Africans as to what would happen to native languages was faced realistically. "We will go on using them at home," was the customary reply; a point of view whose validity is demonstrated when we recognize how few of the many hundred mutually unintelligible languages of Africa, even those spoken by few, have disappeared under contact. "You cannot study science or philosophy or medicine if you only know an African language, no matter how well you can read or write," was how one Ghanaian put it.

This comment gives point to the apprehension with which Africans contemplated the efforts of the South African government to recast the curricula in African schools so as to make the native languages the medium of instruction. "How can you do multiplication in them?" asked one African. "It's like trying to multiply using Roman numerals. It can't be done." He was referring to the mode of counting in these Southern Bantu tongues where, for example, the number 358 in Venda is "hundreds-three-and-tens-five-and-three-and-five" (*madana mararu namahumi matanu namararu natanu*).[3] On the other hand, the point of view expressed by an American missionary in the Congo, in regretting the introduction of French as a medium of instruction in the schools there, illustrates an earlier position on the matter: "I have been teaching for thirty years, always using Chiluba, and have turned out many Christians who have become good artisans and even teachers." "But can a boy or girl who knows only Chiluba go to a University?" "It is not my task to prepare them

[2] Melville J. Herskovits: *Notes on African Field Research,* p. 57/D550.
[3] Ibid., p. 57/D453.

for University. My task is to enable them to read the Word of God."[4]

Certainly language problems in Africa are of such complexity that they cannot be solved by reference to any formula. When the question of reducing the spoken tongues to writing for use in schools was broached, the matter of orthography, the characters to be used in writing and printing a given African mode of speech, provoked strong controversy. *Ad hoc* usages, introduced by those who first reduced a given tongue to writing came to be so completely accepted, that the proposal to bring them into line with international linguistic standards called forth typical responses of cultural conservatism. Yoruba is a prime example of this, with its special signs that are used nowhere else, or Zulu, where the use of a "k" for the sound of "g", due to faulty transliteration of early texts, became firmly established.

Controversy over orthography, however, was but a beginning. If literacy was to be attained in a native language, and text-books provided, in which languages were they to be printed? It has been estimated that to print in a language having less than 100,000 speakers, a figure not met by the users of many African languages, is uneconomic. The fact that many African modes of speech have significant tone means that diacritical marks have to be used to indicate differences in pitch, and this adds to printing costs. The problem of selection thus took on overtones of local identification. But even if a consensus was finally reached, and a language or certain languages chosen, the question at once presented itself, what would it profit a child who spoke one African language to achieve literacy in another? Was it a step toward learning to use a European tongue?

[7]

We have touched on only a few of the problems raised by the development of schools in Subsaharan Africa. Many of those we have not considered are common to all countries in transition. There is the need for more teachers with professional

[4] Ibid., p. 57/D240.

training, which in turn involves budgetary considerations as the schools compete with other public agencies, and with business and the professions, for the personnel they require. Another is the lack of adequate physical facilities, and equipment of all kinds. In Africa, it is true, these problems were intensified because schooling there developed at a relatively late date, and because of the rapidity with which, once introduced, the demands for it spread. But even here, the situation was not too different from that in other economically less developed countries, which had suddenly to provide educational facilities that older, established systems had possessed for decades.

General problems of expanding opportunities for schooling are not our concern here. They are essentially technical, whether in the educational or financial sense. They involve no basic human adjustment or cultural readjustment, once schooling has become an accepted part of the social landscape. They rather represent the inner dynamic of a system which, after it has taken firm root in the culture, develops facets common to other systems. The questions they raise can be resolved by techniques that have been used in solving similar problems elsewhere.

One aspect of this dynamic which we must consider, however, has to do with the progressive development of schooling to higher levels. In a sense, this is an inevitability in any educational system, even the most informal kind. In most nonliterate societies, it exists as a function of age and accumulated experience, though in some cases formal instruction takes on a character of higher learning analogous to that found among peoples with writing. For example, the process of becoming a diviner in Dahomey and among the Yoruba required about seven years' study, demanding a length of time and intellectual effort comparable to that needed to obtain the doctorate in European and American universities. Also relevant in this context is the post-initiation training of Temne Poro society officials in Sierra Leone.[5]

The move toward making higher education available to Africans came first in the west. In Sierra Leone, where the mis-

[5] Vernon R. Dorjahn: "The Initiation of the Temne Poro Officials," *Man,* Vol. 61, 27 (1961), *passim.*

sions, as we have seen, gave early priority to educational activities, a training school for ministers was established by the Church Missionary Society in 1827, which, in 1875, as Fourah Bay College, began to train candidates for degrees granted by the University of Durham in England. In a sense, this established a tradition which came to have an important place in African higher education, since most centers, whether in British, French or Belgian territories—there being no institution of higher learning in Portuguese or Spanish Africa—had the quality of their degrees guaranteed by metropolitan universities. Except for Fourah Bay, the degrees of British Commonwealth University Colleges, as they were called, were guaranteed by the University of London. Degrees at Lovanium were under the control of Louvain; at Elizabethville they were supervised by committees from the four Belgian Universities; at the Institut des Hautes Études at Dakar, which in 1957 was given full university status, examinations were under the direction of professors from the Universities of Paris and Bordeaux.

A Belgian discussion of higher education in Africa south of the Sahara and north of the Union, which is a special case, noted the larger numbers of staff in proportion to students commonly found when they were instituted. Yet this, it was pointed out, changed as the size of the student body grew. How rapidly the numbers of students increased is to be seen in the following table.[6]

	Numbers and date at opening	*Numbers in year indicated*
Khartoum	188 (1946)	700 (1955)
Makerere	130 (1946)	625 (1957)
Ghana	90 (1948)	349 (1954)
Ibadan	224 (1948)	750 (1957)
Dakar	94 (1950)	1316 (1959)
Lovanium	21 (1954)	236 (1959)
Elizabethville	104 (1956)	171 (1957)
Salisbury	72 (1957)	166 (1959)

[6] A. Girard: "La mission des Universités d'Afrique noire," *Académie Royale des Sciences Coloniales, Bulletin des Séances* (n.s.), Vol. 4 (1958), pp. 596–7.

These numbers, it should be noted, except for the University of Dakar, the Congo institutions, and the University College of the Rhodesias and Nyasaland at Salisbury, represented student bodies that were almost exclusively African. The numbers of Africans at Lovanium, 142 in 1959, and Elizabethville, 24, were on the increase;[7] in 1959 the student body at Dakar included 1000 Africans;[8] the same year, Africans studying at Salisbury numbered 66.[9]

This list does not include students at various Institutes of Technology and other specialized centers of advanced training. Thus the numbers in all institutions above the level of secondary school in what was the Gold Coast advanced from 90 in 1948 to 540 in 1952, 756 in 1953, and 865 in 1954.[1] At the end of 1957, there were 960 students in the University College of Ghana and the Kumasi College of Technology, most of them studying under government grants. Nor does this tell the entire story, since Ghana, in addition, supported 232 scholarship students in British and American Universities.[2] Besides the students at the University College of Ibadan and the Nigerian College of Art, Science and Technology, Nigeria in 1954 sent "about 2,348 private students overseas . . . , of whom about 2,054 were in the United Kingdom and 294 in North America," while "overseas students with scholarships numbered 442."[3] The French Cameroons, which had no institution of learning higher than the *lycée*, at the

[7] Anonymous: "Statistics of University Enrolment," *Belgian Congo 59*, Monthly Information Bulletin, No. 10 (October, 1959).

[8] André Lemaire: "L'Université Française de Dakar," *Le Monde*, No. 4659 (January 14, 1960), p. 3.

[9] Federation of Rhodesia and Nyasaland, Information Department: "President Reviews University College Progress," *Newsletter*, No. 48/59 (November 27, 1959), p. 6.

[1] United Nations: *Non-Self-Governing Territories* (Summaries of information submitted to the Secretary-General during 1955), ST/TRI/SER. A/12 (New York, 1957), p. 238.

[2] Anonymous: "Overseas Scholars," *Ghana Today*, Vol. 2, No. 18 (1958), p. 7.

[3] United Nations: *Non-Self-Governing Territories* (Summaries of information submitted to the Secretary-General during 1955), ST/TRI/SER. A/12 (New York, 1957), p. 251.

beginning of 1957 had 247 scholarship students in French institutions, of whom 67 were studying medicine, 53 law, 24 letters, 21 science and 17 pharmacy. In addition there were 184 Africans in France on scholarships, studying technical subjects at various levels.[4] In 1954, Northern Rhodesia reported that "over forty Africans were taking advanced courses outside the Territory."[5] Kenya had 166 African students at Makerere, while of the overseas students "holding scholarships for higher education," 81 were African.[6] During the academic year 1959–60, Tanganyika sent 180 students to Makerere College in Uganda and 6 to the Royal Technical College in Nairobi, Kenya, 111 to institutions in the United Kingdom, 40 to the United States, 35 to other African countries, 31 to India and Pakistan, 24 to western Europe, and 1 to Australia, for a total of 428.[7]

Because of the circumstances under which institutions of higher learning were developed in Africa, standards tended to be equivalent to those of the metropolitan countries. Through grants from various colonial development funds and internal budgetary allocations, impressive modern structures were erected to house them. Africanization of staff proceeded slowly. To some extent this was due to the opportunities in other callings open to well-trained Africans, though in some cases there was a certain reluctance of European staff to recognize African scholarly potential.

However, there were problems that went beyond having an adequate available supply of Africans with postgraduate training of high quality. In the colonial situation, where developing nationalisms heightened emotional commitments, African university teachers at times showed a tendency to substitute indoctri-

[4] From an official but unpublished list, dated December 31, 1956, provided by the Director of Education of the French Cameroons in Yaounde.

[5] United Nations: *Non-Self-Governing Territories* (Summaries of information submitted to the Secretary-General during 1955), ST/TRI/SER. A/12 (New York, 1957), p. 86.

[6] Ibid., p. 121.

[7] Betty George: *Education for Africans in Tanganyika*, United States Department of Health, Education and Welfare, Bulletin 1960, No. 19, OE 14039 (Washington, 1960), p. 77.

nation for analysis. Yet objective scholarship developed in the writings of Africans, who also made conscious efforts to imbue their best students with academic ideals, and turn their attention to the values and rewards in a career of teaching and research, so that in later years these universities would be able to acquire full African staffs of high quality.

The problem of adapting subject matter to African requirements, which we encountered in discussing the curricula of the lower schools, was also present in the universities. Aside from the fact that for the Europeans who founded these institutions, the validity of the home curricula seemed self-evident, there was also the point of view of the African to be taken into account. Almost everywhere the value of a university degree was recognized to the extent it was like that of the Metropole, and deviations introduced by European teachers were resented as attempts to dilute the purity of the degree, and hence its worth.

The point was made by a representative of Guinea before the Assembly of the French Union in 1950:

> The day you make a distinction between higher studies in the Metropole and those you want to set up in Africa you will not find a single African in the University of Dakar. . . . We don't want people to come and teach us what we already know better than anyone else—the customs and usages of our country. . . . We want to have higher education at home, but we want it to be exactly equal to that of the Metropole. We want a Metropolitan curriculum.[8]

From one point of view, in practical terms, this demand for equivalence is understandable, since the student had to pass examinations set by professors in the controlling metropolitan universities, and were graded by them. Yet at times the insistence on equivalence was so strong that it would go beyond curriculum to traditions which had only symbolic value, such as that attached to wearing the academic gown to lectures and other university exercises by undergraduates in certain university colleges established under British auspices.

[8] Virginia Thompson and Richard Adloff: *French West Africa* (London, 1958), p. 539, *n.* 1.

To equip African territories with the personnel essential for them to function as self-governing states in the broader world, this insistence on quality proved to be of great use. Even more important from this point of view was the training received by Africans in overseas universities. The task set students from Africa to meet the same standards as other students, being taught in a language not their own, in a strange environment, often under financial handicaps, made the results obtained by the outstanding students all the more important psychologically for the Africans, and of no little importance for a growing awareness on the part of administering authorities of the African intellectual potential.

The institutions abroad and at home produced men and women competent in medicine, in public administration, in economics, in law, and as research scholars, in professional skills which countries about to take their places as independent entities in the twentieth century world had to have. It may be suggested parenthetically that this success of Africans in utilizing the training they received in leading institutions of higher learning explains the urgency in the extension of *apartheid* by the nationalists of South Africa to the university level, and the measures taken by the Portuguese to reduce the very meagre base in secondary education for Africans that would permit them to go on to a university.

With the increase of opportunities for higher education, other problems arose. The graduate of a secondary school could no longer rely on being given an important government or business post. As the number of men and women with university degrees increased, the graduate could no longer command a senior post, but was called on to work his way upwards. In time, however, this began to be recognized as normal, and the process of integrating those with higher education into the newly oriented levels of society commensurate with their training resembled its parallels elsewhere.

One point much stressed in the literature requires special scrutiny. This has to do with the so-called "marginal" character of educated Africans, especially those who received training overseas. Emphasis has been laid on their inability to resume ways of life they had left behind, because of newly acquired values, of differences in standards of living, or of the need to resist pressures from traditional sources. It was insisted that this produced individuals at ease neither with African custom nor with European ways.

A considered view gives no support to such assertions. While true enough for individuals here and there, these could not be regarded as typical. The early conditioning of Africans to the home scene was no different from that of men and women everywhere, and the desire of a majority of Africans who completed their studies abroad was to return home and get on with the job in hand. These men and women, indeed, constituted one of the most powerful forces making for the essential adjustments between African and non-African values in the new nations of Africa.

9

The City

THE CULTURAL DIVISIONS of aboriginal Subsaharan Africa fall into two general categories, those areas inhabited by the food-gathering and herding peoples of the eastern and southern part of the continent, and those comprising the societies based on agriculture, found in the western and central portions. In the former, we saw that villages were communal groupings, most often based on ties of kinship, economically self-sufficient, and standing in a loose political relationship to other villages of the same tribal group. Societies to the north and west, on the other hand, were found to have had a considerable number of towns, and even cities of appreciable size. The importance of affiliation on the basis of kinship was not lessened in these towns and cities, their essential pattern was for members of a given kinship group to cluster in the same quarter or ward. Lloyd has called the Yoruban centers "tribal" towns.[1] Markets, held at fixed intervals, were ubiquitous, with the range of products for sale reflecting the division of labor in the economies of this part of the continent.

[1] P. C. Lloyd: "The Yoruba Town Today," *Sociological Review,* Vol. 7 (n.s., 1959), p. 45.

These communities, moreover, were with few exceptions the seats of political control, as well as centers of economic activity.

Those who have studied this aboriginal urban complex of western Africa have been faced with difficult problems of classification and definition. Urban sociologists, who have dealt primarily with cities in Europe and the United States, have defined the city as "a relatively large, dense, and permanent settlement of socially heterogeneous individuals." [2] A number of anthropologists, in studying the city, ordered their analyses along the lines of a continuum which places what was termed a "folk society" at one extreme and the modern urban community at the other, contrasting "isolated-homogeneous" folk-groupings with "mobile-heterogeneous" urban ones.[3]

Analyses based on categories of this type, as they bear on the aboriginal city-town complex of Subsaharan Africa, need not long detain us. Bascom, putting Wirth's criterion of heterogeneity to the test in Yoruba towns, concluded that, "At best, it is a relative criterion which is difficult to apply cross-culturally." [4] In Timbuktu, Miner found that while

> heterogeneity . . . is clear-cut in the presence of three diverse cultures . . . the different culture groups are woven into a system of diverse economic and status groups which constitute elements in the division of labor. Compared to Western cities, the heterogeneity of Timbuktu appears . . . to be more a product of diverse cultural origin and less a result of elaborate division of labor.

For him, without qualification, "Timbucktu is a city." He found it difficult to apply the criteria of the folk-urban continuum to his data, since they showed that the ways of life in this community were by no means as secular, impersonal and uncohesive as is necessary to fit the model of an urban center advanced under this hypothesis. "Beyond the simple expedient of noting the pres-

[2] Louis Wirth: "Urbanism as a Way of Life," *American Journal of Sociology,* Vol. 44 (1938), p. 8.

[3] Robert Redfield: *The Folk Culture of Yucatan* (Chicago, 1941), p. 18.

[4] William R. Bascom: "Urbanization among the Yoruba," *American Journal of Sociology,* Vol. 60 (1955), p. 403.

ence of non-folk traits in Timbucktu, this study can say nothing as to the degree of urbanism there." [5]

Whatever the problem of definition, there can be little question that in West Africa and, to a greater extent than has been realized, in other parts of the continent, the institution of the large settled community long antedated the imposition of European controls. As Bascom comments concerning the Yoruba towns: "Urbanization can . . . be considered a traditional Yoruba pattern and not the outgrowth of European acculturation," [6] a statement that has much wider applicability than to southwestern Nigeria. We have the observations of Arab travelers and of Europeans from the seventeenth century onwards on the early existence of towns in West Africa generally. In the Western Sudan, what Trimingham terms "ruler towns" had the characteristics of "agglomerations of villages," which continually changed their sites as the political scene changed, while other cities, such as Jenne and Kano, which were both trading centers and political capitals, remained stable over their long recorded history.[7] Still others—Segou, Macina, Mopti, Wagadugu, Gao, Zaria—are all repeatedly found on early maps and are named in writings of early chroniclers. In the Congo, the capitals of the Kingdoms of Kongo, of Lunda, of Bushongo excited the admiration of travelers. Even in southeastern Africa, ruins such as Zimbabwe and lesser known ones, such as Khami, argue for earlier concentrations of people, though whatever urban traditions may have existed here seem to have disappeared well before European penetration.

We have no dependable figures on the size of the early African towns. The estimates made by early travelers, Arab or European, are extremely variable, and are seldom more than guesses until late in the colonial period, as illustrated by the figures from Bascom, who searched the available literature for data on the size

[5] Horace Miner: *The Primitive City of Timbuctoo* (Memoirs of the American Philosophical Society, No. 32, Princeton and Philadelphia, 1953), pp. 267–8.

[6] Ibid., p. 448.

[7] J. S. Trimingham: *Islam in West Africa* (Oxford, 1959), p. 191.

of West African towns and cities. Thus, the population of Salaga in northern Ghana was estimated at 10,000 by Müller and Mähly in 1885, 20,000 by Bonnat in 1877, and 50,000 by Baumgarten in 1887, while Johnson said it had upwards of 40,000 before the Ashanti war of 1874.

Of Dahomean cities,

> Abomey, the capital . . . , was estimated at 24,000 by Norris in 1772, and about 30,000 by Ducan in 1845, Forbes in 1849 and Wallon in 1858. Wilmot placed it at 20,000 in 1863 and Burton in 1864 said it did not exceed Whydah, which he gave as 12,000. Other estimates for Whydah range from 8,000 by Norris in 1772, 20,000 by McLeod in 1803 and Burton in 1863, 20–25,000 by Wallon in 1858 and Bouche in 1885, to 60,000 by Baudin in 1874. Allada, between Whydah on the coast and Abomey, was estimated at 7–10,000 by Adams between 1786 and 1800, 15–18,000 by Wallon in 1858, and 8–10,000 by Bouche in 1885. . . .

Estimates of the size of Yoruba cities made from 1856 onwards, show similar disparities. Thus Abeokuta, estimated in that year at 60,000, in 1860 at 110,000, and in 1890 at 100,000, was given in the census of 1911 as 51,255, in that of 1921 as 28,941, in 1931 as 45,763, and in 1952 as 84,451.[8]

Impossible though it has been, even for the parts of Africa longest in contact with the literate world, to give valid estimates of the size of African urban centers, there can be little question that a pattern of urbanization existed, certainly in West Africa, as a base on which to build the new cities of the post-European era. For our purpose, the significance of this indigenous pattern lies in the nature of its inflence on later urban development. This is why the cities of eastern and southern Africa came to be far more European in their planning, appearance and organization. And what is far more important, they required of their African inhabitants a much greater degree of adjustment than where urban life existed before the colonial period.

Mitchell's discussion of the historic background of the cities of "Bantu Africa," is to the point here:

[8] William R. Bascom: "Urbanism as a Traditional African Pattern," *The Sociological Review*, Vol. 7 (1959), pp. 30–1.

> These towns, unlike many towns in West Africa have grown up around a foreign nucleus. . . . They are agglomerations of population which have grown upon the basis of foreign enterprise and the settlements are organized and structured in terms of the social situation out of which administrators, industrialists, mining engineers and other entrepreneurs have come. . . . We must accept that there are certain major determinants of the social system which are fixed by the European administrative and industrial system in which they are set. The legal position of Africans . . . illustrates this, since the basic assumption behind much of the legislation seems to be that the rightful place of Africans is in their rural areas and that their sojourn in the towns is only temporary. . . . The Africans in the majority take the same point of view and most of them view the towns with some misgiving and look upon their tribal area as their true home to which they wish to return as soon as they are able.[9]

In contrast, the cities that developed in West Africa, especially those that grew out of indigenous settlements, remained essentially African except for the districts containing European business and government operations. The architecture of the old cities of the Sudanic belt just south of the desert was little disturbed; as was the multiple, compound centered housing, and the inner organization of the urban centers within the forested regions to the south.

[2]

With European expansion into Africa, the city everywhere became a major element in the African cultural landscape. In some instances, indigenous administrative and trading centers, like Kumasi in Ghana or Segou in Mali were continued. Elsewhere, towns were created to fulfill these functions, as was the case with Luluabourg, established as the capital of Kasai Province in the Congo, or Lusaka, the Northern Rhodesian seat of government. Mining operations were responsible for the founding

[9] J. Clyde Mitchell: "Social Change and the New Towns of Bantu Africa," *Working Paper No. 11* (Round-Table Conference on the Social Implications of Technological Change, 19–25 March 1959, International Social Science Council, Paris, 1959), p. 4.

and rate of growth of other centers. In some, growth was extremely rapid. Enugu, capital of the Eastern Region of Nigeria, was founded in 1909, following the discovery of coal nearby. In 1953 it had almost 63,000 inhabitants,[1] and by 1960, 80,000.[2] Lunsar, in Sierra Leone, in the thirty years from 1929 to 1959 grew from a hamlet of some 30 persons to a town numbering between 15,000 and 20,000, drawn there because of the labor requirements of the Marampa iron mines.[3]

The character of these developing urban centers changed with the growth of new African needs, and with the introduction of industries producing consumer goods for an expanding market that made it profitable to produce on the spot instead of importing commodities. Jinja, in eastern Uganda, provides an example of this. In 1901, the center of the British Government in the African kingdom of Busoga was moved there from Inganga. This was not only because Jinja was healthier, as the then Commissioner for Uganda, Sir Harry Johnston, stated in a dispatch to the Foreign Office, but also because its situation at Ripon Falls commanded "a very important transport route along the Nile," and already had a telegraph station and "a certain aggregate of European settlers." [4] During the same year, land grants were made to the missions; with the passage of time, the importance of Jinga as a trading center and the introduction of cotton into Busoga as a cash crop brought more persons, Asians as well as Europeans and Africans, to service this development.

In 1949, the construction of the Jinja hydroelectric power station stimulated further growth and initiated a period of industrial development. Not only was African labor imported during the building of the dam which was to provide power, but various

[1] Nigeria, Department of Statistics: *Population Census of the Eastern Region of Nigeria* (Lagos, 1953), p. 45.

[2] Anonymous: "Warm Greetings for Mr. Macmillan," *London Times,* (Jan. 16, 1960), p. 7.

[3] Anonymous: "Race Relations and Industry," *West Africa,* No. 2220 (December 19, 1959), p. 1114.

[4] Quoted in Cyril and Rhona Sofer: *Jinja Transformed* (East African Studies, East African Institute of Social Research, No. 4, Kampala, Uganda, 1955), p. 12.

subsidiary projects were begun. Between 1948 and 1951, the African population increased 239%, from 4,400 to 14,900; the Asian, 34%, from 3,800 to 5,100; the European, 300%, from 200 to 800. The total number of inhabitants grew 148%, from 8,400 to 20,800. How powerful the stimulus of industrial development could be is shown by the fact that in 1924 the total had been 5,037, reduced to 3,120 by 1930, perhaps as a result of an outbreak of plague in 1926, and of the slump in trade that resulted from the extension of the railway from the east coast through to Kampala, which lessened the importance of Jinja as a Victoria Nyanza lake port.[5]

The degree to which Africans were attracted to the urban centers following the introduction of European economic patterns is exemplified by Usumbura, the capital of Ruanda-Urundi. The facts take an added significance because in this territory the ratio between the urban and the total population in 1953 was .93% and 2.81% for Ruanda and Urundi, respectively, as against a proportion of 33.71% for the industrialized Katanga Province of the Congo, and 21.51% for the then Belgian Congo as a whole. The urban population of the entire territory increased 42% in the five years between 1950 and 1954; during this same period, the Africans in Usumbura, the largest center, about doubled in number. This particular city, at the northern end of Lake Tanganyika, lies at a crossroad, and thus attracted Africans of widely differing tribal groups, with only a minority of its African residents, 876 out of a sample of 2,295, being from Ruanda and Urundi.[6]

This pattern does not differ greatly from that which was to be found in other parts of the continent, as a survey of Accra, made in 1953–5, demonstrated. The city developed out of settlements that date from the sixteenth century, which composed the nuclei of the later urban center. In 1891, the three towns which came to make up the municipality had 19,999 inhabitants, and in 1901, 17,892. Succeeding counts showed a steady increase:

[5] Ibid., pp. 14–15.

[6] L. Baeck: "Étude socio-économique du centre extra-coutumier d'Usumbura," *Mémoires,* Académie Royal des Sciences Coloniales, Vol. 6, fasc. 5 (Brussels, 1957), pp. 9–13, 33–7.

18,574 in 1911, 38,049 in 1921, 61,558 in 1931, 135,926 in 1948. In 1954 the figure was 192,047, and included the inhabitants of a new suburban area.

The Africans of Accra in 1948 came from 60 different tribal groups. Of each 1,000 persons, more than half, or 516 were Ga, who were in the area before the city was founded; 111 were Ewe, from the central region to the east; 150 were from Akan-speaking peoples other than Ashanti, plus 17 from Ashanti. Of each 1,000, 28 were from the Northern Territories, while 160 belonged to groups not indigenous to Ghana. Migrants from outside the borders of Ghana, in addition to the Ewe, included 6,064 from southern Nigeria or 4.7% of the total population; 4,407 Hausa derived from various parts of West Africa, 3.4%; and 2,282 Zabrama or 1.8%. In all, 21,813 persons living in Accra had come from the Sudanic region north of the country, primarily from what at that time were French territories.[7]

The consistency in the rate of urban growth for Subsaharan Africa as a whole was supported by data from other centers. Dakar grew from 30,000 in 1926 to 230,000 in 1955, Conakry from 13,000 in 1936 to 50,000 in 1951, Abidjan from 800 in 1910 to 127,000 in 1955. Kumasi increased from 18,853 in 1911 to 75,000 in 1955, Ibadan from 387,173 in 1931 to 459,196 in 1952, Leopoldville from 39,531 in 1930 to 299,806 in 1955, and Nairobi from 13,145 in 1927 to more than 250,000 in 1956. Salisbury, with a population of 25,594 in 1931 had 167,630 in 1956; Johannesburg went from 282,971 in 1921 to 1,030,200 in 1957.[8]

Behind these statistics lay the human factor, the response of those who, by the circumstance of change in their habitat, were compelled to resolve the discontinuities between their ante-

[7] Ioné Acquah: *Accra Survey . . . 1953–1956* (London, 1958), pp. 16–17, 30–5.

[8] Northwestern University, Program of African Studies: *Africa* (Studies of United States Foreign Policy, No. 4, Committee Print, Committee on Foreign Relations, United States Senate, 86th Congress, 1st Session, No. 4, Washington, 1959), pp. 35–6; Inter-African Labour Institute: "The Housing of Workers in Urban Living Conditions in Africa," *Bulletin,* Vol. 6, No. 2 (1959), p. 67.

cedent and the urban settings—discontinuities that were present everywhere, even for those who came from regions where the phenomenon of urbanization had existed before the arrival of the Europeans. This is why the problems of motivation, of adjustment, of cultural reintegration that the African had to meet come into such sharp focus when we consider his reactions to life in the new cities and towns. The effect of this change on broader facets of African life were consequently subject to much speculation. Many held, for example, that urban living would be the reagent whereby tribal loyalties could be distilled into national political identifications; that here adaptation to the needs of an industrial establishment could be achieved most rapidly and effectively, and that in the cities a growing middle class would guarantee future steady growth.

[3]

Various reasons have been advanced to explain why Africans moved to the city, but there are few analyses based on direct querying of those who have migrated to urban centers. Schapera grouped the reasons for migration from Bechuanaland to the Union of South Africa in three categories. The first of these comprehended social and psychological factors; the depth in time of the migration pattern, the desire for adventure and for change, and escape from domestic and communal demands. Economic needs, particularly the acquisition of new wants, made up the next category. Of 297 men who were questioned as to their reasons for going to the Union, all but six gave economic reasons —to pay taxes, to buy clothing, cattle, or other goods, to get money for their parents. Finally there was the influence of labor agents, of administrative spurs to migration, and of pressure from the chiefs.[9] Denis, who indicated many of the same reasons for Central Africa, stresses two categories, one the traditional setting

[9] I. Schapera: *Migrant Labour and Tribal Life, a Study of Conditions in the Bechuanaland Protectorate* (London, 1947), pp. 115–55.

which discouraged remaining at home ("*facteurs répulsifs*") and the second, the positive attractions of the urban center.[1]

What are the historical roots of the growth of these new towns and cities? In the early days of colonial control, among several devices of the governing authorities to mobilize African man power, the most effective was the requirement that taxes be paid in currency rather than in kind. The need to obtain shillings or francs or escudos brought village Africans to administrative or trading or mining centers, and thus initiated a trend that increased with the growth of industrialization and large-scale agricultural enterprise. As waves of migrants followed each other, a growing number became accustomed to living and working there, and some of them took up permanent residence, establishing themselves and their families in towns and cities, and becoming what we may call proto-urban dwellers.

As the crude earlier techniques of impressing labor gave way in all but southern Africa to more regularized methods, the objectives toward which they were directed began to gain acceptance. Thus, by 1952, among the Mambwe of Northern Rhodesia, wage labor had become "an accepted part of man's life. . . . A man would be considered odd if he did not wish to earn money." There were by then many additional reasons why money was wanted more than in earlier periods. It was still needed to pay taxes, but it had also come to be used for marriage payments and court fines, for bicycles and their licenses, for bus fares, European clothing, household goods, brick houses, and "luxuries" such as guns and radios.[2]

More than this, women exerted "considerable pressure on the men to go out and work," since in the Copperbelt a single woman could not go to the towns. Women, like men, were able to earn money, and a married woman thus profited from the opportunity to accompany her husband there.

[1] J. Denis: *Le Phénomène Urbain en Afrique Centrale* (Académie Royale des Sciences Coloniales, Mémoires in-8°, n.s., t. xix, fasc. 1, Brussels, 1958), pp. 156–73.

[2] Ibid., pp. 44–5.

> A trip to the Copperbelt is an experience that a young woman never forgets. For at least once in her life she is free from the everlasting duties of fetching water and stamping meal, and acquires the outward appearance of European women, if not their leisure.

It is understandable that some women would "go to extraordinary lengths to get to the towns." [3]

With time, unforseen consequences of the efforts to force Africans into wage labor and into urban centers appeared—consequences which, in the light of later events, can be seen as the logical outgrowth of earlier policies. The introduction and development of public health measures, plus new crops and improved agricultural methods, made for a pressure of population on the land unknown in earlier days, which gave rise to regulations governing land reallocation, or the "villagization" adopted in Kenya after the Mau Mau uprising of 1952–4. Since the boundaries of the areas allocated to Africans in these territories were so drawn that there was insufficient land to support the existing African population, the growing number of landless Africans made available a labor pool for European farms, for the mines, for factories, for domestic employment and for use as unskilled or semi-skilled labor.

This and similar developments, differing from region to region, greatly contributed to urban growth in the more highly industrialized societies of Subsaharan Africa, principally South Africa, Southern Rhodesia, and the Katanga. In time, the trend toward urbanization was reinforced by measures calculated to channel the flow of Africans and thus assure a controlled supply of labor. To this end pass laws were promulgated, and the requirement to register periodically with urban authorities. These were moves to promote economic development, but also to consolidate and protect the status enjoyed by the dominant racial minorities. But, as we shall see, in bringing about large urban concentrations of Africans, this system laid the ground work for

[3] W. Watson: *Tribal Cohesion in a Money Economy* (Manchester, 1958), p. 40.

organized reactions to the established social and economic differentials, and centered in the cities organized political protest through nationalist movements.

The growth of African urban populations, however, should not be attributed solely to pressures of this kind. Though such pressures may have been effective instruments in the multiracial territories, they cannot explain the drift to the cities where there were no permanent non-African settlers, or where the pressure of population on the land was not critical or was even nonexistent. The movement toward urban centers became shot through with factors of prestige, of new identifications, new wants. No matter how poor the level of material accommodation it might offer the African, or how inferior his position in the urban social and economic hierarchy, the enticements of city life—not unique to Africa—and the incentive of returning home with coveted possessions, far outweighed the trials and the insecurities of the experience. Fellow villagers, newly sophisticated in ways of dealing with men and women, once back home, proved a powerful influence on other men who learned about their adventures in the cities so full of dazzling sights.

One study in which the incentives for migration to an urban center were analyzed dealt with the African population of Brazzaville, particularly in the quarter of Poto-Poto. Five categories of motives were presented. First came the economic ones. As with Leopoldville, just across the Congo River, Brazzaville had come to be an important labor market, where, moreover, a wide range of manufactured objects could be bought cheaply. Here the migrant hoped to accumulate the goods he needed to establish himself as a man of substance. That those who were attracted to Brazzaville soon discovered how, too often, the higher cost of living cancelled out the benefit of higher wages, is beside the point. The fact remains that about 25% of the Africans who were queried gave this kind of economic reason for going there.

Considerations of family ties and kinship obligations, the second category, entered in 25% to 30% of the cases. The reasons given by those in this category for coming to the city illustrated the complexity of the problem:

A paternal or maternal uncle takes with him some of his young nephews, whom he sends to school, or helps learn a trade: this is a kind of long-term investment; the nephew understands, in accordance with the accepted formula, that he must "be appreciative" when the proper time comes. An old man wishes to surround himself with young relatives, so that he can the better evaluate them in selecting his heirs. An older brother summons a younger to aid him in taking his risks. An older sister married to a government official or a clerk, brings a younger sister or brother to help her with her housework. A successful man is surrounded by those under obligation to him who rely on his power and contribute to enlarging it.

A third series of reasons for migration to Brazzaville expressed, in various ways, the desire to achieve higher social status. Some persons, having been stimulated by what they learned in their village schools, came to further their education in order to qualify for work that paid higher wages, demanded less physical exertion, and led to preferred social standing. Some 10% fell into this class. About the same proportion had come to Brazzaville for reasons in the next category, that it was a refuge from supernatural dangers that threatened in their villages, or provided an escape from the demands of the local administration. Finally about 5% had come for such reasons as the inducements offered in the course of various labor recruiting campaigns for industry.

In addition to the positive pull of the city, then, there was also a negative aspect, the escape the city offered from the limitations and irritations of village life. "The colonial economy," we are told, "has not been able to absorb the individuals it has liberated in destroying traditional economic systems." The resulting movement to the city was an attempt by the people themselves to resolve the difficulty.[4]

[4]

Beyond the statistics lay the problems of adjustment, not only to life in the city, but to the repercussions of migratory move-

[4] Georges Balandier: *Sociologie des Brazzaville Noires* (Cahiers de la Fondation Nationale des Sciences Politiques, No. 67, Paris, 1955), pp. 40–3.

ments in the rural areas from which the migrants were drawn. In large measure, those problems arose from the fact that the African city dweller, as the saying went, had one foot in the city and one in the village. This, indeed, was the policy in the more industrialized southern and eastern parts of the continent. In South Africa, a worker who came to the city was actively discouraged from bringing his family with him; if he came to work in the mines, his family had to remain behind.

A careful protrayal has been given us of the background of the migratory urban worker who moved from what at the time of the study was French West Africa to the then Gold Coast. Here, where migration was free, the impact on the course of life in the Zabrama communities from which 40% of the adult males migrated to the cities, and 10% to the mining areas,[5] was not too great. Ties were maintained with those left at home. Even during their stay in town, the migrants sent back part of their savings. If married, they contributed to the support of their wives and children; if bachelors, they sent remittances to their immediate kin.[6]

These migrants made up 40% of the wage earners of Ghana, some 160,000 out of a total of 405,000. They were an important factor in all occupations. They constituted 98% of the workers employed by the Accra Town Council; 36% of those in the Public Works Department of that city. 75% of the laborers hired by cocoa farmers were from the north, as were also 55% of those working in the mines, 37% of those employed in timber-working and in forestry, 22% of the industrial labor force, 40% of the police, and 20% of the employees of one large commercial concern, the Union Trading Company.[7] They were also independent traders. Thus of 6,096 licensed traders in Accra, 1,649, or 24%, were Zabrama. On the ferry at Yedji, an important point on the

[5] Jean Rouch: "Migrations au Ghana (Gold Coast), (Enquête 1953–1955)," *Journal de la Société des Africanistes,* Vol. 26 (1956), p. 76; English translation by P. E. O. and J. B. Haigham (Accra, 1954), mimeographed, p. 17.

[6] Ibid., p. 136; English translation, p. 48.

[7] Ibid., pp. 102–3; English translation, p. 31.

route of migration, 14,805 out of 35,665 migrants crossing from south to north in March 1954, declared themselves to be traders.[8]

From the earliest times, the migrant was set apart by preference and custom. The *zongo,* or foreigners' quarter, had long existed in each Ghana town, with its own organization and its particular status. The nature of the social life lived by the migrants in these urban quarters differed according to their ethnic derivation. Hausa, who traditionally traveled with their families, showed about equal numbers of men and women, and half of the Fulani, of the Northern Territory migrants, of the Liberians, and of the Wangara had their wives with them. In contrast were the Mossi and Busanga, where there was one woman to three or four men. Even more striking was the sex ratio among the Zabrama, where there were but 65 women per thousand.[9] Statistics of this kind also reveal the roots of certain of the pathological aspects of African urban centers. Thus, the fact that among Kotokoli migrants there were 511 women per thousand, a very high proportion, was explained by the fact the "many of these women come specially to Accra to become prostitutes."[1]

Despite limited contact between migrants and Ghanaians, and the attitudes of superiority and inferiority mutually held by migrants and native residents, relations between the two were, on the whole, cordial. Some of the migrant groups, notably Yoruba and Hausa, were more prone to settle permanently than others. In contrast, 59% of the Zabrama queried in Accra had been there less than a year, 71% less than two. The conditions under which the migrants lived were dictated by their economic position rather than by the ethnic groups to which they belonged. Since they were mainly on the lower rungs of the economic ladder, their standard of living was low. This was accentuated by the wish to put aside as much of their earnings as possible, so that they could return to their homes laden with gifts. On the day the migrant reached his village, he was like a king, distributing the presents he had brought with him until he had almost nothing

[8] Ibid., pp. 121, 107; English translation, pp. 40, 35.
[9] Ibid., p. 147, transl., p. 54.
[1] Ibid., p. 147, transl., p. 54.

left for himself. This done, he would turn to the cultivation of his fields, until it was time for him to leave for another tour of work.

The full significance of these details emerges only when they are compared with their counterparts elsewhere in the continent. A summary of studies of urbanization up to 1952 is helpful for this overview:

> Industrialization . . . has led to migration from rural areas to towns; to the growth of urban populations characterized, in their early stages, by a preponderance of youth over age and men over women; to the development of overcrowding and slum conditions in towns; to the emergence of a labouring class with certain characteristic attitudes and problems; and to the formation of new types of associations.

This resembles the consequences of the growth of cities everywhere in the world. But in Africa, particular kinds of development resulted from the fact that, ". . . the immigrant labourers are of a different race and speak different languages from the . . . Europeans and Indians who provide the capital."[2]

With this as a beginning, we may attempt to subsume similarities and differences. We shall be aided in this if we do not restrict ourselves to the institutionalized aspects of the life of the African migrant to the city, but analyze the phenomenon within our terms of reference, which hold the human factor paramount. We must, of course, consider the institutional framework, without which it would not be possible to order our data to account for the psychological forces in play.

Migration to the cities everywhere in Africa induced imbalance in the sex ratio, both in the villages from which a disproportionate number of men were drawn, and in the cities, to which fewer women migrated. Movements of workers tended to be periodic, in the sense that only a small proportion of those who came to the city made the social and psychological commitments

[2] Meran McCulloch: "Survey of recent and current field studies on the social effects of economic development in inter-tropical Africa," in *Social Implications of Industrialization and Urbanization in Africa South of the Sahara* (D. Forde, editor), Tensions and Technology Series, UNESCO (Paris, 1956), p. 209.

essential for establishing permanent residence there. The nature of life in the city demanded some reordering of traditional relationships. Migrants were faced with the need to adapt themselves to a whole series of cultural discontinuities, or suffer demoralization. This applied more especially to the migrant who had one foot in the city and one in the bush, oscillating between his home and his place of employment.

Mitchell, for "Bantu Africa," derived two principal "determinants or imperatives" of difficulty in adjusting to urban living. The first was the discontinuity between "tribal background," and "the novel conditions" of the new setting. He laid particular stress on those aspects of the urban scene that arose from the technological phases of life in the towns. Since "the technological system itself is only part of a larger cultural whole" it followed that "certain basic patterns of social relationships . . . are defined by the culture as a whole." The second determinant he distinguished as demographic, and this, "because of the peculiar relationships of town to rural areas . . . set certain limitations to the pattern of social relationships within them."[3]

Exceptions will inevitably be found, even to the most carefully drawn generalizations. Migration was relatively less important in the mining districts and towns of the Katanga and the Copper Belt than in South Africa or in Kenya. In the former two, a determined effort to develop a stable labor force was to be sent in the provision of housing for family living and of schooling for workers' children. Thus in Elizabethville a project enabled Africans to build their own houses with materials furnished at cost, in order that home ownership might encourage them to become permanent city dwellers.[4] Whatever the labor policy, or the degree to which urban labor had been migratory, a certain proportion of those who came to the city remained permanently.

[3] J. Clyde Mitchell: "Social Change and the New Towns of Bantu Africa," *Working Paper No. 11* (Round-Table Conference on the Social Implications of Technological Change, 19–25 March 1959, International Social Science Council, Paris, 1959), p. 1.

[4] Cf. F. Grevisse: "Le Centre extra-coutumier d'Elizabethville," *Bulletin du Centre d'Étude des Problems Sociaux Indigènes,* No. 15 (1951).

Their children, accustomed to urban life, knew little or nothing of indigenous rural ways. The development of a class of permanently unemployed young men in the cities of South Africa, notably the *tsotsis* of Johannesburg, affords us our most extreme example of how settlement in the city can bring on its own particular forms of social pathology. Such types were not found elsewhere. Evidently the Africans who migrated to the cities, the mines, or plantations of West Africa had a far less radical adjustment to make than those in the urban centers of the east and south.

Here we touch on an essential point which differentiates the character of the migratory movements of western Africa from those elsewhere in the sub-continent. In West Africa, the migrant was a free agent, coming and going as he desired, and moving from one kind of work to another as opportunity offered. If he decided to become a permanent urban resident, this was his affair, for no regulations governing his movements existed which were not applicable to others, without regard to race. His economic betterment was limited by circumstance and his own ability, but no legal ceiling was imposed on him. Where he might live was dictated by his resources and his wishes; a point emphatically made by Ghanaian official who, as Ghana was becoming independent, characterized a housing development for workers in Accra as, "not housing for Africans, but for people." [5]

It is scarcely necessary to contrast this with patterns where pass systems not only controlled the movements of Africans from one part of a given country to another but, as in South Africa, regulated the labor market by dictating the kind of work a given African might perform in the city. Binding the man to continue this particular kind of work and no other, such a system set up an effective barrier to the kind of economic and social advancement in search of which the man had come to the city in the first place. Where an African might live was governed by regulations aimed especially at him, and even there he could live only at the pleasure of an official who was a member of the dominant racial

[5] Melville J. Herskovits: *Notes on African Field Research, 1953–1960* (manuscript, 1953–1960), p. 57/D170.

group.[6] When he put down any roots in the city, they struck stony soil that could only permit a stunted growth.

Accommodation to city life taxed not only social and psychological, but even physiological resources. A study by Scotch of blood pressure among the Zulu of South Africa showed significant differences in incidence of hypertension between those who lived in the rural areas of the "reserves" and those who lived in the City of Durban. This was matched by an index of maladjustment, such as the number of persons who felt that they had been bewitched or were victims of sorcery in the two settings. The contrast in the extent to which high blood pressure was found in rural and urban Zulu was described as "striking." There was a statistically significant "greater frequency of elevated blood pressures . . . among urban Zulu for all age groups and both sexes," while as regards "mean blood pressure values, urban males and urban females are significantly higher for all age groups."[7] The explanation, drawn in terms of acculturative stress, seems clear:

> When informants were questioned in the rural areas as to what were the major problems of life, almost all answered by saying that poverty and migratory labor were the big problems. In the city, however, respondents went on and on when asked the same question. Not only was there poverty, but degradation and humiliation in the treatment of Africans by Europeans, frequent arrests, high rates of illegitimacy, divorce and separation, alcoholism, and open competition for few jobs. From the foregoing it is quite evident that the Africans themselves recognize that there are greater and more kinds of stress in city life than in rural. It is of interest that in response to the question of where they would prefer to live, the country or the city, a significantly greater percentage of city dwellers expressed a preference for living in the country than the percentage of country dwellers who stated that they would prefer to live in the city.[8]

[6] Ibid., pp. 57/D531–535.

[7] Norman A. Scotch: "A Preliminary Report on the Relation of Sociocultural Factors to Hypertension among the Zulu," *Annals of the New York Academy of Sciences,* Vol. 84 (1960), pp. 1001–2.

[8] Ibid., pp. 1003–4.

The reasoning behind the measures that in eastern and southern Africa came to restrict the migrant and the African urban dweller was well expressed in 1942 in an official Circular of the Government of Angola, over the signature of its Governor:

> The rendering of work in Africa cannot continue to depend upon the whim (*arbitrário*) of the Negro, who is by temperament and natural circumstances, inclined to expend only that minimum effort which corresponds to his minimum necessities.[9]

With such a point of departure, the regulation of the labor supply was dictated by the demands of industry. This resulted in a disorganization of village life with serious social consequences stressed by almost every student of labor migration and urbanization in these parts of Africa.

[5]

Like so many other post-European developments, the modern African city emerged under a system of colonial controls whereby the relations between rulers and ruled were determined by differences in physical type. Because of this, colonial thinking in all Subsaharan Africa became, to some degree, racial thinking, and was accentuated by the fact that race became a symbol of status. The "government compound," as it was called in some parts of West Africa, was removed from the center of the city. Where the country was hilly, it was situated atop a rise that gave a view of the countryside and was held to be more healthy than the lower-lying "native" quarters. In the older cities, the pattern was superimposed on the pre-existing community; the newer ones were planned to fit the model.

"Health" was not all. The more experienced colonial powers had learned the value of withdrawal, particularly of formality in the encounters between subject peoples and their rulers. The senior European officials who lived in these government quarters

[9] Quoted in Marvin Harris: "Labour Emigration among the Moçambique Thonga: Cultural and Political Factors," *Africa*, Vol. 29 (1959), p. 62.

descended into the African city only on stated occasions. Those in the higher ranks were to be seen only at a distance, usually in ceremonial dress, invested with an aura of power and prestige.

As the cities grew, the quarter where the government civil servants lived became the nucleus around which other Europeans established themselves. In West Africa, where Europeans were few, their impact on the life of the city was through controls exerted over economic or educational or other activities. In eastern and southern Africa, where the European community was more numerous, its impact was felt in such ways as the amount of land reserved for its dwellings, gardens, and accessory buildings. The districts inhabited by the Africans inevitably became satellites of the European-controlled center. The African presence in the life of these central sections on any but the lowest economic levels was regarded as intrusive.

An instance of how the African urban patterns of racial separation dominated planning may be seen in the 1940 mapping of the projected development of the city of Leopoldville.[1] Leopoldville is situated at the lower end of the great widening of the Congo River known as Stanley Pool. Its western portion lies on a bluff above the river, where the Congo narrows to form the beginning of the long series of rapids reaching to Matadi. In this higher section of the city, the palace of the Governor-General was erected and, in accordance with the general pattern, this was where the Europeans came to cluster their residences. This part dominated the lower-lying commercial center, and the *Cités Indigènes,* inhabited by the Africans. On the map, its status was formally recognized; it was called *Zone Residentielle des Blancs.* The districts along the river were reserved for European commercial structures, for a cultural center, a hospital for whites, and administrative buildings. Behind this a broad belt of parks separated the central portion and the European residential zone from the African city, which was planned to have its own commercial, social, and cultural centers, and its own hospitals. A narrower green belt was to lie between it and the part of the Euro-

[1] Belgian Ministry of Colonies: *Plan Décennal pour le Developpement Économique et Social du Congo Belge* (Brussels, 1949), Carte No. 16.

pean city reserved for industry, whose labor force would thus be close at hand.

When this map was drawn, the principle of separation in location and internal functioning of the European and the African sectors of the population was accepted with little question by the vast majority of Europeans and, it should be noted, unchallenged by most Africans. In the Belgian Congo, Africans at this time were not permitted to be in the European City after nine o'clock at night without a pass. Europeans, too, were prohibited from visiting in the African city at night without permits. This reasoning was extended to explain regulations governing both groups, and consequently said to be nondiscriminatory. Where the European community was small, measures of this sort seem never to have been formally instituted, but in the multiracial territories their objective was protection of the minority from the African majority.

In Leopoldville, the contemplated changes were never fully executed. Rising discontent among Africans was met by lifting many restrictions on their freedom of movement, and extending their range of social activity within the city by the revocation of the official color bar in restaurants and cafes in 1954. Accordingly, the "green belt" between the European and African cities remained as it had been before the Ten Year Plan had been drawn. There was, however, little or no change in the pattern of segregation in housing. Toward the end of the colonial period, some attempts to place African functionaries in housing built for government employees were resisted by the Africans themselves. This was on the dual grounds that under existing conditions they would be held in suspicion by their fellow-Africans because of their closer relations with Europeans, and would also be subject to uncomfortable surveillance by officers of the Government, in ways not possible if they continued to live in the African city.

What was happening in Leopoldville was taking place in differing degree elsewhere in Subsaharan Africa, though not in those countries committed to strict and continuing racial separation. In West Africa, racial desegregation began concurrently with programs to Africanize the government services. That is, officials who were Africans were housed in government compounds in accordance with the perquisites of their rank. This in effect broke the rule of housing segregation. The biases of individual Europeans continued, however, so that Africans who were the first to move into official houses frequently experienced covert discrimination, despite official policy.

In British East Africa, where the size of the European community was larger, change came more slowly. In Kenya, it was only after the Mau Mau uprising that Africans began to be admitted to restaurants frequented by Europeans in the central portion of the capital city, Nairobi. The housing barrier, however, continued, and many Africans were subject to pass laws, though these and comparable measures were clearly in the nature of a rearguard action. Similar developments were observable in Northern Rhodesia.

In the extreme south of the continent, in contrast, the earlier patterns whereby city structure reflected and enforced racial discrimination were not only continued, but intensified. The city of Salisbury, capital both of Southern Rhodesia and the Federation of the Rhodesias and Nyasaland, offers an instructive example of the force of this tradition in the face of attack. This was the result of its geographical location, marginal to countries belonging to the two categories differentiated on the basis of response to Ghana on the one hand, and to South Africa, on the other. Southern Rhodesia, moreover, while politically attached to the less committed northerly territories belonging to the Federation, had long-standing ties of mutual interest and shared views with her neighbor to the south. Here, too, we move into the most industrialized area of Africa, where the need to assure a continuous supply of wage labor was of major importance.

However, Southern Rhodesia is not South Africa, and the growing conviction that the Federation had to prove that multiracial states could function and prosper in Africa led to the introduction of certain modifications in race policy. The establishment of a multiracial university, at a time when in the Union separation of the races in all institutions of higher learning was being pressed, was one indication of this. Some lifting of the industrial color bar was also to be observed, and a complicated revision of the franchise, allowing multiple voting on a qualitative basis, was set up with the aim of encouraging more Africans to participate in government. Along the same lines was the admission of Africans into the Southern Rhodesian House of Assembly. Yet the earlier pattern of the city was maintained. The "townships," as the African quarters were termed, were enlarged. Of symbolic import was the denial, as late as 1959, of housing, in the European residential section of the city, to an African junior Minister in the Federal Cabinet.

A comparable degree of residential differentiation was in fact, if not by statutory regulation, present in the cities of Portuguese Africa. *Assimilados* could live wherever their means permitted, but they were few in number and their means were limited. Around the more favored portions of such centers as Loanda in Angola, or Lourenço Marques in Mozambique, were grouped the African quarters. Here the disparity in the quality of housing available to Europeans and Africans which exists everywhere in eastern and southern Africa, stood out in starkest relief. Thus in Loanda the African quarters were without hygienic facilities. Overcrowding, poor housing, and unpaved streets that were deep in dust during the dry periods and in mud during the rains were the physical expressions of a system of rigorous control over the African populations, that often resorted to physical brutality and forced labor.

Such measures of control were rarely brought to public notice, except in occasional news reports, or the findings of scholars. The following comment on the "impressions of interracial harmony" that might be gathered by the casual visitor to Lourenço Marques in 1956 and 1957 indicates how effectively the controls operated:

> In Moçambique "Europeans Only" notices are not needed in order to maintain an almost perfect separation between the African mass and the Europeans. For example, a bus ride in Lourenço Marques costs the equivalent of one-fourth of the average African's daily wage. Whites transact their business at the post office and bank through African runners and servants. At the movies, soccer games,

> restaurants, hotels and other semi-public places, prices and clothing act as efficient color filters. There is no need for establishing native "locations" as in the Union; perfect residential segregation follows automatically from urban zoning laws and rents. Whites can indeed walk safely in Lourenço Marques' African quarter in the dead of night, but this is because the Africans who live there are forbidden to step out of their houses after nine o'clock.[2]

As late as 1957 it was reported that two Nyasaland truck drivers who failed to make way for the car of a Portuguese official were taken to a police post and beaten so severely with a *palmatoria* that their hands were "like bunches of bananas." [3]

Measures of racial separation and control of African life by a European minority achieved their most explicit form and most rigid implementation in the cities of South Africa. With the coming to power of the Nationalist Party, dominated by Afrikaans-speaking members of the European community, these measures, which had been initiated by preceding governments having majorities from the English-speaking community, were given more rigorous application. Under the doctrine of *apartheid*, the traditional patterns of segregation that marked African cities were extended to all sections of the population. That is, not only were Europeans segregated from non-Europeans, but Asians and Coloureds, or mixed-bloods, were removed to separate quarters. Africans were by law deprived of their urban freehold rights, and those who had earlier acquired holdings, or were living close to the heart of the city, were moved to new "locations" situated miles from the center. In the large cities, particularly in Johannesburg, housing was also provided for the squatters who, in earlier years, had erected mud block or more flimsy shelters that from the beginning became noxious slums.

The pattern of segregation was carried so far as to embrace urban African ethnic groupings. Thus, in planning the Bantu townships of Daveytown, established in Benoni, Transvaal, one portion was allocated to the Shangaan-Tonga-Venda groups. A

[2] Marvin Harris: *Portugal's African "Wards,"* Africa Today Pamphlets: 2 (New York, 1958), p. 4.

[3] Anonymous: "Nyasaland African Drivers Beaten . . . in Portuguese Territory," London *Times* (September 14, 1957).

second was split between the Xhosa, the Swazi, the Ndebele, and the Zulu, each occupying its own subsection. A third was given over to the Sotho, the southern and northern subgroups, each being allocated a separate part. This separation was to be thoroughgoing:

> Each sector must be looked on as an entity of its own and be provided pro rata with school, church and trading sites. In the case of intermarriage, it is usual, even in terms of international law, for the wife to assume the nationality of the husband. However, if any great difficulty should present itself the choice must be left to the family, the deciding factor usually being the medium of the native language through which the parents desire their children to be educated.

The reference here was to procedures under the Bantu Education Act, which as we have seen stressed the use of African languages in the schooling of African children.[4]

Striking correlations existed in Subsaharan Africa between the proportion of Europeans in the population of a given area, the degree of internal tension found there, which tended to increase with greater numbers of non-Africans, and the rigor of the rules of urban segregation. The relation between these three factors accordingly made for restrictions that became more numerous and more firmly enforced as we move from north to south along the eastern coast.

The key to an understanding of these differences is to be sought in the fears of a socially, economically and politically privileged minority faced with an indigenous population of overwhelming superiority in numbers, steadily growing in their capacity to challenge the inequities of their situation under the rules established by the minority itself. Obviously, this is not the entire explanation. We are dealing with a complex psychosocial phenomenon which cannot be referred to any single cause. But the factor of fear merits further exploration.

One example of this is found in a 1957 incident in a South African town named Standerton, in the Transvaal. As a result of

[4] J. Edward Mathewson: *The Establishment of an Urban Bantu Township* (Pretoria, 1957), p. 32.

moves to extend the pass laws to African women as well as men, almost a thousand women had been arrested during a protest march, charged with taking part in an illegal procession. As the day neared for the trial, rumors began to circulate in the European community that the African women would demonstrate to show their defiance of the law; that the African men would demonstrate in sympathy with them, and that there would be riots; that there would be a "blood bath" and that the town was therefore "no longer safe for white people." On the morning of the trial the African women, babies strapped to their backs, moved through the police "show of force," while "back in town, servantless householders waited, peered through windows and prayed. Some husbands stayed at home." No trouble developed, however, and in the afternoon the word came that the women had been discharged. As one Johannesburg newspaper editorialized: "While we do not wish to make too much of this phenomenon, . . . it shows that one does not have to dig far beneath the surface to find tension." [5]

In seeking to understand reactions of this kind, the continual conflict in values must be given a prominent place. The contrast between the social and economic position of the racial minority, and that of the indigenous majority over whom they ruled generated deep ambivalences. These were masked by a telltale stridency in defending practices which were out of line with the ideological heritage brought from Europe. The disparity between ideal and act was a nagging reality. For example, the European doctrine of the equality of all before the law had its own interpretation in southern Africa, where one measure of treatment was reserved for Europeans, and another for Africans.

The pervasiveness of such discrepancies could not but arouse feelings of guilt, particularly where an accepted democratic ideology could be and was frequently appealed to—and was actually operative in enough cases to keep it alive in the minds of all elements in the population. These feelings of guilt translated themselves into resentments and fears, and sometimes

[5] Anonymous: "Standerton's Ordeal," *Johannesburg Sunday Express* (July 21, 1957), *passim.*

brutality in situations where the gap between the image of decency and actual behavior stretched beyond the limits of acceptable rationalization. The accusations raised against Africans about the dangers of their "reverting to savagery" were to be heard most frequently, and stated with the greatest conviction, in those parts of the Subsaharan continent where racial inequalities in opportunity and reward were most marked. Conversely, questions of this sort were rarely raised in the western portions of the continent, as Africans came more and more to participate in the direction of their own affairs.

[6]

The world-wide movement of peoples to towns and cities, though not peculiar to Africa, was accelerated there. Where these centers did not exist, they were created. Where they developed out of earlier centers, they changed both in form and function. Moreover, urbanization in Africa took on a particular character. Here city dwellers not only had to solve the usual problems of urban life everywhere—questions of housing, of health and hygiene, of recreation, of juvenile delinquency—but the complexity of these problems was compounded by other factors. In the areas of permanent non-African settlement, city life sharpened a sense of differentials based on race, on standards of living, on education, on economic opportunity and the like, since in the city these were experienced at close range, and thereby served to multiply the frictions arising out of continuous propinquity. Even where multiracial tensions were minimal, the rapidity with which those who migrated to the towns had to adapt themselves to life in the new setting introduced special problems into what is at best a difficult enough process, even in those parts of the world where the city in its later forms had been long known.

So encompassing did this process of change seem to be, so different the new urban setting from the traditional scene, that it seemed eminently reasonable to assume that far-reaching changes, if not complete breaks with the older tribal ways must result. An early student of these changes described them in this passage:

> Over the heart of a poor and primitive continent civilization has laid a finger of steel; it has stirred a hundred tribes together; it has brought them new wealth, new ambitions, new knowledge, new interest, new faiths and new problems.[6]

In the preceding chapter, we have seen how the logical appeal of the concept of cultural marginality, applied to Africans who had studied in institutions of higher education, led to the conclusion that the need to resolve conflicts between aboriginal and acculturated experience must result in social and personal maladjustment. In the case of the new urban masses, who had lower status, similar reasoning led to what seemed to be the equally inevitable conclusion that Africans who left their tribal milieu for life in towns and cities or on the mines, to become wage laborers in industry, or domestic servants, or mine boys, must suffer in a similar way.

To this process various terms, of which "detribalization" was perhaps the most widely used, came to be applied, and for a decade or more had extensive currency. Given the customary assumptions, the cogency of such terms seemed undeniable. Like most catchwords, however, they meant different things to different people, particularly since they were rarely defined with any degree of precision. Thus, questions that seldom entered initially began to be asked concerning the extent to which, under "detribalization," changes in African material culture—housing, furnishings, clothing, implements and the like—could be equated with changes in the nonmaterial aspects of life, particularly in religious and moral sanctions. For though it is far simpler to carry over rural patterns of nonmaterial culture into city life, changes in material aspects are much more readily discernible. It was undoubtedly for this reason that discussions of African urbanization selected items of material culture in drawing indices of acculturation. This approach was rooted in the ethnocentrism of

[6] Godfrey Wilson: *An Essay on the Economics of Detribalization in Northern Rhodesia,* Rhodes-Livingstone Papers No. 5 (Livingstone, 1941), p. 9.

the industrialized societies and their emphasis on the importance of technological change. It is easy to see how acceptance of material culture by urban Africans came to be regarded not only as a total acceptance of the new culture, but also as a rejection of the old.

Taken literally, "detribalization" could only mean disaffiliation with those groupings into which urban Africans or their forbears had been born. This disaffiliation was understood to be psychological as well as behavioral; it was the "abandonment of traditional behaviour patterns."[7] From a more positive point of view, it characterized "detribalized" Africans as having taken over new primary loyalties and values, along with new ways of living and new occupations.

In the strict, but not the connotative meaning of the word, whether the detribalized person lived permanently in the city or not was secondary, and so was his degree of adjustment to his new setting. Yet few individuals or groups in Africa could be regarded as truly detribalized. Strictly speaking, the word could reasonably be applied to the Americo-Liberians, or to the Creoles of Sierra Leone, though in both cases length of residence and current loyalities made it inappropriate. Perhaps the only truly detribalized populations of African origin are to be found in those New World Negro societies where the sense of African affiliation has long been quite absent.

The colonial policy of the French during the first half of the twentieth century, and the continuing policy of the Portuguese, usually called "assimilationism," may be regarded as aimed at inducing selective detribalization. In the former case, attempts were made to create a special group, schooled so as to make up a nucleus of highly acculturated persons who, as Frenchmen, could participate in ruling the territories from which they came, and thus minimize social, political and economic frictions. In Portuguese practice, the policy of assimilationism, or admitting to Portuguese citizenship Africans who could satisfy the criteria for

[7] A. Moreira: "The 'Elites' of the Portuguese 'Tribal' Provinces (Guinea, Angola, Mozambique)," *International Social Science Bulletin,* Vol. 8 (1956), p. 477.

inclusion in a category termed *assimilados,* set up criteria which were authoritatively described as follows: An *assimilado,*

> must be over 18 years of age, fluent in Portuguese, in receipt of earnings from a trade, profession or appointment or in possession of property adequate to provide for himself and his dependents; he must be of good character, with the educational background and habits presumed for the purposes of full liability to the public and private law applicable to Portuguese citizens. . . ." [8]

The fact that in 1956 no more than 1% of the Africans in Portuguese possessions had this status suggests the extent of "detribalization" incident on African-Portuguese contact.

Terms of this kind, in actuality, gloss over the complexities of adjustment to the urban setting; for those engaged in the scientific study of change in Africa they are meaningless. Balandier, examining the concept of the *évolué,* in connection with his study of Brazzaville, found it to be "singularly equivocal and imprecise." This was not only because it was wrongly used to classify those whose response to contact with non-African culture was quite different, but more importantly because of its ethnocentric component "because it implies a particular kind of a relation of the Black and the White, that of teacher to pupil. . . ." [9]

Another such term was "élite." A UNESCO symposium held in 1956 revealed the difficulties in employing it as a tool for research, by demonstrating how ambiguous were its uses. Tardits, one of the contributors to this symposium, in analyzing the aspects of the term most prominently put forward by social theorists, characterized one of these as "not . . . a selective criterion but merely a label" which "may therefore be said to serve no useful purpose in this context." Another important theory he held to be no more than the identification of an "élite" as a group that wielded political power.[1] He concluded that in view of the difficulty of delineating the term, "the criteria by which the section of

[8] Ibid., p. 464.

[9] Georges Balandier: *Sociologie des Brazzaville Noires,* Cahiers de la Fondation Nationale des Sciences Politiques, No. 67 (Paris, 1955), p. 34.

[1] Claude Tardits: "The Notion of the Elite and the Urban Social Survey in Africa," *International Social Science Bulletin,* Vol. 8 (1956), pp. 493–4.

the population to be studied are determined must be clearly defined," in each situation to which it might be applied. Yet even where, as in his investigation of the response of younger Africans living in Porto Novo to European culture, he defined his élite in terms of degree of schooling, he found his analysis complicated by the fact that, "the coexistence of illiterate, semiliterate and literate members of the same group is one of the characteristic traits of present-day Dahomean society."[2] However, the validity of the designation "*élite*," has not been unanimously challenged. The Smythes, defining the word in more flexible terms as "the class of persons who are in positions of leadership, power and influence,"[3] used it as a key concept in analyzing the upper stratum of late colonial and postcolonial Nigerian society.

There was no disagreement as to the disutility of the word "detribalization." On this point, the Smythes conclude,

> Despite class feelings on the part of the élite, the popular notion that a Western education somehow separates an African irrevocably from his tribal identification was not borne out in this study. It is true that the educated élite live in Western houses, usually at some distance from their home villages, and they have forsaken long-revered . . . aspects of indigenous culture. It is also true that their way of life is far different from that of the villagers. However, they did not consider these changes as removing the lasting appeal of allegiance to the tribe.[4]

So unsatisfactory was the term "detribalization" for Rouche, that in his study of Zabrama migration to Ghana he was moved to state:

> The transplanted communities, far from being "detribalized" are, on the contrary, "super-tribalized." The town, the mechanized life, do not weaken their tribal cohesion but strengthen it. . . . This "super-tribalization" appears especially in the prototype of the migrant . . . who has organized himself into subdistrict and village communities which do not allow him to leave his social stra-

[2] Claude Tardits: *Porto-Novo, les Nouvelles Générations Africaines entre leurs Traditions et l'Occident* (Paris, 1958), p. 17.

[3] Hugh H. and Mabel M. Smythe: *The New Nigerian Elite* (Stanford, 1960), p. viii.

[4] Ibid., p. 109.

> tum throughout his whole stay; who, in his system of chieftainships, has transplanted the traditional systems of his native country; who, in his relationships with other communities of migrants remains faithful to old alliances or old enmities; who, in his relations with the native peoples of the Gold Coast remains in a position of "splendid isolation" which allows almost no exchange of culture.[5]

In Freetown, we are told, "Instead of using such blanket terms as 'detribalization' it will be preferable to isolate the system of relationships obtaining among members of a given group and analyse changes within that system."[6] In a later discussion of the point, we read, "a careful examination of the extent to which immigrants maintain tribal customs and acknowledge tribal loyalties shows the foolishness of such generalizations."[7]

The force of ethnocentrism is such, however, that despite the unanimity with which these overall designations were criticized by serious students of urbanism in Africa, they continued to be used. Almost from the beginning, research on urbanized Africans proved that such designations simplified the question and obscured the realities of a very complex phenomenon. These early data, like the materials of the studies that followed them, disclosed how many different levels of adjustment were to be found in a given urban group at a given moment.

In 1948 Hellmann, who made a study of an African slum-yard in Johannesburg, commenting on the uncritical use of "detribalized," stated that "The growth of this concept" was "dangerous because the term is not defined and is not used to convey any definite meaning but rather a host of vague impressions." She therefore set up three criteria to guide its use in her study:

> . . . permanent residence in an area other than that of the chief to whom a man would normally pay allegiance; complete severance of the relationship to the chief; and independence of rural relatives

[5] Jean Rouch: "Migrations au Ghana (Gold Coast)—(Enquête 1953–1955)," *Journal de la Société des Africanistes,* Vol. 26 (1956), p. 164; English translation by P. E. O. and J. B. Haigham (Accra, 1954), mimeographed, p. 60.

[6] Michael Banton: *West African City, a Study of Tribal Life in Freetown* (London, 1957), p. 18.

[7] Ibid., p. 121.

> both for support during periods of unemployment and ill-health or for the performance of ceremonies connected with the major crises of life.[8]

Later in her discussion, she wrote:

> The rapidity and completeness of the process of detribalization has been exaggerated. The importance of the process of cultural absorption and the changes which it is bringing about can, on the other hand, hardly be exaggerated. By this I do not mean to imply that Native culture is being Europeanized *en bloc* or that all aspects of Native culture are being influenced to the same degree by western civilization. For, despite the extent of cultural absorption which is taking place, Native culture is not being submerged by European culture. Rather, it is adapting elements of European culture, incorporating them into Native culture, and often modifying them so as to create a new composite culture.[9]

This means that we are dealing with a basic process in the adjustment of individual behavior and of institutional structures to be found in all situations where peoples having different ways of life come into contact. This process we term *reinterpretation,* whereby sanctions and values of a given tradition under contact with another are applied to new forms, combining and recombining until syncretisms develop that rework them into meaningful, well-functioning conventions. In the same region where Wilson studied the economics of detribalization,[1] Mitchell, a decade later, analyzed another aspect of the urban situation, with results which plumbed further depths of complexity. His attention was attracted by "an apparent paradox," in a dance called the *Kalela,* that he came upon in the African quarters of the Copper Belt towns of Northern Rhodesia. This was the paradox:

> The dance is clearly a tribal dance in which tribal differences are emphasized by the language, and the idiom of the songs and the dress of the dancers are drawn from an urban existence which tends to submerge tribal differences.[2]

[8] Ellen Hellmann: *Rooiyard, a Sociological Survey of an Urban Slum Yard,* Rhodes-Livingstone Papers, No. 13 (Capetown and Livingstone, 1948), p. 110.

[9] Ibid., p. 115.

[1] Godfrey Wilson: Op. cit.

[2] J. Clyde Mitchell: *The Kalela Dance,* Rhodes-Livingstone Papers, No. 27 (Manchester, 1956), p. 9.

It is not possible here to follow the ramifications of institutional and personal relationships that made up the reinterpretative adjustments which arose in developing the new orientations laid bare by this study. We may, however, note yet another formula that Mitchell found inadequate when applied to his data. This formula held that, in urban collectivities, such as "schools, churches, trade unions, political parties" and the like, "the more that Africans identify themselves with these groups the less important tribal affiliation becomes." [3] While, as in the concept of "detribalization," there was enough semblance of validity in this statement to carry some conviction, the principle of cultural change, which holds that adjustment to a new setting builds upon pre-established alternatives in an old way of life compels us to look beyond the surface of appearances.

The study of the Kalela dance demonstrated that the transient nature of the African experience in these Copper Belt towns caused the dance to operate "as a category of interaction together with tribalism," to mediate social relationships between the Africans. "The . . . relationships among a group of tribesmen in their natural home," it was found, "form part of a complete tribal system," whereby they "fix their relationships to one another in terms of kinship links, by clanship, and by their membership of villages." That is, though adaptive behavior, altered preceding patterns of tribal affiliation, these patterns did not necessarily disappear.

Mitchell's research was directed primarily toward an understanding of how the relevant social structures, and the relations between members of an urban society, had changed as a result of living in the Copper Belt towns. Where the total range of activity was taken into account, and other aspects of life less immediately related to the new economic situation considered, such as religious and political behavior, language, or music, the force of custom was seen to be even stronger, and the "detribalizing" factors tended to recede further into the background.

[3] D. F. McCall: "Dynamics of Urbanization in Africa," *Annals* of the American Academy of Political and Social Science, Vol. 298 (1955), pp. 158–9.

It is essential, if confusion in the study of African urbanization is to be avoided, that *change* be carefully dissociated from *demoralization.* Concomitantly, it is most important to recognize that not all cultural elements, particularly those in the area of values or, as in the case of music or language, those that lodge deep beneath the level of consciousness, are as susceptible to change as material culture and technology. The studies from southern and eastern Africa cited are particularly pertinent because of the greater discontinuities between rural and urban life there than in western and central Africa.

We may thus profitably examine the relevance of concepts such as "detribalization" to the life of urban Africans of these other regions, in the light of the adjustments between rural and city ways that have here been made. Writing on Nigeria, Lloyd observed,

> In a continent in which urbanization is usually correlated with the disruption of traditional tribal forms of social grouping, it seems paradoxical that in southwest Nigeria the commercial revolution should have preserved an even fortified these groupings.[4]

In Ghana, Busia found that in the Sekondi-Takoradi area, traditional marriage forms, puberty rites, the "housemaid" system whereby a girl is sent to live with relatives as a preparation for marriage, have all persisted in this urban complex.[5] According to Nicol,

> The old gods are not completely lost in the cities and industrial towns in spite of the urbanized African being a Christian or Moslem. Occasionally a trade union or particular body of artisans adopts a particular god relevant to its calling and sacrifices to it annually, much as guilds and trade unions in Catholic countries choose a patron saint. An example often quoted is that of Ogun, the Yoruba god of iron. He has been adopted by taxi and lorry drivers

[4] P. C. Lloyd: "The Yoruba Town Today," *Sociological Review,* Vol. 7, n.s. (1959), p. 61.

[5] K. A. Busia: *Report on a Social Survey of Sekondi-Takoradi* (London and Accra, 1950), pp. 30–7.

in cities as their patron god; he receives an annual and—from the pedestrian's point of view—absolutely necessary sacrifice from his subjects for safety on the road.[6]

Research in Freetown, Sierra Leone, on the elements in the population coming from the tribal groupings of the Protectorate and the rural territory of the coastal Colony, defined the adjustments to city living there. Certain facts brought out in this investigation, though lightly passed over, indicate how essential for perspective on life in the city is the understanding of the entire gamut of pre-urban patterns. Clothing is a case in point. While the tribal immigrant woman might wear European dress on the street, or the version of it worn by the women born and raised in the city, once within her own compound, she could be expected to go about in traditional garb, uncovered above the waist. The "Moslem monopoly of the respected roles in tribal society," was reflected in behavior at funerals, and in preferred modes of dress.[7] Though, like most studies of urbanism in Africa, this one was focused on social orientations, some attention was given to the retention of what was called "pagan practices." Many of these, it was stated, "continue in Freetown," and though details were not included, we are told that the "relatively respectable trade of herbalist" continued in force, together with divination by the "look ground man" and the practice of magic.[8]

Belief in magic, in the efficacy of aboriginal medicines, and in divination is, indeed, one of the most persistently and widely retained traditions in the African urban scene. There is supporting evidence from all parts of the subcontinent that the force of these beliefs has been strengthened by the psychological insecurity of those removed from ancestral or other traditional safeguards. Thus, on the Witwatersrand, the most intensively in-

[6] (Abioseh) Davidson Nicol: "Some Observations on the Assimilation of Traditional African Culture in the Culture of Mass Society," *Newsletter*, American Society for African Culture, Vol. 3, No. 3, Supplement No. 17 (November 30, 1960), p. 4.

[7] Michael Banton: Op. cit., p. 135.

[8] Ibid., pp. 138–9.

dustrialized district in the whole of Subsaharan Africa, all three of these aboriginal beliefs flourish.

> The practice of African medicine and, to a degree to which it is difficult to estimate, the practice of magic, is universal. . . . There is a widespread belief in the existence of magic and in the magical power of human beings and, in the urban environment, new spells, new medicines, new cures, are all adapted or applied to new situations and exigencies. . . . When distress and misfortune befall an urban African family, the African doctor is called and warns the members of the family to observe African ways of life. . . . African beliefs . . . are evident even in the conduct of those who, to all outward appearances, have taken over western standards of living, education and mores.[9]

To complete the picture, the reinterpretation of the indigenous belief that specialized aspects of magic and medicine are the same brings it about that in this South African city "many Africans seek the services of both qualified European doctors and attend the municipal clinic besides consulting their own special types of Native doctors and diviners." [1]

Another aspect of urbanization that throws light on the attitudes of Africans living in towns and cities is found in the ubiquitous voluntary associations. For West African cities, these fall into four categories—tribal unions, friendly societies, occupational groups, and entertainment and recreational associations. They can be divided into "traditional societies," "traditional-modernized groups," where earlier ways have been "modified or expanded to suit modern purposes," and those which are "wholly modern in organization and objective." [2]

The African city differs in many essential respects from the definitions and descriptions it has been given in studies which,

[9] L. Longmore: "Medicine, Magic and Witchcraft among Urban Africans on the Witwatersrand," *Central African Journal of Medicine,* Vol. 4 (1958), pp. 242–3.

[1] Ibid., p. 244.

[2] Kenneth Little: "The Role of Voluntary Associations in West African Urbanization," *American Anthropologist,* Vol. 39 (1957), pp. 581–91, *passim.*

consciously or not, have drawn forced parallels to Euroamerican cities at the cost of underestimating or disregarding the power of antecedent tradition. It is of the first importance to shed the ethnocentric concepts that have gained currency, and without such preconception seek to understand the nature of the African city, and the kind of adjustments Africans have made to it.

10

Toward Self-Government

IF THE twentieth century be called the Century of Self-Determination, for Subsaharan Africa the critical period was the half-decade between 1955 and 1960. In the larger perspective of world history, this same half-decade brought the system of Western European colonialism, which had been developing for over the preceding four centuries, in sight of the end of its road. The ten preceding years had been the time of Asian self-determination; now it was the turn of Africa. Rarely has the course of events moved with greater speed, or to a more clearly discernible conclusion.

At the end of 1954, in all Africa south of the Saharan latitudes, only three states were self-governing and full members of the United Nations—Liberia, Ethiopia, and the Union of South Africa. Of these three, only the first two were in African hands; in the Union the indigenous majority was permitted no say in the government. Southern Rhodesia, where a similar internal situation existed, had the status of a self-governing colony, regulating its domestic but not foreign affairs, and with certain powers, never invoked, reserved to Great Britain. The vast area lying between the desert and the Congo River were, with two minor exceptions, under French and British control; the heart of the continent, the Belgian Congo, was governed from Brussels. The territories lying to the east were British. Portugal, in the face of growing anticolonial world sentiment, had changed the juridical, but not the functional status of her overseas possessions from colonies to provinces of the Metropole, with the reins of government held tightly in Lisbon. Spain held the island of Fernando Po and, on the mainland, Rio Muñi.

In 1955, what had been the Anglo-Egyptian Sudan became independent. By this time the Gold Coast had for several years possessed an African ministry, responsible to a popularly elected African legislature for its internal affairs, under a British governor. This system of devolution of power established a pattern that was to be followed in bringing other British possessions to self-government. In 1957 the functioning reality was given legal sanction, when the Gold Coast was transmuted from a British possession into the State of Ghana, absorbing through plebiscite the former Trust Territory of British Togoland. A year later, in 1958, the roll of independent countries was increased by the addition of the Republic of Guinea, which voted against joining the French Community.

Then the floodgates of self-determination opened. 1960, which came to be called "the year of Africa," must be regarded as marking the climax of this movement, if only because of the number of states that gained their independence in this year. On January first, by United Nations action, the French Trust Territory of the Cameroons became the self-governing Republic of Cameroun. In April another Trust Territory, French Togo, was granted its independence, and on July first a third, Somalia, was released from tutelage. On June thirtieth the independence of the Congo Republic was proclaimed.

The movement then swung to French territories. In October, however, the most populous country of Subsaharan Africa, Nigeria, took over from the British the remaining powers not already in African hands—foreign relations and defense. As in Ghana in 1957, this act turned functional into juridical reality. Nigeria became a full member of the British Commonwealth and the United Nations. November saw the final symbolic vestige of earlier controls disappear, when a Nigerian Governor General assumed office. This move was similar in intent, though not in form, to the adjustment that took place in July when Ghana, becoming a Republic, replaced its British Governor General with an elected Chief of State.

In the intervening months, France disappeared as a colonial power in Subsaharan Africa. The French Community, in which all French African territories but Guinea opted to accept membership in the 1958 referendum, vested in France control over defense, foreign relations, and, except for internal matters, over finance. These territories became Autonomous Republics, not independent in the sense of Liberia, the Sudan, Ghana, Ethiopia, or Guinea, which as sovereign nations had control over all their affairs, external as well as internal. The status of these Autonomous Republics precluded their holding membership in the United Nations, a factor that by this time was becoming of increasing importance to African states.

In the Community, as originally envisaged, the relations of each Autonomous Republic with the others were to be channeled through central organs, located in France. Predictably this generated dual reactions. Balanced against the positive pull of earlier patterns of administrative centralization was the negative force of suspicion, generated by colonial policies of divide and rule, which caused African leaders to be deeply apprehensive of this arrangement. The concept of "balkanization," as this type of geographical and political fragmentation had come to be called, was frequently discussed in this context. One result was the coming together, in a manner not originally planned, of the constituent states of Senegal and Soudan, to form the Federation of Mali. As first contemplated, it was also intended to include the Republics of the Upper Volta and Dahomey, but these eventually decided to join another grouping, termed the Council of the Entente, in a looser union with the Ivory Coast and Niger. Parallel motives brought about discussions among the four members of the Community that had made up the former French Equatorial Africa. Three of them, the Republic of the Congo, the

Central African Republic, and Chad, entered into agreements relating chiefly to a customs union. The Gabon Republic, economically most prosperous, remained aloof.

The Federation of Mali, like Madagascar, after protracted negotiations, declared itself to be fully independent in April. This introduced a new element into the Community, bringing its structure closer in character to that of the British Commonwealth. In July, however, without prior discussion, the countries of the Entente announced their intention to assume the same status, and declared themselves fully independent. At about the same time the four French territories of central Africa took similar measures. All of them, together with Senegal and the Soudan, which in August split into the Republics of Senegal and of Mali, were thereupon admitted to the United Nations, which thus gained thirteen full members to swell the total to nineteen from the subcontinent, all except South Africa under the full political control of the indigenous population.[1]

How much the African situation had evolved in five years can be seen if we contrast 1960 with the beginning of this half-decade. In West Africa, all but four colonial administrations had disappeared. These were Portuguese Guinea, the Gambia, an anomalous splinter of land whose ecology no less than its history made its future an enigma, Sierra Leone, scheduled for independence in 1961, and the British Trust Territory of the Cameroons, which was in process of deciding its future alignment by plebescite. Except for Rio Muñi and Fernando Po, which remained under Spanish control, and the island of São Tome and the enclave of Cabinda, still Portuguese possessions, no foreign political administration functioned between the Cameroons and the Congo. South of the river, the former Belgian Congo, which in June became the Congo Republic, though racked by internal dissension, could no longer be classified as a colonial dependency.

In British East and Central Africa, in the Portuguese territories of Angola and Mozambique, and in the High Commission

[1] Mauretania became independent in November of this same year; it is not included in our discussion because it lies outside the area of Subsaharan Africa.

territories of Bechuanaland, Basutoland and Swaziland, ultimate controls were still vested in Europe. The legal status of South-West Africa, mandated to the Union of South Africa by the League of Nations after the First World War, was still in dispute. The Federation of the Rhodesias and Nyasaland, and Kenya, Uganda and Tanganyika, were moving with increasing rapidity toward self-government, with full African participation; in South Africa, soon to be declared a Republic, Africans were becoming more and more restive; only in the Portuguese territories was there no internal organized movement toward change in the position of the Africans, though here, too, stirrings were to be detected.

The difference between the countries which lay to the north and south of the line drawn along the northern borders of Angola, Southern Rhodesia and Mozambique, were becoming more marked. South of it, the European populations were holding to their political position of dominance, determined to resist any drive toward effective African participation in government. Here the tale was one of increasing tension, the prognosis one of open interracial strife. North of our line, between Southern Rhodesia and the Ethiopian border, the dominant minority groups were becoming increasingly resigned to inevitabilities which grew more and more apparent.

We can obtain an even more striking perspective on how far-reaching was the change-over during this half-decade if we approach it in terms of its geographical and demographic dimensions. In 1954, those parts of Africa lying between the Sahara and South Africa not under various forms of colonial control included only about 450,000 square miles, peopled by some 18,000,000 inhabitants. At the end of 1959, with the addition of the Sudan, Ghana and Guinea to Liberia and Ethiopia, the area of self-government had increased to something more than 1,500,000 square miles, with populations numbering more than 37,000,000. Two years later, better than half of this area, more than 4,500,000 square miles of a total of about 9,000,000, and an even larger proportion of the population, over 90,000,000 inhabitants of an estimated 160,000,000, were in this category. This meant that ir the "African year" of 1960 alone, territories encompassing over 3,000,000 square miles, with an aggregate population of over 53,000,000—about three times the population, and seven times the area of all independent Africa five years earlier—had become self-governing.

The dramatic events of these years must be recognized as the climax of forces in play from the beginnings of the partition of Africa to the close of the Second World War and the post-war period. The responses to colonial control which, with increasing African familiarity with the world scene gave rise to nationalist movements that aimed at overthrowing the system. The counter-nationalisms African nationalism stimulated represent one aspect of this complex. Appeal to methods of constitutional change as a means of attaining independence, as against the direct use of force is another. Still another factor of continuing political significance was the increasing cultural awareness of the Africans, expressed in the affirmation of African values and the search for a unified image of its historic past. On the European side of the political line between colonial rulers and African subjects, criticism of colonialism and colonial controls was registered in the metropolitan countries.

In this chapter, we shall analyze and assess these emergent forces. We shall endeavor to understand how they made for a consolidation of past and present experience that, on the level of culture in general no less than on that of polity, could make for the establishment of an Africa which would itself shape its particular future.

[2]

The most important force in this swift movement toward self-government was the pressure of the various nationalist groups. Irrespective of their beginnings or leadership, more and more Africans came to know and incorporate into their own thinking the political ideologies and the economic and social aspirations of the outside world. The significance of these movements went beyond their role in preparing African countries for independence, and enabling them to control their own affairs. One result of their activities was the experience gained by their leaders in the practical politics of government, which they put to use, once in power, for developing the political systems of their countries.

The movement toward African self-determination began long before it crystallized into identifiable and cohesive organizations, with specific programs. The dissatisfaction of Africans with their position as colonial subjects found expression as early as the nineteenth century, and continued with increasing vigor into the twentieth. When first expressed, its protest tended to be particularistic, and was contained within the framework of the colonial system; that is, it did not question the system itself. The direct attack on colonialism came much later. Thus a leading editorial in the Lagos *Times,* in 1881, stated: "It is gradually becoming an anxious question with many—how long shall we be tied to leading-strings? . . ." and later, "it is time for us boldly to ask England to associate us with themselves in the matter of regulating and superintending our own affairs." Though those the writer represented were "not clamouring for independence," he made clear his conviction that "a time will come when the British Colonies on the West Coast of Africa . . . will be left to regulate their own internal and external affairs." [2]

Here it is important to clarify the concept of nationalism, since its use in the African context, though consistent, differs from its established meaning in political philosophy. In political theory, as generally stated, nationalism is inseparable from the idea of nationality, or nationhood.

> The growth of nationalism is the process of integration of the masses of the people into a common political form. Nationalism therefore presupposes the existence, in fact or as an ideal, of a centralized form of government over a large and distinct territory.[3]

[2] Cited in Jean Herskovits Kopytoff: *Liberated Africans and the History of Lagos Colony to 1886* (unpublished Ph.D. thesis, University of Oxford, 1960), pp. 410–11.

[3] Hans Kohn: *The Idea of Nationalism* (New York, 1944), p. 4.

The same authority later defined nationalism as "a state of mind, in which the supreme loyalty of the individual is felt to be due to the nation-state."[4] Africanist usage, however, consistently held the word to mean movements striving for independence from colonial rule, and left the factor of devotion to a nation-state to one side.

Hodgkin, in defining the term, took the more common Africanist position:

> My own inclination is to use the term "nationalist" in a broad sense, to describe any organization or group that explicitly asserts the rights, claims and aspirations of a given African society (from the level of the language-groups to that of "Pan-Africa") in opposition to European authority, whatever its institutional form and objectives.[5]

Coleman, in writing of Nigeria, employing the term exclusively for protest movements, differentiated "traditional" from "modern" manifestations. The former class included:

> movements of resistence to the initial British penetration and occupation, early revolts provoked by the imposition or operation of alien political or economic coercions, and nativistic or messianic movements which provided psychological or emotional outlets for the tensions and frustrations produced by rapid cultural change.

He distinguished "modern" nationalism by the fact it comprehended "sentiments, activities and organizational developments aimed explicitly at . . . self-government and independence . . on a basis of equality in an international state system."[6]

Not all Africanists accepted this position. Balandier remarked on the "ambiguous character" of the word nationalism when used to designate

> any kind of organization, however rudimentary, which evades the control of the dominant Power, any protest against political in-

[4] Hans Kohn: "Nationalism," in *Encyclopaedia Britannica,* Vol. 16 (1957), p. 149.

[5] T. Hodgkin: *Nationalism in Colonial Africa* (London, 1956), p. 23.

[6] James S. Coleman: *Nigeria: Background to Nationalism* (Berkeley and Los Angeles, California, 1958), pp. 169–70.

> feriority, any movement stimulated by a "racial" policy locally adopted.[7]

Hailey, sensing a need to distinguish the African from the conventional European usage, expressed preference for the word "Africanism."

> In Europe nationalism is a readily recognizable force, even though it may not be easily definable, but as a concept it has associations which make it difficult of application in the conditions of Africa.

For him, only in the cases of South Africa; of Liberia, marked by "its determination to preserve its national identity, even to the extent of refusing to accept foreign aid in the development of its resources" during its earlier years; of the Basuto, who "continue . . . to display a strong feeling of pride in their national life"; and of the (then) Gold Coast, which "has developed a conception of nationhood which though artificial in its origin now has something of the quality of a genuine national ideal" did he find the word "nationalism" applicable.[8]

There can be little question that claims for a more restricted use of "nationalism" had a certain validity, but the fact remained that the main current in discussions of African questions continued to follow the broader definition, and the usage that Hailey urged was never taken up. Even where "nationalism" in its European sense became applicable to new nations such as Ghana or Guinea or Nigeria, its use was eschewed by African leaders, who were already committed to the stated ideal of broader political entities. Here, the word will be used to distinguish "those movements that have arisen in reaction to foreign control," and thus to designate "attempts to attain self-government by the conversion of colonial dependencies into independent political entities."[9]

[7] Georges Balandier: "Contribution à l'Étude des Nationalismes en Afrique Noire," *Zaïre*, Vol. 8 (1954), p. 379.

[8] Lord Malcolm Hailey: *An African Survey, Revised 1956* (London, 1957), pp. 201–2.

[9] Northwestern University, Program of African Studies: *Africa* (Studies of United States Foreign Policy, No. 4, Committee Print, Committee on Foreign Relations, United States Senate, 86th Congress, 1st Session, No. 4, Washington, 1959), p. 22.

It is astonishing how late in the period immediately preceding self-government the movements for African independence came to be recognized as a factor in colonial policy. No mention of these movements occurs, for example, in the first edition of the Hailey *African Survey,* the most comprehensive analysis of African affairs before the Second World War. Nor does the word "nationalism" appear in its elaborate index. How quickly the nationalist groups moved into positions where they had to be taken into serious account is shown by the 1956 revision of this study, where we find the manifestations of "Africanism" discussed at some length.[1] Even at this late date, however, the subject was treated along broad lines, and not in terms of the specific organizations which were exerting cumulative pressures.

The development of African nationalisms was directly related both to the opportunities of Africans for access to European education, and to the administrative policies of the several colonial powers. It is not by chance that the first two Subsaharan African countries to gain their independence in the twentieth century, the Sudan and Ghana, came out of British tutelage. By the same token, the territories where African nationalism was least developed as late as the end of the "African year," 1960, were those under Portuguese rule, where Africans were most debarred from schooling and lived under the most rigorous political controls. Between these poles were the positions of the French and Belgians. The former followed a policy of relative assimilationism through the creation of what at the time was termed an "élite of black Frenchmen." The paternalistic Belgian position permitted Africans no political experience even on the local level, and until 1954 limited their education to crafts training, elementary school and, for a few, secondary and trade schools and training for the priesthood, while university education was actively discouraged.

Hodgkin has listed a number of other factors that contributed to the rise of African nationalism. One was "the new towns"—the factor of urbanization, with the realignment of customary behavior it brought in its train. Another, "the new associa-

[1] Lord Malcolm Hailey: op. cit., pp. 253–60.

tions," comprehended the various kinds of clubs and self-help organizations that resulted from the growth of urban centers, and provided forums for the expression and propagation of nationalist sentiment. A third was found in the many separatist religious sects that developed out of conflict with Christianity and Islam; while a fourth was the growth of labor unions in industrial centers and among workers on agricultural projects and in the mines. Finally, he distinguished two other factors that represented a kind of feed-back phenomenon. The one comprised the various parties and congresses that fostered the organized anticolonialist nationalisms whence they had arisen; the other, the ideologies that were propagated in the process.[2] In addition, we may note still other factors. These included pride in the past, as evidenced by the history of such precolonial native African states as Ghana and Mali and Kongo; convictions as to the worth of African cultures and the need to have a political base for the expression of their values; an increasing knowledge of the history, ideology and practices of Euroamerican democratic institutions; the experiences of Africans in the fighting forces of World War II, especially in the Far East; the independence of India, Indonesia and other nations of Asia; and first hand contact with the Communist regimes of the Soviet Union, Eastern Europe, and China.

[3]

In reviewing the origins of African nationalism, it is to be noted that the first proponents of organized effort were not Africans, but British West Indians and American Negroes. Their original formulation was in terms of Pan-Africanism, perhaps because at the time a sense of the diversity of the African scene was submerged in a combination of racial identification and lack of knowledge of modes of life in the continent. The most significant result of this pattern of thinking about Africa was to be found in the influence, decades later, of the name given this protest movement. Such concepts as a "United States of Africa," were nurtured by the doctrine of Pan-Africanism, as were efforts made by

[2] T. Hodgkin, op. cit., *passim.*

African leaders to establish regional groupings of states for greater political and economic effectiveness, and to check trends toward what was later to be called the "balkanization" of the subcontinent.

Padmore, who was at once a student and active promoter of the Pan-African movement, ascribes its origin to "a West Indian barrister," Henry Sylvester Williams of Trinidad, who "took the initiative in convening a Pan-African conference in London in 1900." It was conceived as

> a forum of protest against the aggression of white colonizers and, at the same time, to make an appeal to the missionary and abolitionist traditions of the British people to protect the Africans from the depredations of the Empire builders.[3]

Some thirty delegates attended, apparently none from Africa; they were mainly from England and the West Indies, with a few American Negroes. So striking was this, in the light of later developments, that one student of the movement went so far as to state that, "At the outset, Panafricanism was a simple manifestation of fraternal solidarity between Negroes of African descent from the British Antilles (West Indies) and the United States of America."[4] The principal result of this meeting, as one of its organizers expressed it, was to "put the word 'Pan-African' in the dictionaries for the first time."[5]

As an instrument of anticolonial protest, and as the direct progenitor of the nationalist movements in British Africa at least, we must look to the later Pan-African Congresses, whose "rather hurriedly conceived beginning"[6] lay in the effort by W. E. B. DuBois to put the case of the colored peoples before the Versailles Peace Conference of 1919. It was held in the face of government opposition, principally from the United States and the United Kingdom. Padmore quotes an account of it from a New York

[3] George Padmore: *Pan-Africanism or Communism? The Coming Struggle for Africa* (London, 1956), pp. 117–18.

[4] Pillippe Decraene: *Le Panafricanisme* (Paris, 1959), p. 9.

[5] W. E. B. DuBois: *The World and Africa* (New York, 1947), p. 7.

[6] W. E. B. DuBois: *Dusk of Dawn* (New York, 1940), p. 276.

newspaper. It was described as "the first assembly of its kind in history," which had

> for its object the drafting of an appeal to the Peace Conference to give the Negro race of Africa a chance to develop unhindered by other races. Seated at long green tables in the council room were Negroes in the trim uniform of American Army officers, other American colored men in trench coats or business suits, polished French Negroes who hold public offices, Senegalese who sit in the French Chamber of Deputies. . . ." [7]

According to DuBois, there were 57 delegates, including sixteen American Negroes, twenty West Indians, and twelve Africans.[8]

DuBois, in retrospect, felt that "the results of the meeting were small," but Padmore believed that it had repercussions of some consequence. Its proposal, "to place the former German African colonies . . . under international supervision to be held in trust for the inhabitants as future self-governing countries," was embodied in the Mandates system of the League of Nations, albeit "in a much diluted form." And though the ineffectiveness of this system is a matter of historical record, the initial move of the Congress was important since out of the Mandates system came the Trusteeship Council of the United Nations, with real supervisory powers, and specifically charged with bringing the trust territories to self-government. In the light of later developments, the demands of this 1919 Congress were modest, as we can see from its stipulation that

> the natives of Africa must have the right to participate in the Government [*sic*] as fast as their development permits. . . . to the end that, *in time*, Africa is ruled by consent of the Africans.[9]

To what extent the view of these early Congresses coincided with the thought of the time can be grasped when we compare the opinion of a contemporaneous major figure in fashioning British colonial policy: "The verdict of students of history and sociology of different nationalities . . . is . . . unanimous that the era of

[7] Op. cit., p. 123. [8] Op. cit., p. 262.
[9] George Padmore: op. cit., pp. 123–5. (Italics added.)

complete independence is not as yet visible on the horizon of time."[1]

There were more Pan-African Congresses. A second and then a third were held in London in 1921 and in 1923, while in 1927 there was a fourth in New York. After this the movement languished until after the Second World War, when in 1945 the Fifth Congress was convened in Manchester, England. By this time the Africans, whose participation in all the earlier meetings had been minimal, were ready to take over; mainly students, they had created an effective organ of protest in the West African Students Union. Names that later came to be widely known outside Africa appear on the roster—Kwame Nkrumah was the principal *rapporteur;* Jomo Kenyatta was *rapporteur* for East African affairs; Peter Abrahams, the writer, was publicity secretary; Padmore and Nkrumah were the joint political secretaries. It was exigent in its program:

> We are determined to be free. . . . We demand for Black Africa autonomy and independence. . . . We are unwilling to starve any longer while doing the world's drudgery. . . . We shall complain, appeal and arraign. . . . We will fight in every way we can for freedom, democracy and social betterment.[2]

Despite the importance of this movement as a catalyst of anticolonial sentiment and as a prime mover in the drive toward African self-government, it should be kept in mind that it was oriented toward British Africa. There were two reasons for this. In the first place, it will be remembered that the initiative in establishing the earlier Congresses came from British West Indians and American Negroes. Their language was English; consequently it was natural for them to document their case with materials in this language, and to orient their arguments toward British colonial issues rather than toward those of the French, Belgian or Portuguese possessions. Secondly, particularly in later periods, these Congresses were dominated by Africans from British possessions—or, in the case of those from South Africa, a

[1] Lord Frederick D. Lugard: *The Dual Mandate in British Tropical Africa* (London, 1922), pp. 197–8.

[2] G. Padmore: op. cit., pp. 152–70, *passim.*

former British possession—because in these territories, even at this time, many more Africans had received secondary and higher education than in those governed by France, to say nothing of those under Belgian, Spanish and Portuguese rule. In terms of preparation to face the metropolitan power, therefore, the position of the British Africans, compared to other Africans, was analogous to that of the West Indian and American Negroes of the earlier Congresses in relation to the Africans in British African possessions.

[4]

Let us recall our generalization that the development of African nationalism as a conscious drive for independence is to be closely correlated with the opportunities of Africans to obtain secondary and higher education, and on the political plane, with the policy of the Metropole. In the case of French Africa, the sharpness with which the great mass of the population was differentiated from an élite of "Black Frenchmen," both by education and status, influenced the character of the nationalist movements in those parts of Africa which, after the end of direct French rule, came to be known as "countries of French expression." An analysis of the situation in French West Africa at the beginning of the Second World War affords us some pertinent insights. At that time,

> nationalism had not yet taken root . . . but there existed a simple sense of racialism, chiefly felt by Africans most in contact with foreigners. A small vanguard had come into being that took pride in its African heritage and was not content to remain indefinitely in a static position midway between the French and the rural population. Specifically, members of this group wanted abolition of military conscription (and the restriction of the use of African volunteers to the Federation); total suppression of the regime of disciplinary penalties known as the *indigénat;* elimination of prestation labour; exemption of women and children from poll taxation; wider use of native languages; more responsible and higher-paid positions for Africans; and greater security of African land tenure.[3]

[3] Virginia Thompson and Richard Adloff: *French West Africa* (London, 1958), p. 25.

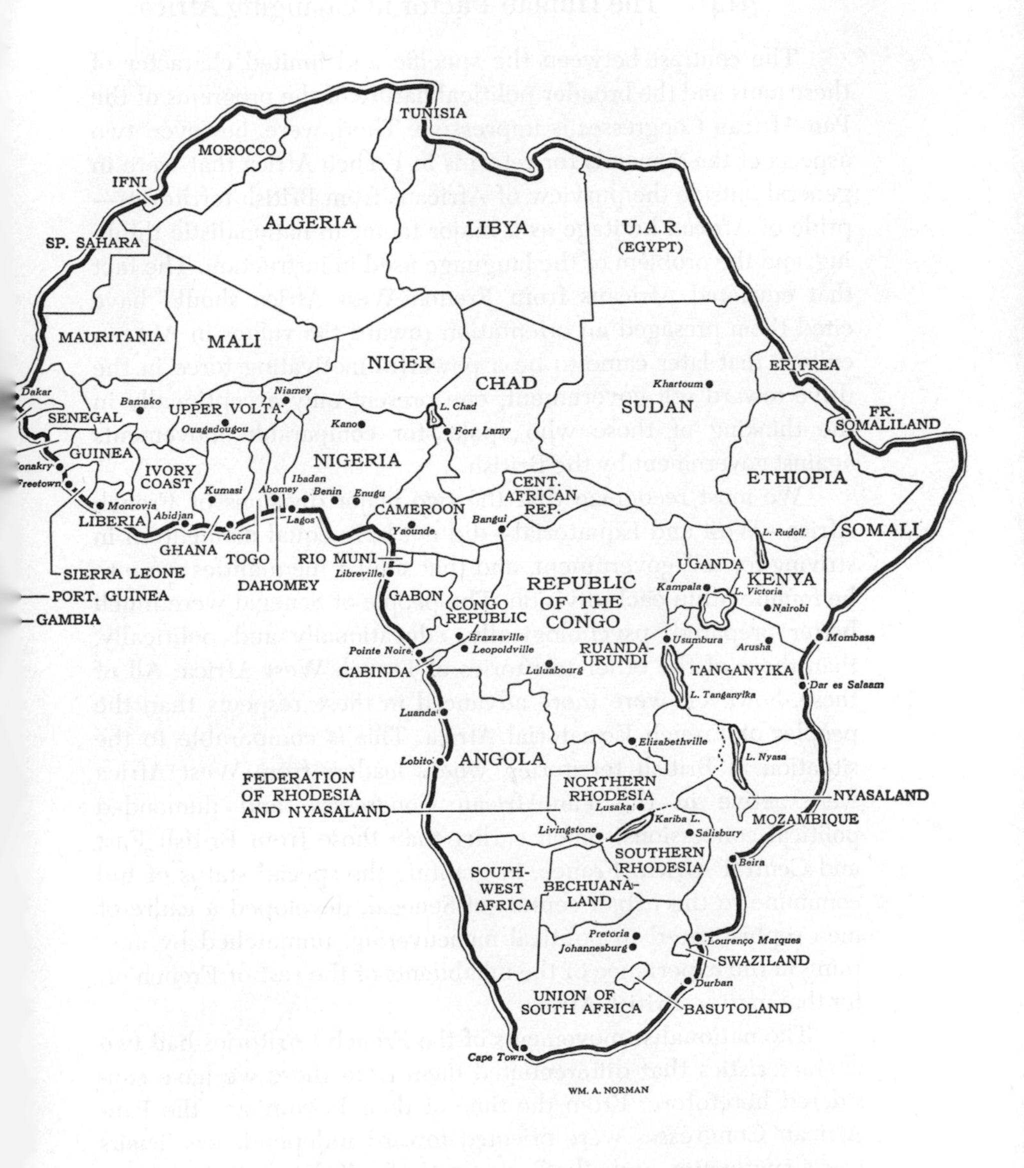

AFRICA AT THE END OF 1960

The contrast between the specific and limited character of these aims and the broader political nature of the programs of the Pan-African Congresses is impressive. There were, however, two aspects of the demands for reforms in French Africa that were in general outside the purview of Africans from British territories—pride of African heritage as a major factor in nationalistic thinking, and the problem of the language used in instruction. The fact that educated Africans from French West Africa should have cited them presaged an orientation toward the values in African culture that later came to be a powerful motivating force in the drive toward self-government, one present only exceptionally in the thinking of those who spoke for comparable movements against government by the British.

We must recognize that the two major divisions of French Africa—West and Equatorial—did not have equal momentum in striving for self-government, and that similar inequalities were to be found within each division. The people of Senegal were much better prepared, psychologically, educationally and politically, than those of the other territories of French West Africa. All of these, however, were more advanced in these respects than the peoples of French Equatorial Africa. This is comparable to the situation in British territories, where leaders from West Africa were active in the Pan-African Congresses, and demanded political concessions, much earlier than those from British East and Central Africa. France, in granting the special status of full commune to the urban centers of Senegal, developed a cadre of men sophisticated in political maneuvering, unmatched by anything in the experience of the inhabitants of the rest of French or, for that matter, British Africa.

The nationalist movements of the French territories had two characteristics that differentiated them from those we have considered heretofore. From the time of their beginnings, the Pan-African Congresses were oriented toward independence. Theirs was a single aim, and all other aspects of self-determination were subordinated to it. Kwame Nkrumah's paraphrase of the Biblical quotation, made late in the period of nationalist striving, "Seek ye first the political kingdom, and all else shall be added unto it," is a concise, accurate expression of their objectives. French African nationalists, however, in fact if not in conscious strategy, employed what turned out to be a flank attack on the common objective. Questions of political independence, as such, did not enter prominently into their discussions until rather shortly before they attained autonomous status or, in the case of Guinea, full independence. For one thing, their contacts with the French labor movement, particularly the left-wing Confédération Générale du Travail, turned them toward preoccupation with the problems of workers, and toward an internationalist approach to political problems, with its emphasis on economic factors. On the other hand, another group of French African leaders, because of the nature of their training in French institutions of higher learning, became intellectuals in the French tradition, and as such were oriented toward the humanistic values in their African cultural endowment.

How the best laid plans can lead to unforseen results is illustrated by the fact that it was precisely the policy of developing an African élite of "Black Frenchmen," that resulted first in the restudy of African culture, then the concept of *négritude,* and finally active participation and leadership in the drive for political independence.

"The British African nationalist leader writes constitutions," a student of African affairs once asserted, "the French leader writes poetry." And, as late as 1954, this was the impression given by an African labor leader in Dakar: ". . . his attitude was that of a labor man and not an African." The group he headed "are not nationalist, but work as a labor organization within the general setup; they do not even try to elect their own people, as a party." Or, again, at that time, a Conseil de la Jeunesse du Sénégal could be described as "a cultural movement—theatre, sport, lectures, but with emphasis on native custom. They get some government support, but are not political." [4]

We may first consider the influence of the labor movement. African trade unions in French territory, like those of British Africa, were developed with the aid and support of the trade

[4] Melville J. Herskovits: *Notes on African Field Research, 1953–1960* (manuscript) (September 8, 1954), pp. 1–2.

union organizations of the metropolitan countries. Unlike those of British Africa, however, which followed the British pattern of local control rather than the centralization of authority that marked French practice, the unions of French Africa for a long time remained integral elements of their parent organizations in France. This meant that they were inculcated with the strong ideological bent of the several segments of the French labor movement, which at that time included the Communist-oriented C.G.T. (Conféderation Générale du Travail), the Catholic oriented C.F.T.C. (Conféderation Française des Travailleurs Croyants), and the F.O. (Force Ouvrière).

We are not directly concerned here with the intricate moves that, in the labor field, as in politics, marked the post-World War II period in France. French African labor leaders, like French African politicians, played a part, though a minor one in the instance of labor, in the respective hierarchies in France. Not being cut off from metropolitan participation, as were Africans in British territories—no African political leader sat in Parliament at Westminster, nor was one a member of the Executive of the Trades Union Council—identifications of a different order could be and were set up. In consequence, what turned out to be identical objectives reached at about the same time, were marked by different strategies and ideologies.

The influence of the C.G.T. on French African labor unions can be held to account for the facility with which political orientations geared to establishing a party-dominated state, took root. It would be wrong, however, to conclude that the model was totally accepted. The attempt to impose a rigid Marxian interpretation of class warfare on the African anticolonialist movement alienated the powerful political party, the Rassemblement Démocratique Africain. Its leader, F. Houphouët-Boigny, later shed his Marxist affiliation and, as a member of successive French cabinets, did much to hold French Africa close to France. However, this did not bring about a complete political commitment for, at the strategic moment, he led his country, the Ivory Coast, and the three associated states of the Entente, abruptly to independence.

This orientation of the C.G.T. also figured prominently in causing Sekou Touré—the labor leader whose influence was to be predominant in making his country, whose President he later became, the sole member of the Community to vote for full self-government in the referendum of 1958—to form an independent African labor organization, the Conféderation Générale des Travailleurs Africains (C.G.T.A.). "It is time that we wear our own glasses," he is reported as having declared. At the heart of a dispute "that broke a large segment of the African workers from the C.G.T." of France, was "the feeling that the special interests and characteristics of Africa conflicted with those of France." Another reason was that the C.G.T.A. leaders "questioned one of French Communism's basic tenets, which makes the proletariat the privileged arm of the revolution." In Africa, these leaders felt, the classical Marxian distinction between worker and peasant was meaningless. Moreover, "African leaders came to see . . . as just another form of European imperialism . . . many of the tactics of the French C.G.T. leaders, which maintained African leaders in a subordinate position." [5] As one grass-roots labor leader from the Soudan explained after the Cotonou conference of trade-union officials, held in January, 1957, African unions were no longer to be "under the thumb of the French syndicates, who do not face the same problems as the workers in a non-self-governing, underdeveloped country." [6]

We now turn to the other aspect of the development of nationalism in French Africa. During all this time, the intellectuals, on their side, were working out an ideology based on concepts of the worth of aboriginal African culture. The outstanding expression of these ideas was to be found in a periodical published in Paris, entitled *Présence Africaine,* which came to dominate the field as did no single publication among British Africans. French writers and scientists, such as André Gide and Théodore Monod were among its sponsors, as was the West Indian poet, Aimé Cesaire. But of the original editorial committee,

[5] Ruth Schachter: "Trade Unions Seek Autonomy," *West Africa,* No. 2075 (January 19, 1957), p. 55.

[6] Melville J. Herskovits: op. cit., p. 57/D74.

all but four of the twelve were Africans, and in 1955, when a "new series" was begun, the committee of sponsors disappeared, and the enlarged *Comité Présence Africaine* was even closer to being entirely African. By this time, too, Africans from other than French-speaking territories were being included, such as Biobaku from Nigeria, Busia and Codjo from Ghana, and Davidson Nichol from Sierra Leone.

It is of some interest to note the orientation given this publication in the prefaces to the first issue by Gide and by the editor, Alioune Diop. The first stressed the impact of Africa on France, the second of Europe on Africa. Both were marked by a broad humanism which recognized the contributions all groups can make to the common store of knowledge, art and ethics. As Gide put it:

> However rich and appealing our civilization, our culture, we have finally come to admit that it is not the only one. That our ways of living, our values, our religions, our beliefs are not unique; and that if they appear superior to us, it is largely because we have been fashioned by them. . . . Hence as concerns Africans there are three periods, three attitudes, and we have reached the last. First, exploitation; then pitying condescension; then, finally, that understanding which brings it about that we do not only seek to aid, to elevate and progressively to teach, but also to allow ourselves to be instructed.

Présence Africaine, therefore, "proposes a vast program: to welcome all that which aids the cause of the Africans, and any African voice that is worth hearing."[7]

Diop began his preface with a Toucouleur proverb, "To eat enough to live is not the same as to eat enough to get fat." Then followed his statement of policy:

> This review is not influenced by any philosophical or political ideology. It is open to the collaboration of all men of good will (white, yellow and black), who are willing to help us define the African's creativity and to hasten his entry into the modern world.

[7] André Gide: "Avant-propos," *Présence Africaine*, No. 1 (1947), *passim*.

Each issue was to have three essential parts. The first would "contain authoritative studies of the culture and civilization of Africa by well-known scholars" and also "searching examinations of the methods of integrating the black man into western civilization." Then, "most important in our eyes," was to come a section devoted to "texts by Africans (novels, short stories, plays, etc.)." Finally there was to be a part "devoted to a review of art and thought concerning the Black world." The article emphasized the reciprocity of interaction between African and European in a series of dichotomies—the "active, productive and creative beings" of Europe, and "the much more numerous men of overseas, who are generally less active and barely productive (at least their productivity does not correspond to the rhythm of modern times)." [8] As regards African friendship for France, and admiration for the achievements of Europe, the tone of this argument parallels the modesty in the initial aims of the British African nationalists.

Yet the pressure of events was upon this humanistic movement no less than on the political ones centered across the English channel, and in the very next issue we find the beginnings of expressions of protest against colonialism, phrased, characteristically for this review, in poetry. Two examples, from the pen of David Diop, can be given. The first is entitled *Le Temps du Martyr:*

The White man has slain my father
For my father was proud
The White man has ravished my mother
For my mother was beautiful
The White man has bent the back of my
brother on the sun-scorched roads
For my brother was strong
Then the White man turned to me
His hands reddened by blood
Black
Spat his contempt in my face

[8] Alioune Diop: "Niam n'goura, ou les raisons d'être de Présence Africaine," *Présence Africaine,* No. 1 (1947), pp. 7, 12–13.

And in the voice of the master:
"Hey, boy, a chair, a towel, water!"

The second, *Souffre Pauvre Nègre* . . . is in a similar vein:

The lash whistles
Whistles over the sweat and blood
on your back
Suffer poor Black
The day is long
So long carrying the white ivory of the
White, your master
Suffer poor Black
Your children are hungry
Hungry and your tumble-down hut is
empty
Empty of your wife who sleeps
Who sleeps in the Master's bed
Suffer poor Black
Black black as Misery.[9]

In succeeding years, the pace of political developments and the pressure of the economic effort came to be reflected in later issues of *Présence Africaine*. Political and economic questions tended, however, to be discussed on the broad planes of world conflict and ideological implications. The relations between Negro peoples everywhere came into prominence—an entire number was devoted to the African-derived cultures of the New World. The question of retentions of African custom in the Americas was debated in its pages, because of the light it would throw on whether African traditions were strong or fragile under contact with European ways of life. The Bandung, Cairo, and Accra Conferences were given prominence, documents that issued from them were reproduced, their significance for the African scene analyzed.

These discussions were keyed to the facts that would lay bare the historical and conceptual framework, so as to reveal their essential meaning for the African. Thus the theme of under-

[9] David Diop: "Trois Poèmes," *Présence Africaine*, No. 2 (1948), pp. 235, 236.

development, as brought into relief by the circumstance of the Cairo conference of 1957, was treated along lines that posed the problems in ways quite different from those found in most discussions of the subject. Here the basic question was how a people, in accepting aid from technologically more developed nations, might avoid domination by those who would make their contribution an instrument of power over the recipients or, how Africans "can control and utilize technology in accordance with their own interests." Increasingly, in succeeding numbers of the periodical, political questions were stressed. Political issues were no longer touched on only by implication, but directly and with a strong affirmation of objectives.

> The indispensable initiative peoples must hold, on all levels (political operations, economic and social vitality, scientific, cultural and spiritual intuition and creativity), is essentially of a political order. It necessitates independence. Beyond this stage other problems, in turn, pose themselves. Because political independence is not an end, but an indispensable step.[1]

The approach which followed the statement, "We are underdeveloped," clearly showed the orientation:

> First of all, spiritually. Whether we be animists, Moslems or Christians, our faith cannot be vigorous except through its own institutions and accomplishments, nourishing itself on its own tests and challenges, unless it has some of the security, the assurance and the responsibility that a sovereign state gives its citizens. There is no durable faith outside a spiritual civilization with confidence in itself.

The discussion continued, with the point that all the religious beliefs of Africans, indigenous or introduced, had been at the very least changed by the colonial system, to the end that the prestige of a Europe "jealous of its supremacy, could be furthered." The restoration of confidence Africans must have in themselves, and the re-establishment of a psychologically secure

[1] *Présence Africaine:* "Le sous-équipment et les leçons du Caire," No. 17 (1958), pp. 3–4.

personality "infers, aside from political independence, the free creation of ample means for cultural expression: books, newspapers, radio, cinema, architecture, art schools . . . etc." Yet it was not only political independence that was held to condition "cultural equipment," but also "technological and economic power."

The tightly-argued premise was followed to its logical, humanistic conclusion.

> Political independence is almost at our door. The solidarity of underdeveloped peoples begins to be understood, and recognized on various levels as a modern necessity. But when will we realize the west has never wished and indeed cannot conquer our underdevelopment and our weakness? When will we realize that it is necessary to pay dear, very dear, in building a strong and respected world? That what is needed is a creed (*mystique*) to reach this objective and to compensate for the capital we lack? [2]

This *mystique* had already found expression in the concept of *négritude*. It is a word that defies translation, since "negroidness" has quite another connotation, being essentially related to physical characteristics, and "negro-ness" is outside the range of English usage. It was the creation of two poets, one a West Indian, Aimé Cesaire, the other a West African, Léopold Sedar Senghor, who was later to become President of the Republic of Senegal and who, in public addresses, continued to allude to "notre petite Négritude" in speaking of the spirit of his country. We shall consider this in more detail in later pages.[3]

The two wings of nationalism in French territories, the trade union wing and the humanist, must not be thought of as having been in opposition. They merely represent two different strands in the anticolonialist fabric. They were striving toward the same ends. The channels of communication between them were always open, in some cases the same personalities functioned in both. Perhaps because of the Marxist influence on both labor and intellectual circles of France, these aspects of the independence movement shared an orientation toward internationalism that went beyond just the concerns of Africans, or populations of

[2] Ibid., pp. 4–6. [3] *Infra*, pp. 466–70.

African descent. Nonetheless, in the broader base of their thinking, and in the sharpness of their philosophical formulations they were unique among the nationalist movements of the Subsaharan continent. The fact that, in the main, the independent French-speaking countries of Subsaharan Africa were less emphatic in their verbal rejection of association with the former colonial power than the English-speaking countries may, indeed, be attributed to the influence of these formulations. For the French-speaking African intellectuals, having given thought to their own cultural values, were able to place humanistic and technological achievement on a philosophical and ideological base that enabled them to face their former rulers with well-reasoned convictions of their own inner worth, and without having to reject the European contribution in order to secure the validity of their African cultural commitment.

[5]

In the Spanish and Portuguese portions of what has been called "Latin Africa"—those parts of the Subsaharan continent into which Romance languages were introduced—nationalist movements were virtually nonexistent. As regards Belgian territory, the transition from colonial status to independence was so rapid that organized agitation for self-government had barely begun before it found itself successful.

In 1957, the situation in the tiny splinter of Rio Muñi on the mainland, and on the island of Fernando Po, comprising Spanish holdings, was assessed in this way by one Spanish writer:

> There is no visible movement for autonomy, and less for independence. However, this apparent state of affairs should not confuse us: among the black *élite*, and sporadically among the masses, a consciousness of belonging to a world different from that of the whites, the lesson of success in other negro territories ruled for the most part by their indigenous inhabitants, and in addition a certain distaste or uneasiness, whether justified or not, perpetuate a sort of racism which could easily transform itself into nationalism, especially since it is not entirely a localized phenomenon.

To this analyst, there were ample potentialities for such a movement in Spanish Guinea and Fernando Po.

> The danger for Spain, is that this nationalism, stimulated, propagated and perfected, will become inclined toward an *anschluss* between Guinea and a neighboring territory of greater size, ruled by negroes whose associations have been with other European powers. For example, Fernando Poo with a Nigerian member of the commonwealth—whose structure is favorable to additions—and continental Guinea with a Cameroons, emancipated by the United Nations, holding to a relationship with the French Union.

He also noted that the greater part of the population of Fernando Po was composed of Africans who had come from elsewhere, while the element "relatively aboriginal (the Bubi)," which was "at the same time the most pro-Spanish and most assimilated," made up a minority "with regressive tendencies." As concerned the immigrant majority of the population, consisting, since 1934, of Nigerians, with a mixture of Cameronians and Fang of Rio Muñi, he wrote, "It is a majority that today may only want to make a living but tomorrow may be like the *uitlanders* in the Transvaal." Certain aspects of the colonial situation—bureaucratic inefficiency, unwillingness to adopt reform, indifference of the Metropole to these overseas possessions, the position of the great land owners and other "elements of limited vision"—led to the conclusion, that "the absence of a movement for autonomy in Spanish Guinea does not constitute a symptom of absolute tranquillity." [4]

That no Portuguese student or statesman discussed Portuguese Africa in comparably realistic terms demonstrates the romantic view as well as the authoritarian controls of Portuguese colonialism. Despite the obvious realities, Portuguese writers continued to affirm that the absence of any overt expression of African nationalism betokened an African appreciation of Portuguese racial tolerance, and of the historical civilizing mission of

[4] José Condero Torres: "Las Dependencias Españolas," in *Enquête sur l'Anticolonialisme* (Estudos de Ciências Políticas e Sociais, Centro de Estudos Políticas e Sociais, Ministério do Ultramar, Junta de Investigações do Ultramar, Lisbon, 1957), pp. 146–9.

Portugal. How seductive was this romanticism, which was inspired by the grandeur of a distant past, can be deduced from its appeal for even such a critical and humanistic scholar as the Brazilian writer Gilberto Freyre. After a tour of Portuguese dependencies, Freyre evolved the concept of *lusotropicalismo*, based on the hypothesis of a unique endowment of the Portuguese for dealing harmoniously with tropical peoples and incorporating them into the Portuguese world.[5]

Before 1960 there were, in fact, few indications of overt African discontent in Portuguese territory. Among the relatively small number of *assimilados* who had become Portuguese citizens, there was some reaction to the disabilities of the great mass of Africans, but the rigorous controls over any public expression of discontent reduced this to grumbling in private. There existed no organized popular movements, such as marked the areas of West Africa under British and French control, in the colonies or in the metropolitan capital where, for these other West Africans, the seeds of nationalism were planted. In 1958, a student of Portuguese Africa wrote:

> Through an administrative system which penetrates into almost every African village, a series of native labor laws, and the necessity for the male *indígena* to possess a *caderneta* (an identification card and pass-book), Portugal maintains a sufficiently close surveillance over the African population in Angola and Moçambique to have avoided in recent years disturbing incidents like those that crop up from time to time in other European colonies (the Portuguese claim that this tranquility is the result of the more idealized aspects of their policy).

The nature of the controls by means of which the Portuguese maintained this tranquillity were varied. For one thing,

> The presence of African informants, sepoys (the sepoy, generally chosen from the ranks of African soldiers, is an indispensable element in policing the colonies), and reliable chiefs in the midst of the African population have helped contain dissatisfaction and

[5] Gilberto Freyre: *Aventura e Rotina* (Rio de Janeiro, 1953), pp. 9, 521–2.

nascent sentiments of Africanism. Censorship, border controls, ruthless police action, and a supervised educational system have prevented the formation of an effective leadership capable of arousing resistance to the Portuguese administration. Literature and phonograph records—the latter used to circumvent the high illiteracy rate in the provinces—of suspicious nature are confiscated, and the amount of political literature circulating in Angola and Moçambique is small. It is not unknown for Africans educated in Portugal to be kept from returning home. Africans suspected of agitation, including those who have made unhealthy associations in the Congo or the Rhodesias, are quickly jailed, frequently beaten, and usually sent to a penal camp or exiled to a remote point in the colonies, in Angola to the desert-bound fishery town of Bahia dos Tigres.[6]

Because of censorship and surveillance, it was not possible to obtain at first hand a picture of the type and degree of reaction in Portuguese Africa to the growth of nationalism elsewhere in Africa, and to the attainment of independence by other African countries. Portuguese Guinea, in 1960, had the Republic of Senegal to the north and the Republic of Guinea on its southern border; Angola, with its large Bakongo stock in the north and in Cabinda, its Balunda on the east, was particularly vulnerable to the spread of ideas from the Congo Republic. Mozambique, with none of its neighbors except South Africa independent, bordered on Tanganyika, in which responsible government had been instituted and which was to become fully self-governing in 1961, and on Nyasaland, which in 1959 had had an uprising against continuation in the Federation. Bases of operation consequently came into existence for Africans from Portuguese possessions working for the self-government of their people. The newly independent states were hospitable to refugees from the Portuguese areas, and in Conakry, Accra and Leopoldville colonies of exiles carried on continuous agitation. Movements, comparable to those that the French and British Africans had for many years been permitted to promote in their respective Metropoles, thus began their work on the soil of Africa itself.

[6] James Duffy: *Portuguese Africa* (Cambridge, Massachusetts, 1959), p. 303.

In the Congo, the generalization that the rise of African movements toward self-government was an offshoot of governmental policy and educational opportunity finds additional confirmation. Its first institution of higher learning was established in 1954; up to this time, the number of Congolese permitted to go abroad for higher education, if we except those sent to Rome for training as members of the Catholic priesthood, or the few who went to the United States to study in Protestant denominational colleges, totaled at most five or six. No Congolese had an opportunity to learn how a parliamentary system worked, since controls were exercised entirely from the metropolitan capital, and no form either of indigenous or, it should be recalled, European political expression was allowed. African labor unions were supervised by Belgian political officers; no African groups inclined to political action were sanctioned. The inclusion of a few Africans in the Advisory Councils of the Governor General and the Provincial Governors summed up the totality of African political participation.

Perhaps nowhere else on the African continent was an indigenous population more affected by the shock of initial contact with the outer world than in the Congo basin. Here the slave trade to the New World, which West Africa also knew, was compounded by the excesses of Arab raiders from the east, and by sharp competition in all the central portion of the country between them and Europeans for allies among the indigenous tribal groups who would deliver their human commodity in the quantities required. Traffic in Congo slaves continued by illicit means even beyond the end of the period of the effective operation of the trade. Through Angola, New World slaving to Brazil and Cuba, the last two countries there to abolish slavery, went on until the penultimate decade of the nineteenth century. Toward the east, the Arab slave raiders were active even longer. How powerful they were may be seen in the tale of Henry M. Stanley's negotiations over the expedition to rescue Emin Pasha, wherein Tippu-Tib is described as "an uncrowned king of the region between Stanley Falls and Tanganyika Lake, commanding many thousands of men inured to fighting and wild Equatorial life,"[7] a judgment confirmed in the contemporaneous accounts of Belgians who fought to suppress the Arab slavers.

Elsewhere in Africa, the end of slaving operations ended this drain on African human resources, but not in the Congo. Here it coincided with the establishment of what, in the ethnocentrism of the time, was named the Congo Free State—free, that is, to European entry. The civilizing mission proclaimed as the reason for its creation scarcely cloaked a degree of economic exploitation which stopped at nothing to obtain raw materials, and which was not sparing of Congo human resources. This was particularly true of the drive to obtain rubber in profitable quantities. Coercive methods of such severity were employed as to move the outside world to protest, as in the debate in the British Parliament in 1903.[8] Increasing pressure for reform resulted in 1908 in the transfer of the Congo by Leopold II to the Belgian government.

We must take into account the manner in which this phase of Congo history came to be sublimated in later years, if we are to understand the argument for controls over Africans that prevented any expression of African critical opinion. Such controls were not unique to the Congo, but here their importance derives from the fact that this reasoning was part of a broader pattern of rationalization of Congo affairs. Leopold II, who countenanced procedures that were denounced by his contemporaries, came to be translated into a far-sighted, beneficent ruler, whose only concern was to civilize and uplift the peoples under his care. Belgian discussions of colonial questions, marked by the kind of critical appraisal that, for example, characterized British assessments of British colonial policy, particularly in reports issued by Royal Commissions, were rare.

Belgian works on the Congo showed little sense of underly-

[7] Henry M. Stanley: *In Darkest Africa, or the Quest, Rescue, and Retreat of Emin, Governor of Equatoria,* Vol. I (New York, 1890), p. 63; cf. also pp. 69–72.

[8] Great Britain: "Congo Free State," *Parliamentary Debates,* Fourth Series, Vol. 122 (May 7 to May 26, 1903), *passim.*

ing problems. In 1954, an official press release from Leopoldville, under the heading "Realism-Continuity" quoted a Belgian official as saying,

> Our colonial policy . . . was pursued with a remarkable continuity by the Independent State first, and then by Belgium. Since the beginning of its colonial effort, Belgium has held uniting the European and native elements to be the essential element of its civilizing mission.[9]

Policies being implemented were held to be the best, indeed, the only possible means to evolve a society in which both Africans and Belgians would live a good life. Race relations were proclaimed to be nowhere better, discontent less, advancement more rapid. All warning signs were ignored, and criticism by non-Belgians of colonial aims and administrative procedures were acutely resented.

Yet the signals that all was not well, that African discontent was a reality, were not lacking. Despite censorship, word of clandestine movements and illegal activities did emerge. Among the most important of these were the abortive uprisings, in 1940 in the lower Congo, and further to the east in 1944. The latter, in which Congolese soldiers of the Force Publique were involved, represented the coming together of various "prophet" movements of the central part of Africa, and of the Kitawala, or Watch Tower movement.[1] Though these and other movements were suppressed, they were rarely mentioned by Belgian writers, despite the clear indication of continuing unrest in the fact that, over the years, several thousand malcontents were, according to official reports, being held in "exile"—that is, banished to remote parts of the Congo—because of political activity. Nor did the Belgian Government pay attention to the uneasiness of its own administrators on the scene. The statement of Governor General Jungers, widely quoted in the Congo by Belgians before independence, "The hand extended too late risks being rejected," is one exam-

[9] *Congopresse:* "Réalisme, Continuité. La politique coloniale belge tend a éveiller chez l'Africain le sens démocratique," *Pages Congolaises,* édition B, No. 38 (Brussels, 1954), p. 1.

[1] Leon Debertry: *Kitawala* (Elizabethville, Congo, 1953), pp. 7–13.

ple.[2] Another is the reaction, in 1955, of the Governor General to speeches and articles that exalted the wisdom of Belgian colonial policy and cited the state of affairs in the Congo as proof, when in a private interview he said, "One of these days we are going to have trouble—it must come . . . people will say, 'Where is your perfect colony?' "[3]

The absence of a realistic appraisal cannot be ascribed to the blindness of able men, but rather to a distaste for unpalatable economic and social truths. As late as 1956, the Belgian Government considered sufficient a promise of independence to the Congo no later than 1985. On the level of human relations, no less than of politics, there were serious miscalculations of African reactions. In some quarters, these miscalculations did not go unquestioned. Already, in 1954, we find a Belgian scholar asking: "We have drawn ten-year plans for the economic and social development of the Congo and of Ruanda-Urundi. Why not think of *a plan of political development and emancipation*?"[4]

This failure, especially in human relations, moved the Belgian government precipitately, after the Leopoldville riots of January 1959, to accelerate its five-year timetable so as to bring policy more into line with Congolese aspirations. In the final years of Belgian rule, Congolese reaction had forced revision of earlier regulations. Debated since 1948,[5] the *Statut de Ville* was proclaimed in 1957, permitting the inhabitants of certain Congo urban centers to vote for burgomasters, African and European, though the head burgomaster of each city was to be a European. Earlier decrees permitted Africans to be served in restaurants and cafés; official separation between the African and European quarters of Congo cities had been modified to allow greater freedom of movement; teaching in the *écoles laïques* was in French and secondary education was being accelerated; the university

[2] Congo Belge, Conseil de Gouvernement: *Discours du Gouverneur General E. Jungers; Statistiques* (Leopoldville [?], 1951), p. 7.

[3] Melville J. Herskovits: op. cit., p. 6.

[4] A. A. J. Van Bilsen: *Vers l'Independence du Congo et du Ruanda-Urundi* (Brussels, 1958 [?]), p. 36.

[5] Jean Labrique: *Congo Politique* (Leopoldville, 1957), pp. 247–50.

center of Lovanium was functioning and a second, an Official University, was being established at Elizabethville; more Africans were enabled to visit Belgium.

As events proved, however, these measures were inadequate for the task of coping with the unsuspectedly strong Congolese resentment against the Belgians and their policies. It became clear that Africans had acquiesced in the paternalism which reduced them to the position of a child race subject to authoritarian rule, only because of their political impotence. Schooling, even on the lower levels, stimulated them to look toward recognition of the right to determine their own destinies. At the very end of the colonial period, the Belgian Parliamentary Commission inquiring into the Leopoldville riots assigned two causes to these events. One was unemployment, but the other, stressing the need for "the amelioration of human relations," named specifically the scorn customarily shown by Europeans for Africans.[6]

There were, however, stirrings which indicated that Congolese nationalism was a force to be reckoned with. Study circles were active in the cities; in the countryside the radio stimulated discussion; the tales told by those who after 1953 were taken to Belgium had an effect quite different from the results officially anticipated when the policy of showing Congolese the Metropole was instituted. Events elsewhere during the years immediately preceding Congo independence gave point to aspiration. The independence of Ghana, the establishment of the French Union, with suffrage exercised by Africans living just across the Congo river, who were experiencing Africanization under an autonomous government, all had their effect. In Luluabourg, almost an entire issue of a weekly newspaper published by a local group of élite was given over to the findings of the 1958 Accra All-African People's Conference.[7]

The origin of Congolese nationalism, as an identifiable movement openly expressing its aims, can be precisely delineated. In

[6] Belgium, Chambre des Représentants: *Rapport* (on events in Leopoldville in January, 1959, Session 1958–1959, March 28, 1959), p. 9.

[7] *La Lumière:* "La Conférence d'Accra" (December 15, 1958 and January 1, 1959), *passim.*

1955, A. A. Van Bilsen, who had traveled in West Africa, noted a "law" which, he said, the French and British had come to understand, to the effect that since

> political maturity of a people precedes its capacity to administer itself, it is a mistake to refuse political rights on the pretext that this must wait until the Africans are capable of guaranteeing that all levels of administration can function.[8]

This led Van Bilsen, the following year, to issue a statement that, in the Congo, catalyzed African aspirations, but in Belgium caused a storm of protest. Its title, *A Thirty-Year Plan for the Political Emancipation of Belgian Africa,* is self-explanatory; the reaction to it in Belgium can be sensed in the fact that the year following this same student was moved to write another article, a "Plea for the Thirty-Year Plan." [9]

Reaction in the Congo soon followed. The journal of a group of Congolese intellectuals in Leopoldville, *Conscience Africaine,* some five months after the Van Bilsen "Plan" appeared, carried a "Manifesto," the first published Congolese demand for self-government. "In the history of the Congo, the last eighty years have been more important than the thousands which preceded them," it began. As for the future: "We believe that the Congo has been called to become, in the center of the African continent, a great nation." Demands were modest. The concept of "equal, but separate" was rejected—"we wish to be civilized Congolese, not 'black-skinned' Europeans." The aim of creating a "new complete civilization," in which the "growing number of Congolese, with the desire to take more responsibility and more initiative in the future of their country" could fulfill their aspirations, was set forth. Emancipation, though total, was to be progressive, and a timetable of thirty years in which to reach this goal was held to be acceptible. As for relations with Belgium, it was suggested that the new multiracial independent Congo would of its own volition enter into a Belgo-Congolese federation. Appeals to

[8] A. A. J. Van Bilsen: op. cit., p. 50.
[9] Ibid., pp. 164–202, 203–74.

both Belgians and Congolese for mutual tolerance and cooperation, for national unity, and for resolution of the question through further discussions, completed the document.[1]

Shortly thereafter, the ABAKO (*Alliance des Bakongo*), a Leopoldville association composed of Bakongo, which, like other groups in the Congo forbidden political organization, had as its original stated purpose to promote the development of their language and the study of their history, met to consider the *Conscience Africaine* document. Their manifesto was more intransigeant. For them, political emancipation meant a break with the existing order. Government must be representative, and the consultative bodies must be changed into organs having the power to make decisions. Only through a complete break with Belgium could total emancipation be achieved. They demanded approval of the formation of Congolese political parties, not affiliated in any way with those of Belgium, as a means of achieving national unity.

Here, for the first time, we find explicit rejection of the passive role the African had been allotted. "No one of our society was present at the Congress of Berlin" which conferred the

> semblance of independence the independent Congo State retained for 24 years. . . . And in the meantime, everything was done for us. . . . Even in being independent, the Congo did not have a Sovereign of its own race, or at least chosen by them; nor did it have a government to its liking; its citizens were never citizens.

The ABAKO asked for: "1. Political rights; 2. Complete liberty, that is to say: freedom of thought, of opinion and of the press; freedom of assembly, of association, of conscience and of religion." The concept of a Belgo-Congolese community was rejected. "How can one conceive of the Congo, 80 times larger than Belgium, as becoming its 'tenth province'?" Equalization of pay was demanded, the question of the nationalization of industry raised. The "Congolization" of the services and the extension of

[1] *Conscience Africaine: Manifeste* (Numero Special, Juillet-Août, 1956), *passim;* for an English translation of the entire document see Alan P. Merriam: *Congo, Background of Conflict* (Evanston, 1961), pp. 321–9.

educational opportunities were further requirements. Only on the basis of consent and mutual respect, as the final quotation in this *Manifesto,* taken from Van Bilsen's "Plan" made clear, could association with Belgium be continued.[2]

The echo of this opening salvo had scarcely time to reverberate before the bastion fell. Almost the entire tale of organized Congolese nationalism is told in the four years between the issuance of these first manifestos and the achievement of independence. Even then, most of this time the political situation was quiescent. A year after the ABAKO statement appeared, high Belgian officials could dismiss it as an extremist document which, in contrast to the *Conscience Africaine* statement, need not be taken too seriously. On the Congolese side it was a period of clarifying alignments, and gathering forces for the next step. Political parties appeared which varied in number and shifted their base of intent and objective almost from month to month. The centralization of power as against distribution of it among federated states became, and continued to be, a major issue. As independence came closer, internal discord, based on long-standing tribal animosities which had been held in check by colonial controls, came to the surface.

These were portents of things to come, but the attitudes revealed in the Leopoldville riots gave a clear indication that, whatever the degree of inner unity or disunity, and regardless of inexperience in parliamentary procedures, the Congolese would countenance no delay in achieving the direction of their own affairs. In the face of this determination, the Belgians gave way. A year afterwards, a round-table conference in Brussels, where Africans for the first time sat on equal terms with Belgians, set the date and conditions for independence, and six months later, the transfer of power was effected.[3]

[2] Jean Labrique: op. cit., pp. 266–75; for text in English cf. Alan P. Merriam: op. cit., pp. 330–6.

[3] For detailed accounts of these happenings see Alan P. Merriam, op. cit., Ch. III–V; and Colin Legum: *Congo Disaster* (London, 1961), Ch. 5–10.

[6]

We have seen that the development of African nationalism, particularly as it is related to the rapid attainment of its political aims, derived impetus and encouragement from European support for African aspirations. There can be little question that without an ideology of responsibility and obligation toward colonial peoples in the metropolitan countries, African self-government would have been vastly more difficult to achieve. We are not being naive about the economic and political drives operative in the establishment and maintenance of the colonial system, when we recognize the significance and force of this metropolitan climate of opinion on colonial issues. We need only contrast the Portuguese record in this respect, or the prevailing view in South Africa among the dominant European minority, with that in Britain, France and, at the end of its African empire, in Belgium, to make the point.

The value of such European sympathies is dramatically illustrated by the rise of African nationalism in British East and Central Africa, compared with the failure of Africans to obtain political participation in the Portuguese territories and in South Africa. Here we find African nationalism confronted with what can best be called "counter-nationalism," that is to say, the determination of the many non-African permanent residents not to relinquish their position of dominance.

In eastern and southern Africa, African nationalisms and European counter-nationalisms were centered on the fact of race. When Africans came to have some say in politics, as in Kenya and Tanganyika, and to a modest extent in the Federation of the Rhodesias and Nyasaland, political groupings proceeded to organize on racial lines; multiracial parties were difficult to form and even more difficult to keep alive. In South Africa, where African political activity was prohibited, African organizations existed which tolerated European association, and certain multiracial protest movements came into being. From the point of view of the African activist, the latter were largely impotent. The pressure of events caused even moderate Africans to turn toward "Africanist" movements, which rejected any form of joint effort with non-Africans, Indians no less than Europeans, and to denounce "congress" groups for agreeing to cooperate with them.

Yet another aspect of African nationalisms in the multiracial societies differentiated them from the movements elsewhere in Africa. In West Africa, efforts to achieve independence were directed toward the metropolitan government. The non-Africans on the scene were regarded as agents of the colonial power, instruments in the implementation of policy, not responsible for it. This was also true in the Congo, though in no comparable degree, on the level of human relations. In the multiracial colonial territories, on the other hand, the role of the Metropole came to be that of mediator among various racial groups. On the local secne, for example, the District Officer, a Colonial Office appointee, was in many respects looked upon as one who cushioned the policies instituted by territorial legislative bodies controlled by European settlers. African nationalist effort was directed primarily against the counternationalist moves of the dominant minority rather than against the colonial official. In South Africa, where the *apartheid* policy was that of the Government of an independent country, there was no liberal opinion of a Metropole to be effectively enlisted, and the terms European and Government were synonymous. In only a slightly lesser degree, this also applied to Southern Rhodesia.

Another dissimilarity, especially in the tactics of nationalism, is to be noted in the efforts made by nationalists to attain their objectives in western and central Africa, as contrasted with those of the multiracial states, though here we are dealing with differences that overlay a basic similarity. The unities of nationalist effort derives from the fact that in all the Subsaharan continent, the chief recourse of African nationalist movements, with few exceptions, was to political, or more precisely constitutional means. The preindependence history of Ghana, of Nigeria, of Sierra Leone was marked by conferences in London which resolved issues in dispute by means of constitutional revisions. In the French territories after the Second World War, developments moved from the Brazzaville meeting of 1944, through the establishment of the French Union in 1946, to the achievement of a commonwealth-type structure of the Community in 1960, with constitutional provision for former French colonies to determine for themselves the degree of their association with France. The final sanction for Congo independence followed the Belgo-Congolese round table discussions of January 1959.

Constitutional discussions also followed the pressures of African nationalism in the multiracial territories, but here they included recourse to violence. The reasons for this are not far to seek. The objectives of African aspirations, the roads to opportunity were in these countries blocked by a force near at hand. Local vested interest made sluggish response to a world opinion that, for some decades, had been coming more and more to favor the doctrine of self-determination for all peoples. In West Africa there had been the Aba tax disturbances in 1930, the Gold Coast riots of 1946, violence incident on labor difficulties in the Ivory Coast in 1950; there were also, in addition to earlier uprisings, the much more serious reactions in the Congo—in Matadi, Leopoldville, Stanleyville and elsewhere—during 1959. But there was nothing in West Africa that approached the violence of Mau Mau in Kenya, or the scope of the 1959 incidents in Nyasaland, or the uprisings in Angola that began in 1960, or the continuous unorganized attacks on Europeans in South Africa.

But even more exacerbative than actual violence was the constant fear of it in the multiracial countries. In West Africa, or in the Congo before 1959, the small European minorities went their way without fear. Whatever may have been the attitudes of Africans, there was little overt hostility; physical aggression was rare, or altogether unknown. On the eve of Ghana's accession to independence, some few Europeans could be heard to whisper that the newly-freed Africans in their exuberance might become arrogant or insulting to Europeans in the streets, but all accounts testify that such apprehensions were quite unfounded. In the case of the French territories except Guinea, or of Nigeria, statements of this sort were not even heard. Even in Guinea, where the abrupt French withdrawal could have been expected to set up racial tensions, all was quiet. Wrote one observer of events in Conakry:

> If few Europeans left their houses, and I did not encounter one of them on the street, . . . their apprehensions, however understandable, were quite unfounded. Rarely has collective action, having such enormous historic consequences, been carried through with less feverishness.[4]

The attitude in these countries was one that looked to the future. It was, so to speak, a positive, hardheaded approach that continued to focus attention on the task ahead, and regarded the Europeans as of proved or potential usefulness when they brought needed skills, expert advice, or capital resources. There is no evidence that they were objects of overt resentment because of the role their countries had played in the colonial past.

The difference in attitude toward Europeans found in western Africa and in the eastern and southern parts can also be traced to the history of African responses to colonial penetration. In West Africa, a number of the indigenous peoples, with their tight political organization and their established record of expansion through conquest, met the Europeans with organized military resistance. The contemporaneous accounts of the British expeditions against Benin or Ashanti, or the French conquest of Dahomey give evidence that operations of considerable scope were needed to impose European control. Conquest by force of arms was known and understood in these African societies. Once they had recovered from the initial impact of colonial subjugation, they learned the ways of their rulers and, within the framework of the new situation, used what they learned to their own advantage.

At the southern end of the continent there was comparable organized resistance to initial European incursion. Yet both here and to the north, where resistance was slight, the wider gap between aboriginal political, economic and social organization and that of the non-Africans who imposed their rule, plus the presence

[4] *André Blanchet:* "Un envoyé du gouvernment français met la Guinée devant les consequences de sa 'sécession,'" *Le Monde,* Vol. 15, No. 4256 (September 30, 1958), p. 1.

of non-African permanent settlers, made for a slower, more tortuous adjustment. When achieved, this found the alien elements in a position of such strength that it was impossible to resolve the situation as in West Africa. The disparity in numbers did lead to organized expressions of resentment through force. The 1915 uprising led by Chilembwe in Nyasaland aroused European fears to such a pitch as to give this occurrence a psychological importance which far transcended its military or political significance. At the other end of the spectrum, the Mau Mau uprising in Kenya merited the term "war" frequently applied to it. With its suppression came substantial changes in the way of political, social, educational, and economic betterment.

This interplay between African nationalism and European counter-nationalism moved along certain lines that resembled one another to a marked degree in the various parts of the multiracial areas. Everywhere the African majority appeared on the offensive, and used the potential threat of its numerical strength to wring concessions from the minority in power, even while measures were being enforced to suppress organized activity that might threaten its rule. To the north, in British East and Central Africa, African moves came more and more to resemble the appeal to principles of constitutional change that had proved effective elsewhere. In South Africa, economic weapons, especially the boycott, began to be employed. During the "Year of Africa," the success of the drive toward full African participation in government was the issue which dominated thought, planning and action in the multiracial states.

11

Politics and Polarities

WITH INDEPENDENCE ACHIEVED, fresh problems began to press for solution. In the new African states, many of these problems could be traced to the interaction of two closely related factors—the internal effects of changes in the structure of power, and the play of antecedent tradition on the new situation. Patterns of social control, little in evidence during the period of foreign rule, proved far from extinct. They now reappeared in earlier form, or as reinterpreted to accommodate innovations introduced during colonial times.

Foremost among the new problems was the need for capital to build an infrastructure for the kind of industrialized pecuniary economy that became an important goal of the new order. There was little or no capital in the hands of the indigenous population that could be tapped. Economic development under colonial rule had been the work of outsiders, primarily those from the metropolitan countries. While their operations continued after independence, the increasing rapidity in the pace of economic growth and the urgent need to encourage the growth of an indigenous capital structure caused the new governments to seek economic aid outside, and to impose new controls on the domestic front, to mobilize human as well as natural resources. This was not without its crosscurrents. Even while outside aid was being sought, the cry of "neo-colonialism" began to be raised. The position of non-Africans in the economic life of the new countries, and the introduction of foreign capital, private or governmental, to facilitate economic growth, came in for re-examination. In all this could be discerned the emergence of nationalism in the classic sense of the term, with, here and there, overtones of African chauvinism.

Among the new nations themselves, and within them, rivalries that long antedated European occupation once more came into focus as, with self-government achieved or assured, subgroups began to envisage the possibility of finding themselves dominated by another ethnic group instead of the colonial system. Here, also, the problem of the future of indigenous rulers arose. What was to be the relationship of the traditional chiefs to the new political leaders, and of earlier political institutions to the parliamentary forms instituted to govern regions whose boundaries were a heritage of the maneuvering of European powers in Africa? The question of the amalgamation of African states into larger units took on a new dimension, as African national leaders began to seek position for their nations and themselves on the international scene.

On the ideological level, the concepts of Pan-Africanism, of the "African personality" and of *négritude* began to provide a symbolic frame for shaping African objectives, as the African states moved to gain for themselves the recognition their peoples had been denied under colonialism. For societies having the strong tradition of communal control, the attraction of socialist philosophy and doctrine, and especially the methods of left-wing parties in attaining and holding political control, encouraged discussion of a peculiarly African kind of democracy. It was said that models evolved to fit specific African needs, and not borrowings from other countries, would shape African forms of political organization.

We have seen how, in the colonial period, the course of events in Africa was charted by the interplay between the policies and practices of the governing powers and African aspirations. The struggle of Africans for independence itself was shaped by the presence or absence of permanently settled non-African populations, and by the positions taken by the respective colonial powers toward the African drive for self-government. This interaction with outside forces was multiplied, and on some levels intensified with the attainment of independence, or where self-government was imminent. What this meant was that Africa, even that part of it which had not as yet achieved the status of self-governing nations, came into widening contact with the outside world.

Here the role of the United Nations was critical. It not only presented a forum for those who were striving for control over their own destinies, but after independence provided a sounding board and a base of operations in world politics. For these new nations, this was a spectacular demonstration of the achievements of leaders who had transformed Africans from colonial subjects to sovereign peoples, whose voices were to be given the same attention as any other member state.

This can be seen as a logical outcome of two historical movements toward the self-determination of peoples, one ideological, the other technological. The first, crystallized by the Fourteen Points of Woodrow Wilson, was brought into sharp focus by the statement of the Four Freedoms two decades later. The second sprang from scientific developments in communication, and the emergence of weapons so powerful that they threatened the destruction of much, if not all, life on the earth's surface.

There can be little question, too, that the rapidity with which Africans won independence and an important position in world affairs resulted from circumstances which made them beneficiaries of events they had not initiated. These events had developed entirely outside their own historic experience. What can only be regarded as a series of historical accidents triggered unforeseeable results, whose capstone was the rivalry between two world power blocs.

The heightened tensions of the Cold War, which coincided with the growth of African nationalist movements, were not without their effect on developments in Subsaharan Africa while it was still largely under colonial controls. Once independent, however, the Subsaharan African states could take a position between the two major contenders, particularly when they increased their strength by forming a kind of diplomatic third force jointly with the nations of Asia and North Africa. Their declared position of "positive neutrality" allowed them to bargain on highly favorable terms with both sides in the Cold War. As a result, at each turn of events their support was sought by powerful states. They were no longer pawns in the game, but active participants in international affairs, whose reactions were carefully weighed.

As we review the performance of African statesmen, it is evident that they demonstrated no lack of astuteness in making the most of their opportunities. Without the circumstance of the Cold War, however, they could not have attained the position of influence which they commanded as members of the world bloc. Their emergence from colonial status was of itself nothing new, but rather part of an historical process experienced by many peoples in other parts of the world. The contrast between their position on the world scene and that of nations of comparable size in Latin America or in Asia is significant. The reason cannot be sought solely in differences in resources, or in forms of organization, or in overall cultural orientation, or even in the personalities of the heads of state, but also in the historical moment when independence was achieved. It was the timing that was important; the timing, that is, in the light of the international situation at the moment of the "African year."

In all these developments, internal and external, the human factor continued to provide the clues essential to an understanding of the changes observed in individual behavior and institutional setting. The peoples of Subsaharan Africa were reacting to the events of the time in terms of their total cultural heritage, and through it shaping, transforming, and adapting their traditional ways in the light of their response to the innovations brought to them. Culturally, no less than politically, independence made of them free agents. They were free not only to take over or change what had been brought to them, but they could re-establish patterns that under colonial control had been discouraged or suppressed. Thus we again see that, in considering the approaches to the questions which faced the newly independent African peoples, and the solutions that were advanced, we must not only give full attention to the impact of the new on the old, but also understand how, and to what degree, when released from the psychological and political pressures of colonial rule, the old influenced the acceptance of the new.

[2]

So orderly was the transition to independence in most of Subsaharan Africa that there were few major discontinuities to be observed in the new self-governing nations. Even on the political plane, the break was abrupt only in the sense of the formal transfer of power. In Nigeria, as in Ghana, and to a noteworthy extent in the former French territories, Africans had been performing the functions of government before complete control was placed in their hands, while an appreciable number of Europeans, particularly in the technical services, were retained in their posts after African countries became self-governing. Thus, four years after independence, the top echelon of the Ghanaian army was British. In the non-Official sector, changes were even less marked. European, Indian and Lebanese business and professional men continued in their private capacities much as before. Differences in standards of living were no longer so closely correlated with race. Earlier disparities in income, housing, and education began to lessen—the gaps were beginning to narrow.

But some discontinuities were present, even in the smoothest of transitions. The manifest expression of this was the change in the composition of the non-African technical and trading population. During the colonial period this was largely composed of citizens of the metropolitan power. As a matter of implicit policy, incursion by those who were not citizens was not encouraged. With independence, access to African territories was determined by policies set by African governments. In consequence, for various reasons, prominent among which was the psychological need to exercise free choice, foreigners from a wide range of countries were called in as technical experts. The economic ties with the former Metropole were neither cut, nor even significantly loosened. A large proportion of export and import trade continued to be carried on through earlier channels, and educational relations were little altered. Nevertheless, the degree of reliance on any single country was markedly reduced, and a broader base of international trade was established. In this respect, the African scene was being changed by the freedom of choice that came with the end of colonial status.

The "Year of Africa," especially the events in the Congo that followed on independence, revealed an important contribution made by the African nationalist movements that had gone almost completely unrecognized. It would, in all probability, never have been so clearly understood, had not Congo events stood out in such stark contrast to the peaceful transition from colonial rule to independence that prevailed in West Africa. This contrast, however, highlighted the role of these nationalist movements in preparing African colonial peoples, psychologically no less than organizationally, for the changes to come, when the direction of their affairs would be in their own hands. The difference in the degree of orderliness in the transfer of power could be directly correlated with the extent to which nationalist movements had the time to organize, manoeuvre, and thus undergo a process of natural selection of political leaders. This was the case in West Africa. In the multiracial territories of British East and Central Africa, the pressure of the nationalist movements in their own countries and the sweep of events in the continent as a whole caused the dominant European minorities to face up to an inevitable shift of power. Gradually these minorities began to give ground, so that more and more Africans came to participate in government, and thus learn by doing.

In the Belgian Congo, however, nationalism had no opportunity to serve the apprenticeship it served elsewhere. There was no time either to exert pressures on the colonial administration to place Africans in positions of responsibility, or to perfect an organization which could provide experienced, responsible leadership for self-government, when it came. Because the reins of colonial control had been held so tightly, the habit of independent thought, of initiative, of protest, and above all of self-confidence, had atrophied.

These qualities had not been absent in the precolonial societies of the Congo. They had to be there, since they are essential to any people who, as a self-governing entity, must make their own decisions. What underscored the discontinuities when independence came was the fact that they had to reassert themselves suddenly, in a broader geographical and operational matrix then any indigenous Congolese system. With the earlier base long suppressed, so that it could no longer be drawn on, the aptitude to adjust to the new requirements was also dulled. Thus, with independence, a political vacuum resulted that brought on the anarchy which marked the beginnings of the new self-governing Republic.

It is of interest to contrast the Congo experience with that of Nigeria, which shared with the Congo problems stemming from the presence within its borders of numerous ethnic and linguistic groups. Both countries are large, the population of Nigeria being approximately three times that of the Congo. Each was presented with the task of continuing a unity which was artificial from every point of view—ecological, ethnic, historical. In essence the question was whether some kind of a federal system, with allocation of specific powers to the various regions, should be instituted, or whether there should be a strong government at the center. Both countries were faced with rivalries between ethnic groups dominating administrative regions which were in large part constructs of colonialism, and unknown during precolonial times.

In the Congo, there was barely time to broach these questions, let alone bring them to some kind of resolution. Tribal loyalties and ancient hostilities generated fears that erupted as colonial controls were relaxed, so that actual warfare, often with weapons that antedated the introduction of firearms, broke out between the Baluba and Benelulua in the Kasai even before independence. Political parties with local affiliations sprang up everywhere. A few were at most regional, and none could claim a membership that was country-wide. As Merriam summarized it,

> Almost every party formed in the Congo had its origin in a tribal group, and since there are many tribes there were many parties as well. Local interests were paramount and . . . never ceased to be a powerful factor in politics.[1]

The ABAKO may be taken as an example of this trend. It was originally a Bakongo cultural society which first openly took on a political character when it drafted its manifesto in reply to the *Conscience Africaine* statement.[2] When restrictions on political parties were lifted, it took its place among the other parties that were being formed. One of its stated aims was the restoration of the Kongo kingdom, which was to reunite all members of the Bakongo into a nation comprising the lower Congo basin—the Bakongo not only of the Belgian Congo, but of the Congo Republic, formerly a part of French Equatorial Africa, of Portuguese controlled northern Angola, and the Cabinda enclave. Such a state, which would cut off the rest of the Congo from access to the Atlantic, was scarcely calculated to win support among non-Bakongo Congolese. As a party organization, ABAKO effectiveness was unchallenged where the Bakongo were in the majority. This was shown in the Leopoldville elections of 1958 for burgomasters. The voting, which was primarily along ethnic lines, showed heavy majorities for the ABAKO candidates.

The dispute over the question of a federal structure of government as against centralization—the "struggle between unitarians and federalists" that "divides nationalists throughout Africa," [3]—had other overtones. Regional economic self-interest was the salient factor. So much of the wealth of the Congo was in the Katanga that the dominant Balunda, encouraged by the Union Minière and other interlocking financial interests, expressed resentment against the diversion of substantial revenue for the

[1] Alan P. Merriam: *Congo, Background of Conflict* (Evanston, 1961), pp. 114–15.

[2] *Supra,* pp. 333–5.

[3] Colin Legum: *Congo Disaster* (London, 1961), pp. 96–7.

support of undertakings elsewhere in the Congo, and particularly for the cost of the central government in Leopoldville. It was this complex of economic interest and lack of identification with the country as a whole that, in the case of the Katanga, caused it to secede shortly after independence. An accompanying factor, was the long-standing dissatisfaction of Congolese in the several provinces against the extreme centralization of authority in Leopoldville, the seat of the Government General, which represented the Ministry of Colonies in Brussels and worked through a hierarchy of Belgian officials to regulate every detail of life in the colony.

The dichotomies of center versus provinces, richer versus poorer sections, tribal versus national affiliations were serious enough, but they need not necessarily have presented insurmountable obstacles to establishing a viable political system. However, those conflicts were aggravated by a complete lack of political experience and the deep Congolese distrust, and even hatred, of those who had so often treated them with contempt, or ordered them about as if they were children. With fear, insecurity, and hostility let loose, chaos inevitably came with independence. Merriam, in his description of the coming of independence to a remote Kasai village, Lupupa, has given us an illuminating view of the lack of understanding of the larger issues, and the degree of commitment to the local scene that prevailed in most of the Congo.[4]

In Nigeria, the early nationalists had recognized the need for unity. The 1938 "Nigerian Youth Charter" stated as a principal aim "the development of a united nation out of the conglomeration of peoples who inhabit Nigeria," and committed itself to "combat vigorously all such tendencies as would jeopardize the unifying process."[5] The presence of regional, even tribal affiliation, created perhaps even more of a problem in Nigeria than in the Congo. Each of the regions was controlled by a single ethnic majority—the Hausa in the North, the Yoruba in the West,

[4] A. P. Merriam, op. cit., pp. 173–204.

[5] Obafemi Awolowo: *Awo, the Autobiography of Chief Obafemi Awolowo* (Cambridge, England, 1960), p. 121.

the Ibo in the East. But all these regions touched on the so-called middle belt, a part of the Northern Region inhabited by the "pagan tribes," that is, many culturally and linguistically separate societies united only through their fear of being dominated by more populous neighbors. The Western Region included the Bini, a large population, proud of their cultural achievements and their historic past, desirous above all for status as a separate region. In the Eastern Region, numerous peoples of the Niger Delta who did not belong to the politically dominant Ibo wished to establish themselves as a region on an equal footing with the three then constituted. The Central Government kept a measure of balance between the Regions; in human terms, it performed the important task of providing a common meeting ground for leaders from various regional and ethnic backgrounds, and allowed political maneuvering on the national level to develop a sense of identification with the nation as a whole.

We have seen how, in British territories, nationalism developed early in the colonial period, and how Nigerians were prominent in this movement. With educational opportunities that enabled them to base their claims to self-government on legal no less than moral grounds, they could take advantage of an early expressed aim of British colonial policy, the preparation of Africans for self-government. With this as a fulcrum, Africans moved much more rapidly than expected on all levels, local as well as national, toward greater participation in the direction of affairs. Consequently, the actual transfer of power was no more than a matter of taking a final step in a long process. The form of the independent government had been hammered out in long debate, political parties had experience and a tradition; the coalitions that had to be formed were not *ad hoc*.

Despite the relative smoothness of the transfer of power, the newly independent countries of Subsaharan Africa continued to have their problems. We can discern a clear correlation between the degree of continuity and the amount of tension that marked the actual event. The case of Guinea is to the point. When Guinea, alone of all French Africa south of the Sahara, voted to leave the Community and take over full control of its affairs, the angry reaction of the metropolitan government of France was expressed in prompt retaliatory measures, designed to serve as an object lesson. Within two months, all French officials were withdrawn, all programs of economic and technical aid cancelled. The withdrawal extended to such matters as the destruction of records in district offices, the removal of the furniture from the palace of the Governor, the destruction of such instruments of communication as could not be taken out.

This policy hardened the determination of the country to go it alone, if necessary, and to obtain aid wherever available. Another result was the appearance of xenophobia. While directed primarily against the French and those countries that were held to be associated with her, this manifested itself in a general suspicion of all outsiders. Attempts to reimpose colonial status were feared. Withdrawal from the franc zone led to currency restrictions accompanied by tight financial controls that placed serious difficulties in the way of growth, and inhibited the development of foreign trade essential to the healthy functioning of the internal economy.

Here it was not so much a total lack of experience in government that made the break from colonial status to independence so severe; it was rather the hostile reaction of the governing power. The consequence was more severe dislocation in the structure and functioning of government in Guinea than in the other countries that had been under French rule but elected to remain within the Community. But on the international level, the cut off of Guinea from outside associations spawned needs that had not been anticipated, and that had to be met by a process of trial-and-error.

Later, the other countries of the Community profited from the political crudity of the earlier break with Guinea. When they declared themselves sovereign states, two years later, there was no shock. The step involved a series of moves rightly assumed to be acceptable. Only in the cause of Mali, the former French Soudan, did certain comparable discontinuities arise. Here, however, they were secondary, caused by a break with Senegal, partner in the Mali Federation, after a series of political moves in which

French military and commercial interests were held to be implicated, with charges and countercharges of undue intervention.

The transfer of power from French to African control was achieved without bloodshed. Even in Guinea the engagements were verbal. No African or non-African life was sacrificed to the attainment of the new status. Accession to power was rather in the nature of a peaceful reshuffling of functions. On a scale of discontinuities where the Congo was at one extreme and Nigeria or the Ivory Coast, like Ghana before them, at the other, Guinea and Mali lay midway. Yet the presence or absence of discontinuities must not be accorded more importance than it merits. It was critical in influencing the degree to which change-over could be effected smoothly or traumatically; it affected the way Africans responded to the fact that their constitutional revolutions were marked by a minimum of personal danger and sacrifice on the part of actionists who took part in them.[6] It was out of this that the shape of self-governing Africa crystallized.

One further point should be made clear. In discussing the transition from colonial status to independence, the consideration of how the factors of continuity and discontinuity operated carries no ascription of value. The point is important because it was at the core of the argument for gradualism the colonial powers advanced in the early days of their rule, an argument which the dominant non-African minority in the multiracial countries also continued to urge during the later period of colonial rule. As a rationalization of the desire to maintain control, it was argued primarily on an emotional basis. Insistence on the validity of the doctrine of gradualism grew stronger as the force of the African drive increased, and as the power of African nationalism grew to be such that the decisions no longer lay in the hands of the non-Africans. For the Africans, self-determination became a supreme value, particularly since with self-determination they would no longer suffer the stigma and hold the status of a child race, dependent on others for guidance. This value, and all the resentments its denial awakened, must be seen as an essential

[6] Cf. André Blanchet: "Les nationalismes africaines frustrés d'une révolution?" *Preuves,* No. 112 (June 1960), *passim.*

constant in the analysis of the forces set in motion by the emergence of a politically independent Africa.

[3]

With independence, African governments faced three major problems in organizing their internal political systems. All three of these problems had been foreseen during late colonial times, but the decisions, now in the hands of Africans, could no longer be made by fiat. The first has already been touched upon. It had to do with how local identifications could be transmuted into national loyalties. As commonly phrased, this was *the problem of "tribalism."* The second was how to integrate traditional political institutions, particularly the traditional rulers, into the new structures of government. This was most often designated *the problem of the chiefs.* The third had to do with *the kind of governmental system* that could best function to promote the social and economic aims of the new nations. All were interrelated, but since their resolution was predicated on the governmental structure that had evolved in each country, it is useful first to examine this phase of the process of adjustment.

When self-government was under discussion, during the period between the end of the Second World War and the beginnings of African participation in government, the consensus was that under independence, the colonial territories would take over the political institutions of the countries that ruled them. In essence, this implied the continuation of such parliamentary bodies and responsible ministries, and of forms of local administration as had been introduced from the Metropole. The will of the people, it was assumed, would be expressed through a secret ballot which offered alternative programs, conceived in the national interest, arrived at by the interplay of political parties in public debate. "The loyal opposition" would function as in England. When the word "democracy" was used in the context of political developments in Africa, it thus meant a system in the Euroamerican democratic tradition.

In fact, many political institutions of the administering colonial powers did carry over. For example, the number of parties in the former British territories was smaller than in those under French or Belgian control. The party system flourished as self-government approached; only where political activity was forbidden, as in the Portuguese territories, or earlier in the Congo and Ruanda-Urundi, were they absent. Even in South Africa, where only those of unmixed European ancestry enjoyed the franchise or exercised parliamentary or administrative authority, the African element in the population had its Congresses that, in their own extra-political way, worked toward a change in the position of Africans in South African society.

Coleman has analyzed the political systems of the continent as these existed in 1959 and 1960, within the framework of a threefold set of categories. The first comprised what he termed the African controlled systems, with three subgroups, consisting of the emergent African systems, such as Sierra Leone and Uganda, the new African states, excluding the Congo, and the historic African systems of Ethiopia and Liberia. The second grouping included the Congo, Kenya and Tanganyika, which had what were called transitional systems. Finally came the systems under European control—the Portuguese territories, the Federation of Rhodesia and Nyasaland, and the South African complex. Only four countries were without political parties—Ruanda-Urundi, the Portuguese provinces, Ethiopia and the Republic of the Sudan, a number shortly afterward to be reduced to three as self-government for Ruanda-Urundi came close to realization.

This was more than a classification of the party systems; it also indicated trends. Thirteen territories were listed as having one-party systems. Six had what was termed "comprehensive nationalist" parties, confined to Africans only, and included most of the multiracial territories. Fourteen had competitive party systems, those in Southern Rhodesia at the time, and in the Union of South Africa, being limited to the European population. In the years 1958 and 1959 political parties were numerous, varying from those in total control of their respective legislative bodies, as with the True Whig party of Liberia and the segmented *Rassemblement Démocratique Africaine* and its affiliates in the then

Autonomous Republics of the French Community, to those which, as in the Southern Cameroons or the Gabon, had bare majorities or less, and participated in coalition governments.[7]

Political developments in the half decade preceding the "Year of Africa" forced a reconsideration of views about the future political systems of the emerging nations. In 1955, Apter observed "It remains an open question whether or not the structures of parliamentary government are suitable for the development of African social organization from tribal to national systems of social interaction." [8] The problem came to be recognized as basically part of a larger process of cultural adaptation, wherein parliamentary democracy is governed by the same principles as control the transmission of any other cultural elements.

There was another current in the formation of African political systems that, until independence, had gone almost unnoticed because its influence had been extra-official. We have seen how one group of African trade-unionists in French territory was subject to Marxist discipline in their association with the parent left-wing unions of the Metropoles. In British territories, African nationalist leaders were encouraged in their aspirations by members of the Labour Party, and at intervals received active support from British Communists. This was also true of the Congolese, whose leaders received moral and political aid from comparable groups in Belgium.

The support given African protest and aspirations by left-wing parties, particularly those which formed a part of the world-wide Communist movement, whether Russian or in the dependent Communist states, or Chinese, or affiliated parties elsewhere, attracted African leaders in many ways. They were deeply impressed by the way in which such Communist countries as Russia and China had, through disciplined direction of energy, transformed their economies, and with the position they had assumed in world politics. They were also impressed with the way the one-

[7] James S. Coleman: "The Politics of Sub-Saharan Africa," in *The Politics of the Developing Areas,* G. A. Almond and J. S. Coleman, editors (Princeton, 1960), pp. 266, 286–7.

[8] David Apter: *The Gold Coast in Transition* (Princeton, 1955), p. 3.

party systems of these totalitarian states functioned internally. Nor could they fail to respond to the unqualified support for anti-colonialist movements given by the Communist bloc.

Marxist doctrine, as received by a non-industrial population in a colonial setting, where the class structure of the indigenous peoples was of minor significance beside the enormous differences between European rulers and African ruled, weighed heavily in shaping the socialist policies of a number of the new states. Similarly, the tight controls of the Communist parties and labor unions in Western Europe, and the organizational lessons learned from them, offered ready-made blueprints for the continuation in power of the leaders who had become heads of state. These influences fused with indigenous elements, to develop the one-party systems, and what in the economic field came to be called "African socialism."

[4]

The fallacy that the political structures of self-governing Africa would be replicas of their Euroamerican models, or would take over foreign socialist or communist forms whole-cloth, arose from an underestimation of the vitality of aboriginal political institutions. It seemed logical to assume for most of the Subsaharan colonial world, that institutions that had borne the brunt of the initial impact of colonialism had disintegrated. Where some structural features were retained, they were under control of European administrators; often they had been replaced by non-traditional local heads and councils selected by the colonial authorities, and held accountable to them.

For those who looked below the surface of the African colonial scene, there was evidence that these imposed governmental forms had neither destroyed or completely superseded earlier institutions. In some instances, as in Northern Nigeria, for example, the policy of indirect rule, which so influenced British colonial practices,[9] continued earlier governmental institutions and con-

[9] Lord Frederick D. Lugard: *The Dual Mandate in British Tropical Africa* (London, 1922), *passim.*

solidated the power of the traditional rulers. In 1949, a British writer with extensive experience as a colonial civil servant stated that the "main duty" of the British in Africa, after having assumed that the peace would be kept, was "to interfere as little as possible with native life. Leave them alone, was the watchword." [1] All colonial governments, even the Portuguese, whose direct controls were strictest, realized that the European political officer could not, by his own effort, administer the large numbers of people placed under his jurisdiction. In many parts of the continent where formal governmental structures were rudimentary or absent, and there were no traditional territorial, or even village chiefs, these were arbitrarily appointed and held accountable for carrying out the orders of the government in the administrative units for which they were responsible.

Traditional rulers carried on as best they could over all the Subsaharan continent. Where they were accorded a measure of recognition by colonial governments, they exercised what prerogatives they were permitted, without openly voiced objection to the restrictions laid on them. Protest was not allowed to come to the surface, nor the resentment that lay beneath their behavior as they received government officials and passed on to the people the demands of the administrators. In more instances than not, their traditional position was accepted by those over whom they continued as nominal rulers. Where a traditional chief was not acceptable to the Europeans, and they named another to take his place, all played the game. Many a *chef medaillé* in the Belgian Congo, appointed to replace a traditional village head, was accepted only as a representative of the Belgian administration. Loyalty was reserved for him who had been displaced, for in the eyes of the people, he was their rightful ruler.

This same attitude prevailed in French West Africa. In 1939, Delavignette estimated that there were 32 tribal or provincial chiefs, 2,206 canton chiefs, and 48,049 village chiefs.

> Since the French conquest, all these exercise temporal power by virtue of their confirmation in office by the administration. But only

[1] W. R. Crocker: *Self-Government for the Colonies* (London, 1949), p. 137.

> those among them who also belong to the traditional governing families are regarded by their people as the true chiefs, wielding moral and religious authority as well.

Even where the chief selected by the administration was a member of one of the branches of the line from which election was made under customary law, there were difficulties.

> It was only natural that the French should choose as chief the candidate most amenable to their orders and pass over those they considered to be too old or incompetent, and the one selected might or might not be his people's choice. . . . When the French thought that they were following the traditional procedure and confirmed in office the candidate they believed to be the chief sanctioned by custom, they found he did not hold moral authority over his people unless they voluntarily accepted him as their chief.[2]

The matter, however, was not as simple as this. Among the Busoga of Uganda, the so-called "civil service chief" was caught between the demands of conflicting roles:

> While the various specific duties of a chief have a clearly civil service character, his total rôle as a chief is unlike anything found in Western civil service systems, at any rate in modern times. . . . The Soga power system is to a great extent monolithic. There is essentially only one centre of authority: the hierarchy of civil-servant chiefs and, extending beyond it, the similarly monolithic authority system of the Protectorate Government. . . . The chief is not only the most powerful person in his area but also the wealthiest person and the person with the highest social prestige.[3]

Many other complicating factors entered. A generation of men with higher education, or with specialized technical skills essential in the African economies of the day, came to question the competence of the traditional rulers in secular matters. The participation of some chiefs in party politics, and the active support of nationalist movements by others, was one response to this challenge. In French territory, we are told, "The African *élite* was be-

[2] Virginia Thompson and Richard Adloff: *French West Africa* (London, 1958), pp. 204–5.

[3] L. A. Fallers: *Bantu Bureaucracy* (Cambridge, England, n.d.), p. 197.

ing drawn to the chiefs by an intensified pride in all indigenous institutions, which they increasingly stressed as a means of combating the assimilation trend in French Policy."[4] In pre-independent Ghana, too, the ambivalences which marked attitudes toward the traditional system were found everywhere; "all these show the predominantly characteristic feature of chiefship in Ashanti today—its insecurity."[5]

With independence, Ghana moved to bring the chiefs under the control of the central government; their traditional religious role was recognized, but they were rendered relatively impotent politically. In Guinea, they were stripped of all power in favor of the Party organization that came to rule the country. The rationale for this was phrased as follows:

> The Africans are accustomed to certain democratic forms, since in Africa of earlier days it was the elders who spoke for the country. When you travelled in the interior and, in a village, explained the program of the party, it was usually the oldest man of the village who first responded, then he turned to the elders of the Keita (clan), then to the elders of the Camara and to those of the Bangoura, etc. . . . But democracy, within our Party, is not a democracy of clan or family, it is a basic democracy where the entire population contributes directly and freely to the action and enrichment of the worth of the country.[6]

Yet historical continuity was explicitly claimed: "In analyzing our past acts, . . . (it is clear) . . . that the fundamental guiding principles of our policy have a specifically African base and orientation."[7]

In still other countries traditional rulers were incorporated into the new governmental structures. Thus, in each of the three

[4] Virginia Thompson and Richard Adloff: op. cit., p. 209.

[5] K. A. Busia: *The Position of the Chief in the Modern Political System of the Ashanti* (London, 1951), p. 214.

[6] Sékou Touré: *La Lutte du Parti Démocratique de Guinée pour l'Émancipation Africaine* (République de Guinée, Vol. IV, Conakry, 1959), p. 41.

[7] Sékou, Touré: *L'Action Politique du Parti Démocratique de Guinée; la Planification Économique* (République de Guinée, Vol. V, Conakry, 1960), p. 275.

Regions of Nigeria, an upper house composed of traditional heads of the pre-European states, became a part of the legislative system. The symbolic Yoruba religious head, the Oni of Ife, was named as the first Governor of the Western Region. At the time of independence, the Prime Minister of the Northern Region, a principal member of the important pre-European hierarchy of the Sokoto Emirate, belonged to the Fulani ruling caste whose power had been strengthened by the British policy of indirect rule. In some instances, where a "chief" had been named in a society that had not known the institution of chieftainship, as among the Wachagga of Tanganyika, the innovation was accepted and, in the new system, he became their elected head.

The South African approach to the position of the traditional ruler in changing African society was unique on the continent. Its official sanction was bolstered by a misreading of cultural theory which, contrary to all scientific findings, assumed a generic relationship between physical type—"race," the word most often used—and traditional institutions. Since the South Africans in power held that the ways of living developed in the past by a people were best for them, it seemed logical to assume that subsequent changes in their modes of life must be undesirable. Membership in an ethnic grouping that had inhabited South Africa since before European occupation was officially held to be fixed by circumstance of birth, and immutable. An official government White Paper declared that under *apartheid*, "the latent power of the Bantu's own system is harnessed to play the leading part in the programme for the development of the Bantu community."[8] The separate indigenous groupings were to be re-established each as a distinct political entity. Each was to be ruled by its own chief but, as an innovation, would have a representative in urban areas nominated by the tribal authority in consultation with the European Minister of Bantu Administration and Development, to look after the interests of its members who had migrated to the cities.[9]

[8] Union of South Africa: "Promotion of Bantu Self-Government," *Bantoe*, No. 5 (May 1959), p. 14.

[9] Ibid., p. 20.

Africans and others opposed to this program came to call these proposed political subdivisions "Bantustans." Officially they were projected as autonomous parts of the Union, eventually to become a kind of commonwealth in miniature. That is,

> . . . if the various Bantu national units show the ability to attain the required stage of self-sufficiency they will eventually form a South African commonwealth together with White South Africa which will serve as its core and as guardian of the emerging Bantu states.[1]

The powers of the chief and his councillors were, however, limited, and strictly controlled by non-African Commissioners, who were responsible to the Minister. Eventually, it was promised, each ethnic group would reach a place where it would have control of its own internal affairs.

In devising this system, no Africans were consulted, inasmuch as Africans were excluded on all levels from making or even implementing policies concerning their affairs, except that, with governmental approval, they could levy taxes on themselves. The reactions of the Africans were similar to those seen in territories where local rulers were named by government, as in Angola and Mozambique, or earlier in the Belgian Congo. In the main, Africans resigned themselves to a cynical acceptance of the unavoidable, and showed a studied disdain for the nominated chiefs, considered creatures of the government, whose acts could not represent the people's wishes. At times, distaste broke into open disaffection, as in the 1960 incidents in the Pondo reserve.

The policy of *apartheid,* conceived as recognition of the need of all Africans to revert for their own good to aboriginal patterns, and enforced by all the powers of the state, provoked a reaction antithetical to the intention of its originators. Elsewhere in Africa, the extension to Africans of control over their own affairs was followed by a rediscovery of the values in the pre-European cultures. In South Africa, however, Africans saw an officially imposed return to the ways of their ancestors as a

[1] Ibid., p. 16.

deliberate measure to keep them permanently from achieving participation in the society of which they formed a part. Their protest against this was a protest against restriction of opportunity, rather than a repudiation of their traditions. Psychologically, however, it was a factor of importance in the total situation, of which the attitude toward chieftainship was but one manifestation.

Elsewhere, the establishment of local government was regarded by colonial administrations as providing experience in the exercise of responsibility. Institutions on this level customarily followed the pattern of the Metropole, so that the county system was taken as a model in British East Africa, and the *canton* in French West African territory. This fact is important for us, since we are concerned with the role local government played in integrating aboriginal political patterns with the European practices that were introduced.

The transition, especially in British territory, appears as a series of steps, each dictated by a recognition of changing needs. We have seen how the system of indirect rule continued earlier institutions in a fixed mold. On the local scene, the chief still ruled, but under the supervision of the District Officer. A later stage saw the establishment of Native Authorities. According to Cowan, these "were at least in some degree based on tradition, which lent their activities a certain respect in the eyes of the people." Shortly before independence, "a new type of secular authority, the elected council, . . . appeared with powers previously held by both former sources of authority." This new form lacked "traditional sanction." It was "composed of ordinary citizens, whose mandate, unlike that of the District Officer, may be withdrawn at the next election." As a result, there was "a strong element of doubt and confusion in the voter's mind as to the legitimacy of this new organ." [2]

In its particular form, this innovation of elected councils in

[2] L. Gray Cowan: "Local Politics and Democracy in Nigeria," in *Transition in Africa: Studies in Political Adaptation* (G. M. Carter and W. O. Brown, editors, African Research Studies No. 1, Boston University, Boston, 1958), p. 50.

Nigeria differed from comparable developments in other parts of Subsaharan Africa, but the reactions to it represented an aspect of the process of adaptation that was to be discerned no matter what forms were involved. As Cowan put it:

> Though tribal institutions can no longer undertake the tasks that have to be done, the chief will continue to be an influence in local affairs so long as the mass of the people still feel that he represents legitimate authority. Thus regardless of the position the system of popular representation assigns to him, his place will not lose its importance for some years to come.[3]

In Kenya, what Rosberg called "tribal parochialism" was a prime factor in restricting the effectiveness of African nationalist efforts. There were "numerous tribal and sub-tribal groups," among all of whom there was found a "consciousness of separate identity." The strength of this feeling was compounded by later developments, since

> these tribal units became the primary focus of administration and policy. The government appointed chiefs and headmen from the tribes as agents of control; courts were created which administered customary law and there were no possibilities of developing inter-tribal law. Eventually local native councils were established, . . . but the majority of these embrace only a single tribal area.[4]

The political systems of the West African indigenous kingdoms have from time to time been equated with the feudal regimes of Europe, and the African ruler with the medieval feudal lord. The first to make the comparison was Rattray:

> The student of the English law of Real Property who comes to examine the Ashanti law relating to that subject, will at first be astonished to find that a system, which he had been taught to believe was peculiar to his own country, had an almost exact replica in West Africa among the Ashanti.

[3] Ibid., p. 60.

[4] Carl G. Rosberg, Jr.: "Political Conflict and Change in Kenya," in *Transition in Africa, Studies in Political Adaptation* (G. M. Carter and W. O. Brown, editors, African Research Studies No. 1, Boston University, Boston, 1958), p. 113.

He denied that this similarity was the result of European influence:

> The human mind and human intelligence, . . . seem often to have reacted in a like manner to a similar stimulus, and the Ashanti, under certain conditions not unlike those existing at the time of the Norman conquest, seem to have evolved an almost exactly similar land code.

He pointed out that "the tenant had to swear fealty to his chief, and the chief to his king"; that "reliefs, in the language of feudal tenure . . . have their exact parallel in Ashanti," and continued with a long list of other homologies.[5]

Rattray's interpretation was challenged by Busia, who detailed "important differences between the Ashanti system and English medieval feudalism." His conclusion as regards land tenure, the point which attracted Rattray's attention, was as follows:

> The system of land-tenure in Ashanti . . . was based on kinship solidarity, allegiance to tribal stools, and the supremacy of the ancestors, . . . It was essentially different from the English feudal system of land-tenure based on the universal ownership of the king, individual tenancies and fiefs, and contractual relations of lord and vassal guaranteed by legal sanctions.[6]

The feudal concept was especially congenial to Marxist thinking, which gave it a new lease on life. In a speech already cited, we find Sekou Touré asserting that, "Before colonial domination, Africa had a feudal regime," though he continued, significantly enough, "which was its own particular kind."[7] Russian scholars ordered their evaluations of African societies along the same lines. Potekhin, while conceding Rattray's position that, "it is obvious that Ashanti feudalism cannot be regarded as identical with the feudalism of medieval England," nonetheless objected that Rattray "did not attach sufficient importance to the difference in the relationship between the aristocracy and the rank-

[5] R. S. Rattray: *Ashanti* (Oxford, 1923), pp. 223 ff.

[6] K. A. Busia: op. cit., pp. 57–60.

[7] Sékou Touré: *L'Action Politique du Parti Démocratique de Guinée*, p. 275.

and-file community members of the Ashanti on the one hand, and the British feudal lords and the peasantry,—on the other." "Here," he said, is where "the essence of the matter lies," and concluded that

> Professor Busia and his followers came to deny Ashanti feudalism precisely because they did not try to see its true economic import obscured from them by the public rights or even sacral form of the relations between the rank-and-file community members and the aristocracy. Yet these relations are based on feudal exploitation. In various degrees they exist even in our days. . . .[8]

Controversy over terms is usually sterile. Enough analogies can be found between African social and political forms and those found elsewhere to make a case not only for applying "feudalism," but also "democracy," "communism" and many others to them. Too often, however, the aim in drawing the comparison has been to support a position rather than to illumine the facts. Hence the stress on feudalism in Marxist analyses of Africa. Lacking the classical bourgeois-proletarian components of the class struggle, indispensable to the Marxian dialectic, the African social structure, was equated with European pre-industrial feudalism.

The facts are that social stratification has long characterized many African societies, and in them the chief as ruler exacted tribute. But analysis of the relation between chief and commoner shows resemblances to European feudalism to be no more than analogies. There has always been a large component of democracy in African systems, if by this we mean governmental forms based on common consent, and expressing the will of those governed. The right to depose an unpopular chief, the prerequisite of popular acquiescence for action by the ruler found everywhere, and reaching from the village level, give evidence of a tradition of rule by consent. But this is not the democracy of Europe and America, with its pattern of majority rule and its parliamentary structure.

Communal forms and values are everywhere present in African life, but this is not the communism of state control and ideol-

[8] I. I. Potekhin: "On Feudalism of the Ashanti" (Paper presented to the XXV International Congress of Orientalists, Moscow, 1960), pp. 7–8

ogy in the Marxist-Leninist tradition. Indeed, the African leader who moved closest to the communist model of party control over the state in shaping his government, made this point explicitly:

> We are not a communist regime, we must state this without any complex or false shame, we are much more concerned quickly to obtain our total emancipation within the frame of an Africa that is entirely free and truly united than to adapt our conditions and our realities to any other given political system.[9]

It has long been possible to anticipate that Africans would reshape their political systems on the basis of their own particular historic experience and their needs of the moment. They would, in short, do what all peoples over the entire history of man on earth have done—adapt what has come from outside their societies to their own physical, psychological and cultural requirements. Little more than three years after Ghana obtained her independence, the Speaker of her parliament no longer wore his wig, the President sat on an adaptation of the traditional chief's stool, the post of Leader of the Minority was abolished.

[5]

Under the colonial system, Africans had no voice in the bargaining among the powers that ruled them. Independence brought them into international politics, and thus added a new dimension to their political life. The United Nations provided the forum. As we have seen, the world tensions that marked the period when the new African nations came to self-government placed them in a most favorable position to be heard. Their support or their neutrality became a goal aimed for by the concerted diplomatic efforts of the great powers. They were courted by proponents of current controversies—the Cold War, the Arab-Israeli dispute, internal dissension in the Congo. It was undeniably a strategic moment in world history for them, and they were quick to grasp the advantages it held.

Africans were not quite as new to this world political setting

[9] Sékou Touré: *L'Action Politique* . . . , p. 296.

as might seem at first glance. As petitioners before the Trusteeship Commission of the United Nations and the Fourth Committee of its Assembly, they had had considerable firsthand contact with this body. Some had gained insight into how international affairs were conducted through membership in the secretariats of various multilateral bodies. With the approach to independence, Africans were assigned to embassies of the Metropole to be trained for the foreign service of their countries. African nationalist leaders had gained experience in stating their case during visits to countries outside the Metropole, in Europe, North America, and Asia.

The first states to gain independence after the Second World War joined those that had earlier been self-governing to bring together African leaders at meetings like the All-African People's Conference, held in Accra in 1958. This was but one of a number of conferences of varying scope held in this single year. A list of these meetings shows how rapidly African peoples entered international activities. In addition to the one named, it includes an Afro-Asian Peoples' Solidarity Conference in Cairo, a Conference of Independent African States in Accra, a Pan-African Students' Conference in Kampala, the initiation of a Pan-African Freedom Movement for East and Central Africa in Tanganyika and, on a broader level of intergovernmental operations, an African Caucusing Group in the United Nations and a United Nations Economic Commission for Africa in Addis Ababa. All these, while concerned primarily with the problems of Africa, permitted Africans of different backgrounds to get to know one another, and plan the strategy of joint action, which later was used with skill.

By the end of 1960, it had become evident that the problems of the countries of Subsaharan Africa lay on several levels of international commitment. There were, first of all, those which affected them as members of the world community, some quite outside the scope of African concern as such, as when matters bearing on other world regions came before the United Nations. Next came questions that arose as the result of their affiliation with other new nations that had formerly been under colonial rule. Here the repercussions of the Bandung Conference of 1956 were manifest. For while participation by Africans from Subsaharan Africa had been minimal at this Conference, the impulses it set in motion led to united action on colonial matters. Finally, there were the important questions of the relations between the countries of Subsaharan Africa itself, which, with the unrest in the Congo after it had become self-governing, brought the African nations full circle into the arena of Cold War conflict.

There is little in the first category of problems that distinguished the African approach from that of others. The positions they took were dictated by their interests and their sympathies. Aside from the routine diplomatic maneuvering on this level, there was another, more humdrum problem that each new African state had to face. This was the question of diplomatic representation. For though membership in the United Nations symbolized their new status, the workaday business of diplomacy had to be carried on in the capitals of the world if African countries were to function in the international field in a manner commensurate with the prominence of the position they had assumed. Missions had to be staffed, but there was no backlog of experienced personnel to be called on for ambassadorial and other posts. The interchange of embassies involved resolving questions of precedence and prestige and, above all, costs. How large this could bulk can be seen from the Liberian experience. In the 1952 budget, for example, the sum of $1,122,639 was spent to support diplomatic missions, 13% of the total income of $8,500,000 for the fiscal year.[1] However, a special factor enters here. Burdensome as support for these peaceful modes of contact may seem, it was made possible by the minimal military budgets of these countries, which were limited to the needs of internal security.

In our second category of problems fall those questions arising from a community of interests with other newly independent states. Important here was the concept of African unity, cast in a continental rather than a Subsaharan framework. We have seen

[1] Republic of Liberia: *Report of the Treasury Department for the Fiscal Year 1952,* William E. Dennis, Secretary of the Treasury (Monrovia, November 14, 1952).

how loose were the bonds between North and Subsaharan Africa, when considered in the long historic view. Under the influence of the Asian-African formula, however, a kind of association, primarily political, began to develop. The guiding concept was that of African unity, and all the independent countries of the entire continent, which joined to form a bloc in the United Nations, sent representatives to all-African, non-regional conferences. As in the broader Asian-African context, the issue of colonialism provided the underlying motive for united action.

Within the African section of this larger grouping, however, there was beneath the surface much questioning, and some apprehension. Suspicions deeply rooted in the history of the slave trade with the Arab states of North Africa had not everywhere been dispelled. The attitudes and behavior of North Africans toward the Subsaharan peoples, the personal ambitions of leaders, the strong affiliation of the nations of the northern tier with the Arab world, were disquieting. Once again, the new African countries were presented with the problems of reconciling earlier experience with later developments; of resolving polarities in this crucial issue of their international relations, as well as their internal affairs.

But more searching, and more absorbing for the new nations, were the questions that had to do with the developing relationships among the countries of Subsaharan Africa. The centripetal force of anticolonialism was here continuously in evidence, and the eradication of all non-African controls over Africans was put foremost. Statements made at the All-African People's Conference were unequivocal. "Africa is the continent of tomorrow. Europe is the continent of yesterday." "We have decided to be free, not tomorrow, but *now*." "South Africa is the situation which no longer requires mere resolution but action." One of the resolutions adopted by the Conference stated: "That independent African States should pursue in their International policy principles which will expedite and accelerate the Independence and sovereignty of all dependent and colonial African territories." And from the then Prime Minister of Ghana: "The independence of

Ghana will be meaningless unless it is linked up with the total liberation of Africa."[2]

At this time, also, the question of what came to be called "neo-colonialism" began to be raised. This gave an ideologically powerful, because familiar, name to suspicions that by some strategy the newly won independence might be nullified. It was, essentially, an expression of African distrust of the powers who had ruled them, and of any associated countries. An example of this is the question raised by a Nigerian student at the time of independence, whether the favorable notices Nigeria was receiving in the world press were not designed to drive a wedge between his country and the other African states.[3] Africans found it difficult to believe that political controls had been relinquished without covert plans to retain economic controls for the benefit of the Metropole. The implications for Africans of any move to establish an association of European states were carefully studied, to discover whether these were not designed to maintain African economies in their classical colonial role as a source of raw materials for European industry and as a vast market for the products of European factories. As it was put by one African leader, himself an economist:

> It would be a mortal error for the nations of the Third Force (*Tiers-Monde*), especially for those which have only just recovered their liberty, to believe they had come to the end of their struggle when Independence was proclaimed. This is without doubt a capital step in the struggle, but it is only the first one which, it is true, makes it possible to attack basic tasks, confront burning questions and to apply audacious solutions. A certain number of recently emancipated States have clearly understood that sovereignty is not real in this world unless it is justified technically and economically.[4]

Given the premises of their position, Africans were not without grounds for their uneasiness. German proposals in which the

[2] All Africa People's Conference: *News Bulletin*, Vol. 1, Nos. 1–7 (Accra, 1959), *passim*.

[3] Melville J. Herskovits: *Notes on African Field Research*, p. 60/D134.

[4] Mamadou Dia: *Nations Africaines et Solidarité Mondiale* (Paris, 1960), p. 40.

concept of "Eurafrika" was initiated,[5] were explicit on the position of Africa in such an alignment. The African aid programs of the Organization for European Economic Cooperation raised the question of the motives for the southward extension of the interests of this purely European association. The possibility that the North Atlantic Treaty Organization, despite its expressed exclusion of Subsaharan Africa from the area of its operations, might be considering Africa as a strategic resource in its planning, was not overlooked. Suspicions were not lulled when Africans read, reprinted in an official Belgian journal, a statement to the effect that

> From the economic standpoint, the symbiosis of Europe and Africa is governed by very simple facts. The soil of Africa is too poor for Africa to be able to dispense with Europe. The subsoil of Africa is too rich for Europe to be able to dispense with Africa.[6]

They were accentuated when the Prime Minister of Portugal asserted, "Africa is the complement of Europe, indispensable to its defense, a necessary support for its economy."[7] This was the complete antithesis of the flat statement by the then Prime Minister of Ghana, that Africa "is not an extension of Europe or any other continent."[8]

The slogan of neo-colonialism became an instrument of the first order for Cold War maneuvering. It offered obvious advantages in playing on suspicions directed against those who had been colonial rulers, and who were affiliated with various multinational organizations which in this frame of reference, it was urged, were planning to impose a new economic hegemony on Africa. Utilizing the position of "positive neutrality" that became the expressed policy of the African states toward the Cold War,

[5] Anton Zischka: *Afrika, Europas Gemeinschaftsaufgabe Nr. 1* (Oldenberg, Germany, 1951), pp. 12–13, 60–100.

[6] Phillipe Lalanne: "For a United Eurafrica" (abstracted from an article in *Western World Magazine,* October, 1959), *The Belgian Congo Today,* Vol. 9 (January, 1960), p. 10.

[7] Antonio de Oliveira Salazar: "A Posição Portuguesa em face do Europa, da América e da África" (radio address delivered May 23, 1959), *Notícias de Portugal,* No. 630 (May 30, 1959), p. 4.

[8] Kwame Nkrumah: *News Bulletin,* All African People's Conference, Vol. 1, No. 1 (Accra, 1958), p. 6.

the slogan was calculated to turn suspicion into accepted fact, and in certain cases succeeded in committing those who had adopted a policy of neutrality to a position of potential partisanship. It was necessary to counteract the danger of "balkanization" of the continent, seen as an instrument of "neo-colonialism," and to remove the obstacles to intercourse between segments of ethnic groups separated when boundaries had been drawn in the chancelleries of Europe. Efforts to prevent fragmentation were numerous. African statesmen frequently mentioned the dangers of Africa becoming a collection of "South American republics." Discussions of economic viability—how large a nation must be to become prosperous, or even to survive—took on added urgency as the number of independent African countries increased.

The question of "balkanization" had been debated by Africans long before they had attained independence, and attempts were made to resolve the difficulty once independence was gained. They included unions such as that of Ghana and Guinea in 1958; the Mali Federation of 1959; the Entente of four West African countries of the French Community; and a parallel arrangement entered into by countries of what had been French Equatorial Africa. There was also the consultation of the heads of the Ghanaian, Guinean and Liberian governments, held in Liberia in 1959, as an expression of intent to achieve closer cooperation on matters of mutual interest. In the interracial Federation of Rhodesia and Nyasaland, the question of union as against separate identity for the three component territories was debated on economic, political and racial grounds. African leaders contended that in British East Africa, a union of the three territories, Uganda, Kenya and Tanganyika, must be achieved before independence, if they were ever to be incorporated into a single nation.

It was not long before an initial obstacle emerged in the way of moving toward the realization of some form of a united Africa, either on a continental or regional basis. It lay in the gap between a political ideal and the willingness to surrender newly-won identities. After years of dependency, self-government came to hold deep symbolic value. At the start of Nigerian independence, the point was repeatedly made: "We want to enjoy our independence, before we begin to think of giving it up." Or, as the leader of the Nigerian independence movement, Nnamde Azikiwe, declared in 1959.

> It would be capital folly to assume that hard-bargaining politicians who passed through the ordeal of victimization and the crucible of persecution to win their political independence will easily surrender their newly-won political power in the interest of a political leviathan which is populated by people who are alien to one another in their social and economic relations.[9]

It was heady to participate in United Nations debates. Whose voice would speak when full members surrendered their individual positions to enter a larger political entity? When a smaller state allied itself with a larger, what measure of control over its own affairs would it exercise? Where states contemplating entry into a larger grouping had strong leaders, personality factors invariably entered. In brief, a long road led from the fear of fragmentation or "balkanization" to the realization of African unity.

There was still the carry-over, from colonial times, of attitudes based on contact with the differing languages, customs, institutions and, above all, values, of the respective governing powers. Until Africans who had grown up under these differing kinds of influence attempted to come together, it was scarcely realized how much this phase of the past could mean. Within any given country, communication among ethnic groups speaking different African languages was usually achieved in the tongue of the Metropole which they had all been taught. Hence the continuing use of English as the official language of Ghana and of the Federal Government of Nigeria, or French in Guinea or the Ivory Coast or Dahomey. But when those from countries termed in French "anglophone," and those of the "francophone" group had to communicate, the difficulty was increased. The cultural dynamic of the colonial period was not to be denied, either on the international or the national level.

Again, the position of the African states in the broader area

[9] Nnamde Azikiwe: *Zik, a Selection from the Speeches of Nnamde Azikiwe* (Cambridge, England, 1961), p. 173.

of international affairs was dramatized by the events in the Congo following independence. The wave of lawlessness which the new government was ill equipped to suppress, and the dispatch of Belgian troops to protect Belgian nationals led to an appeal to the United Nations. Military detachments were made available by African member states, and by European countries without colonial commitments. It was not long before African states took the position that the Congo problem was an African matter, and attempts to solve it at solution must be placed in their hands, though within the framework of the United Nations.

We are not concerned here with the course of events in the Congo itself, but rather with understanding some of the underlying motives involved. One of these had to do with the position taken by African spokesmen on the issue of legitimacy, and the alignment of support in the internal political controversy that developed in the Congo. The proposed constitution under which the Congo was freed followed the Belgian model. Under this constitution which, for reasons not germane to the point we are considering, was never ratified, the President dismissed the Prime Minister, and gave his support to an extraconstitutional regime wherein administrative responsibility was in the hands of the armed forces and a group of élite whose professional training, though incomplete, made them the best available source of administrative personnel.

The Cold War was openly injected into this situation when the Eastern Bloc and China gave direct aid to the deposed Prime Minister in his effort to re-establish his authority. The dispute was not calmed when the Congolese opposed to him expelled the diplomats of the Eastern European countries. The African states and African leaders insisted all the more that what they regarded as the legitimate government be re-established.

This political issue in especially relevant to the continuing influence on African opinion of cultural concepts and attitudes that derive from the traditions of the respective European colonial countries during whose rule they were acquired. The President of the Republic of the Congo, in dismissing his Prime Minister, followed Belgian constitutional practice, whereby the King may dismiss a government acting against the best interests of the country. But to the leaders of the other African countries, legitimacy meant what it was in British practice—and in French practice before the Fifth Republic—whereby only Parliament can dismiss a Prime Minister, and this because of his failure to obtain a vote of confidence. Since the Prime Minister of the Republic of the Congo had not been repudiated by a vote of the elected representatives of the people, action to remove him was, to them, a flagrant violation of the principle of legitimacy. In terms of the historic processes involved in the initial move of dismissal, their position can be viewed as a case of secondary cross-cultural misunderstanding.

The "Year of Africa," brought the peoples of the Subsaharan continent into world affairs in a way that could not have been foreseen even a decade earlier. Not only were the majority of the indigenous peoples self-governing in the fullest sense, but they found themselves in a maelstrom of international currents that forced on them decisions on questions that in former years would never have touched them. They showed a remarkable lack of diffidence in taking up their new role, and on both national and international questions, they learned rapidly to maximize their opportunities. That they had assimilated much more knowledge and skill during the colonial period than even they had realized was patent; it was equally patent that their experience as subject peoples had altered, but by no means destroyed the indigenous traditions which they had brought with them into that experience.

12

Economic Change

CONCERN over what came to be called the "underdeveloped" portions of the world coincided with the march toward self-government. There was a growing awareness by the peoples of Asia, Africa and Latin America of the disparities between themselves and the industrialized countries of Europe and North America in income, standards of living, and levels of schooling, health and hygiene. The fact that the list of "developed" countries included the colonial powers led to the conclusion that the exploitation by these powers of the mineral, agricultural and human resources of their possessions was the instrumentality by which they had achieved their position. Political independence represented for colonial peoples a means of recapturing control over their own resources, and thus acquiring for themselves the material benefits that had previously gone to their rulers.

The demands of the inhabitants of the "underdeveloped" areas caused economists and planners to shift their attention from almost exclusive preoccupation with the mechanisms that controlled the play of economic factors in Euroamerican societies. The effects of the infiltration of industrial and pecuniary institutions into what were termed "backward" economies could no longer be ignored. Under the pressure of changes in political power, the increasing economic potential of colonial and nonindustrial countries came more and more into the foreground as functioning parts of the broader economic system. During the decade 1949–59, Africa grew steadily in importance, "both as a supplier of certain primary products and as a market for imports from the rest of the world . . . associated with and . . . reflected in the growth of the domestic economies in which both government development plans and private initiative . . . played a part." [1]

It is not difficult to understand why this interest in the problems of economic growth developed as late as it did. In African colonial territories decisions concerning policy, particularly economic policy, rested with the Metropole. As we have repeatedly seen in earlier chapters, lines of communication and action in all fields led to centers of power in Europe. In colonial economies, the influence of mercantilism persisted long after this economic philosophy had ceased to dominate economic policy. It persisted, in fact, even after the principle that the colony existed for the benefit of the country that governed it was revised to include aid programs of various sorts, financed from the Metropole.

In Africa, as long as the conditions making for overt political self-assertion [2] were not present, little attention was given to internal factors in the economies of colonial possessions. Since these were dependencies of the Metropole, it seemed clear that the significant factors were to be sought not in the colonies, but in the metropolitan centers where the decisions were made. This was reinforced by the ethnocentrisms of the day, which accepted concentration on the economies of the industrialized, pecuniary societies of Europe and America, and held the peoples of colonial areas, especially those of Africa, to be outside the stream of progress.

It thus became almost an article of faith that whatever their "primitive" economies may have been, these "backward" systems

[1] United Nations: *Economic Survey of Africa Since 1950* (No. E/CN.14/28). (New York, 1959), p. 1.

[2] *Supra*, pp. 307–8.

must in the long run give way before the more "developed" ones, with their superior technologies. African labor had been given some study chiefly by colonial administrators who had the responsibility for maintaining the work force at a required level. Few economists gave more than cursory attention to the aboriginal economies, whose fit to theoretical models was too loose. Attempts at analysis were consequently restricted almost entirely to a few economic historians who studied the evolution of economic institutions, and to an equally small number of anthropologists engaged in determining the range of variation in economic behavior manifested by human societies.

Typical of early interest in the problem of economic under-development was a report by a group of experts who, in 1951, presented certain *Measures for the Economic Development of Under-Developed Countries.*[3] Frankel, who analyzed its findings, made a point that is particularly pertinent to our present discussion. The report was significant, he said,

> because of the *unconscious* expression which it gives of the climate of economic opinion in the middle of the twentieth century. Indeed, it is in itself a very interesting case study for economists, political scientists and even for philosophers, of preconceptions which are apparently current not only in the offices of government, but also in the more cloistered retreats of academicians—preconceptions which seem at times to be developing into something like an "Official Concept of Progress." [4]

Because of the built-in evaluation in the term "under-developed," economists were at some pains to clarify their use of the word. In a standard handbook on the subject we read,

> Under-development refers simply to a low level of economic and technical achievement; it does not refer to other achievements or qualities. . . . settled government and the sway of law have obtained for many years in some of the poorer countries of the world;

[3] United Nations: *Measures for the Economic Development of Under-Developed Countries* (No. E/1986 ST/ECA/10). (New York, 1951), *passim.*

[4] S. Herbert Frankel: *The Economic Impact on Under-Developed Societies* (Oxford, 1953), p. 83.

> in others the achievement or restoration of law and order is . . . the most essential pre-requisite for economic growth.

As for distinguishing underdeveloped countries from others, "the characteristics which are common to these countries are specified by the definition itself: poverty in income and accumulated capital and backwardness in technique by the standards of North America, Western Europe and Australasia." However, "the dividing line is arbitrary, and no analytical significance can be attached to it." [5] The ethnocentric element also came in for analysis:

> The problem is not to wipe the slate clean in the underdeveloped countries, and to write our economic and technical equations on it, but to recognize that different peoples have a different language of social action and possess, and, indeed, have long exercised, peculiar aptitudes for solving the problems of their own time and place; aptitudes which must be further developed in the historic setting of their own past to meet the exigencies of the present and the future.[6]

The changes to be looked for, as a society with a pre-industrial type of economic and technological system moves into a "modern" system, have been described as follows:

> A high and sustained rate of increase in real product per capita, accompanied in most cases by a high and sustained rate of increase of population; major shifts in the industrial structure of product and labor forces, and in the location of the population, commonly referred to as industrialization and urbanization; changes in the organizational units under whose auspices and guidance economic activity takes place; shifts in the structure of consumer expenditures, accompanying urbanization and higher income per capita; changes in the character and magnitudes of international economic flows. . . . Behind all this is the increasing stock of useful knowledge derived from modern science, and the capacity of society, under the spur of modern ideology, to evolve institutions which

[5] P. T. Bauer and B. S. Yamey: *The Economics of Under-developed Countries* (Cambridge, England, 1957), pp. 4–5.

[6] S. Herbert Frankel: op. cit., p. 96.

permit a greater exploitation of the growth potential provided by that increasing stock of knowledge.[7]

These specifications suggest the aims implicit in programs laid down by administrators, or explicit in the many "plans" for African economic development advanced by academic economists and by various official boards and commissions that addressed themselves to the problem. Beginning with the period of the Second World War, moves toward directed economic change became more numerous. Initially, they were made by colonial governments, but with the growth of nationalist movements, African participation in planning increased. After independence, the new governments not only continued the movement, but bent every effort to accelerate it.

[2]

In order to assess the nature and force of African responses to economic change, we again turn for insight to the concept of additive as against substitutive innovation. Though the institutions of money and markets were well known in the western half of the Subsaharan continent, in contrast to their rudimentary development or absence in the eastern and southern portions, the changes required of all African societies when they converted to "modern" economic systems were so great as to make the difference between the traditional and the new almost one of kind. Yet the process was additive rather than substitutive, though reinterpretations did occur. Two outstanding examples were the reconciliation of earlier patterns of labor with the requirements of an industrial establishment, and of earlier communal traditions bearing on the acquisition and distribution of wealth with the rewards of individual enterprise.

Colson has presented the broad outlines of the aboriginal system and the adjustments required as it moved into the new

[7] Simon Kuznets: "Notes on the Take-off" (Paper presented at the meeting of the International Economic Association, September, 1960) MS p. 1.

setting. Life in Africa was, and even after decades of colonial control continued to be

> conditioned by certain attitudes toward property and persons . . . characteristic of a nonindustrial stable society, in which opportunities and power depend upon status within social groups rather than upon control of investments; where, indeed, the safest form of investment, and often the only one, is still to be found in the building up of claims against persons.

The older patterns persisted, despite the exposure to new ways incurred in "moving toward . . . an economy largely tied to foreign markets," as in West Africa, or in Central Africa, "where . . . most of the people are caught in a web of labor migration which draws them out of the rural areas for a part of their working lives," or in South Africa, where they "have been overwhelmed by the inability to make a living in the overpopulated and eroding reserves while at the same time they are not encouraged to settle permanently in the individual centers where they earn their livelihood."

These patterns persisted because they continued to meet common human needs:

> security of life and property, provision for the nurture and maintenance of their children, assistance in sickness and old age, the mobilization of assistance for economic activities beyond the scope of the individual, and provisions for assistance to handle unforseen accidents such as entanglement with the law, the necessity to meet a civil claim, or the payment of medical and funeral expenses.

The disintegration and disappearance of some of the larger social units, especially those having political functions, was to be anticipated, since "the various central governments have assumed the obligation of guaranteeing the safety of persons and property throughout the territories over which their mandates run." But this was by no means the whole story. The central governments were not concerned with the entire range of social obligations that existed previously to "provide for the other needs catered to by the old system," and consequently, "the African must continue to rely upon the willingness of his fellows to assist and protect him." [8]

Here again, innovation and customary practice were fused into a new system. For even in those aspects of changing African economies where the difference between induced and indigenous patterns was not so great, values, no less than behavior, had to be reoriented. This was true no matter what ideology dictated the innovations with which the Africans were faced. Adjustment was necessary whether change derived from the system of individual initiative to which the Africans were exposed during the period of colonial control, or came from socialist doctrine. The African business or professional man, called upon to fulfill his traditional obligation to members of a numerous kinship grouping, had to resolve conflicting claims of two systems of value, just as a family brought by government decree into productive and distributive cooperatives such as were initiated in Guinea and Ghana. Africans also newly experienced the impersonality of industrial societies, the conventions of formal credit, the institutions of banks and of labor unions. They were presented with other innovations that had no counterparts in earlier practices, such as production of cash crops disposed of through marketing boards and destined for consumption in distant lands quite beyond the horizon of the producer.

Certain elements of the new system, particularly its technologies, were readily accepted. Medical science, once its aims were understood and demonstrated, found resistance rapidly diminishing. The Africans came to value the knowledge which ensured the safe delivery of their infants, the alleviation of physical suffering, the prolongation of life. Scientific medicine was thus added without conflict to their earlier therapies. More striking was the acceptance of other aspects of the system, such as the use of money, response to the profit motive, the institution of markets to facilitate exchange in those parts of the continent that had not known them, adjustment to wage labor and the in-

[8] Elizabeth Colson: "Native Cultural and Social Patterns in Contemporary Africa," in *Africa Today* (C. Grove Haines, editor, Baltimore, 1955), pp. 70–1.

centives toward upward mobility in a new social scale. Commitment to the goals of large developmental projects, the most advanced types of equipment, the utilization of rail, motor and air transport, the building of a communications network, are further examples.

The realignment of values was by no means confined to the members of the new middle and upper classes, nor to urban as against village communities. It was general, and continent-wide. This does not mean that African societies were being completely transformed. There were regions where innovation was resisted, and where life continued much as in pre-European days. On the whole, however, change was relatively more pervasive in the economic and technological sectors of the culture than in others, and the response to innovation more demanding.

The challenge of the situation was well summarized in these terms:

> It is the fate of many African countries to achieve responsibility of independence at a time when the reach of government has extended into most fields of economic life and in a period when technological change is so varied and vast that adjustments to it are not easy even for peoples with several generations of industrial development behind them.[9]

The adaptations to this new dimension in the structure of economic life called for searching analyses of all factors involved in the process, past and present, and planning for the best use of existing and expanding resources.

These analyses, however, were too frequently dominated by concepts and conclusions that continued to be extraneous to the African historical background. Discussions of African economic development by administrators and scholars from Western Europe and the United States tended to regard as essential the development of a middle class which would exercise the functions of the entrepreneur through individual initiative. The thinking of socialist planners passed through the Marxist conceptual screen, being based on the principle of social evolution, which referred

[9] United Nations: *Economic Survey of Africa Since 1950* (No. E/CN.14/28). (New York, 1959), p. 3.

development to a series of stages through which all social institutions must of necessity pass, and on the formula of the class struggle. As a result, there were practically no studies of economic development which, beginning with the established institutions and values of a given African people, projected against these the lessons to be learned from the experience of the more technologically and industrially complex societies, drawing the balance which would with maximum effectiveness promote economic growth.

A growing consciousness of the need for a broader approach is discernible in some of the reports that were drawn. Thus the Mission of the International Bank for Reconstruction and Development, in its assessment of Nigerian needs, balanced the plusses and minuses in aboriginal custom that it felt had a bearing on the attainment of the desired ends. They noted with approval the "strong local loyalties" of Nigerians, and the possibilities of building a cooperative movement on this traditional base. On the other hand, the Report debited the fact that these loyalties did not require the same canons of morality toward outsiders as they did toward members of a local or kinship grouping. "This is reflected," we were told, "in many instances of apparent disregard for personal rights and private property, flouting of oral or written contractual obligations and exploitation of one Nigerian by another." An added point was that:

> The need for self-help is not understood by the African businessman who looks to the government, and the government alone, for financial assistance in the expansion of his business instead of joining with others in a partnership or other forms of common enterprise.[1]

The attempt to relate such problems to earlier custom reflected an awareness of the historical and traditional background, but the conclusions cited could not stand the test either of cultural or of historical relevance. Thus the fact that the patterns of the society which shaped the relationships between the individual

[1] International Bank for Reconstruction and Development: *The Economic Development of Nigeria* (Baltimore, 1955), pp. 21, 22.

and his kin and local groups had for generations caused people to set up various "forms of common enterprise" involving private partnership was quite ignored by the Mission, most likely because the formal institutions were shaped by tradition. Moreover, the fact was overlooked that in the history of Nigerian private enterprise during the colonial period, the Nigerian businessman could only under exceptional circumstances obtain a bank loan, and had therefore to turn to government, which controlled most of the sources of aid.

More typical of underlying assumptions and customary recommendations was the Ten Year Plan for the economic development of the Belgian Congo during the decade 1949–59. The authors felt no need to look into any traditional or human factors that might figure in affecting procedures or results. In an introduction to the Plan, the then Minister of Colonies wrote:

> In the Belgian Congo, public authority has the responsibility for more than 10 million natives. These are incapable, by themselves, of assuring a sufficiently rapid evolution of their methods of production and a progressive elevation of their standard of living. They count on us.[2]

The course to be taken was then outlined:

> What are the remedies? Always the same: mechanization and rationalization. These first of all impose themselves on the European industries which must be multiplied since they are the most active ferment in this economy and the surest guarantee of better conditions for the natives. They impose themselves also in the agricultural setting, where they will make the villages more attractive, increase their productive capacity while reducing the time that must be given to agriculture and the preparation of food, and raise the standard of living.[3]

We are here concerned with the repercussions of such plans for economic improvement, and of other economic and technological developments, on the lives of the people; the kinds of

[2] Pierre Wigny: "Introduction" to *Plan Décennal pour le Développement Économique et Social du Congo Belge,* Vol. I (Brussels, 1949), p. xii.

[3] Ibid., p. xviii.

adjustments Africans had to make to new modes of getting a living. We have already treated certain aspects of this complex, particularly those which had to do with the establishment of an economic infrastructure for the new order. In earlier chapters we have dealt with land use, education, and urbanization. Throughout these discussions, too, has run the thread of the influence of a new communications grid, and of the introduction of European forms of money and its use.

In the pages that follow, we will consider certain problems of the readjustments that lie below the institutional level. Perhaps the most important of these are the changes in motive and aspiration necessary to create the stable industrial labor force essential to economic development. Another is the response of Africans in the self-governing countries toward projects designed to facilitate economic growth. Other problems, such as fostering a tradition of individual saving as a means of building up resources for an adequate capital structure on a national scale, and the related question of developing a middle class, need not be discussed again. But there are two phases of the developing economies of Subsaharan Africa which are fundamental to the understanding of economic change, but have not been given the attention they merit.

[3]

A central problem in economically underdeveloped areas is to hold workers to the job. Here the factor of motive is paramount. As an early analysis showed:

> . . . the response which an indigenous people make to the new conditions introduced by capitalism depends upon three determinants of individual motives: the need of money, which decides in the first place the extent of the effort the native will make to produce for exchange; the preference for one set of living conditions over another shown by various labourers; and the desire of some natives to travel outside their tribal area, which should probably be regarded as an initial rather than a permanent stimulus.[4]

[4] I. C. Greaves: *Modern Production among Backward Peoples* (London, 1935), p. 113.

Those who attempted to develop a stable labor force had to devise a "permanent stimulus," since the introduction of many had succeeded chiefly in bringing forth what economists came to call the "target worker." Men were willing, typically, to accept employment for a limited period. Then, once enough was saved for certain specific wants, they would leave, to return to a mode of life that was based on an economic system wherein subsistence, prestige and security were to be had without reliance on pecuniary rewards.

The difficulty was recognized early in the period of the extension of European economic activities to colonial Africa. Thus, in 1929, it was noted:

> The African, where his inclination is unfettered, is finely unresponsive to merely economic considerations. It is no use raising his wages to induce him to work four days in the week on an estate instead of three. The probable effect will be to make him work two, seeing that two days at the higher rate will give him all the cash he proposes to hire himself to work for.[5]

Some two decades later, in East Africa, another student reported that:

> Conversations with travelling labourers will usually elicit the fact that they have a definite sum in view, and that they hope to earn that amount and then go home again. The sooner that this can be done, therefore, the quicker the worker's return to his village. Consequently, the offer of more money seldom has much attraction for him; increased wages enable him to leave earlier, but do not persuade him to remain longer. This accounts for the statement frequently made that the offer of a higher wage means less work and not more.[6]

The problem of how to cope with this unstable labor market was given several answers. Orde Browne, one of the first analysts of the labor problem in Africa, assessed the various means of direct or indirect coercion in use, or that could be put to use once

[5] Lord Sidney Haldane Olivier: *White Capital and Coloured Labour* (London, 1929), pp. 109–10.

[6] G. St. J. Orde Browne: *Labour Conditions in East Africa* (London, 1946), p. 5.

the institution of chattel slavery had been abolished, so that "to the self-sufficing life of the village should be added some requirement which could be met by work for an employer."

> The needs of the local government might be . . . met by a levy as a form of tax in kind, or a proportion of the able-bodied males might be forced through their chiefs to go to work with private employers, or heavy taxation might be imposed so as to provide a stimulus, or partial exemption from taxation or duties might be offered as a reward for the returned worker.

Alternatively there was the system which,

> consisted in reliance upon the natural motive provided by the increasing variety of imported articles which the native desired; as his need for money to buy novelties grew, so his incentive to go to work to earn it would be greater; there was also the love of adventure and the wish to see more of the world.[7]

All these methods had their palpable deficiencies. The imposition of taxes, payable only in currency or compounded by forced labor, while it got roads built and perhaps houses for colonial officials and other restricted projects completed, could scarcely provide labor for large-scale, continuing industrial undertakings. Another recourse, made effective by threat of punishment, was contract labor, which permitted an employer to compel a worker to stay on the job for the period of his contract. The methods varied. In Liberia, tribal heads who recruited for employers were expected to see to it that the men they were paid to furnish did not leave. In the South African mining industry, African workers were forcibly confined to the mine compounds to prevent desertion.

With time, employers experimented with the alternative of inducement. On the Firestone plantations in Liberia, or on the mine compounds of the Union Minière du Haut Katanga in the Congo, workers who remained on the job beyond a specified time, or who recontracted, enjoyed a higher wage. Fringe benefits, such as good hospital facilities, schools for the children of

[7] G. St. J. Orde Browne: *The African Labourer* (London, 1933), pp. 29–30.

workers, an assured supply of food, and well-built houses, were set up as additional incentives to facilitate the establishment of a dependable labor supply.

All these methods were to some extent successful. Their success varied with time and place, and with the schedule of wants dictated by aboriginal patterns of living. Elkan has produced data showing that in Uganda, in 1956, the rule seemed to be that "an inverse correspondence between the income from the sale of farm products in an area, and the proportion of its men in employment." Thus, for example, among the Baganda, with an average farm income of Sh. 218/-, 16% of the working population were wage earners; among the Basoga, with farm incomes averaging Sh. 165/-, 11%. On the other hand, the Toro, averaging Sh. 61/- farm income, sent 41% of their working population into wage labor, while 35% of the Kigezi labor force who averaged Sh. 17/- income from farming, worked for wages. The Ankole, however, did not follow the rule. With an average farm income of Sh. 49/- sent only 16% of the available workers out as wage earners.

How complex the problem was can be seen from Elkan's comment on these data:

> Except in a very general sense, the proportion of men who enter employment is not so much a function of their farm incomes as of their relative opportunities for earning an income as farmers or in employment. In other words, there is nothing strange about an association between low farm incomes and a low employment ratio if the area is poorly endowed by nature or badly served by transport and its inhabitants do not have good employment opportunities, perhaps because they are not physically strong or because they are in some way peculiarly backward. Even if their land is admirably suited for development and employers are only too anxious to employ them, they may eschew these opportunities if for some reason they have low material aspirations or wants; but this is an unusual situation, though not uncommon amongst purely pastoral peoples, like the Masai in Kenya.[8]

The broader question is summarized in these terms:

[8] Walter Elkan: *Migrants and Proletarians, Urban Labour in the Economic Development of Uganda* (London, 1960), pp. 35–7.

> The impermanence of urban labour in Uganda . . . [is] . . . to a greater or lesser degree . . . found in every part of tropical and southern Africa . . . In Africa . . . towns are growing rapidly, but although some of their houses may be built to last a lifetime, those who stay in them seldom stay so long; sooner or later they return to their original homes.[9]

The shortness of period of employment and the resultant magnitude of labor turnover has been stressed by all students of the subject, and holds for all parts of the continent. Thus in Ghana (then the Gold Coast), during the years 1954–5, out of an African labor force of 17,917 employed by six gold-mining companies, 46% or 8,314 had been newly engaged, while 8,968 or 50% had left their jobs. In the case of one diamond mining company, 62% were newly engaged, 58% [*sic*] having resigned or been dismissed.[1] In his study of migrant labor in the Union of South Africa, Schapera found that of 813 men, coming from five different Bechuanaland groups, 32.3% had remained in the Union up to one year, 25.7% were away one to two years, 16.1%, two to three years; that is, a total of 74.1% had returned home within the three years preceding the study. For the rest, 7.1% of these men had been away for three to four years, 5% from four to five, 7% for from five to ten, and 6.8% more than ten years.[2] In Johannesburg, a study of records in the Johannesburg Pass Office showed that,

> so great is the influx and outflow of Native labour that the number of Natives entering registered non-mining employment in Johannesburg after August 1, 1936 "could numerically have replaced the entire working force actually engaged on the initial date by 31 January, 1938, i.e. within eighteen months.". . . Over the whole seven-year period, the total number of new workers registered was sufficient to replace the average working force every twenty-eight months.[3]

[9] Ibid., p. 129.

[1] Gold Coast Government: *Report of the Gold Coast Mines Board of Inquiry, 1956* (Accra, 1956), p. 36.

[2] I. Schapera: *Migrant Labour and Tribal Life, a Study of Conditions in the Bechuanaland Protectorate* (London, 1947), p. 59.

[3] Sheila T. Van der Horst: "Native Urban Employment (a Review Article)," *South African Journal of Economics*, Vol. 16 (1948), p. 253.

As increasing numbers of Africans moved more permanently into industry, mining and large-scale agricultural undertakings, the labor force became more stable. In 1960, a preliminary analysis of reports on absenteeism and labor turnover in six African countries concluded that "the absenteeism and turnover rates are lower than had been expected and similar in towns to those observed for industrial countries."[4] In addition to becoming accustomed to wage labor, inducements of various sorts began to make for a diminution in the rate of turnover. Thus, in 1953, one of the gold-mining companies in Ghana that had some years before faced the monthly turnover of about 100 men, reduced this to five by the simple expedient of allocating to their workers the surface land for farming, which by contract had in any event to be kept cleared of undergrowth. This meant that the wives of these workers, who came mainly from the Northern Territories, could settle down into the regimen of gardening and marketing to which they had been accustomed, and could provide a more normal home life for the men.[5] Similarly, in the Katanga,

> On the mines of the Union Minière . . . the number of workers with at least ten years of service rose from approximately 2,000 in 1941 to approximately 9,500 in 1955, a percentage increase from 14 to 45. And whereas in 1925 it was necessary to recruit 96 fresh laborers each year to have 100 constantly at work on the mines, in 1955 the corresponding figure was 7.

Turnover as a rule continued high, and percentages of 110 per year were reported from the Witwatersrand, Southern Rhodesian, Nigerian, Ghanaian and Angolan mines, and from plantation enterprises everywhere.[6]

Whatever tendencies might have been apparent, the problem remained a complex one. There is little question that the target worker inhibited the formation of a permanent labor force.

[4] Commission for Technical Cooperation in Africa South of the Sahara: *Report* of the Secretary-General to the Sixteenth Session of CCTA, Lagos, 3, 6–11 February 1961, p. 93.

[5] Melville J. Herskovits: *Notes on African Field Research,* pp. 53/D78–79.

[6] George H. T. Kimble: *Tropical Africa* (New York, 1960), Vol. I, p. 587.

More important, yet almost always overlooked in studies of African labor, the fact remains that total commitment to wage labor came to be actively discouraged by employers. The reason is clear. Wage scales could be depressed when the support of the worker's family could be assured by his kinship group in the village. The summary of the situation of the African worker made by an international commission to study African labor is to the point:

> But whether he is (in the restricted sense . . .) a "target worker" or not, whether he has ventured into the wage economy with the vague intention of remaining in it indefinitely, his Native village or land unit remains in many areas an effective alternative to town life; no social or economic factors have yet arisen which link him and his fellows to industry and to town life. . . . That he should try to retain such security as his rural background has to offer him is therefore normal. That his work in the wage economy should be conditioned by the complex of circumstances, largely unfavourable to him, which exist there is equally natural. It is against this general background that the efficiency of the African worker must be considered.[7]

[4]

Let us review some of the special aspects of tradition which raised difficulties in utilizing available labor power for the economic development of Subsaharan Africa. The example of an indigenous manufacturing system may serve our purpose.

We may recall that iron smelting and the manufacture of iron implements has been known in Africa for a very long time, and is so widespread that it was long thought the technique had been invented there. In aboriginal practice, ironworkers, like other craftsmen, have always belonged to a kind of guild, membership in which is customarily based on kinship, with craft secrets and practices validated by supernatural sanctions.[8]

This aspect of ironworking had been studied in some detail

[7] International Labour Office: *African Labour Survey* (Geneva, 1958), p. 142.

[8] Cf. *supra*, Ch. 3, 4, *passim*.

among the Lobi peoples living along the west branch of the Volta River, in the Republic of Upper Volta, where knives, hoes, and other implements were manufactured. Because here, as in nonindustrial societies the world over, lines of specialization are blurred, these men were not the full-time specialists of industrial societies. Though primarily artisans, the blacksmiths made their living only partially by the sale of the products of their forges, which they worked principally during the dry season when the fields could not be cultivated. This does not mean that within this general framework specialization was entirely absent. Some ironworkers made only arrowheads and knives; others made hoes, others axes, and still others ornaments. A system of apprenticeship was in effect, though the apprentice was usually a member of the kinship group of the ironworker.

The fact that ironworking was not a full-time occupation is particularly revealing, since these men could support themselves entirely by their craft. Their numbers were small in relation to the total society of which they formed a part. In one series of districts, enumerated about 1930, there were 60 ironworkers out of a population of 19,618; certain other districts had 39 of these specialists in a total population of 17,737. This number of ironworkers did not begin to supply the demand for the implements they produced, as shown by the fact that for generations, hoes and bush knives had been imported from neighboring peoples, while European trading firms later found it profitable to stock implements made in Europe on the native model.[9]

Evidently motivations here differed from those in the economies of Europe and America. Those accustomed to thinking in terms of the patterns of production and exchange in industrial societies, whether based on the profit motive or on the rationalization of economic resources by the state, would find it perplexing to understand why these ironworkers did not relate the exercise of their special competence to an obvious demand. Why did they fail to supply this demand by complete, full-time specialization, and by training more apprentices to enlarge their op-

[9] Henri Labouret: *Les Tribus du Rameau Lobi,* Travaux et Mémoires de l'Institut d'Ethnologie, Vol. XV (Paris, 1931), pp. 69–70.

erations to take advantage of their potential market? All the conditions for expanding production were present, yet they were ignored. The answer lies in cultural conventions and values which were rational and of self-evident worth to those who followed them, just as they are difficult for Euroamericans to grasp and accept.

The adjustments required by a new rhythm of work offer another example of how aboriginal patterns influenced reactions of workers to the demands of labor in industrialized undertakings. Especially in tropical Subsaharan Africa, the rhythm in indigenous societies has always been that of the seasons. There are daily rhythms, but these do not dictate changes in economic activity as do the longer fluctuations of seasonal change. Just what time of the day men and women go to the field, or on just what days they will work, will be determined by the demands of the season and of the day. The total objective is of primary concern. If a crop is successfully harvested, it does not matter just how the time to grow it was allotted. The ironworkers among the Volta River peoples divided their time seasonally between ironworking and agriculture. The same seasonal shift in productive activity is to be seen where, because of climatic conditions, house-building, house-repairing, or the making of mats or mortars or other utensils is deferred until the dry season. Moreover, cycles of economic activity are closely related to ritual cycles. Except for emergencies, these are held almost without exception in the dry season. This follows the logic of the culture, since the demands of agriculture are too exacting during the rains to allow for the proper execution of forms of worship, and while foodstuffs to fulfill ritual and social obligations are not available.

The daily rhythm that continues irrespective of seasonal change dictates the allocation of time to tasks immediately at hand. The day may be thought of as broken into segments delimiting the hours between rising and retiring. The limits of these segments are set by mealtimes. In West Africa, and to a degree over all the Subsaharan continent, the breaks come at about ten in the morning and late afternoon. At times the large meal is eaten at or after nightfall. It must be recalled that day comes without a prolonged dawn, and darkness falls early. There is no time for cooking breakfast in the morning. Waking with the dawn, the African takes a hurried bite of some left-over food before occupying himself with his routine tasks. At the other end of the day, after the principal meal has been consumed, he rests.

The contrast between this seasonal and daily work-rhythm, even with its local and individual variations, and the pattern of labor in the industrial establishment, is obvious. Except in the case of large-scale agricultural undertakings for an export market, the seasonal factor does not enter. The routine of work in extractive and industrial operations, the rhythm of work, is fixed not by natural conditions, but through decisions reached far from any contact with the worker, and as much beyond his control as are the seasons. The variety of economic activities in which he engages under his own economic system is also entirely lacking. In industry, his task remains the same from one day to the next; he is not free to vary the monotony of his work by moving from one aspect of a job to another. The worker in a mechanized society has developed recreational and other compensations for this monotony. The African, moving into the industrial complex, finds it hard to discern long-range adequate rewards, when he compares this new situation with what he has left behind.

There has been some tendency to define the industrial routine as disciplined, in contrast to an assumed carefree round held to characterize nonindustrial societies. In reality, these are different kinds of discipline, each deriving its validation from differing ecological and cultural sources. We soon see, from this point of view, that no question of the presence or absence of discipline, as such, enters in either type of economy. The discipline of the worker in Africa, as in all nonindustrialized societies, is largely self-imposed, while that of the industrial operative is imposed from outside. To the worker born in an industrial society, this outer source of discipline is taken for granted, as is any other culturally established mode of behavior. But the problem of reorientation necessitates radical adjustment for the worker accustomed to patterns under which the allocation of time and expenditure of energy are self-determined and governed by well understood rules of reward and failure, and who is newly brought into the impersonal industrial scene. The degree of social, no less than of personal disorganization that resulted from such attempts to make an adjustment of this sort can be measured in the record of African urban social pathology. We may take it as an indication of the plasticity of the human organism that the amount of demoralization has not been greater.

Adjustment to the daily rhythm imposed by industrial work was equally hard. Here it was not a question of an imposed as against a self-determined routine, but of a difference in the cultural patterning of primary, biological drives. One of the more severe adjustments demanded of the African worker has arisen from a factor in the daily life of all human beings, so taken for granted that it would be surprising if it did consciously enter in the planning and execution of projects for economic development. It is the schedule of mealtimes in the industrial scene, in contrast to the traditional schedule.

Habits associated with food consumption reflect some of the deepest conditionings of the human organism. It is a truism of social science that, while hunger is a universal drive, the foods which satisfy the drive, and the intervals at which hunger is appeased, are culturally determined. The applicability of this principle to the foods consumed is quite well recognized, but the importance of the fact that hunger, a biological phenomenon, operates on a cultural timetable, is not. Therefore, where the African worker was furnished his native foodstuffs, as came to be the rule in establishments where he was either fed, or supplied with provisions for his wife to prepare at home, only half of the requirement for adaptation to the industrial routine was met. The nonobservance of customary mealtimes caused acute discomfort to the worker and strongly affected his attitude toward his new situation. It was astonishing to be told by Africans in European employment that one of their principal hardships was adapting to a new schedule of meals. Yet one need only contrast a routine of meals eaten before going to work, at mid-day, and in the early evening, with the indigenous pattern of mid-morning and mid-afternoon meals, to see the point.

The stubborn adherence to established mealtime patterns nullified the effort of a group of industrial plants in Durban, South Africa, to provide low-cost, nutritional lunches for their African employees. Under this plan, a substantial meal of meat, vegetables, and bread was furnished the men for nine-pence. It was necessary for a majority of the workers to subscribe, to make the plan effective. At first, some 85% of them accepted the arrangement, but in a short time the number fell to a fraction of those who had originally agreed to it. The plant managers called meetings of their workers, urging them to take advantage of what was nutritionally and financially to their benefit. The number of subscribers again rose, but soon dropped as the workers returned to their usual fare of a loaf of bread and a bottle of soda pop. The head of one industrial plant expressed his bewilderment at the reaction of the Africans when he summed up with, "There's no figuring them." And while a desire for freedom of choice may have entered into the reaction of the Africans, it is also likely that it was based on their eating habits that did not dispose the workers to eat a large meal in the middle of the day.[1]

Another problem concerns the changes involved in the mobilization of the labor force. In the main the industrialized economies are based primarily on individual effort, whereas African societies are communally oriented. Accordingly, the Euroamerican worker acts as an individual; even his trade-unions are aggregates of individuals who are agreed on group action. In African economies, on the other hand, the individual acts primarily as a member of a group, whether based on kinship or residence or both. The ubiquity of African cooperative effort testifies to this. The problem of cultivating considerable tracts of land in West Africa during the short period at the beginning of the rainy season is met quite effectively by group labor of this sort. The hoe, in the hands of one man, is not too efficient an instrument for large-scale endeavors, but many hoes in the hands of many men will in a day ready a large field for planting. Or, again, in the eastern part of the continent and other cattle-keeping regions,

[1] Melville J. Herskovits: *Notes on African Field Research,* p. 57/D479.

where herds must be taken daily to pasture, it is the boys of the village who together care for the animals belonging to all their elders.

A further aspect of this tradition of group labor has to do with the direction of work. Europeans and Americans who came to Africa soon discovered how deeply the concept of the responsible leader was lodged in the customary work patterns of Africans. To have a given task performed, one does not hire workers as individuals. If he thinks he has, he soon finds that he is negotiating the problems that arise with one man who has been selected as leader, and who may alone be held to account for the quality and amount of work done. To reprimand an individual worker is to invite trouble; it is the responsible head alone who must see to it that those in his group do their work, and it is he alone who may take his men to task. A worker coming from a society where work-patterns of this sort prevail must make a far-reaching adjustment, to function under a system oriented to individual responsibility. He is, indeed, likely to feel lost where the social support he has always expected and received is lacking.

Gang labor was one expedient resorted to in recognition of the African cooperative work tradition by those charged with the operation of large-scale projects in industry, agriculture, or mining. But this proved to be only a half measure, because the African pattern was only half understood. The leader of the African work group is only secondarily accountable to the employer. His primary responsibility is to the members of the group he directs, and with which he identifies himself. The system whereby a group of men, working as individuals for a common employer, are directed by a leader who is also hired, as an individual, by the same employer, has only a specious resemblance to the democratically controlled indigenous work group.

[5]

The force of antecedent tradition did not nullify the dynamic of cultural change. The number of wage earners, and the degree of their commitment, steadily increased. Hodgkin, in

1955, estimated that in Africa south of the Sahara and north of the Union, excluding the Portuguese territories, there were "between four and five million wage earners," a figure that represented some 5% of "the total population of colonial Africa," though this number included many "target" and migratory workers.[2] Greater numbers of Africans became permanent residents of urban centers; more and more of them made long-term commitments to the modes of life and to the work rhythms of the factory and mine and large-scale agricultural production; a middle class, composed of professional, academic and business men and women was now a feature of the economic and social landscape. The total effect of these impulses from industrialization was thus one of continuously increasing complexity. Measures of the wider economic community to cope with the demands of the new system on the individual—labor unions, cooperatives, business men's associations—were adopted, to be incorporated into or modified by the traditional cultures, whether consciously with the intent of achieving the acceptance of an innovation, or unconsciously by seeking to reconcile antecedent values with those newly presented.

The organization of workers into trade-unions was the most far-reaching of those responses. In certain of its characteristics, the short history of these organizations was not unlike that of their forerunners in other countries. In Africa, as elsewhere, the organization of workers was opposed by the entrepreneurs, who regarded such organizations as a threat to their own competitive vested economic position, their profit margin, and to their plans for industrial growth. African workers found the power of the state arrayed against them in the classical alignment of government and industry, though this developed mainly in the multiracial states of the east and south, where industry was an important sector of the economy, and it became a real factor only after the Second World War. It was from these conflicts in European economies that the concept of the class struggle emerged in western Europe. That industrialization in Africa brought nei-

[2] T. Hodgkin: *Nationalism in Colonial Africa* (London, 1956), pp. 118–19.

ther the European sense of class differences, nor the European kind of industrial conflict poses a problem that merits examination.

Three reasons may be called on to account for the particular ways in which African workers reacted to the need of protecting their interests in this new world of economic change. One of these inhered in the nature of the psychological readjustments required of African workers joining the industrial labor force: it became necessary that the "foot in the village" join "the other in the town." Secondly, trade-unionism, particularly in the multiracial territories, was like everything else shot through with the racial factor. Finally there was the rallying cry of anticolonialism, and the militant counter-nationalisms of the European minorities in the multiracial territories, which brought political issues to the forefront, and caused all types of African organized effort, including that of labor, to focus on the goal of self-government. These three reasons go far to explain the conclusion of one economist that inasmuch as in Africa, "the economic situation displays certain genuinely novel characteristics"—as does its social setting—it follows that "institutions growing up within the labor force, such as trade-unions, may really be extremely different in function and character from the institutions which bear the same name in other economies." [3]

Labor organizations were late in being formed, predictably following the trend in industrialization and urbanization, which gathered momentum only after the Second World War. The original and revised versions of the Hailey *Survey* provide a useful perspective on this development. In the 1938 edition, the discussion of the work force centered about such problems as impressed labor and private employment, labor migration, welfare, wages, the role of the pass laws and the like. The one comment on labor unions was the following:

> It may be questioned whether African workers are in general sufficiently advanced in capacity for organization to form effective trade unions, or whether, in territories where the state has assumed full

[3] Walter Elkan: "Migrant Labor in Africa: an Economist's Approach," *American Economic Review*, Vol. 49 (1959), p. 190.

> responsibility for their working conditions, such unions can serve any useful purpose.[4]

By 1957, however, the movement had developed to such proportions that an entire section was devoted to the machinery for adjusting trade or industrial disputes.[5]

Hailey felt that the development of African trade-unions was in sharp contrast to that of Europe, where "the movement originated within the ranks of labour itself." In Africa, the system "came at a stage when African labour had not as yet found it possible to combine on any considerable scale for the purpose of collective bargaining with employers." According to this approach,

> the stimulus . . . came from two different sources. . . . There was in Europe a school of thought which was strongly impressed with the need for the improvement of conditions among African workers, and which saw in the trade-union the most effective machinery for achieving it. At the same time, some of the Colonial Administrations had already had experience of the immature attempts of Africans to combine for collective action and they felt that the trade-union could provide a more responsible basis for negotiating trade differences.[6]

In British West African territories, moves toward encouraging the establishment of labor unions began about 1940. In areas under French control, though forced labor was not abolished until 1946, trade-unions were made legal in the West African colonies as early as 1937, with membership being restricted at first to those who were literate in French. They were legalized in French Equatorial Africa in 1944. As late as 1946, organizations of workers could exist in the Belgian Congo only with official sanction, and functioned under close supervision. Portugal did not allow her African workers to organize. In South Africa, unions of Africans were not permitted to strike or to negotiate directly with

[4] Lord Malcolm Hailey: *An African Survey, a Study of the Problems Arising in Africa South of the Sahara* (first edition, London, 1938), p. 698.

[5] Lord Malcolm Hailey: *An African Survey, Revised 1956* (London, 1957), pp. 1439–53.

[6] Ibid., p. 1439.

employers, while racially mixed unions were banned in 1957 as a part of the *apartheid* policy.

Despite these late beginnings, the trade-union movement grew steadily. Some 507,000, or about 11% of Hodgkin's 5% of the total estimated labor force of 4,712,000 working full or part time as wage earners, belonged to unions. In 1955 the all-Nigeria Trade Union Federation was made up of 39 affiliated unions with a total membership of some 95,000. In 1957, it comprised 278 registered organizations with a paid-up membership of 198,265. In French West Africa, there were 68,550 unionists in 1953; by 1956, the number had almost tripled, rising to about 180,000. In South Africa, on the other hand, the strengthening of the *apartheid* policy made for a counter-movement. It was reported that in 1946 the Transvaal alone had 65 African unions with a membership of 97,000; at the end of 1953, the estimate for the whole of the country was 22 African unions with a membership of about 10,000.[7]

There were various reasons why the form of the European labor union was not easily acceptable to African workers, particularly when, as in British and French territories, metropolitan labor bodies attempted to transplant the structure and values of their organizations to the soil of Africa. For one thing, the very fact that so large a proportion of the African labor force continued to be "target" workers, or signed on for seasonal employment, or was employed in agriculture or as domestics, categories most resistant to organization, made it difficult to establish and maintain unions. For another, while African wage workers were quick to see the advantage of organized protest at a time of crisis, once a dispute had been settled it seemed pointless to go on paying dues.

Where unions did take root, their practices deviated from the usages of their parent organizations. Thus, in the industrialized Copper Belt of Northern Rhodesia, it was difficult even to find union headquarters, methods of keeping accounts were rudimentary, the money received was handled casually, and dues-

[7] International Labour Office: *African Labour Survey* (Geneva, 1958), pp. 231–9.

paying members were few. This did not mean an inability to mobilize strength when a dispute arose. In 1953, after a strike vote had been taken by the African employees at the Roan Antilope mine at Luanshya, the workers and their families, to the complete surprise of management and government, during the night left the company houses they occupied on the mine compounds and camped in the bush for three weeks, until their demands were met.[8]

The attitudes of African workers toward their leaders also diverged from the conventional model in industrialized societies. From the European point of view, African labor leaders were prone to mishandle union funds, as is conveyed in the report of the Commission appointed to inquire into the riots that marked the 1949 strike at the Enugu collieries in Eastern Nigeria. The leader was shown to have taken for his own use a good proportion of union money subscribed by the miners for a strike fund, to purchase a house, a car and other personal items—"a lavish expenditure on purposes entirely for his own advantage," as the Commission put it. Yet there was little evidence of resentment that the Commission could detect. The workers seemed to feel that since their leader's efforts had obtained for them the wage increases they had demanded, he consequently merited whatever he had taken.[9]

The reaction of the Commission was clearly stated:

> The evidence that has been adduced before us convinces us that the Trade Union leaders, in the great majority of cases at all events, have shown little sense of . . . responsibility. . . . It will not help the workman if he continues to choose as his representatives . . . types . . . not in the slightest degree interested in advancing the material prospects of the workers of the territory.[1]

[8] Melville J. Herskovits: *Notes on African Field Research,* p. 57/D533.

[9] Great Britain, Colonial Office: Enquiry into the Disorders in the Eastern Provinces of Nigeria, *Proceedings of the Commission* (London, 1950), Vol. II, pp. 688–713, and *passim.*

[1] Great Britain, Colonial Office: *Report* of the Commission of Enquiry into the Disorders in the Eastern Provinces of Nigeria, November, 1949, Colonial No. 256 (London, 1950), p. 14.

Perhaps more perceptive as to the attitude of the workers was the comment of one British labor leader: "They treated him as though he was one of their chiefs!"

How workers equated chiefs and labor leaders is illustrated by the case of a local union in Ghana, whose members, in 1958, voted to remove their leader from office. The entire affair followed the procedure that regulates the destoolment of a chief among the Akan peoples, both as to the charges involved and the measures taken to carry out the decision. A principal charge was that the union head had left his district without the consent of the membership, an obligation parallel to that of a chief who wishes to travel. At the meeting where the action was taken, the shoes of the deposed official were removed, as are the sandals of a rejected chief, and he was insulted and abused by the members, again following closely on the customary procedures of destoolment. It was further explained that, as a general rule, the custom in European unions, or other bodies, of reaching decisions by taking a show of hands for or against a given proposition had little meaning for these African unionists. "They talk it out until agreement is reached, as they have always done in council meetings."

The second reason for the special character of African unions is the role of race differences, which is important, however, only in the multiracial parts of Africa. In French Africa the problem did not arise because unions in the African territories were affiliated closely with the corresponding unions in the Metropole. More to the point, however, both in French and in British West Africa, and to a degree in the Belgian Congo, was the fact that the labor force was almost exclusively African, the numbers of non-Africans being so small as to keep the factor of race from becoming significant.

In the multiracial territories of eastern and southern Africa, the permanent non-African population was too numerous to allow all its members to enjoy the higher types of employment. In these countries, there was potential or actual competition between Africans and Europeans for certain categories of jobs.

This held for the so-called poor whites in the Union of South Africa. Before the period of expansion that followed the depression of the 1930's, they would have been in active competition with Africans—and, to an even greater extent, with the Coloreds—had the play of economic forces not been contravened by social convention [2] and later, by governmental action, in giving preferment to Europeans on all levels of employment.

As in other phases of African life, the factor of race gave a particular dimension to all trade-union activity in these parts of the continent, injecting a sociological component that rendered it difficult for labor organizations to concentrate their efforts on their primary economic objectives. Thus, in the Rhodesian copper mines, African labor leaders not only had to bargain with their employers, but also had to take into account the claims of a powerful union of European workers whose efforts were bent on reserving to themselves all categories of skilled labor. It is not without irony that, because of the established differentials in wage scales on the copper mines, these European workers should have used the trade-union slogan, "An equal day's pay for an equal day's work," to prevent the upgrading of African workers.

In order to maintain their position, the European unions also were compelled to face two ways. Like the Africans, they had to deal with the employers, but they also had to keep an eye on the place of the African union, in this case so as to maintain the large differentials in base pay and fringe benefits between European and Africans deemed necessary in a multiracial society. Indeed, a major preoccupation of these unions seems to have been the protection of their job categories against any inroads by African workers. Thus, on the railways of South Africa and of the Federation, it was taken for granted that no African could be entrusted with driving a locomotive, despite the fact that Africans in the neighboring Belgian Congo and elsewhere seemed to have no difficulty doing this, or operating far more intricate machinery.

The significance of the third influence which gave African labor unions a special character, the fact that they developed in a

[2] Carnegie Commission: *The Poor White Problem in South Africa* (Stellenbosch, 1932), Vol. I, pp. 164–80, Vol. II, pp. 59–64.

setting of colonial control, was well expressed by Hodgkin, when he observed,

> the fact that the economic claims and interests of different sections of African society—traders and entrepreneurs, farmers and fishermen, labourers and clerks—may be divergent is of subordinate importance, so long as for all sections the colonial regime is regarded as the main obstacle in the way of economic advance.[3]

He comments on the fact that since unions in British Africa were concerned "less with *equality* of rights, and more with the rights of *African* workers as such," this gave their demands a "strongly nationalist flavor," and made it natural that they should "seek to ally themselves with nationalist political parties and congresses."[4]

For labor unions to be involved in politics was nothing unique to Africa. Wherever workers organize to advance their own interests, their activities sooner or later, in some measure, enter the political field, since it is here that power is wielded, power that comes into play where differences between any two segments of a society must be resolved. To the extent political issues become paramount, they will be prominent in the activities of unions; and since in Africa the paramount political issue was colonialism, the efforts of the unions predictably took on the anticolonialist character.

In West Africa, this tendency toward anticolonialism in the trade-union movement was reinforced by the fact that the principal employers of labor were the respective colonial governments. The two largest and best organized Nigerian unions were those of the railway workers and the teachers. The Enugu coal mines were government owned. In the then Gold Coast, of seven "larger and more active organizations" listed for 1956, five were composed of government employees, working for the Gold Coast Railway, the Public Works Department, the Kumasi municipality, and those in the Health and Education Department, as against the two unions in the private sector—the mines, and the

[3] Thomas Hodgkin: *Nationalism in Colonial Africa* (London, 1956), p. 115.

[4] Ibid., p. 132.

United Africa Company.[5] This meant that a strike to obtain higher wages or better working conditions at once involved the administering authorities and, taking on political overtones, became part of the struggle against colonial rule.

The African unions in the multiracial territories of British East and Central Africa, of the Congo under Belgian rule, and in the Union of South Africa, were under closer surveillance and restraint, but their political orientation was the same. The seventeen country-wide constituent unions of the Kenya Federation of Labor were all composed of Africans, "a situation due to the practice of race discrimination in wages and employment conditions." In the African view, though the Kenya government

> insists that trade unionism must be separated from politics. . . . this view is of course rejected by the labor unions who insist on their right to take an active and positive interest in all matters affecting workers as a class, and as citizens.

This, we were told,

> is an example of flagrantly undemocratic practice. One group, the white settlers, not only have an active voice in government, but it sometimes seems as though they set government policy; another organized group . . . of Africans not only has no voice in government, but is even forbidden to engage in political activity to defend its own interest.[6]

The close alignment between government and industry in the countries that had gone farthest toward industrialization, where both were under European control, led to the firm conviction among African workers that economic advancement was not to be separated from the attainment of political power. The fact that unions in all these countries had to be approved by government before they could function, and all operated under legal restraint, established the association even more firmly to the African worker.

We have had occasion to mention the political education

[5] International Labour Office: *African Labour Survey* (Geneva, 1958), p. 235.

[6] Tom Mboya: *Kenya Faces the Future* (Africa Today Pamphlets, No. 3, New York, 1959), pp. 24–5.

that unionization provided African workers. The number of African political leaders who came out of the trade-union movement gives ample evidence of this. From the Rhodesias and Kenya to Sierra Leone, Guinea and Mali, to take examples at random, leaders who had been active in the formation and direction of labor unions found that their positions provided effective steppingstones to wider political activity, aimed primarily at achieving self-government.

In the groups which they headed, they had at hand not only a base from which they could move in proclaiming their wider aims, but a core of determined and disciplined activists who were willing to agitate for these aims, often in the face of governmental repression. Negotiations with employers provided valuable experience in the give-and-take of compromise, and allowed contacts with members of the dominant race in their societies with whom they later had to deal politically. Moreover, they were brought close to the inequities of a differential wage scale. Here, too, leaders learned the realities of the human aspects of the industrial system, a segment of experience which they would put to good use when they assumed the responsibilities of administering their countries.

With independence at hand or in sight, the unions took on new political functions. Experienced trade-union leaders became members of the governments of their countries, or participated in directing its parastatal organizations. Especially in countries under a one-party system, or where a single political grouping so blanketed opposition that it was in effect a one-party system, the unions came to occupy a special position. They influenced, and in one instance at least, made foreign policy, as when, in 1959, a proposal of the International Confederation of Free Trade Unions to establish an African section was opposed by those committed to the isolationism of Panafrican doctrine that African affairs were the concern only of Africans. Accordingly, an All-African Federation of African unions, unaffiliated with any world body, was organized.

Within the countries having single-party systems, unions were brought under even closer governmental control than during the colonial regimes. They had been an effective agent in the struggle for independence. Through the instrumentality of strikes that were essentially political, they had done much to accelerate the revolutionary movements of their countries. With independence, they were integrated closely into the new power structure. This is outlined in the discussion of the role of labor in an official Guinean handbook:

> The General Confederation of Guinean Workers, at its Second Congress of July, 1959, underlined in its resolution on policy its firm determination to ally itself with all levels of society that are working for national and social liberation in the struggle against all forms of exploitation of the workers. The workers of Guinée made a most important contribution to the fight for independence. Today, they bring enthusiastic support to the task of rearing an economic structure in the country which will be related to the progressive amelioration of their own living conditions.[7]

[6]

Directed economic change, in the sense of "deliberate development policy by African governments" appeared late in the colonial period, during the decade 1949–58. While this " 'development plan era' started immediately after the war," it did not "actually get under way in most cases until 1949 or thereabouts. . . ."[8] These new plans differed from earlier economic policies in the motives that actuated them, and their modes of implementation. That is, while they undoubtedly arose out of enlightened self-interest on the part of the metropolitan government, the welfare of the colonial populations entered to an unprecedented degree. This stimulated the formulation of new goals that were to figure importantly in making for the increase and intensification of planned economic development.

This reorientation was quite explicitly enunciated in the British House of Commons when the 1940 Colonial Develop-

[7] Mamadou Traore Rayautra: *Connaissance de la République de Guinée* (Conakry, 1960), p. 23.

[8] United Nations: *Economic Survey of Africa Since 1950* (No. E/CN.14/28). (New York, 1959), p. 185.

ment and Welfare Bill, which superseded the Colonial Development Act, was under discussion. In the debate, it was declared that the primary purpose of the earlier Act of 1929,

> was not to help colonial development for its own sake, but in order to stimulate that development mostly to bring additional work to idle hands in this country. It was devised as part of our scheme to solve our own unemployment problem. . . . The Bill we are discussing . . . breaks new ground. It establishes the duty of the taxpayers in this country to contribute directly, and for its own sake, toward the development in the widest sense of the work of the colonial peoples for whose good government the taxpayers of this country are ultimately responsible.[9]

The operations of earlier projects, both in the private and public sectors, tended to differ from later ones. Except for certain large plantation developments, notably in Liberia, the Ivory Coast, the Cameroons and the Belgian Congo, large-scale private schemes were directed toward the exploitation of African mineral resources, to ensure the high returns that were held essential to attract risk capital. Most of the agricultural projects in the public sector, perhaps with the exception of the Gezira Scheme, were oriented essentially toward filling needs of each Metropole. The original aim of the *Office du Niger,* in the Sudan, was to grow cotton for the metropolitan market.[1] This was also the purpose of the Portuguese cotton-growing project in Mozambique. The East African Groundnut Scheme in Tanganyika was organized to supply the urgent postwar need in Europe for vegetable oils. Much of the effort of private development, particularly in the mining industry, aimed at supplying needs for strategic materials. This explains the vast expansion in the enterprises of the Union Minière du Haut Katanga, and in some measure, also stimulated the development of the Firestone rubber plantations, though the initial impetus here was to provide a hedge against Far Eastern suppliers.

In all these earlier developments, Africans entered only as

[9] Barbu Niculescu: *Colonial Planning, a Comparative Study* (London, 1958), p. 6.

[1] *Supra,* Ch., pp. 159–62.

lay figures. Their role was to provide a labor force. Whatever benefit they might derive in the way of a higher standard of living was incidental and, in fact, was not conspicuously marked. Where such a consideration entered in the thinking of planners and directors, it was not central to their primary economic objectives. The exception to the rule, the Gezira cotton-growing scheme of the Sudan, was one of the earliest consistent attempts to develop a region rationally through the functioning of what in 1919 was called a "three-cornered partnership." In 1925, the Chairman, in reporting to his shareholders, expressed the position of the controlling Sudan Experimental Plantations Syndicate in these words:

> I should just like to remind you that you are not only owners of a great agricultural enterprise, but you are also associated with probably one of the greatest colonial development schemes going on at the present time. This is not only a scheme which will be materially advantageous to Great Britain and the cotton industry but one also which is adding very largely to the welfare of the natives in the areas with which it deals.[2]

At the time it was made this statement lay at the extreme liberal end of the spectrum of thinking about colonial economics. As a rule, African needs in the way of food or housing or training for positions on the managerial level, or education for the children of workers, came last in any list of priorities, and most times did not enter at all. And just as subsequent programs of the colonial governments, which aimed at what were termed welfare objectives, established attitudes toward continuation of programs of social welfare after African countries had gained their independence, so the earlier experience with "schemes" of various sorts convinced Africans that foreign economic effort was essentially exploitative in character. This contributed largely to the ambivalences in the political field that later could be seen to underlie the position of African leaders toward "neo-colonialism."

African economic development after the Second World War came to have international implications directly related to Afri-

[2] Arthur Gaitskell: *Gezira, a Story of Development in the Sudan* (London, 1959), p. 82.

can and non-African maneuvering in the Cold War struggle. It was not long before questions of economic growth took on a position of major importance in all of changing Africa. As a result, a vast literature came into being, which treated of the various plans that were evolved, how they were structured, financed, implemented, and their results. Detailed statistics were prepared to show the lines along which African economies were moving, the extent to which the stimuli from outside effected the creation of an infrastructure on which further growth could be reared, and ways of testing theoretical constructs to permit anticipation of results in the various sectors of these economies.

Hance has given a kind of balance sheet of these post-World War II efforts. "Before the war," he stated, "what is termed tropical Africa, that part lying south of the Sahara and north of the Union,

> accounted for only 2.4 per cent of free-world exports, so the 1956 figure [of 3.4 per cent] represents a 42 per cent improvement. . . . The value of exports increased from about $429 million in 1938 to $1,709 million in 1948, $2,550 million in 1951, and over $3,200 million in 1956. Imports increased in value from about $427 million in 1938 to over $3,100 million in 1956, reflecting, with allowance for inflated prices, both higher consumption levels and a greatly enlarged investment in developmental programs. Intra-tropical exchange . . . also increased, notably in the supply of food to the deficit rain-forest areas.

However, these figures are to be read with the contrasts in the economic position of different territories in mind. "There is no continuous frontier" marking economic advance, but instead a "series of economic 'islands' in which the bulk of the economic output is rather highly concentrated." [3]

Against these gains were to be balanced the obstacles to accelerated growth. Certain aspects of the physical environment, "the absence of a well-developed transport and distribution system, and inadequate production of power," were three formidable deficiencies. Others were "the inadequacy of statistical, eco-

[3] William A. Hance: *African Economic Development* (New York, 1958), pp. 3, 5.

nomic, and social information; the shortage of investment capital; quantitative and qualitative labor shortages"; these in addition to some of the noneconomic aspects of the problem we have discussed in preceding chapters. Finally, two phases of the situation were of broadest import, "the imbalance between population and resources in many African areas, and the imbalance in the rate of agricultural advance as compared with other occupations." [4]

The various development programs that were announced in the period after the Second World War addressed themselves to problems of this kind. They were particularly concerned with establishing an infrastructure which, because of the fact that its great cost had to be met while normal budgetary needs continued, could not be financed without aid from outside. A table prepared by the United Africa Company gives percentages of expenditure under development plans that illustrate this point. For various countries from 1951 to 1960, transport and communications claimed from between 13% to 46%; agriculture from 4% to 26%; electricity and water from 4% to 29%, housing from 1% to 12%; health expenditures varied between 4% and 9%, funds for commerce and industry between 1% and 11%, while from between 6% and 23% were devoted to public works.[5] These percentages do not include the more industrialized countries, South Africa and the Rhodesias, which received the bulk of private investment, and were also heavily favored in loans granted by international agencies.

Hailey classified under four headings the sources of capital for the many developmental programs that sprang up in Subsaharan Africa during the later colonial period. These were allocations from colonial budgets, grants-in-aid from metropolitan countries, loans made or guaranteed by the Metropoles, and loans issued by the colonial governments themselves. Toward the closing period of colonial rule in the French and British West African possessions, French Equatorial Africa, and the Congo, loans and other forms of economic aid were also provided by various international bodies, and by the United States. After in-

[4] Ibid., p. 15.
[5] Cited in George H. T. Kimble: op. cit., Vol. II, p. 405.

dependence, countries of the Communist bloc entered the scene, while the International Bank for Reconstruction and Development, which had directed its attention initially to South Africa and the Federation, extended its African operations. The International Finance Corporation, the United Nations Technical Assistance Program and the United Nations Special Fund also began to function in Africa, and new United States agencies, especially the International Co-operation Administration, came increasingly to give the technical assistance it had felt restrained from extending while most of Subsaharan Africa had colonial status. On the level of planning and the compilation of data, an important step was taken under the auspices of the United Nations, when an Economic Commission for Africa was set up in 1958, with its headquarters in Addis Ababa, a move that had been urged for some years previously, but had been blocked by the colonial powers.

With independence at hand or achieved, the ambivalences toward economic assistance, we have mentioned came into full play. On the one hand, African governments saw raising the standards of living through economic growth as their immediate task, an objective which, because of the condition of their national economies, could only be achieved with the aid of foreign capital. Against this, however, stood the sense of national identity, and their determination to protect this against all forms of outside interference. The Cold War became a major factor here. African leaders saw danger in too close commitment to either side. Yet aid had to come from the industrialized nations if it was to come at all, and there were no uncommitted industrialized nations to which the Africans could turn.

This was emphasized in many of the addresses presented to the Second Conference of African States, held in Addis Ababa in 1960. In his opening address, the Emperor of Ethiopia warned that African nations "must be prepared to assert their ability to maintain independence without exchanging it for financial support or for subsidies." The Liberian Secretary of State, in urging co-operation among African countries, declared that this could ensure,

> such economic strength that the danger of subtle control from more advanced states will be considerably reduced if not altogether eliminated, and through aid we will be able to provide for greater improvement and more rapid advancement of our respective countries.

The Minister of Foreign Affairs of the Republic of the Sudan, noting that, "our prosperity is admittedly dependent on the aid we get from abroad—technical and financial," made the point that "the outside world should not take us as pawns in the cold war that is distorting the face of the world." Finally, the anticolonialist resolutions of this Conference asserted "that assistance to the emerging states should be without political conditions," and that their leaders should be urged "to consider seriously this question before committing themselves to action which might prejudice the future of their countries." [6]

On one central point there was no ambiguity. There was no question in the minds of African leaders that economic development was essential. The leader of the Ghanaian independence movement, for whom "the first objective is political independence," continued:

> Once this freedom is gained, a greater task comes into view. . . . The economic independence that should follow and maintain political independence demands every effort from the people, a total mobilization of brain and manpower resources. What other countries have taken three hundred years or more to achieve, a once dependent territory must try to accomplish in a generation if it is to survive. Unless it is, as it were, "jet-propelled," it will lag behind and thus risk everything for which it has fought.[7]

The *Preface* to the 1960 proceedings of the national conference of the Parti Democratique de Guinée states, "It is necessary . . . to create conditions for rapid economic and social development which, thought out and directed toward general betterment, must be conceived and realized by and for the people." At this assembly, the President of the Republic, the party head, laid down this principle:

[6] Conference of Independent African States: *Proceedings* of the Second Meeting, Addis Ababa, June 14–16, 1960 (Addis Ababa, 1960), pp. 26, 33, 57, 104.

[7] Kwame Nkrumah: *The Autobiography of Kwame Nkrumah* (Edinburgh, 1957), p. x.

> A society incapable of caring for its economic development has no way of caring for its social development. . . . It is clear that political independence which does not result in total economic liberation is a snare.[8]

The principle that economic growth was essential to the development of Africa found acceptance in the multiracial states no less than in those controlled by Africans. In the former, indeed, it was used as an argument against African agitation for participation in government. The argument repeatedly advanced was that too hasty moves on the part of the Africans in this direction would have the effect of discouraging foreign investment. Reactions of investors to the Sharpeville incident of 1960 in the Union of South Africa, or to tensions in British East and Central Africa, to say nothing of the Congo, were cited as cases in point, to read the lesson that this must handicap Africans no less than other racial groups.

Symbolic referents soon appeared. Sentiments crystallized about the larger developmental projects. The Volta River scheme in Ghana became one such; another was the development of television in Nigeria, evident in the pride with which the Western Region proclaimed its priority as having been the first in West Africa to have established a transmission system. Aspects of the infrastructure, such as roads, especially when they were paved, or bridges, that brought immediate economic benefits to the people, were likewise given symbolic value.

Among the most prized developments was the establishment of institutions of higher education. Makerere College in Uganda was originally intended to serve all three British East African territories; it was not many years after its establishment that first Kenya and later Tanganyika moved toward setting up their own colleges. The same was true of French West Africa. Under colonial status, the University of Dakar served the needs of the entire region but shortly after the Ivory Coast attained independence, it began to develop its own University, and Guinea also moved to achieve this. In British West Africa, insistence on an institution of

[8] Sékou Touré: *L'Action Politique du Parti Démocratique de Guinée; la Planification Économique.* République de Guinée, Vol. V (Conakry, 1960), pp. 5, 75, 76.

higher learning for each territory came some years before independence.

It would be wrong to overlook the political dimensions of economic development. As we have seen, suspicions of the ex-colonial powers made the new African states wary of continuing economic dependence upon them. In practice, however, ties of this kind were not readily broken. With the notable exception of Guinea, economic relations that had existed continued much as before. But many African governments were particularly on their guard against entering into economic commitments with groupings that included former colonial states. The cry of neo-colonialism warned against such organizations as the European Economic Community, whose proposals to extend aid to African countries were scrutinized closely, and debated as initial moves to replace political with financial controls. There began to be heard overtones of a growing African economic isolationism, and views were expressed on how African peoples could best serve their economic objectives by pooling resources and themselves developing productive capacity and distributive mechanisms, in order to substantially reduce their need for assistance from the outside.

Torn between the political ideal of neutralism and the indispensability of economic aid, obtainable only from the major powers involved in the world struggle, Africans came to be attracted by a kind of vague ideal of national autarchy, even while realizing the practical difficulties of such a policy. The ideal was reinforced by memories of the colonial experience, which imposed the classical system of colonial areas as sources of raw materials for processing in the Metropole. For aid, African leaders turned, wherever possible, to international organizations in which they had a voice, such as the various organs of the United Nations, or to multilateral partnership agreements with nationals of a number of countries. By these, and other less direct means, they hoped to avoid the dangers of economic subservience to a single power, or group of powers, in obtaining the capital they must have if they were to achieve their economic goals.

13

Rediscovery and Integration:

Religion and the Arts

THE CHANGING SITUATION in Subsaharan Africa, particularly the drive toward self-determination, caused the missions to accept the principle of devolution of church control into African hands.[1] The same process, but not as a conscious movement, had marked the spread of Islam. Though the organization of worship and the locus of religious sanction were different, African converts increasingly became "contact agents," as Trimingham calls them, with "Negroes spreading Negro Islam." [2]

Independent African Christian churches, particularly outside the missions, were established as an expression of protest against the close direction and control by the missionaries, and date from a fairly early period in mission activity. Yet it would be wrong to ascribe the development of separatist churches to this cause alone. For one thing, the tendency to evolve separatist cults was not confined to African Christians; we have seen how

[1] *Supra,* Ch. VII, *passim.*

[2] J. S. Trimingham: *Islam in West Africa* (Oxford, 1959), p. 31.

this was also present among Africans who were adherents of Islam. Because it represents a tendency in the structuring of traditional worship, in this as in so many other phases of African change we must again turn to aboriginal patterns for the causes.

When we take the more inclusive approach, we find that many of the separatist groups are to be thought of as reinterpretations of the prophet movements widely prevalent in Africa long before European control. Schlosser, who has collated much of the data on these movements, named thirty-one prophets inspired by Islamic teaching, the earliest going back to the eighth century. Thirteen prophets, whose doctrines were drawn from the indigenous belief systems, arose in various other parts of the continent, while twenty-one others represented reactions to Christianity.[3]

Some of these Christian cults were directly stimulated from outside. This was the case of both the Ethiopian and Zionist movements in South Africa.[4] It was also true of the Watch Tower Movement[5] in the Rhodesias and later in the Belgian Congo where, as we have seen, it became the militant Kitawala sect. One of the first documented examples of an indigenous Christian prophet movement was the church established in West Africa by William Wade Harris, a Liberian, who in 1910 emerged as a prophet after having had a vision in which he was called to preach. Harris, whose principal influence was exerted in the Ivory Coast, acquired a West African following of between 100,000 and 120,000 adherents.[6]

These responses to mission activity give us striking instances

[3] Katesa Schlosser: *Propheten in Afrika* (Braunschweig, Germany, 1949), *passim.*

[4] Bengt G. M. Sundkler: *Bantu Prophets in South Africa* (London, 1948), pp. 38–59.

[5] Raymond Leslie Buell: *The Native Problem in Africa* (New York, 1928), Vol. I, pp. 242–3.

[6] Gaston Joseph: "Une Atteinte à l'Animisme chez les Populations de la Côte d'Ivoire," *Annuaire et Mémoires du Comité d'Études Historiques et Scientifiques de l'Afrique Occidentale Française* (1916), p. 348; A. Roux: "Un Prophète: Harris," in *Le Monde Noir* (Th. Monod., editor), *Présence Africaine,* Numéro special, 8–9 (Paris, 1950), *passim.*

of continuity in the psychological resilience of African peoples, who in pre-European times took over deities and other supernatural agents and the rites associated with them from societies, friendly or hostile, with whom they came into contact. Essential for an understanding of the process is the dynamism in African belief, where the universe is conceived as being in continuous process of change, and where the dictum of any supernatural power can be swayed, or even challenged by man. "The Dahomean does not feel that the powers which have given man the gbo (the magic charm) have stopped their gifts, . . ." even though "new charms and medicines are not made known in the same way and with the same frequency . . . as in the time of his forbears." Thus, it was not difficult for the Dahomeans to accept vaccination. It was held to be new magic to circumvent Sagbata, the earth deity whose most dreaded punishment is smallpox. In discussing the power of Earth and Sky to punish, one Dahomean said, "The white man has brought us a 'counter' against Sagbata, but he hasn't yet found one against the thunderbolts of his little brother." [7]

This resilience is as manifest in African reactions to Islam as to Christianity. Baba, a Hausa woman, herself the wife of a *malam,* or Koranic scholar, discussed in her autobiography the hold which the *bori,* the autochthonous spirits, have even on these devout Islamic teachers:

> All the rulers like the *bori*—if they didn't, would their work be any good? . . . So do the *malams,* secretly. The *malams* call on the *bori* in private, in the darkness at night. Everyone wants the spirits, kings and noblemen want them, *malams* and wives shut away in their compounds—it is with them we work in this world, and without them would our labour be any use? The work of the *malams* is one thing, the work of *bori* experts is another, each has his own kind of work, and they must not be mixed up.[8]

[7] Melville J. and Frances S. Herskovits: *An Outline of Dahomean Religious Belief* (Memoirs of the American Anthropological Association, No. 41, Menasha, Wisconsin, 1933), p. 67; the reference, "his little brother," is to Hevioso, the god of thunder.

[8] Mary F. Smith: *Baba of Karo, a Woman of the Muslim Hausa* (New York, 1954), p. 222.

For a comparable response of a Christian convert, we turn again to Dahomey, a quarter century after the reinterpretation of vaccination as a new form of magic was recorded. In the compound of the head of one of the craft guilds, a man who at that time was also chief priest of an important cult group, chromolithographs of Catholic saints were to be seen hanging near magic charms. It was a Sunday morning, and the cult head was in church. In a courtyard of the compound, where the initiation rites for a major deity of the Dahomean pantheon were held, an elaborate altar to this god glistened under its offerings of palm oil and other sacrifices. "You are Catholics?" a senior member of the family was asked. "Yes." "And your father, the cult head?" "He, too." "You say he is at mass now. Does he go to confession, and take communion?" "Of course." "What does the priest say about his god?" "That," came the answer, "is no business of the Church." [9]

The process of bringing different religious strands together, which can be observed in the many separatist movements that dot the Subsaharan continent, has received less attention in the regions under the influence of Islam than within African Christianity. One reason for this is that the Islamic separatist movements had their beginnings at a much earlier period, and consequently had achieved the cohesiveness of "denominational" rather than schismatic congregations. In effect, the manifestations of separatism are of such long standing that they have of themselves taken on their own orthodoxies. Yet we have seen that the process has been a continuing one, institutionalized in what has been called the steady "maraboutization" of the Islamic community in the Sudanic belt.[1] Information as to the character of the beliefs and rituals of the more recent local sects has tended to be restricted to the informal, popular reinterpretations of aboriginal custom by African followers of Islam. We can, however, gain some insight into the nature of the institutional changes in the Islamized areas as they functioned on a tradi-

[9] Melville J. Herskovits: *Notes on African Field Research, 1953–1960* (manuscript), p. 53/D196.

[1] *Supra,* pp. 187–9.

tional non-Islamic base, by seeing how it was described among the Nupe of Nigeria.

Here Islam represented something "utterly novel to people reared in traditional Nupe culture." The formal character of Islamic prayer was quite different from the "variable and informal addresses" directed toward the aboriginal deity. The daily routine of prayers, holding rituals inside a building, individual instead of group worship, the Moslem priesthood, as the body of holy or learned men who conduct religious services can be called, were all foreign to earlier Nupe religion. The differences were "resolved by Nupe-izing the orthodox Moslem practices." Open-air mosques, consisting of a ring of stones, were laid out, usually under a shady tree, and daily prayers were recited in Arabic. But "over and above the stereotyped prayers, the Nupe have others which ask for special benefits and are meant to take care of such contingencies as a drought or the threat of an epidemic." These permitted the direct appeal to the deity which characterized earlier Nupe relations with the gods. More than this, "any household or kin group which faces some deep anxiety or threat will arrange . . . a ceremonial meal at which a fowl is killed and a mallam, specially invited, utters a brief prayer." A Nupe invocation would follow, however, so that this rite "differs only in minor details from the communal meal of the pagan ceremonial." [2]

The most detailed study of the syncretic and reinterpretative aspects of African response to religious impulses from outside the continent found in the many separatist Christian sects that have arisen since early in the colonial period, and the first of its kind, was that of Sundkler, who treated the separatist Christian churches in South Africa. They were formed mainly because of a reaction to the strict controls over Christian converts by the missionaries, and the meager opportunities for Africans in the missions. These South African separatist churches had a relatively long history. Thus, in 1882, an African leader in the Wesleyan Mission Church, criticized by a European missionary because of

[2] S. F. Nadel: *Nupe Religion* (London, 1954), pp. 236–8.

his "strong Tembu nationalistic sympathies," left the church and two years later founded the "Tembu Church." The syncretistic factor, even at this early date, was apparent. "The cause of this important secession was not only opposition to European control but also to a positive desire to adapt the message of the Church to the heritage of the Tembu tribe." [3]

These, and similar movements that followed them, were sporadic; it was not until 1892, on the Witwatersrand, that the "Ethiopian" church was founded. Because Johannesburg was a center to which mine workers from many different ethnic groups were attracted, this church was not identified with any one of them. "The church leader on the Rand had a wider horizon and appealed to many tribes." The founder, referring his authority to passages in the Bible, such as Psalms 68:31, "Ethiopia shall soon stretch out her hands unto God," interpreted this to mean, "The self-government of the African Church under African leaders." [4]

These leaders had heard of the African Methodist Episcopal Church in the United States. At a conference of all independent church heads held in Pretoria in 1896, it was decided to seek affiliation with this body, and an emissary was dispatched to Philadelphia to open negotiations. This is not the place to recount the tortuous course of events; as it turned out, "American Negro missionaries were. . . . just as much foreigners and strangers in the eyes of the Ethiopians as the white missionaries." Though the influence of the Americans continued to be important, both in the religious and educational fields, African dislike of any form of outside controls made for further schisms.[5]

Fission was accelerated and given new form in 1904 by arrival on the scene of representatives of the Christian Catholic Apostolic Church of Zion, Illinois, out of which "a whole series of Zionist Churches . . . emerged." With individual autonomy, they proliferated. Their many names—"Zion," "Jerusalem," "Apostolic," "Full Gospel," "Pentecostal"—represented

> only individual variations on a theme once intoned on the shores of Lake Michigan, United States. The practices of these Churches,

[3] B. G. M. Sundkler, op. cit., p. 38.
[4] Ibid., p. 39. [5] Ibid., pp. 42–3.

> . . . show, however, that much . . . happened in the transfer from Lake Michigan to the streams and ponds of Zululand.[6]

Both in its historic past and its later forms, we have in the South African syncretisms a clearly discernible continuum. The two poles are respectively the aboriginal religions on the one end, and the mission-controlled or, in the mission sense, the orthodox Christian churches on the other. Between these are the independent Zionist groups, which incorporated much of aboriginal belief and practice in their theology and ritual, and the Ethiopian churches, which leaned toward more conventional Christian dogma and rites. Of the latter, Sundkler writes:

> Seen from a Zulu point of view, the Ethiopian programme appears at the same time Christian and African. The ideology and theology appear as roughly the same as those preached in the Mission Church. But the Ethiopians have thrown in their lot with their African kinsmen against the whites.

As for the Zionists, though they were regarded on the reserves as being, "a third race, over against both the heathen and the Christian community," they nonetheless were "a conservative force insofar as the fundamentals of Zulu society are concerned."[7]

This form of protest against control by missionaries, which originated in, and was bolstered by the tradition of prophet movements and the polytheism of the aboriginal faiths, explains why the Christian separatist movements appeared over all the continent beginning with the early days of direct contact with the mission churches. Two difficulties present themselves when we seek to analyze these earlier sectarian divisions. For one thing, it is not easy to divorce doctrinal differences from reactions against foreign control. For another, it is difficult to obtain contemporaneous information concerning the theology and rituals of the separatist churches, which means that the degree and character of their syncretisms cannot be accurately assessed.

That there was a degree of both these elements, even in the earliest reported instances, cannot be questioned. We have seen

[6] Ibid., p. 49.

[7] Ibid., pp. 93, 95, 98.

the history of the South African sects to be a tale of protest; Sundkler's evidence concerning the beliefs and rituals of the churches he studied establishes the progression from Christian to native Zulu, through the elaborate reinterpretations of both Christian and Zulu practices in the Ethiopian and Zionist segments of the continuum. In another early separatist movement, the Independent Native African Church, founded in Lagos, Nigeria, in 1891, the element of protest was clearly evident in the resolution adopted at the organizational meeting, where it was resolved:

> That this Meeting, in humble dependence upon Almighty God, is of the opinion that Africa is to be evangelized, and that the foreign agencies at work at the present moment, taking into consideration climatic and other influences, cannot grasp the situation. . . . That a purely Native African Church can be founded for the evangelization and amelioration of our race, to be governed by Africans.[8]

The signers were professing Christians; it would have yielded important insights to know the form of the services and the moral code by which the members were expected to live so as to learn what pre-European elements, if any, were brought into doctrine and ritual; but the documents tell us nothing of all this.

Protest against the lack of opportunity for religious self-expression was similarly present in the better known separatist cults, such as those of Chilembwe in Nyasaland (1915), or Kimbanguism and Kitawala in the Belgian Congo (1921 and 1940), or Matsuanism in the French Congo. Their inner syncretic aspects, however, have too often been masked by popular assertions about their "dark rites" and "orgies," which rumor, not discouraged by the missions that hold them renegade, or government, which saw them as subversive, attributed to them. In both the Belgian Congo and French Equatorial Africa, since separatist

[8] Cited in Jean Herskovits Kopytoff: *Liberated Africans and the History of Lagos Colony to 1886* (unpublished D.Phil. thesis, University of Oxford, 1960), p. 489.

sects were strictly suppressed,[9] their adherents kept details of their beliefs and practices from outsiders.

The problems of reinterpretation and syncretism become the more complex when the forces of intertribal acculturation and internal dynamics are taken into account. One such case is that of the Basuku in the southern Kwango region of the Congo Republic. Between 1922 and 1959, three movements developed, each of which had its own ways of nullifying the powers of practitioners of evil magic, to whom the Basuku belief-system assigns a place of major importance. The first of these movements, which is said to have originated either in Angola or the east, was called *Mbianda.* It continued until its efficacy in ridding the people of these practitioners, the *baloki,* was called into question, when a serious epidemic broke out. *Mbianda* was replaced by another "medicine" called *Lupambulu,* derived from the Kasai, perhaps from among the Baluba. This was not a "prophet" movement nor, despite the fact that it was banned by the Belgian government, was it political in character. It was, to the Basuku, another new medicine that would rid the people of the *baloki.*

When in 1954, an African Catholic priest went about the countryside, calling on the people to abandon their "fetishes" and to take Holy Water, the Basuku responded by accepting Holy Water as a means not only of neutralizing the power of magic, but of protection against the evil designs of its practitioners. Holy Water became a new kind of "medicine" against the *baloki,* to be carried in small bottles on journeys; it was used to protect travelers at night; it was sprinkled in the four corners of houses to render them safe from evil spirits, or on fields to ensure a good harvest; it was rubbed on bows before going on a hunt, or a few drops were poured into the barrel of a gun.

Yet, "contact with European culture appears largely irrelevant in explaining these movements." The first one occurred before Europeans were significantly on the scene; the second,

[9] Cf. Jules Chome: *La Passion de Simon Kimbangu* (Brussels, 1959), *passim.*

though perhaps influenced by administrative action, showed "no element of acculturation to European ideas." Even in the case of Holy Water, "the similarity of pattern between Holy Water and the previous movements is too striking to assign great importance to direct acculturation forces." [1]

Another instance of the operation of intertribal and internal forces in influencing a syncretic development is found in the MBuiti movement, which arose among the Fang of the Gabon. Unlike the Kimbanguism of the nearby Republic of the Congo, it was not messianic, but represented a reaction to "stimuli arising from the contact of Bantu peoples," and was essentially a reworking of the Fang ancestral cult. Only later did the changing colonial situation give it a messianic character. It began about 1915, when the Fang, a conquering people, began to feel the restraints laid on their warlike activities by colonial controls. In Fang thought, their medicines had failed them, and their gods and ancestors no longer heeded their petitions. This prompted a "quite matter of fact search . . . for new traits and complexes with which to strengthen their own failing religious institutions." In this search, the followers of MBuiti turned toward the religions of neighboring peoples, and then to Christianity. In the latter case, these Fang "had to activate their aboriginal idea of God in order to give to Him a central position in their thought and ritual. Equally they have had to deal with the figures of the Virgin and Christ."

Certain difficulties arose, however. Since they hold the relation between a man and his father's brother to be of the closest, Jesus was conceived as the nephew rather than the son of God. And in this patrilineal society, where the mother-son relationship is not held to be important, the Virgin was believed to have been the daughter, wife and sister of Jesus rather than his mother. Stress is also laid on Jesus as the "son of man" rather than the "son of God." He, as "a man that was born and died . . . not only made God evident on earth but made God himself evident."

[1] Igor Kopytoff: *Suku Religion: A Study in Internally Induced Reinterpretation* (Ph.D. thesis, Northwestern University, Microfilmed; 1960), p. 173 and *passim.*

Moreover, for the Fang, success is dependent upon a man having a phantom "witch spirit," a being who is essentially dangerous and unreliable. Jesus, who performed miracles and was powerful and successful, was thus thought of as demonstrating the power of God as against the power of this potentially malignant spirit.[2]

Materials such as these, which show African reaction to the new faiths brought to them by the proselytizing world religions of Islam and Christianity, bring to the fore a number of points of significance. It is striking how early the Africans asserted themselves against foreign controls. The most determined protest was in the instance of the Christian missions, where these controls assumed strict institutional form that left little place for African modification. But in the political field also, it is easy to see, after the fact, how many were the unrecognized indicators of discontent.

These materials, above all, demonstrate the power and persistence of the indigenous world view. One or two examples may be given. In the long run, missionary opposition to plural marriage proved ineffective in the face of African custom, so that the approach of self-government found certain Christian denominations considering the possibility of reconciling polygyny, which Africans pointed out was in the Biblical tradition, with the dogma of monogamy which the missionaries preached. The retention of the ancestral cult, which began to reappear openly in Christian sects and had never been given over by Islamized Africans, further demonstrated the power of traditional beliefs that, in repeated instances, have come to the surface after having been suppressed for many years.

We see in these data another facet of the flexibility of African psychology in the face of innovation. They show how African groups took over the beliefs and rituals of new faiths, and integrated them into their own systems. An instance of this can be cited from among the Ashanti of Ghana. This concerns the priest of an indigenous deity named Mframa, at a village named Mframaso, "the place of Mframa":

[2] James M. Fernandez: "The Idea and Symbol of the Saviour in a Gabon Syncretistic Cult" (manuscript, 1960), *passim*.

> Like most other Africans, he saw no incompatibility between Christianity and his own creed. The Christians bothered about only one of God's sons: his own *abosom* were all God's sons. A poor God indeed it would be who could achieve but one son. At any rate the old man proposed to build both a church and a school in Mframaso, and saw no reason why he should not worship God in the church every Sunday after his morning *abisa*.[3]

The specific syncretisms found in New World countries, particularly in New World Catholic countries, where African gods are identified with, or related to the saints of the Church, are not present in Subsaharan Africa. Yet the mechanism that produced this result was at work, in the Ashanti case just given, while an identical response was found among the Maguzawa Hausa of Northern Nigeria, where the aboriginal local spirits were identified with the *jinn* of the Koran.[4] Protestant syncretisms resembling those of the New World were more widespread in Subsaharan Africa. They were to be found in the position of Jesus and the Holy Ghost in the theology of the independent churches, the importance of baptism and the River Jordan, the incidence and manner of trance and possession.

Finally, we find another aspect of adaptation in the relation of religion to secular phases of life. This is the reason why it has been so difficult for students to distinguish the nationalism of the separatist churches from their religious function, why in some of the independent countries, rituals on state occasions have included both Christian or Moslem prayers, and the sacrifice of animals in the traditional manner. In broad scope, this factor in itself represents a kind of syncretism. But what it demonstrates, like all the other manifestations of the processes of cultural interchange, is that the Africans, to the extent they were free agents, accepted innovations within the full frame of their own cultures; and where they were not free, they maintained these traditions as

[3] M. J. Field: *Search for Security; an Ethno-psychiatric Study of Rural Ghana* (Northwestern University African Studies, No. 5, Evanston and London, 1960), p. 95.

[4] Joseph H. Greenberg: *The Influence of Islam on a Sudanese Religion* (Monographs of the American Ethnological Society, Vol. X, New York, 1946), *passim*.

best they could, reconciling them with their new ways of life when they were able to do so.

[2]

A similar tale of rediscovery and integration is told when we consider the creative arts—carving, painting, literature, music, drama, and the dance. For many years after the penetration of Africa by the colonial powers, expressions of African artistic talent were described in terms that ranged from "childlike" and "grotesque," to "savage" and "bestial." In mission or lay schools, in the reactions of the European officials who came into contact with African life, it was impressed on the Africans that their art was crude, their tales naive, their music cacophonous, their dances lascivious. For the Africans who went abroad, this evaluation was confirmed when they saw their carvings and other forms of art exhibited only in ethnographic collections as items of the material culture of their people, and not in art museums. Sometimes the appraisal was made explicit in discussion and criticism, at times it was reflected in the unspoken attitudes of Europeans, but it was rarely absent. It is understandable, then, why those Africans who did not reject their heritage were placed on the defensive, apologizing for their own pleasure in their arts where, as was more often the case, they did not conceal it.

The influence of Islam was exerted particularly in the important fields of the graphic and plastic arts, and music. The graven image was not tolerated in Moslem worship. Innumerable figures and masks were either surrendered, or searched out and destroyed, while music, especially drumming, and aboriginal ritual dancing were frowned upon, or prohibited. But whether the European depreciation of things African was primary, as in most of Subsaharan Africa, or an overlay on Moslem prohibitions, as in the Islamic belt, the results were the same.

Rediscovery and integration in the case of the arts takes on a special character, since it was here that Africans were first able to restore to themselves a sense of cultural achievement. This phase, in which initial reactions began to be reconsidered, was stimulated by the recognition that had for several decades been given African wood carving as a major art form by the painters and critics of Europe and the United States. This "discovery" is ordinarily dated from about the end of the First World War, and is usually ascribed to the group of young artists in Paris "who were rebelling against traditional European art . . . in their search for new forms," and who came to "recognize the aesthetic qualities in these primitive carvings." [5] The impact of African art on these artists was immediate. We see it in the paintings of the Post-Impressionists, whose canvases on occasion not only show the influence of this art, but in some cases represent a transfer of African mass and design to another medium.

In point of fact, African wood carving by no means burst on the art world as a sudden revelation, as may sometimes be inferred from accounts of this development in histories of art, but goes back farther than is ordinarily indicated. According to Paulme,

> African sculpture had been first acclaimed as an art by a group of painters living in Paris at the beginning of our century: Vlaminck, Matisse, Derain among others spent much time in the old Trocadero museum. In London, Derain made long visits to the ethnographic section of the British Museum. . . . By 1908, the collection of Henri Matisse counted a score of "Negro" statues; Derain, Braque, Picasso owned African masks.

A comparable movement had been developing in Germany. In 1912, the painters Kandinsky and Franz Marc brought out a publication called *Der Blaue Reiter,* which figured "a Cameroon wood-carving, a Benin plaque, a mask from Gabon." In 1915, the first book on the aesthetics of African sculpture, the *Negerplastik* of Carl Einstein, was published in Munich; in 1919, a Paris art dealer presented the first exposition of African (and Oceanic) sculpture. Thus, before 1914, African aesthetics "was not a field by any means entirely ignored; its existence was known, its richness was suspected." [6]

[5] Paul Wingert: *The Sculpture of Negro Africa* (New York, 1950), p. vi.

[6] Denise Paulme: *Les Sculptures de l'Afrique Noire* (Paris, 1956), pp. 1–2.

The movement by now was in full swing, but those who promoted the appreciation of African art drove more deeply into the thought of their day than they could have realized. In marking African wood carving with the stamp of aesthetic worth, they opened new vistas of art appreciation, and stimulated a re-examination of aesthetic theories that broadened the scope of art history to include the entire range of aesthetic activity. Forty years after its discovery, this importance of African art was described as due to "the role it . . . played in the complex drama of modern art," in which it served "essentially to confirm the pioneering efforts of those artists who were seeking to revitalize art and to inspire them further towards the development of nonrepresentational art." [7]

This, then, in summary, was the impact of African art on Europe and America. But we are primarily interested in understanding the effect of this "discovery" of African wood carving, and its recognition as one of the major arts of mankind, on the thinking of Africans themselves. For African intellectuals, particularly after the Second World War, who in Paris and London were exposed to the idea that for creative expression the artist must seek out the mainsprings of his own cultural tradition, the values laid on African art had immediate relevance. As members of groups denied significant achievement, whose cultures had been consistently depreciated, this was a profoundly moving revelation. This facet of African culture, not only accepted but acclaimed, became a symbol of identification, of pride. Beyond this, it led to a growing affirmation of African traditional values, perhaps one of the greatest contributions to a changing Africa.

As might be anticipated, the "discovery" of African art, as it was taken up by art critics and art historians, gave rise to various misconceptions. Since those who wrote about African art knew little about African life, and nothing at all of the cultural milieu of the artist and his works, some of the errors made were egregious. For example, the stereotype that developed early as to the degree of stylization that marked this art could have been easily dis-

[7] Paul Wingert: op. cit., loc. cit.

pelled by firsthand acquaintance with the African setting. One need only see from a distance an African woman carrying a calabash of provisions atop her head, silhouetted against the sky or watch the flexed posture of Africans while dancing to understand that African carvings, long apostrophized as being felicitous, but naive stylizations, were indeed often startlingly representational and realistic.

The assumption that this art, or at least the finer carving, was of the past, gave rise to further error. Two early authorities asserted that pieces of high quality were rare because "this art had long been dead in Africa," and hence "only the ancestral heirlooms, centuries old and sacred, were to be desired."[8] African art was also pronounced incapable of being understood by non-Africans. "We can never hope to plumb its expression fully. . . . For us its psychological content must always remain in greater part obscure."[9] This was before the demonstration by Griaule, in his study of Dogon masks, how deep the sensitive and disciplined observer can strike into the inner values of an art.[1]

A final mistake in this complex of appreciation and incomprehension of African art was the labeling of the better-known styles as "classic." Needless to say, there was no foundation for this except the convention of regarding African art as of the past. It imposed an artificial cut-off point, and helped to distort perspective in thinking about the dynamics of African art. More than this, since the category "classic" included only the wood carvings from those regions which were represented in the earlier collections and in art dealers' show-rooms, it excluded art produced elsewhere in Africa, and was also the cause of the incorrect assignment of provenience to many pieces. Thus much of the art of peoples living in Sierra Leone and Liberia, Dahomey, the Niger Delta and the British Cameroons tended to be ignored, while the label "Dahomean" was given to carvings obviously Yoruba, the

[8] Paul Guillaume and Thomas Monroe: *Primitive Negro Sculpture* (New York, 1926), p. 2.

[9] James Johnson Sweeney: *African Negro Art* (New York, 1935), p. 11.

[1] M. Griaule: *Masques Dogon* (Travaux et Mémoires de l'Institut d'Ethnologie, Vol. 33, Paris, 1938), *passim.*

classification being based on the political boundary between Dahomey and Nigeria and not on ethnic realities.

The total complex of ideas about African art which affirmed that its finer forms were of the past, that its meaning and the aesthetic impulses that gave rise to it were beyond the comprehension of non-Africans, and that only its "classical" examples had artistic value, had other consequences. The enthusiasm for African wood carving allowed no interest in other media in which African artists worked. Only slowly was recognition given the wealth of forms in the African aesthetic tradition. For Africa itself, this was not too important. Especially as regards the decorative arts, objects of everyday use—cloths, baskets, mats, wooden utensils—continued to be embellished with the traditional designs. But it was paramount for understanding the nature and functioning of African aesthetics, since it thwarted recognition of the total range of African art forms. Certain work in metal and the rare stone carvings did gain early acceptance. But it was years before the place of metal working as an African art form was grasped, and many more years before the breadth of its distribution recognized.

Even more damaging was the way this complex of ideas masked the understanding of the continuities, both past and present, in African art. True, the Benin bronzes were granted artistic value almost as soon as they were acquired by European museums, after the sack of Benin; and when, in 1938, the bronze heads of Ife were uncovered, they were hailed as masterpieces. But we must recall again, in this context, that the "high" art of Benin was ascribed to Portuguese influences, if not origin. For a technique and a tradition to become as widespread as artistic metal working was eventually found to be—that is, throughout all of West Africa, the Cameroons and the Congo basin—obviously much time was needed. Moreover, as art forms they were nothing new. The discoveries in Northern Nigeria of the terra cotta Nok heads and, later, of other statuettes, archaeologically dated as coming from periods going back almost three thousand years, changed concepts regarding the time-depth ascribable to African three-dimensional art forms, and made for more intensive archaeological analyses and renewed study of existing collections.

These discoveries, and the subsequent re-examinations of earlier theories, fixed attention on the proximal end of the time scale of African art development. With the growing knowledge that African cultures showed an unrecognized vitality in the face of contact, came the observation that contemporary African artists were continuing to do creative work in their chosen media. They were not, as some kind of "primitive" automata, merely copying "classical" forms representative of a tradition that had died when its religious and mythic sanctions were disturbed. Skilled carvers were discovered working on traditional objects, and were encouraged to continue professionally when they found that there were new outlets for their art. Some of the carvers, applying themselves to satisfy patrons whose tastes they could not fathom, earned the reproach that the pieces they carved, or cast, were not of high quality. What is important, however, is that, as in all societies, there were among these artists those who were of the highest competence, and that what they created had a degree of excellence that matched the work of the artists of pre-European days.

This, however, was but part of the picture. African artists, like other Africans, reacted to the changed conditions under which they lived. They were exposed to new values and learned new techniques. They emerged from a situation in which what they created was for local use, and in accord with the demands of the traditional economy. The culture-bound discussions of African art never took the human element into account. The ways in which the African artist supported himself were rarely if ever mentioned. The artist, as a personality, was never discussed. It was seldom indicated that pieces were traditionally commissioned and paid for by those who needed a statuette in the shrine of a god, or a magic charm, or by a secret society that needed masks for an approaching rite; or that brass or bronze figures were commissioned and paid for by persons of high rank to place on their ancestral altars, or to enhance their prestige by owning and displaying them. Presumably the African artist produced his masterpieces solely because of some archetypal urge; his needs as a human being for food and shelter, for discharging his family and social obligations, were quite ignored.

Here, however, we encounter a factor of some importance in aiding us to understand the kind of continuities we find in African art during the late colonial and postcolonial periods. In earlier times, since the African artist produced for those who lived nearby, what he made seldom left the community to which he belonged. But with the changes in the religious and social sanctions for his art, and with the introduction of a money economy, his market took on a different character. The African who worked in wood, ivory, or brass began to produce for a clientele he did not know, and which, in fact, acquired what he made through intermediaries.

The existence of this market reflected the interest in African art which, over the years, had spread from its recognition by avant-garde artists and critics to wide acceptance as part of the aesthetic resources of the world. For the professionals and the collectors, this continued to mean objects that were old and had been in actual use. But as the repercussions of this current of art appreciation moved beyond the small group of experts, African art became prized by many who neither knew or were particularly concerned with questions of provenience, or age, or the use to which a given piece may have been put. That a carving had been made in Africa, by an African, sufficed.

We may explore the effects of this development in Africa by first indicating the extent of the so-called aboriginal "art area." In our discussion of the cultural base line, it was pointed out that the figurines, masks and other manifestations of African art came from the contiguous areas of the Congo, the Guinea Coast and the Western Sudan. The plastic arts of eastern and northern Africa were sparsely represented, if at all. Within the art-producing area, also, the proportion of those artists who executed the masterpieces was as small as it is in any culture. Cordwell has estimated that this was no more than 2 to 5 per cent of all carvers.

> Those who do not believe that innovations in classic art were made by . . . a small percentage of the total number of carvers may profitably turn from the volumes that present only the best of African art to publications of colonial governments in the Congo and West Africa from about 1920 to 1940. Here they will see photographs of literally hundreds of carvings, all in traditional style but poor in design, technically imperfect in workmanship, and generally lacking all the qualifications of the works that have been admired enough to be included in books on African art.[2]

With the development of a wider market, pressures were brought to bear on carvers and metal workers to produce in quantity, and inevitably the overall quality of the work deteriorated. Hausa traders hawked mass-produced, nontraditional carvings and metal figurines from Dakar to Leopoldville, while as the level of sophistication among visitors to Africa rose, imitations of earlier pieces, sometimes laid away in village huts to "age" with an accumulation of dust and cobwebs, were more and more frequently encountered. The value laid on the antique by European purchasers came to be recognized by African traders. At times carvings would be made to simulate aging and even ritual use; certain groups of metal workers in the Ivory Coast were reported to have brought in a European metallurgist to teach them electrolytic processes that would give the color and patina of age to their products.[3]

The existence of this wide market did more. It served to extend the recognized wood-carving area far beyond its aboriginal boundaries. Just what the mechanisms of this spread were is in general not known, except that the drive behind it was essentially economic. The Kamba of Kenya provide a good example. Though the origin of Kamba carving for the market was variously ascribed to suggestion and encouragement of a colonial official or a missionary, it would seem that it began with a gifted carver named Mutisya Munge who, before 1914, was a maker of ceremonial wands, but who "added greatly to his range during

[2] Justine M. Cordwell: "African Art," in *Continuity and Change in African Cultures* (W. R. Bascom and M. J. Herskovits, editors, Chicago, 1959), pp. 46–7.

[3] Melville J. Herskovits: *Notes on African Field Research,* p. 60/D65.

the war, which he spent in the carrier corps in Tanganyika." The common view that wood carving was an entirely new development is thus only partially correct, since in pre-European times the Kamba did carve these wands and small replicas of human heads as stoppers for medicine horns. What was new was mass production by groups of specialized carvers. This began as Mutisya Munge brought others into what became a profitable enterprise, and proved to be a valuable new source of income to a people whose herding and farming was confined to a region "arid and prone to droughts." [4]

Quantity production of carvings for the market moved to all eastern and southern Africa. In Northern Rhodesia, carvers migrated with their families to camps near Livingstone, where wood was at hand, and the tourists who came to visit Victoria Falls were ready purchasers. Though each man carved a complete figure, every group specialized in a particular animal—tortoise, lion, giraffe, hippopotamus, among others. The carvers had two outlets. One was retail, and sellers would sit at their accustomed places in the town or at the Falls, with their wares spread in front of them. Because they had learned that tourists especially prized a piece obtained from a carver, they would busy themselves sand-papering a carving to smooth the strokes of the adze, or polishing it to a high gloss. The other market was wholesale, and was composed of middlemen who ordered and purchased, at fixed prices, pieces that were destined for curio-shops in Johannesburg, London, New York, Chicago, Los Angeles, and elsewhere. Similarly, carvings for the market were being made in Uganda and the Union of South Africa.[5]

In West Africa, established guilds were also producing carvings and brass figures for the larger markets, while centers under governmental auspices for the training of apprentices in the traditional arts came into being. In certain museums, African artists and craftsmen were retained, and visitors could watch

[4] Walter Elkan: "The East African Trade in Woodcarvings," *Africa,* Vol. 28 (1958), p. 315.

[5] Melville J. Herskovits: *Notes on African Field Research,* pp. 57/D427–429.

them as they plied their traditional calling. At the Bamako *Artisanat,* in Mali, or at the Benin Native Authority Arts and Crafts center in Nigeria, work of high quality by those who had been trained there was available for purchase. Or, again, in the museum at Abidjan, in the Ivory Coast, weavers and wood carvers turned out cloth, or, on order, copied for prospective buyers rare pieces that were on display.

Stimulated by the growing interest in African art, African artists began to experiment with new forms. In Nigeria, miniature realistic wood carvings appeared, which depicted personalities, European and African, in the colonial scene,[6] and others in a new medium, thorns of the cotton tree.[7] European techniques of painting with water colors or in oils became widely diffused. This was introduced principally through mission schools, and initially produced conventional treatments of conventional themes, usually suggested by European reproductions. Where African scenes were depicted, little of African stylistic convention appeared.

After the Second World War, centers were established where Africans were encouraged to use traditional themes, and their own landscapes. Perhaps the best known of these was the one out of which came the "painters of Poto-poto." [8] They took their name from the African quarter of Brazzaville, Congo Republic, where they worked. These painters developed a distinctive style, and their paintings attracted much favorable attention in Europe and the United States. The demand for their paintings prompted many Africans in the two Congos and even in West Africa to copy their style and subjects. Schools employing similar approaches, some of them antedating the Poto-poto center, were founded near Salisbury in Southern Rhodesia, at Makerere College in Uganda, and at Achimota in Ghana.

[6] William R. Bascom: "Modern African Figurines, Satirical or Just Stylistic?" *Lore* (Milwaukee Public Museum, 1957), Vol. 7, *passim.*

[7] Anonymous: "Carver in Miniature," *West African Review,* Vol. 30, No. 377 (1959), pp. 106–7.

[8] Jean-Paul Lebeuf: "L'École des Peintres de Poto-Poto," *Africa,* Vol. 26 (1956), *passim.*

On the surface, this development seemed to be owing exclusively to European influence. This was only partially true. The use of canvas and paper, and particularly the framed composition, were entirely new. But the influence of antecedent tradition was by no means absent. In pre-European Africa, painting was widely used for house decoration. The characteristic motifs were commonly seen not only in painting, but included the geometric patterns in bas-relief found on Ashanti dwellings in Ghana, and the heraldic bas-reliefs on the outer walls of the compounds of Dahomean chiefs, the stylized designs on the houses in the cities of the whole belt of the western Sudan from Kano to Timbuktu, the pebble mosaics on the walls of Basuto round houses, almost at the southern tip of the continent. The widespread rock paintings of earlier days seem also to have been a source of the elongated, pencil-like figures that appear in many of the later compositions of African painters who worked in water colors.

The paintings on inner and outer house walls are in some societies closely tied in with the social structures, as in the elaborate designs placed on the compound walls of the Ibo titleholders in the Niger Delta. How striking an art form this can be is to be seen in the published reproductions of such wall figures and compositions from eastern Angola.[9] Thus African artists who came to paint in water colors and oils, like those who came to do sculpture in the European mode, had much in their own tradition on which they could, and did draw.

Because African carvers were now producing for an impersonal market, and in quantity, did not mean that there were no creative artists among them, as any firsthand acquaintance with African wood carvers and metal workers proves. In Kenya, a specialist in making the familiar heads of young Masai warriors, and experimenting with the conventional proportions, carved two small figures of distinction, sensitively modelled, and without the "prettiness" of the heads usually seen. In Northern Rhodesia, an elderly carver who specialized in modelling lions, among a

[9] José Redinha: *Paredes Pintadas da Luanda* (Museu do Dondo, Publicações Culturais, No. 18, Lisbon, 1953), *passim.*

group working on tortoises, modified realism into a stylized reworking of masses that gave to the portrayal a dynamic quality seen in no other carving in the area.

Older forms, produced in large numbers, were generally of inferior quality by any standards, aesthetic or technical. But if the carvers were asked why these pieces were not as good as formerly, the answer in a number of West African centers was that if a mask or a figurine were commissioned, and the carver given enough time, he could promise the quality found in the carvings of earlier days. The same was true of metal working. After 1940, the Dahomean brass casters began quantity production of inferior replicas of traditional figures, such as that of a woman, infant on her back, pounding grain in a mortar, or a royal officer with his pipe, or a crocodile; and also new ones, such as a woman with a tray on her head on which a long weighted strand, representing a pole, was balanced. Yet members of the same guild who were producing these inferior and culturally intrusive commercial items were continuing to make pieces of traditional quality for Dahomeans or others who ordered them.

The artistic tradition had no more been broken by the impact of European culture than were other African ways of life. Even if the artistically gifted African wished to reject the tradition of his society, he could not escape its influence on his thinking and his behavior. In art as in religion, rejection or indifference was followed by rediscovery. Painting became more and more African. The retreat from realism that marked artistic development in Europe and America took on a positive, African character for the newer sculptors and painters. In his manipulation of line and mass, and in his compositions, the African artist began to call on his own cultural resources. In some instances, carvers who had turned to Christian theology for their themes began to make figures inspired by concepts and mythic beings in the religions of their ancestors.

A similar reorientation was to be seen among the African public. Where museums had been established, attendance steadily increased, as did a sense of identification with the objects displayed, and open pride in them. In Abidjan and Accra and

Kumasi, in Lagos and Ife and Benin and Jos, in Douala, in Kampala, in Leopoldville and Nairobi and Livingstone, Africans came in a steady stream, explaining to their children the meaning of pieces that were displayed, or discussing the merit of one carving or metal figure as against another. Groups from the outlying country could be seen listening, as one of their number who could read told them what the label said.

This interest was manifest on all levels. Between 1955 and 1960, the Nigerian government, which was then under substantial African control, spent some £70,000 buying back Nigerian pieces of distinction, which were being offered in London auction-halls. Strict laws were passed there, and increasingly in the other independent African states, to check the outflow of art objects defined as "antiquities." Popular interest reached a climax during the celebration of Nigerian independence, when attendance at the National Museum in Lagos reached between fifteen and thirty thousand persons daily.

[3]

In music and the dance, accommodation to contact with the outside world followed the broad pattern we have observed for religion and the graphic and plastic arts. In music, the additive factor was of first importance. Certain styles remained close to aboriginal modes of improvisation and performance, but new instruments, a different social setting, and above all the phonograph and the radio brought elements that had not existed in precolonial days to stimulate musical innovation.

African music, to the casual foreign observers, is no less baffling than any other musical idiom with which the listener is unfamiliar. But, while the musical forms of other parts of the non-European world, especially the Far East, were approached with respectful interest, African music was not taken seriously as an art form. What later came to be accepted as a disciplined intricacy of rhythm was regarded as mere noise; patterns of improvisation were interpreted as absence of set form. So fixed was this stereotype that one writer could state, as late as 1952:

> African drumming, submitted to the most painstaking of auditions, simply does not break down into a structured rhythmic music; there are shifts of time and points and counterpoints of rhythm that make accurate notation impossible.[1]

For a long time, Africans were judged incapable of harmonizing their songs, until recordings proved otherwise. The richness of African musical resources reflected in the great variety of instruments was disregarded, because of the all-important place assigned to percussion.

The "discovery" of African music was to affect ideas about its worth held by the outside world, and in Africa itself, as profoundly as did the "discovery" of African wood carving. In the instance of music, however, recognition came indirectly, through the growing popularity of American Negro jazz, and increasing acceptance of Africa as a major source of this music. At one time the origin of jazz was vigorously debated, entering the more general dispute over the amount of identifiable influence of African cultural elements in the United States. There were even those who denied any African influence. The general public, untroubled by these academic controversies, accepted without much question that jazz was African in origin. For specialists, the debate moved to the point of the degree, rather than the fact, of African influence, as African music and other New World Negro musical styles of undoubted African derivation, such as the rhumba of Cuba, the calypso of Trinidad, and the samba of Brazil, from the Caribbean area and South America became known.

As jazz came to take on importance as a world idiom, it found a prominent place in the musical vocabulary of European and American composers of concert forms. The interest in African music as the source of this idiom grew. This is to be seen, for example, in the large number of commercial recordings of African songs, drum-rhythms and instrumental pieces that were issued. The American Negro spirituals also entered into this stream. Their use as thematic material in Dvorak's symphony "From the

[1] Barry Ulanov: *A History of Jazz in America* (New York, 1952), p. 12.

New World," placed them, and the African influence manifest in them, before a wide musical audience whose range of appreciation did not include the "popular" jazz forms.

The jazz vogue had one misleading effect, however. As a New World form, whatever African characteristics it incorporated necessarily derived from the musical culture of the parts of Africa whence the New World Negro predominantly came, the Guinea Coast and the western part of the Congo area.[2] Consequently, it was the music of these regions that was meant by the phrase "African music."

This, however, was in some respects inaccurate. Western African music, that is, by no means represented the music of all the Subsaharan continent. Further studies of African music, and more recordings from the whole of the subcontinent revealed a wide variety of African musical styles. Merriam was able to map seven musical areas for the African continent as a whole. These are the Bushman-Hottentot, eastern Africa, East Horn, Central Africa, West Coast (including the Guinea Coast and the western Congo), the Sudan-Desert area, and the North Coast, areas whose limits follow in a general way those of the culture areas we have distinguished.

Merriam also showed how the music of those areas outside western Africa, for all their internal differences, diverges from the concept of "African music" based solely on West Coast forms and to a lesser extent on those of Central Africa. He pointed out strong Arab elements in the music of the Sudanic and Desert peoples and in the rhythmic structure of East African music. The "specific uses of drums and drumming, and Islamic influences" made for kinds of music that varied considerably from that "African music" from which the jazz forms were derived.[3]

Yet in terms of the changes in African musical culture with which we are here concerned, this West Coast area was un-

[2] Melville J. Herskovits: *The Myth of the Negro Past* (New York, 1941), pp. 33–53.

[3] Alan P. Merriam: "African Music," in *Continuity and Change in African Cultures* (W. R. Bascom and M. J. Herskovits, editors, Chicago, 1959), pp. 76–80.

doubtedly the most important, whether we consider its impact on the musical world at large, or in Africa itself. We may, therefore, indicate the elements of the musical styles found there. According to Waterman, the "outstanding feature" of this music, which "sets it most apart from that of Europe is the rhythm, a focal value which is implemented in a great number of ways." This being the case, "the appreciation of African rhythm requires a musical sense that, in the individual, conditioned only to the norms of European music, usually lies somewhat dormant. This may be spoken of as the *metronome sense.*" Dominance of percussion instruments, polymeters which enhance the complexities of the metrical framework, off-beat phrasing of melodic accents, and the presence of overlapping call-and-response patterns are other features that give it its individuality.[4]

The importance of rhythm, stressed by almost every writer on West African music, lay in the fact that this was the predominant trait that was carried to those parts of the world where the descendants of Africans live. Nketia, an African musicologist, pointed out that the prominence of rhythm in the newer, post-contact forms of African music represented the continuation of a pattern that had many ramifications in African life. "An African child was taught rhythm patterns through language texts from a very early age." Nketia also provided us with an African assessment of rhythm in European music. "Certain passages in Western music, . . . particularly in some of the music of Brahms," seemed to him to be African, though "just when the composer was going to make something of it he went and spoiled it." The rhythms of Euroamerican music, indeed, in this African scholar's view, were "chaotic rather than organized." [5]

In Ghana, where changes in the musical culture were most carefully studied, traditional association between music and

[4] Richard A. Waterman: "African Influence on the Music of the Americas," in *Acculturation in the Americas* (Vol. II, Proceedings of the 29th International Congress of Americanists, Sol Tax, editor, Chicago, 1952), pp. 211–14.

[5] J. H. Nketia: Discussion of "Characteristics of African Music," by A. P. Merriam, *Journal of the International Folk Music Council,* Vol. 11 (1959), p. 19.

dance continued, as in the introduction of new types of songs to go with new forms of popular dances. When Nketia was a child, he reports,

> the dance in vogue . . . was *utan.* Later it was replaced by *siku—rebewu—opere:* then *adakam,* then *Kenkema.* . . . In the new creations . . . significant elements constituting a new departure from the old tradition, or rather a new addition to the old tradition, are found.

All kinds of changes were to be noted—new instruments, new musical forms, even the adoption of new scales. Much of this new music was recreational, as for example the "high-life" songs, as against earlier music which accompanied social and religious ceremonies.

> Whereas in the past each society formed also a "community of taste," in the contemporary situation different "communities of taste" have emerged. The old was what the African genius was able to produce through the stimulus it received within itself. The new is what the African is producing through the stimulus it received from without.

And while, for a time, it seemed as though there was some danger of the older forms being lost, with "nationalism . . . fostering a new pride" in traditional music, conscious efforts began to be made, as independence neared and after, to preserve this musical heritage.[6]

The phonograph was undoubtedly a prime agent in inducing musical change. Not only this, it was instrumental in developing a degree of homogeneity in the newer music that was greater than had existed in the traditional forms. Before attempting a possible explanation for this, let us again turn to an analysis by Merriam:

> The principle of the importance of rhythm in the music of Africa south of the Sahara is unquestioned; it seems clear that to a considerable extent this geographic area is made a cohesive unit set off from other music units by the use of rhythm and rhythmic devices as key concepts. At the same time, much of our writing on rhythm

[6] J. H. Nketia: "Changing Traditions of Folk Music in Ghana," *Journal of the International Folk Music Council,* Vol. 11 (1959), *passim.*

> in African music has tended to emphasize drums and drumming to the exclusion of other musical instruments and ideas. We seem to have lost sight of the fact that it is African *music* that is percussive and rhythmic. . . . Whether accompanied by drums or not, African song depends upon moving horizontal rhythmic concepts, and when drums are present they but reinforce a device already characteristic of the music system.[7]

If we examine the phonograph records that have influenced African musical change, we find that among the most popular were those imported from the New World, presenting jazz and its associated types. It needs no professional competence, for example, to recognize the close relation of the West African highlife to the West Indian calypso. But, as we have seen, these New World forms were derived from West Africa, with the West African special emphasis on percussion rhythm carried over and given even greater prominence. Building on an antecedent homogeneity in rhythm, the new style, continuing the earlier musical tradition and stimulated by the ubiguitous phonograph record, asserted itself universally.

Certainly in West Africa the phonograph accentuated other earlier musical forms, as in the case of rhythm. Nketia, who has also analyzed the effect of this particular instrument of musical change, shows how this applied to other aspects of earlier musical style. Foreign instruments such as the clarinet and the guitar came to be used. The alternation of solo and chorus in the older music changed to "just a short lead," which might be restated in the course of the song. New style music showed "greater interest in part singing," having three and even four-part harmonies. Finally, the forms of the dance with which the new kinds of music came to be associated differed from the old;

> dance music of the new order has distinctive styles of dancing some of which are to a very large extent intertribal. The styles are much simpler, less correlated with stages in music, less varied and with little or none of the usual symbolic expressions that make traditional dancing so meaningful.

[7] Alan P. Merriam: "Characteristics of African Music," *Journal of the International Folk Music Council,* Vol. 11 (1959), p. 15.

Some more recent kind of dancing was of the ball-room variety, but while

> new style music may be Ball-room inspired. . . . some kinds of it . . . provide a welcome change from the somewhat formal foreign dances. Quite often everybody gets up to dance when after Western and American numbers the players switch on to the new African music.[8]

[4]

Literacy effected marked changes in the spoken arts. Narrative and poetic forms had always existed in profusion, but because they were expressed orally, stories were more akin to drama than written narrative can be, poetry took the form of the words to songs, with a significant degree of interaction between linguistic tone, semantic intent, and melodic line. Jordan has shown, for South Africa, the richness of the resources these aboriginal forms provided later African writers.[9]

New literary forms were slow in developing. Literacy, and progressively higher education, supplied models from world literature that in theme, scope, descriptive detail, and in developmental sequences were as overwhelming as, in its way, technology was. As late as the beginning of the Second World War, Africans wishing to write talked about *War and Peace,* and *The Good Earth.* They were baffled by Freudian allusions, as they found themselves unable to relate the analytic concepts to their own systems of values and the behavior and motivations they knew. They were offended by the Jungian creed of the archetype, which related their own thematic resources to primordial levels. This is not to say that tradition did not enter into the written prose literature; one of the early works, Mofolo's *Chaka,* was an outstanding example of the traditional fascination with historic

[8] J. H. Nketia: "The Gramophone and Contemporary African Music in the Gold Coast," *Proceedings of the Fourth Annual Conference of the West African Institute of Social and Economic Research* (Ibadan, Nigeria, 1956), mimeographed, pp. 194–5.

[9] A. C. Jordan: "Towards an African Literature," *Africa South,* Vol. 1, No. 4 (1956–1957), pp. 90–8; Vol. 2, No. 1 (1957–1958), pp. 97–105; No. 2, pp. 101–4, *passim.*

themes. But perhaps the kind of aboriginal literary expression most readily transferable was poetry, especially in the freer forms where imagery is paramount—forms which African poets, whether writing in French, English or Portuguese, who tended to eschew rhymed verse, for the most part employed. The words to songs, the verse forms of indigenous African cultures, were marked by stress on imagery, and both symbolic and oblique reference.

Another reason why the new African literature developed slowly is to be found in the factor of language. Literacy, as we have seen, was an innovation, and except where African languages had been given phonetic equivalence, creative expression in writing had in the main to be in the language of the schools, the language of the governing power. This presented a formidable obstacle. Never was African facility with languages more needed, as African novelists and poets sought to produce works, in an alien tongue, that would gain recognition comparable to that accorded their art and music.

A subtle psychological factor complicated their approach. Not only did they have to write in the language of their schooling, but from their earliest years in school, the models they were made to follow were European. Given the attitude toward "primitive folklore" that marked the thinking of the curriculum makers, and the broader climate of opinion that depreciated African culture in general, it would have been strange indeed if African narratives had been included. On the contrary, when in 1953 two distinguished African educators and writers published a volume of animal tales for use in the elementary schools of French West Africa,[1] its introduction into the syllabus was blocked by school administrators. Thus little of aboriginal narrative found its way, either in form or substance, into the writings of African authors.

The earliest African written literature is from South Africa.[2]

[1] L. Senghor and A. Sadji: *La Belle Histoire de Leuk-le-Lièvre* (Paris, 1953).

[2] A. C. Jordan: op. cit., Vol. 2 (1958), No. 3, pp. 112–15; No. 4, pp. 113–18.

However, as Africans, with schooling on increasingly higher levels, came into contact with the dominant European culture, they more and more identified themselves with its values. On the other side of the coin were the social and psychological realities of the place assigned to them. The greater their competence within the dominant European culture, and their identification with it, the more severely they felt were the inequalities under which they had to live. The frustration thus experienced became the symbol of the abyss toward which the doctrine of *apartheid* was pushing them.

The writing of Africans from South Africa was marked by the directness with which they phrased their bitterness, and a preoccupation with the relations between Africans and Europeans. In contrast, West Africans tended to move the social setting of their stories into the foreground, and showed a kind of nostalgia for their pre-European life. One South African writer analyzed it in this way:

> Moving from South to West Africa is moving from one plane of response to another. We can see the writer on the South African plane preoccupied from minute to minute, day to day experience—with the local commitment to a political situation. He responds by protesting or escaping and pretending it does not exist or insulating himself against the hurts that are aimed at him. Between these poles, the needle of response may steady down somewhere in the middle, where acceptance meets rejection. When the artist reaches this point, he is being emancipated, and he begins to feel the desperate necessity to enlarge the circumference of his protest to take in the demands of universal man, who is too big for a parochial setting. On the West African plane, the writer is already at grips with the problem of his place in the spiritual struggles of universal man. And if he has not yet begun to do so, he must sooner or later feel the desperate necessity of grappling with his local commitment that has reference to class, poverty, and other immediate social maladies. Here, the development is towards the inner circles of response, where the South African non-white has started.[3]

[3] Ezekiel Mphahlele: "African Writing in English" (a paper presented to the International Symposium on African Culture, Ibadan, Nigeria, December 1960), mimeographed, p. 7.

These generalizations are in line with a more specific analysis of the African novel, wherein the theme of the book by the Cameroons writer Oyono, entitled *Une Vie de Boy* was contrasted with the motifs in the works by the South African novelist Peter Abrahams:

> That the situation of M. Oyono's characters does not . . . affect us with that painful sense of helplessness with which we are assailed in reading South African writing is largely because of the feeling we have in M. Oyono's work that for his Africans there are always other worlds apart from that of the white man in which they are humiliated and destroyed. Mr. Abraham's characters, hemmed in by poverty and by racial laws, have nowhere else to go. . . . In West African writing the theme of oppression appears to have given way to the theme of revolution. Inequalities exist, injustices exist. But the heroes are shown not merely as suffering from them, but as taking arms against them.[4]

By 1959, fairly definite themes could be isolated in the African novel. On the basis of such themes, a classification of these works was made: "the literature of oppression," "the literature of adjustment," and "the literature of exploration," in this last case not geographical exploration, but in the realm of those values in African culture that occupy us here.

These observations were as applicable to Africans writing in French as in English. The contrast was western Africa as against southern and, to a certain extent, the central and eastern parts of the continent. It arose directly from the differing social and political forces of the two regions. If an analogy may be drawn, it can be said that in the "Year of Africa," the South African writers were in the stream of the pre-World War II, Marxist-oriented writers, for whom the subject matter of the novel was the portrayal and combatting of social inequities. Their West African colleagues, on the other hand, were responding to the later neocultural school, that looked to the past in interpreting the present, grounding present experience in the continuities of the past.

[4] M. Talmadge: "Themes in the West African Novel," *West African Review*, Vol. 30, Nos. 383–5 (1959), p. 658.

14

Rediscovery and Integration: The Search for Values

In the changed setting of African life, the search for values can be said to have gained effective momentum only with the attainment of self-government. During most of the time Africans were under foreign control, aboriginal African values, and attempts to balance them against what the Europeans had brought to Africa were rarely discussed. For one thing, the educational system was not calculated to encourage critical analyses of this kind; it was geared to inculcate the positive values in the metropolitan cultures. The cultures out of which the pupils had come were viewed as in process of being superseded by the higher cultures of Europe. There were few Africans prepared to raise questions of comparative worth; and where they did, their audience was minute.

Moreover, as the drive for independence became more intense, all effort was directed toward achieving self-government. Non-political discussion was for the most part confined to criticism of the existing social and economic order, and was therefore thus essentially negative. African revolutionists were no different from revolutionists elsewhere. They were much too preoccupied with immediate issues to speculate about underlying forces. They were so occupied with the next step, indeed, that it was difficult for them to give much thought even to the practical problems of government that would have to be resolved once they reached their goal. The planning of strategy for the political offensive, designed to end colonial rule and expand the areas of African power, left no time to contemplate the relative values of African and non-African cultures, or to raise the questions that were later to be raised. No African political leader or intellectual could remain outside the struggle, to enjoy the luxury of contemplative objectivity while it was going on.

When these questions moved into the foreground of African thought, the answers frequently took polemic form, as reactions to statements about African racial and cultural inferiority. As one African scholar wrote, they were,

> a denial, an angry protest against the inferior and infantile role in which the West had cast the African on the stage of world history and culture. . . . Before the African could come into his own, he had to break out of the shell in which others had sought to contain him; he had to destroy the stereotyped idea of himself as an inferior being.[1]

Theories about the nature of race differences and of racial worth that had lost scientific standing continued to be debated as though they had scientific support, and long-discredited ideas had to be disproved all over again.

Understandably, for the great mass of the African people, the question of values arose primarily as they bore on day-to-day life, and only rarely in their broader compass. Local issues were preeminent; in matters of wider scope they were willing to follow the lead of others. The discussion from which the preceding quotation was taken recognized this: "Protest has been most articulate not among the ordinary people whose lives have been

[1] Ayo Ogunsheye: *"The African Personality: Ideology and Utopia"* (a paper presented to the International Symposium on African Culture, Ibadan, Nigeria, mimeographed, December, 1960), p. 1.

relatively less disturbed by western contacts," but was carried on by "the intellectuals who had been made into second class citizens. . . ." The importance of the attention given by these intellectuals to the problem of values in African culture lay in the fact that, as in all societies, it was they who were to give direction to popular thought. With the paramount political issue resolved, some of them could turn to the philosophical and ethical problems raised by the historic forces of colonialism, and the implications of these problems for the system under which, as free agents, they now lived.

Even formerly, Africans who had remained abroad for extended periods, as students or in other capacities, and had accepted Western values, continued to be Africans. There were two compelling reasons for this. The first, a universal in human experience, was the force of their early cultural conditioning which assured the retention of various deep-seated African patterns of behavior and thought, despite the most intensive exposure to other ways. The other was the factor of physical type, which inevitably entered, even where there was no question of prejudice or of discrimination. What has been termed a high degree of sociological visibility was as inescapable for the African in countries outside Africa as it is for Europeans or Asians in Africa itself.

Being thus set apart, Africans could not fail to be critical of the foreign setting in which they found themselves. An example, perhaps unique in the literature, is to the point:

> The African visitor is sometimes shocked at the behaviour of the English. In conversation, children do not hesitate to contradict the views of their elders. Not only do they not understand the principle that, "Children should be seen and not heard," but they allow their children to talk even more than the parents. It comes as a great shock to an African to hear a child say, "Don't be silly, Daddy!"

As for the English women, they feel they

> must make conversation when they have visitors, and so they talk about all sorts of things, which may sometimes prove a bit boring or irritating to a stranger. But that is the way they are, and they

> feel that they are doing the right thing. We must learn to bear with these differences and recognize that certain of our ways may appear strange to them, too.

The men, to the African,

> appear even more mysterious. It may seem to us that they really play the role of children in the house. They are looked after very carefully and told what they are supposed to like, to eat, and to wear, and to do. They hardly ever talk. . . . Perhaps it is correct to say that the Englishman's home is a castle in which his wife offers him shelter.

Other cultural differences were pointed out; how people in England are always in a hurry, how readily the word "nonsense" is used without meaning.

> But, perhaps, what may seem strangest to us, who respect age, is the English peoples' fear of age. Young women cease to add to their years after a certain age. The old ladies . . . do all sorts of things to make themselves look young. The men are afraid of being considered old. In this culture, age, which ought to be a sign of maturity, and to qualify people for leadership in communal and national affairs, is thought of in terms of senility.

In drawing evaluations of this kind, which in the appropriate terms would describe African reactions to customary behavior in any non-African society, whether in Europe, Asia or America, a reciprocal viewpoint concerning African cultures was bound to emerge in the thinking of Africans. This evaluation of English culture had its parallel in views of African ways.

> . . . These generalizations are similar to some of the statements often made by Englishmen about the African. It is very easy for an Englishman driving through an African village to conclude that women do all the work, and the men sit around all day. We know such an interpretation is not accurate, and so we shouldn't attach too much importance to our first general impressions.

And with prescience, it was stated that:

> Culture contact . . . will, in our lifetime, become the normal state of existence between peoples of all parts of the world. . . . We, who have always been ready to welcome strangers and to learn from them, must now realize the need for a concerted effort di-

rected towards the creation of decent and peaceful human relations.[2]

It was but a step from this line of thought about a non-African society to applying the lessons thus learned to African societies themselves. The assumption by administrators, teachers, missionaries, and writers, repeated over the years, that African ways had at best secondary value, had had their effect. No matter how vigorously Africans denied this, they found the argument, usually drawn from a comparison of African and European technological and economic attainment, difficult to refute. Beyond the emotional negative reaction lay a recognition, even among the most vigorous critics of Euroamerican ways, that the historic processes which had been set in motion could not be halted. When this was acknowledged, it became logical that the old as well as the new had to be freshly viewed, in order that what was desirable in both could be retained.

Gradually a formula to guide reintegration in these selective terms began to be perceptible, even though it was nowhere verbalized as such. Three sources contributed to it. These were, first of all, the aboriginal culture, whose strength proved incontestably greater than had been credited. Then came the impulses emanating from the colonial experience. These derived primarily from western Europe and, secondarily, because of the language factor and the opportunities Africans had realized in the United States and Canada for higher education, from North America. Finally, and last in chronological sequence, came the more heterogeneous series of influences that were derived from Communist eastern Europe and China, and from the Near East and India.

Though we risk oversimplification of the complexities of the integrative process, the influence of each of these three historic forces can be generalized to aid us in our understanding of what was taking place. By and large, it came to be accepted that the major values in African cultures that would be important in shaping the new African nations lay in the fields of human rela-

[2] Robert Gardiner: "Going to England," in *Other People Other Ways*, by Sir Alan Burns and Robert Gardiner (London, 1951), pp. 17–19.

tions and the creative arts. In a sense, this implied a refusal to define "progress" as a matter of technological skills and economic resources alone. It had been on the basis of this definition that the evolutionary theories of the Victorian era had laid claim to European superiority, expressing a point of view that was continued into the postcolonial period in the form of the Marxist doctrine of economic stages.

From western Europe and then from North America, as a second influence, came technological development and vistas of improved standards of living; the drive to extend literacy and broaden the base of a schooled citizenry, and to make use of the resources of scientific medicine. The contributions were, however, by no means all material, for ideals of democratic participation on the political level, and new interpretations of the concepts of human rights and human dignity were also derived from this same source.

The third stream brought reorientations that were essentially political, though economic factors also entered. From Russia came the blueprints for the controlled, single-party state, with the Marxian economic philosophy seen as a prime instrument for mobilizing resources and for maximizing scarce means to attain socially desired ends. Its built-in mechanisms for holding power could not but render it attractive to African leaders. From China came techniques for intensive channeling of the energies of the people into planned production. The experience of Israel in solving ecological and other problems confronting the new African nations, was also influential. India had been in touch with eastern and southern Africa for centuries, but in the present context, India contributed primarily the concepts of passive resistance and later, on the level of international relations, of neutrality in the cold war. From the Arab countries of North Africa came the impetus to extend the political implications of Pan-Africanism by bringing it in line with the idea of Africa as a totality, an invaluable instrument for maneuvering on the world stages.

These were the materials which the Africans had at hand as colonial controls disappeared. Given the eclecticism that lies deep in African patterns of thought, the process became one of selection. In this process, the question of values was critical. In the remaining pages of this book, we will therefore move to examine some of the values that guided the rediscovery of traditional forms and meanings which came to be the integrative element binding the old and the new.

[2]

The historic sense lies deep in the human psyche. The existence of writing has validated this sense as could no other form of communication. Documentation in the form of a scroll, a parchment, an inscription, a book, is independent of the vagaries of memory and, because it is a more trustworthy instrument of transmission than word of mouth, we have tended to neglect the contributions of oral tradition. In a world where knowledge of the past, based on written records, is given a place of high importance in the system of values, the fact that African peoples had not developed writing and were thus, in the restricted sense of the term, unhistorical, came to be of some moment. Psychologically, it meant that Africans were unable to call on a documented past to provide them with the identifications of those who had written histories; legally, they could not support territorial claims by reference to contemporaneous records of their own which, for example in South Africa, would have resolved many disputed claims and counter claims of original tenure.

For a long time, African history was regarded by historians, and by no means exclusively European historians, as the history of the expansion of Europe into Africa. In writing this history, narrowly defined in terms of archival and documentary research, African happenings were incidental to the tale of European occupation and the establishment of the colonial system. What was taking place inside Africa, and to Africans, entered only when there was armed resistance to expansion and control, or where, in the determination of policy, it was necessary to take African reactions into account. African history was thus an extension of the history of Europe. Before the First World War, it has been said, Africa was the safety valve of Europe, in that European tensions were often resolved by a readjustment in the boundaries of African holdings of the colonial powers, which were party to a dispute. Matters of this kind dominated the histories of Africa. Given the assumptions about African cultures that were current, the existence of a recoverable African past, antedating contact with Europe, was dismissed. And though some studies were made of the history of the Islamic northern portion of Subsaharan Africa, these, too, were oriented toward analyzing the impinging rather than the internal forces.

The swing of the pendulum to the other extreme was an understandable African reaction. In earlier pages, we have seen the fixation on the idea that in the process of cultural borrowing incident on contact between African and non-African peoples, Africa was essentially a recipient, and not a donor. With an intellectual climate of interest in origins, and an increasing scholarly and lay interest in Egypt, it followed logically that its role in influencing Subsaharan African developments should seem conclusive. In consequence, if linguistic or cultural resemblances, often farfetched and distorted to fit the theory, could even dimly be discerned, it was taken for granted that all such items must have originated in Egypt.

Initially, contemporary African response to this reading of its past was to rest the pyramid of probability on its apex. Egypt, and by extension the Near East, continued to be the essential point of reference, but whereas in the earlier writings it had been the source of cultural advance, these countries were now declared to have been recipients of this cultural ferment. A powerful variant of this developed from the Pan-African conception of the African future. In this, the fact that Egypt was a part of the continent of Africa, and that its achievements were therefore the achievements of Africans, became a principal tenet, though this was scarcely accepted in Egypt itself. The contributions of Egypt to the human adventure, that is, were not questioned, but rather credited to Africa as a whole. So appealing was this that one African writer charged that the documents which would have demonstrated the validity of this assumption had been suppressed by

European scholars, because of the fear that a knowledge of their contents would undermine colonial controls by revealing the true historic role of Africa.

This, however, was but a short episode in the development of the field of African history. The most important factor in this development was the realization that, despite the absence of indigenous systems of writing, there was not only a tale that must be told, but one that could be recovered, once the problem of developing the requisite methods of attack was solved. The motivation of Africans, given the traditional attitude toward knowledge of the past and in particular the past of the world in which they now moved, was plain. Disciplined by training in the techniques of critical scholarship, they began to produce studies of significance. It must be noted, as well, that the drive to develop a new approach to African history, one that did not make of it an appendage of the history of Europe, was not confined to Africa. It was, in fact, an international scholarly effort, in response to a growing conviction that lack of knowledge of the historical development of African civilizations made for a serious gap in world history.

Gradually a new note began to be heard. Documents that had been available, but had gone unused, telling of events and personalities inside Africa, were re-examined. It was discovered that, even in terms of conventional historical research, far more data were to be had than the community of historians had recognized. From the moldy files of District Offices, from early Gazettes, came information about the beginnings of the colonial period, which students could employ to focus on internal developments in Africa itself, studying problems no longer held to be peripheral. Archival materials in the metropolitan countries began to be more effectively examined and analyzed. Not only were official sources tapped, but also the records of commercial houses and missionary bodies, which were found to have a wealth of data. The search went farther afield; the archives of American missions that from the first days of contact had operated in various parts of the Subsaharan continent, were found to contain documents that threw considerable light on developments there.

Studies to which we have had occasion to refer, such as those of Diké on the commerce of the Niger Delta region during the middle five decades of the nineteenth century, or of Shepperson and Price on the Chilembwe movement of Nyasaland, or M. G. Smith on the government of the Hausa State of Zazzau, or Vansina on the early political organization of the Bakuba of the Congo, are good examples of the kind of new history that was being written.

Precolonial history also began to be documented more and more by the use of Arabic and other non-European sources. The existence of these materials was known, as is evidenced by the publication, in 1932, in Cairo, of a multivolumed work which reproduced large numbers of early Arabic documents on Egypt and Africa in French translation.[3] Documents of this kind began to be reworked, with a focus on events in Africa rather than on the political and military history of Arabic and Moslem invasions. New collections of these were published.[4] Sources in Persian and Chinese bearing on Africa were similarly scrutinized. And for the later history of the Islamic belt south of the Sahara, the work of African scholars began to fill in the picture, principally such as the collaborative studies by Hampata Ba on the Fulani Empire of Macina, or the biography of Tierno Bokar, who from the center of Bandiagara influenced so deeply the development of African Islam during the latter part of the nineteenth century.

The new approach to African history also recognized the need to use all possible materials and techniques in recovering the unwritten past of Subsaharan Africa. To do this it was neces-

[3] Youssef Kamal: *Monumenta Cartogeographica Africae et Aegypti*, 5 Vols. (Cairo and Leyden, 1932).

[4] D. Olderogge: *Zapadnyi Sudan v XV–XIX vv* (Trudy Instituta Etnografii, Novaia seriia, t. LIII, Akademiia Nauk SSSR), *The Western Sudan in the XV–XIX Centuries* (Contributions of the Institute of Ethnography, n.s., Vol. LIII, USSR Academy of Sciences, Moscow and Leningrad, 1960); L. E. Kubbel and V. V. Matveev: *Drevnie i Srednevekovye Istochniki po Etnografii i Istorii Narodov Afriki Iuzhnee Sakhary—Arabskie Istochniki VII–X Vekov* (*Ancient and Mediaeval Sources for the Ethnography and History of the African Peoples South of the Sahara; Arab Sources, VII–X Centuries*) (Moscow and Leningrad, 1960).

sary to supplement and extend the conventional methods of historical study. Oral tradition and archaeological findings began to be given serious attention. Comparative studies of the distribution of particular aspects of the aboriginal cultures; of such stable physical characteristics as blood types; and of historical linguistics, were called on to trace possible relationships between peoples. The contents of the *Journal of African History* reflected this breadth of approach; its contributions included papers of a kind not common to other historical journals. Thus, in a single number appeared a discussion of the economic prehistory of Africa, a study of the Somali conquest of the East Horn from the twelfth century onward, and an analysis of the archaeology of Ife, Nigeria, to name but three. To this approach the name of ethnohistory was given.

This was not achieved without extended discussions of the problems of method. Historians have long recognized documentary materials are of uneven reliability, and have developed criteria for determining the value of a given document as an historic source. But where writing was absent, the questions that arose had to do with the value of different kinds of materials whose testing involved new criteria—those of the archaeologist, of the ethnologist, of the student of myth and oral tradition. The problem was a knotty one. It involved the need for specialists to step outside their specialty, and collaborate with other specialists in utilizing and, where necessary, devising techniques of investigation bearing on a common problem. Above all, it meant adjusting to a new concept of historical probability when research was extended beyond the scope of "hard" documentary materials and archaeological artifacts.[5]

One of the most controversial aspects of the movement to recover the African past had to do with the value of oral tradition. "Euhemerism," as the attribution of historical validity to unwritten accounts is called, after the Greek philosopher Euhemerus who accepted myth as an explanation of historical events, had in its crude form been rejected. Defining history as "the recital in

[5] Cf. Melville J. Herskovits: "Anthropology and Africa—a Wider Perspective," *Africa*, Vol. 29 (1959), *passim*.

chronological sequences of events that are known to have occurred," Raglan and others flatly denied the ability of any nonliterate people to give a credible account of any happening farther removed than one hundred and fifty years from the time it was recounted. "Forms of knowledge which depend, even in part, upon written record, can have for the savage no existence at all." The events in his past, "are, in fact, completely lost." [6] Yet such an ethnohistorical study as that made among the Gwambe of Mozambique, in which traditional statements of migration, given orally, were found to be in accord with those in sixteenth century Portuguese documents,[7] demonstrated how dangerous it is to deny categorically any validity to unwritten history.

Tests of this kind and others opened the way for a reappraisal of verbal history. Vansina laid down certain principles for this new kind of historiography. In studying oral tradition, its cultural context must be thoroughly understood. Where specialists in reciting accounts of the past were to be found, textual renditions were to be gathered from them; if not, as many variants as possible were to be obtained so that one could be checked against another. The "human relationship" in which tradition was recorded could not be taken for granted; leading questions were to be avoided. Once the texts had been gathered, they had to be examined from several points of view. The difference between "fixed" texts, learned by rote, and "free" texts, where the wording was left to the tellers, was to be given careful consideration. The mutual interdependence of texts was to be studied, and obscurities in the recorded versions due to archaic usages and figures of speech clarified. The reliability of the originator and teller of an episode was to be assessed, and judgments of value allowed for. Only then, "when the materials have been studied, one can write the history of a culture." [8]

[6] Lord F. R. S. Raglan: *The Hero, a Study in Tradition, Myth and Drama* (London, 1936), pp. 2, 6.

[7] Edward Fuller: "Ethnohistory in the Study of Culture Change in Southwest Africa," in *Continuity and Change in African Culture* (W. R. Bascom and M. J. Herskovits, editors, Chicago, 1959), *passim.*

[8] J. Vansina: "Recording the Oral History of the Bakuba—I. Methods, II. Results," *Journal of African History,* Vol. I (1960), pp. 46–62.

However, it was not only problems of method that had to be resolved. As Africans became conscious of the importance of recovering their historic past, and alert to the political uses to which it could be put, they came to lay stress on the traditions of that past which, in the period before writing was introduced, was accepted as history by the members of each particular group. A body of oral tradition thus became "official" history. This posed a particularly vexing problem for Africans who, trained in historiography, were expected to shape their accounts in accordance with sanctioned versions of the past.

Departure from recognized scholarly procedures in preparing histories of African societies, a practice by no means confined to Africans, became less the exception as the impact of the newer forms of historical research became felt. There was a countervailing factor involved, as well. With the general recognition of the African historical past, and of the importance of knowing that past, the new ethnohistorians no longer had to combat the denial of African history. Africans were thus freed, psychologically, to approach the study of their own history with the objectivity of any trained historian, and to collaborate with their fellow scholars in related disciplines, and outside of Africa, in the full tradition of international scholarship.

The establishment of the field of African history as part of world history was a major transitional factor in the reshaping and reintegration of the developing system of values in Africa under change.

[3]

Though no attempt was made to define specifically the indigenous values it had become important to retain, they can be deduced from expressions of African opinion throughout the Subsaharan continent. These values lay essentially in the field of human relations. African intellectuals fully recognized that their indigenous economic systems and their technology would not permit them or their children a full participation in the world economy. Acceptance of the fact that African technologies and modes of production and exchange were insufficient did not give rise to the negative reactions that spring from challenge. They were not marked by the emotional "loading" called forth by foreign evaluation of the intangibles of these cultures, such as their systems of kinship or morality.

There is another point to be considered here. Technological and economic change, or "development" as it came to be called, could be put to objective tests of comparative accomplishment. In the instance of technology, it was self-evident that, as the Africans had seen repeatedly demonstrated, a machine could accomplish much more, with the expenditure of far less energy, than could mere man power. Electricity provided better and, in the long run, cheaper light than oil lamps. Scientific medicine, whether curative or preventive, and a knowledge of nutrition, could prolong life and prevent suffering, ease child birth and lower the rate of infant mortality. Economic development, defined in terms of increased production and more effective distribution, could be measured statistically; and Africans, drawn into a system of thought where statistical data are given high value, were as susceptible as any others to their appeal.

In the nontechnical, noneconomic aspects of their new life, however, there were no such criteria. Africans, as they came to be better acquainted with the cultures of those who ruled them, and as they fanned out over the rest of the world, began to sense the variety of values among different peoples, and the many ways in which these values could be expressed. They began to ask why their own traditional values were being placed on a lower level than these others. And once the question had been raised, it answered itself. One machine can be compared to another because the end toward which both are employed—the value in each—is measurable. If one of them is faster, or produces a better finished product at a lower cost, it is the better machine. But to compare family systems, or ethical principles, or political organizations, or art, or music in this manner, is impossible, because we are here dealing with intangible values and ends about which there is no cross-cultural consensus.

This was at once a source of strength and of doubt to Africans. It was a source of strength because affirmation of these intangible values could not be challenged except on the grounds of their difference from other systems. If the validity of criteria necessarily drawn from the cultural conditioning of those who advanced them was not admitted, any presumably objective proofs fell to the ground. The arguments advanced for or against plural marriage, pouring libations, or an ancestral cult, are all in this category.

Doubts arose, on the other hand, as a result of the long years during which, under colonial rule, criteria of worth set in European capitals had been inculcated in the Africans, and their aboriginal values belittled by arguments that carried conviction because of the technological and economic strength of those who advanced them. Political leaders, thoroughly schooled in non-African ideologies and techniques of organization, had keyed their objectives to economic and technological advancement in terms of the twentieth century industrialized state. Consequently, ambivalences arose from the variance between these aims and many of the values toward which early orientation and the need for cultural self-esteem propelled them. The result, as one African put it, was that

> We see the peoples of independent African states for the most part tormented by a basic cultural discomfort: they have not . . . recovered the spiritual basis for re-establishing their unsettled societies, they have not recovered their cultural independence.[9]

Values in aboriginal African society must be inferred from African behavior, African social institutions, African beliefs. These values are never systematically formulated. They are most explicit in the proverbs and moralizing tales, which reveal a system of ethical principles, once the hidden meaning of all aphorisms, and the patterns of their use, are analyzed in cultural context. In some societies the values found in these forms have a high degree of complexity, and cover approved behavior in many dif-

[9] Harris Memel Foté: *Rapport sur la Civilisation Animiste* (a paper presented to the Colloquium on "The Contributions of Animism, Islam and Christianity to the Cultural Expression of the African Personality" (Abidjan, Ivory Coast, April 5–12, 1961) mimeographed, p. 2.

ferent kinds of situations. An instance of this is found in the concept of *ubgenge* of the Barundi of Ruanda-Urundi. It is described as "a variation on the idea of intelligence," and represents the value laid on ability to think clearly and argue cogently—to be astute, to be able "to get oneself out of a bad situation," or, in the conjugal setting, to be a woman who "knows how to escape the anger of her husband."[1]

Certain African values began to be repeatedly formulated in the discussions of Africans concerned with developing a cultural ideology for the new African nations. Two of these could be heard, or read, more often than others. One referred to the traditional interdependence of members of a kinship grouping, and the rights and obligations involved—a pattern of relationships that provided security for the individual, and a stable base for society. The other was respect for one's elders, who had knowledge based on experience. Grouped with these we find the value of cooperative effort.

Another aspect of African behavior, implicit in traditional narrative and reinforced by the experience of conquest, colonial or indigenous, was the principle of circumspection in dealing with all strangers and superiors. It was important to listen with passive deference, to disclose as little as possible when questioned, to reach decisions through discussion and consultation with one's own people, to manifest an outer docility while biding one's time for the moment of redress—all that which goes into the making of psychological resilience. The new esteem the educated Africans came to hold for aboriginal graphic and plastic arts, music, and the dance, and the new regard for aspects of African religion, such as respect for the elders, institutionalized as the ancestral cult, has already been discussed. All these must be viewed as affirmations of a basic metaphysic, of which the fundamental principle is the continuity of experience, under which the past, the present, and the future are conceived to be a unified whole.

Some of the values derived from contact with the outer world conflicted with these. The new values placed on a pecuni-

[1] Ethel M. Albert: "Une Étude de Valeurs en Ruandi," *Cahiers d'Études Africaines,* Vol. II (1960), p. 158.

ary economy, on practically all aspects of technological change, on many kinds of non-African material goods, were rarely challenged. Indeed, one of the induced values that came to be accepted almost without dissent in these sectors of culture was change as an end in itself. Roads, bridges, motor cars, multistoried buildings, power dams, were its more dramatic manifestations. In the same category was the value laid on literacy. The value of recognition as free and independent nations in international dealings was similarly accepted.

Of new values in conflict with the old, we find, not unexpectedly, a good many in the area of internal political organization. African leaders, faced with the challenge of economic growth and the need to establish higher living standards, began to re-examine traditional communal patterns with the objective of shaping them to fit the requirements of a new economic order. This re-examination occurred both where patterns of individual effort had become established, and where socialistically oriented plans sought to use traditional communalism as an instrument to make the new system function. The values laid on age and hereditary status came into conflict with systems of political democracy no less than those of strict one-party control. Indeed, herein lay the crux of the argument over the nature of "African democracy." Related to this was the debate over the question of tribalism and the role of the chief, a debate that arose out of the values ascribed to traditional prerogatives and defined lines of authority, as against the concept of the centrally governed state; a debate, that on a regional or continental scale, had as its major theme the various forms of Pan-Africanism.

[4]

The need to re-establish the position of African culture by affirming its particular values was most vigorously expressed in the concepts of *négritude* and of "the African personality." Following independence, these concepts were transmuted from a rallying cry for African independence to a symbol of African worth. They marshaled the forces toward the integrations that came to be a dominant objective of African thought.

To understand the importance of this aspect of the search for new values, especially as it concerns the concept of *négritude,* we must again turn to the pre-independence period. Its most precise expressions were to be found in statements of the *Présence Africaine* group and of the Society for African Culture, which was formed following the First Conference of Negro Writers and Artists in 1956. One statement of their objectives read:

> Since 1941, in Paris, Africans, Madgascans and West Indians have been preoccupied with affirming the "presence" or ethos of the black communities of the world, of defending the originality of their way of life and the dignity of their cultures. . . . They knew that the problem was not only that of assuring between black and white the theoretical equality of individuals. . . . They knew it concerned a fundamental recasting of the structures of European civilization and African life, and the links which bind us should spring from the cultural level. In short, it involved an emergence of an African personality from the accretion of Western culture, which colonization has thrown into disequilibrium and servitude.[2]

A further expression of *négritude* appeared in the call issued for the Second Conference of Negro Writers and Artists, held in Rome in 1959, explaining the aims of its organizing body, the Society of African Culture. "This association comprises men of the Negro world," it stated, "and its mission is to organize our cultural [*sic:* relations, activities?] in such a way that a) our culture patterns be first interpreted by ourselves, b) that they express both our inner life and the universal vocation of our cultures." The idea that "there can be a nation without a culture of its own" was rejected, and as for its task, the agenda of the Conference was to study "1) the foundation of our culture and its chances of achieving unity and solidarity, 2) the tasks and responsibilities of each discipline and art."[3]

One of the founders of the doctrine, the poet Léopold Sedar

[2] John A. Davis (editor): *Africa Seen By American Negroes* (Paris, 1958), p. 1 of *Supplement* at end of volume.

[3] Ibid., final two pages of *Supplement.*

Senghor, who became President of the Republic of Senegal, defined the concept as a "positive affirmation of the values in African culture."[4] Students of African affairs, however, were disquieted by the overtones in the idea of *négritude,* that there is a quality of creativity and response peculiar to the Negro *race.* They found it difficult to forget the racisms of Europe, with their ascription of cultural superiority and unique cultural aptitudes, which culminated in the mystical Nazi doctrines of the *Herrenvolk.* Proponents of *négritude* rejected the analogy. They asserted that the racial factor, though present, carried no implication of superiority, but only laid stress on the validity of the cultural contribution of Negro peoples, that had for so long not only gone without appreciation, but had been actively disparaged by the rest of the world. Again, according to Senghor, the concept was not racist, but represented insistence on recognition of values that "must be accepted if Europe is to retain the good will of Africans."

The psychological reasons for this reaction were not difficult to understand, but a shift from compensatory emphasis on the positive values in African cultures to claims based on racial endowment seemed disturbingly easy to make. This was perhaps why those who defined the term "racism" as European attitudes toward non-Europeans saw *négritude* as "counter-racism." There was some danger of its developing into a rejection of all that was not African, though as far as those who originally espoused it were concerned, there was little likelihood of their drifting into a position which was the more repugnant to them because of what they had suffered from it.

In its political aspects, *négritude* could be related to the concept of "the African personality," favored by those who had shared the experiences of the Pan-African Congresses. As far as can be determined, the phrase "African personality" originated with President Kwame Nkrumah, of Ghana, but it was never defined by its originator to the degree that has made it possible for us to study the meaning of the concept *négritude.* Both had

[4] Melville J. Herskovits: *Notes on African Field Research,* p. 60/D20.

broad applicability, but the concept of an African personality applied to African states was developed after Ghana had attained self-government, and thus did not function in the development of nationalism in British West Africa. In contrast, *négritude* embraced all who were of African descent, wherever they might live, and its political implications were but a part of its overall humanistic approach.

In retrospect, it is easy to see how, under the pressure of the need to re-establish the validity of African cultures, and of integrating the old with the new, the two concepts should have come together. By 1961, Alioune Diop, in discussing the relation between them, was stressing the fact that *négritude* was a term devised in Paris by those who wished to re-establish the dignity of African culture; that "the African personality" emphasized the validity of the African position in the international scene. Both, he felt, were attempts to seek recognition for the universal values in African cultures, to stress the "originality and dignity" of what African peoples had achieved. In the same discussion, a Ghanaian expressed his conception of the "African personality" as "a symbol of the new and highly significant fact that the Africans have come into their own at home and have emerged as a factor to be reckoned with on the world stage." To have "more than a symbolic content," certain broad lines of implementing the concept must be found. And in this "the values of traditional African societies" could figure, as this image of the African was more widely projected.[5]

[5]

In our analysis of the various aspects of contemporary Africa, the balance of our discussion has swung between continuity and change. The simultaneous presence of the two, never in equilibrium, we found to be nothing new in the African experi-

[5] C. G. Baeta: "Les Fondements Éthiques et Spirituels de l'Humanisme Animiste" (a paper read at the Colloquium on "The Contributions of Animism, Islam and Christianity to the Cultural Expression of the African Personality," Abidjan, Ivory Coast, April 5–12, 1961) mimeographed, p. 7.

ence. Africa had had a consistent history of adjustment to elements introduced from outside. African societies had been neither as static prior to European contact as they were thought to have been, nor as hospitable to the cultures of their colonial rulers as at one time they were assumed to be.

The application of the methods and concepts of the scientific analysis of cultural dynamics to the problem of change in Subsaharan Africa revealed complexities of an order not often recognized. This is not to say that certain kinds of complexities had gone unobserved. Differences in indigenous African cultures were pointed out by early travelers, and their observations were confirmed by later intensive and disciplined study. Similarly inescapable were the complexities in the vast range of linguistic expression. Students of colonial policy and administration were obliged to deal with problems arising out of differences in the contact situation. Almost without exception, research findings showed how dissimilarities in the policies of the colonial powers, as well as the aboriginal linguistic and cultural differences, distinctively shaped the impact of each power on the peoples it ruled.

There was little overview, however, to compensate for the particularist findings that came to mark analyses of African affairs. Common features that were clearly discernible, once one moved across political boundaries and considered Africa in terms of its own cultural and historical realities, were held in the background or ignored. Similarities in the aboriginal cultures could be perceived on various levels—in terms of cultural areas, or of the twofold division of the African subcontinent on the basis of ecological setting and economic organization, or of resemblances throughout the subcontinent. Despite the differences in types of innovation from the several European cultures brought to Africa, and variations in colonial policy, certain identities in African response are distinguishable. These ranged from the accelerating African acceptance of the wholly additive elements not in conflict with antecedent custom, such as the introduction and spread of literacy, or scientific medicine, through substitutive adjustments in the new political structures or in the systems of belief, to deeprooted attitudes making for the retention of basic food patterns, or aspects of the social structures, or indigenous values.

African cultures, in other words, were fed by inner resources which enabled them to maintain their strength under the constraints of colonial control and under domination by a permanently resident ethnic minority. Even where African societies were under greatest pressure, traditional ways persisted in forms and to a degree that went largely unrecognized. The sources of this strength derived from the nature of the cultures themselves, especially their institutionalized mechanisms of psychological resilience. The studied deference toward elders and officialdom was basic in ordering behavior on all levels. Whether in personal relations or politics, indirection in stating and holding to objectives, the high value placed on discretion in act and on diplomatic phrasing in statement, the use of aphorism and oblique reference to make a point in an argument were but a few of the more widespread methods for cultural self-preservation.

This complex of values had stood the Africans in good stead as they adjusted to the internal or external innovations to which they had been exposed through the centuries. Under the forced draft of change in the colonial period, such methods were invaluable for accommodation to the imposed alien institutions and for functioning under the new controls. More than this, they allowed a person to retain his self-respect even when subjected to indignities, for in his own household, the slave was master, and with a turn of the wheel of fortune he might take over a role of initiative and command. Roles, that is, were fluid and flexible; no situation was incapable of change.

One of the unities which marked the dynamics of the colonial period was the mode of African reaction to European culture and, by extension, to Europeans. This falls into three fairly well-defined stages that—though overlapping at any given moment in Subsaharan Africa as a whole—represent a consistent pattern for any specific group or any single territory.

The first stage followed on initial contact, and continued well into the time when Europeans assumed full political control, whether by the conclusion of treaties between native rulers and the representatives of the incoming power, or through the imposition of rule by force. Resistance was frequently encountered, and in some instances was prolonged, but except in the populous kingdoms with centralized governments and organized armies, there was no intensive fighting. Non-cooperation was resorted to instead. Thus, in the case of the Tiv of Nigeria, plans made about 1900 to run a telegraph line through their country had to be altered because they "were 'recalcitrant,' refused to 'submit' and supply labour, and because they stole the wire to make jewelry." It was ten years before they were brought under British control.[6]

In this first stage, the European was looked upon as a being who controlled unfathomed power, remote from those whose destinies he ruled. He was to be listened to carefully, studied, and emulated insofar as comprehension of his ways, and ability to tap his resources, permitted. Any doubts the Africans might have had about his ways were well concealed. These were the days of the isolated district officer, the remote mission station. The strangers were counselors, judges and, where friendship could cross the deep gulf of status and cultural differences, friends. Where possible, good relations with these strangers were assiduously cultivated, for it was they who dealt with the forces of the new world that had come to the African.

With continued contact, and the close observation under which the European lived—unaware as he seemed of it—he was found to have frailties Africans recognized among themselves, and some which were new to them. Africans learned early of the rivalries and jealousies among Europeans, and of wars between European nations, in which Africans were called on to aid. The doctrines of those who came to preach a new truth were not always in harmony, and they made manifest their rivalries in contesting for the allegiance of the Africans they sought to convert. Africans learned about the machines that aided the Europeans in conquering time and distance. They discovered that they, too,

[6] Paul and Laura Bohannan: *Three Source Notebooks in Tiv Ethnography* (Human Relations Area Files, New Haven, Connecticut, 1956), p. 26.

could operate and repair these machines. The new skills of reading and writing widened their horizons, and as opportunities to travel brought them firsthand experience with the outer world, they learned that what had happened to them was not unique. Questions began to be raised concerning their present position and their future status.[7]

Thus far the path trod by all African peoples is clearly to be seen. But from here several paths lay open before them. It was at this later point of better acquaintance with the culture of the rulers that evaluation, and later, action, entered. Evaluation, positive or negative, was accelerated by the increasing freedom of choice which accompanied successive moves toward self-government. The elements of the alien cultures that were accepted, or the degree to which they were continued as reinterpretations, differed with time and place, depending on the extent to which the Africans had access to the culture of the rulers, the kind of relations between rulers and ruled, and the degree of identification with the rulers.

There was almost nowhere a complete retention of earlier custom, not even in remote outposts. Even where rejection took the form of violence, as in the Mau Mau of Kenya, the aboriginal practices that were presumably reinstated deviated greatly from the actuality of earlier days. At the other extreme, it was equally rare to find complete acceptance of what had been introduced. Invariably, probing beneath the surface, one would find some aspect of an innovation, whether in its form, its use, its meaning, or its value, which differentiated it from the form in which it had come from abroad.

Read has outlined the similar course of the educational aspect of African-European contact. The first stage "was marked by conservatism among the Africans toward this new form of education." Next came "a gradual acceptance . . . of some of the new ideas and new ways of living to which they were introduced through the schools." Following this was "the rejection

[7] Melville J. Herskovits: "Some Contemporary Developments in Subsaharan Africa," in *Africa in the Modern World* (Calvin W. Stillman, editor, Chicago, 1955), pp. 277–82.

. . . of certain traditional ideas and former ways of living." It was in this third stage that, as one Christian chief put it, "The white teachers taught us to despise our past." In time, educational opportunities came to be "fully accepted by the Africans." This achieved, there was "a partial reinstatement" in the curriculum "of certain elements in the traditional culture," and this set the stage for the final development, when use was made "of the new selection by Africans of elements . . . which they wished to incorporate in their educational system." [8]

To be sure, the process is highly complex, and we should not underrate the difficulties in seeking to understand it. Considerations of personality and position enter, and we must recognize that even within a small community, considerable variation in degree of adjustment can be found. Epstein, in his study of the dialect called *CiCopperbelti* in the urban centers of Northern Rhodesia, stressed the role of "evaluations in terms of prestige" in its formation. Though prestige was assigned on the basis of "the European way of life," this was defined by "a very complex process of selection." The concept would have to include,

> the behavior of Europeans living on the Copperbelt as it is perceived by Africans, patterns of behavior as they are observed in Hollywood films . . . , and even aspects of the life of American Negroes as it is transmitted through popular African magazines published in South Africa.

Given prestige as a value, a variety of factors, in conferring prestige, promoted "a continuous and unremitting struggle in which different and increasingly refined criteria" could be "variously invoked to advance one's claim to status," and led to "a bewildering assortment of rivalries, allegiances, and cross-cutting ties both within and between groups." [9]

The facts about African response to culture contact make it

[8] Margaret Read: "Cultural Contacts in Education," *Proceedings*, British Association for the Advancement of Science, Edinburgh meetings (1951), pp. 366–8.

[9] A. L. Epstein: "Linguistic Innovation and Culture on the Copperbelt, Northern Rhodesia," *Southwestern Journal of Anthropology*, Vol. 15 (1959), pp. 252–3.

difficult to understand how the idea of the African as a passive recipient of European culture could have gained such wide currency. Yet, as we have seen, this point of view was held almost as an article of faith by perhaps a majority of non-Africans who lived and worked in Africa, and was the stated objective of early colonial policy. It provided the ideological base for the nineteenth century concepts of the white man's burden and the *mission civilisatrice*. To an unrecognized extent, it was also implicit in the interpretation of the Marxist doctrine of social progress as relevant to the African scene. Since this doctrine predicates a series of predetermined evolutionary stages through which all societies must pass, the Africans, whose cultures are from the Marxist point of view on a "primitive" or "feudal" level, must move through this series of stages to reach the higher status of the industrialized communist states.

To positions such as these, as to the one which seeks a return to pre-European ways, cultural theory has long provided an essential corrective. Inasmuch as no society is without its own way of life, it never presents a clean slate on which new experience can be written at will. Culture is learned behavior; there is no exclusive franchise for cultural learning. Any people, given the opportunity and motivation, can learn the ways of any other, and can not only grasp but also internalize its values. To be sure, the early experiences of the individual are not erased by learning a new culture. The changes in the traditional customs of a people who experience contact are the end result of what they take over, as this is projected against their earlier patterns. Hence this end result is never identical with the model. It was sheer fantasy on the part of those Africans—a relatively small number, it is true—who believed that they could recapture the "golden age" of their culture which preceded European contact. It was no less fantasy for Europeans—or for that matter, some Africans—to believe that Africans would become European in their thoughts and acts, because African cultures were eroding to their eventual complete disappearance.

African cultural change has been selective. The results of the process of exercising choice, represented in the greater or lesser number of European elements found in a given African setting, and the forms they have taken in this setting, must in each case be regarded as reflecting the historic situation in which this process occurred. What we find not only depends on the opportunity various peoples had to become acquainted with European culture, but also on the degree of intransigeance or flexibility with which they faced new cultural experiences. The Masai of Tanganyika and Kenya provided a classical example of cultural rigidity. A comparable group from the same general area were the Pakot, whose resistance to change was explained by reference to the fact that, "Their herding life provides all they need and all they want, and they have found almost nothing in Euroamerican culture that will entice them to abandon their old ways." [1] This contrasts with the receptivity to innovation among the Nigerian Ibo, whose culture provided "alternatives which the individual must decide upon in terms of his own skill and knowledge," so that "he rapidly develops experience in making decisions in which he must estimate his own position and opportunities for success." Since

> culture contact by its very nature introduces new cultural alternatives, . . . the Ibo—traditionally accustomed to thinking, acting, and making decisions in terms of a range of alternatives—are more at home in the culture contact situation than members of other societies with different orientations.[2]

Between these two extremes lay the great range of historic possibilities. Yet the result was in no case a series of cultural mosaics. Especially for the Africans who were born into the changing scene, African and European elements in combination made up their cultural world. In other words, what they learned in their formative years, even though this derived from more than one stream of tradition, was for them a unified tradition. Only the

[1] Harold K. Schneider: "Pakot Resistance to Change," in *Continuity and Change in African Cultures* (W. R. Bascom and M. J. Herskovits, editors, Chicago, 1959), p. 160.

[2] Simon Ottenberg: "Ibo Receptivity to Change," in *Continuity and Change in African Cultures* (W. R. Bascom and M. J. Herskovits, editors, Chicago, 1959), pp. 138–9.

scholar is concerned with historical processes and derivations. Africans, like all human beings, take their cultural setting for granted, living their lives within a framework of accepted values and expectations. This is why any analysis of derivations and processes must, in focusing on change, keep in perspective the factor of cultural integration. Particularly in understanding Africa, both continuity and change must be given full place if we are to grasp the new reality in all its fresh meaning.

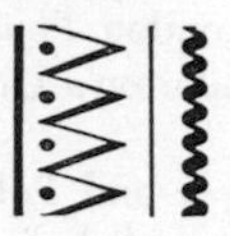

Bibliography

Abdi, Ali, 1961: "Kenya Somalis Put Their Case." *East Africa and Rhodesia,* Vol. 37, No. 1892, p. 538.

Achebe, Chinua, 1958: *Things Fall Apart.* London.

Acquah, Ioné, 1958: *Accra Survey . . . 1953–1956.* London.

Ade Ajaye, J. F., 1958: review of C. P. Groves, "Christianity in Africa," Vol. IV. *West Africa,* No. 2160, 6 Sept., p. 853.

Albert, Ethel M., 1960: "Une Étude de Valeurs en Ruandi." *Cahiers d'Études Africaines,* Vol. II, pp. 148–160.

Alberto, Manoel Simões, 1956: "Populações nativas do Sul do Save, distrito de Lourenço Marques. I. Os Ronga do Maputo." *Boletim Sociedade de Estudos de Moçambique,* Vol. 26, No. 101, pp. 81–108 (abstracted in *African Abstracts,* Vol. 10, July, 1959, No. 420, p. 134.

Alimen, H., 1955: *Préhistoire de l'Afrique* (English translation, "The Prehistory of Africa," A. H. Broderick, tr., London, 1957). Paris.

All Africa People's Conference, 1959: *News Bulletin,* Vol. 1, Nos. 1–7. Accra.

Ames, David W., 1953: *Plural Marriage among the Wolof in the Gambia.* Ph. D. Dissertation, Northwestern University (microfilmed), Evanston, Illinois.

—— 1958: "The Dual Function of the 'Little People' of the Forest in the Lives of the Wolof." *Journal of American Folklore,* Vol. 71, pp. 23–26.

Anderson, Edgar, 1954: *Plants, Man and Life.* London.

André, Capitaine P.-J., 1924: *L' Islam Noire.* Paris.

Anonymous, 1956: *Union Minière du Haut Katanga,* 1906–56. Brussels.

—— 1957: *SABRA Nuusbrief,* July–Aug., No. 25.

Anonymous, 1957: "Nyasaland African Drivers Beaten . . . in Portuguese Territory." London *Times*, Sept. 14.

—— 1957: "Standerton's Ordeal." *Johannesburg Sunday Express*, July 21, pp. 4, 7.

—— 1958: "Prayer and Politics." *West Africa*, No. 2128, Jan. 25, p. 75.

—— 1958: "Overseas Scholars." *Ghana Today*, Vol. 2, No. 18, p. 7.

—— 1958: "Mr. Mboya Asks for More." *The Central African Examiner*, Vol. 1, No. 25, pp. 16–18.

—— 1959: "Blunderbuss." London *Times*, Jan. 14, p. 9.

—— 1959: "Statistics of University Enrollment." *Belgian Congo 59*, Monthly Information Bulletin, No. 10, Oct., pp. 12–3.

—— 1959: "Race Relations and Industry." *West Africa*, No. 2220, Dec. 19, p. 1114.

—— 1959: "Carver in Miniature." *West African Review*, Vol. 30, No. 377, pp. 106–7.

—— 1960: "Warm Greeting for Mr. Macmillan." London *Times*, Jan. 16, p. 7.

Apter, David, 1955: *The Gold Coast in Transition*. Princeton.

Arkell, A. J., 1955: *A History of the Sudan, from the Earliest Times to 1821*. London.

Ashton, Hugh, 1952: *The Basuto*. London.

Aupiais, F., 1938: *Le Missionaire*. Paris.

Awolowo, Obafemi, 1960: *Awo, the Autobiography of Chief Obafemi Awolowo*. Cambridge (England).

Ayorinde, J. H., 1957: *Nigerian Radio Times*, Vol. 4, No. 5.

Azikiwe, Nnamde, 1942: *Land Tenure in Northern Nigeria*. Lagos.

—— 1961: *Zik, a Selection from the Speeches of Nnamde Azikiwe*. Cambridge (England).

Ba, Amadou Hampate and J. Daget, 1955: *L'Empire Peulh du Macina, I (1818–53)*, Études Soudanaises, No. 3.

Ba, Amadou Hampate and Cordaire, Marcel, 1957(?): *Tierno Bokar, le Sage de Bandiagara*. Paris.

Baeck, L., 1957: "Étude socio-économique du centre extra-coutumier *d'Usumbura*." *Mémoires*, Académie Royale des Sciences Coloniales, Vol. 6, fasc. 5. Brussels.

Baeta, C. G., 1961: "Les Fondements Éthiques et Spirituels de l'Humanisme Animiste" (a paper read at the Colloquium on, "The Contributions of Animism, Islam and Christianity to the Cultural Expression of the African Personality," Abidjan, Ivory Coast, April 5–12, 1961). Mimeographed.

Balandier, Georges, 1954: "Contribution à l'Étude des Nationalismes en Afrique Noire." *Zaïre*, Vol. 8, pp. 379–89.

—— 1955: *Sociologie des Brazzaville Noires* (Cahiers de la Fondation Nationale des Sciences Politiques, No. 67). Paris.

Banjo, S. A., 1953: *A West African Teacher's Handbook*. London.

Banton, Michael, 1957: *West African City, a Study of Tribal Life in Freetown.* London, Ibadan, Accra.

Barendsen, G. W., Deevey, E. S. and Gralenski, L. J., 1957: "Yale Natural Radiocarbon Measurements III." *Science,* Vol. 126, pp. 908–19.

Bascom, W. R., 1953: "African Culture and the Missionary." *Civilisations,* Vol. 3, pp. 491–504.

—— 1955: "Urbanization among the Yoruba." *American Journal of Sociology,* Vol. 60, pp. 446–54.

—— 1957: "Modern African Figurines, Satirical or Just Stylistic?" *Lore* (Milwaukee Public Museum), Vol. 7, pp. 118–126.

—— 1959: "Urbanism as a Traditional African Pattern." *The Sociological Review,* Vol. 7, pp. 29–43.

Bascom, W. R. and Herskovits, M. J. (eds.), 1958: *Continuity and Change in African Cultures.* Chicago.

Bauer, P. T., 1954: *West African Trade.* Cambridge (England).

Bauer, P. T. and Yamey, B. S., 1957: *The Economics of Under-developed Countries.* Cambridge (England).

Baumann, A. and Westermann, D., 1940: *Völkerkunde von Afrika* (translated as "Les Peuples et les Civilisations de l' Afrique," Paris, 1948), Berlin.

Baxter, P. T. W. and Butt, Audrey, 1953: *The Azande and Related Peoples of the Anglo-Egyptian Sudan and Belgian Congo* (Ethnographic Survey of Africa; East Central Africa, Part IX). London.

Belgian Ministry of Colonies, 1949: *Plan Décennal pour le Developpement Économique et Social du Congo Belge.* Brussels.

Belgium, Chambre des Representants, 1959: *Rapport* (on events in Leopoldville in January, 1959), Session 1958–9, 28 March. Brussels.

Bingle, E. J., 1952: "The World Mission of the Church—a Survey," in *World Christian Handbook, 1952 ed.* (E. J. Bingle and Kenneth G. Grubb, eds.). London.

Bingle, E. J. and Grubb, Kenneth G. (eds.), 1952: *World Christian Handbook, 1952 ed.* London.

Blanchet, André, 1958: "Un envoyé du gouvernement français met la Guinée devant les consequences de sa 'secession.'" *Le Monde,* Vol. 15, No. 4256, Sept. 30, p. 1.

—— 1960: "Les nationalismes africaines frustrés d'une révolution?" *Preuves,* No. 112 (June), pp. 40–47.

Bliss, Edwin Munsell, 1897: *A Concise History of Missions.* New York.

Bloom, Harry, 1955: *Episode in the Transvaal* (published in London, 1956, under the title "Episode"). New York.

Boettger, Caesar R., 1958: *Die Haustiere Afrikas.* Jena.

Bohannon, Laura and Paul, 1953: *The Tiv of Central Nigeria* (Ethnographic Survey of Africa, Western Africa, Part VIII). London.

Bohannon, Paul and Laura, 1956: *Three Source Notebooks in Tiv Ethnography* (2 vols.). New Haven.

Bosman, William, 1721: *A New and Accurate Description of the Coast of Guinea. . . .* (second ed.). London.
Bovill, E. W., 1933: *Caravans of the Old Sahara, an Introduction to The History of the Western Sudan.* London.
—— 1958: *The Golden Trade of the Moors.* London.
Buell, Raymond Leslie, 1928: *The Native Problem in Africa* (2 vols.). New York.
Busia, K. A., 1950: *Report on a Social Survey of Sekondi-Takoradi.* London and Accra.
—— 1951: *The Position of the Chief in the Modern Political System of the Ashanti.* London.

Calloway, the Rev. Canon, 1868: *Nursery Tales, Traditions, and Histories of the Zulus, in their own Words, with a Translation into English, and Notes* (Memoires of the Folk Lore Society, No. 1). Natal and London.
Carnegie Commission, 1932: *The Poor White Problem in South Africa* (5 vols.). Stellenbosch.
Carter, Gwendolen M., 1958: *The Politics of Inequality; South Africa since 1948.* New York.
Casalis, E., 1861: *The Basutos; or, Twenty-three Years in South Africa.* London.
Castillo-Fiel, Conde de, 1948: "Los Bayeles, una Tribu Pigmea en la Guinea Espanõla." *Africa* (Madrid), Nos. 83–84, pp. 402–406.
Caton-Thompson, G., 1931: *The Zimbabwe Culture.* Oxford.
—— 1957: "The Evidence of South Arabian Palaeoliths in the Question of Pleistocene Land Connection with Africa." *Third Pan-African Congress on Prehistory, Livingstone, 1955,* (J. D. Clark, ed.), pp. 380–4. London.
Chomé, Jules, 1959: *La Passion de Simon Kimbangu.* Brussels.
Christensen, James B., 1954: *Double Descent among the Fanti.* New Haven.
Christiansen, Ruth, 1956: *For the Heart of Africa.* Minneapolis.
Chukwuemeka, Nwankwo, 1950: *African Dependencies: a Challenge to Western Democracy.* New York.
Church of Scotland, 1959: *Report on Central Africa* (including Supplementary Report). Edinburgh.
Clark, J. D., 1957: "A Review of Prehistoric Research in Northern Rhodesia and Nyasaland." *Third Pan-African Congress on Prehistory* (J. D. Clark, ed.), pp. 412–32. London.
—— 1959: *The Prehistory of Southern Africa.* London.
Cohen, Ronald, 1961: "The Success that Failed: an Experiment in Culture Change in Africa." *Anthropologica,* Vol. 3 (n.s.), No. 1, pp. 21–36.
Cole, Sonia, 1954: *The Prehistory of East Africa.* London.
Coleman, James S., 1958: *Nigeria: Background to Nationalism.* Berkeley and Los Angeles.
—— 1960: "The Politics of Sub-Saharan Africa," in *The Politics of the De-*

veloping Areas (G. A. Almond and J. S. Coleman, eds.), pp. 247–368. Princeton.

Colson, Elizabeth, 1955: "Native Cultural and Social Patterns in Contemporary Africa," in *Africa Today* (C. Grove Haines, ed.), pp. 69–84. Baltimore.

Comhaire, J., 1955: "Statistics of the Religions of Africa," in J. J. Considine, *Africa, World of New Men,* pp. 352 ff. New York.

CCTA/CSA (Commission for Technical Cooperation in Africa South of the Sahara/Scientific Council for Africa), 1960: *Report* of the Secretary-General to the Sixteenth Session of CCTA, Lagos, 3, 6–11 February, 1961. Lagos.

Conference of Independent African States, 1960: *Proceedings* of the Second Meeting, Addis Ababa, 14–26 June, 1960. Addis Ababa.

Congo Belge, Conseil de Gouvernement, 1951: *Discours du Gouverneur Général E. Jungers; Statistiques.* Leopoldville.

—— Ministère des Colonies, 1954: *La Reforme de l'Enseignement au Congo Belge, Mission Pédagogique Coulon-Deheyn-Renson* (Conseil Supérieur de l'Enseignement, Publication No. 1). Brussels.

Congopresse, 1954: "Réalisme, Continuité. La politique coloniale belge tend a éveiller chez l'Africain le sens démocratique." *Pages Congolaises,* édition B. No. 38. Brussels.

Conscience Africaine, 1956: *Manifeste* (Numero Special, Juillet-Aout, pp. 1–4).

Considine, John J., 1954: *Africa, World of New Men.* New York.

Cordero-Torres, J. M., 1952: "The Spanish Territories in Africa, 1940–1950." *Civilisations,* Vol. 2, pp. 268–75.

Cordwell, Justine M., 1959: "African Art," in *Continuity and Change in African Cultures* (W. R. Bascom and M. J. Herskovits, eds.), pp. 28–48. Chicago.

Cornevin, Robert, 1960: *Histoire des Peuples de l'Afrique Noire.* Paris.

Cory, Hans and Hartnoll, M. M., 1945: *Customary Law of the Haya Tribe, Tanganyika Territory.* London.

Coupland, R., 1938: *East Africa and its Invaders.* Oxford.

Couturier, Charles, 1957: *Mission de l'Église.* Paris.

Cowan, L. Gray, 1958: "Local Politics and Democracy in Nigeria," in *Transition in Africa: Studies in Political Adaptation,* G. M. Carter and W. O. Brown, eds., (African Research Studies No. 1, Boston University) pp. 44–61. Boston.

Crocker, W. R., 1949: *Self-Government for the Colonies.* London.

Dain, A. J., 1956: *Mission Fields Today, a Brief World Survey* (2nd edition). London.

Dart, Raymond A., 1925: "*Australopithecus africanus:* the Man-ape of South Africa." *Nature,* Vol. 115, pp. 195–9.

—— 1956: "Cultural Status of the South African Man-Apes." *Annual Re-*

port, Smithsonian Institution (publication 4240), for 1955, pp. 317–38. Washington.

Davis, John A. (ed.), 1958: *Africa Seen by American Negroes.* Paris.

Debertry, Léon, 1953: *Kitawala.* Elizabethville.

Decraene, Philippe, 1959: *Le Panafricanisme.* Paris.

De Kiewiet, C. W., 1941: *A History of South Africa: Social and Economic.* Oxford.

Delafosse, Maurice, 1931: *The Negroes of Africa, History and Culture.* Washington.

Denis, J., 1958: *Le Phénomène Urbain en Afrique Centrale* (Académie Royale des Sciences Coloniales, Mémoires in-8°, n.s., t. xix, fasc. 1). Brussels.

De Schlippe, Pierre, 1956: *Shifting Cultivation in Africa: the Zande System of Agriculture.* London.

de Wilde, L., 1949: "De inlandse Landbouwstelsels in Belgisch-Kongo." *Zaïre,* Vol. 3, pp. 994–1002.

Dia, Mamadou, 1960: *Nations Africaines et Solidarité Mondiale.* Paris.

Dieterlein, G., 1956: "Parenté et mariage chez les Dogon (Soudan Français)." *Africa,* Vol. 26, pp. 107–48.

Diké, K. Onwuka, 1956: *Trade and Politics in the Niger Delta, 1830–1885.* Oxford.

Diop, Alioune, 1947: "Niam n'goura, ou les raisons d'être de Présence Africaine." *Présence Africaine,* No. 1, pp. 7–14 (English translation by Richard Wright, ibid., pp. 185–193).

Diop, David, 1948: "Trois Poèmes." *Présence Africaine,* No. 2, pp. 235–6.

Dorjahn, Vernon R., 1961: "The Initiation of the Temne Poro Officials," *Man,* Vol. 61, 27, pp. 36–40.

Doublier, Roger, 1952: *La Propriété Foncière en A. O. F., Régime en Droit Privé.* Saint-Louis (Sénégal).

Douglas, Mary, 1954: "The Lele of Kasai," in *African Worlds* (D. Forde, ed.), pp. 1–26. London.

—— 1958: "Raffia Cloth Distribution in the Lele Economy." *Africa,* Vol. 28, pp. 109–22.

Dowd, Jerome, 1907–1914: *The Negro Races* (2 vols.). New York.

Drennan, M. R., 1931: "Pedomorphism in the pre-Bushman Skull." *American Journal of Physical Anthropology,* Vol. 16, pp. 203–10.

DuBois, W. E. B., 1940: *Dusk of Dawn.* New York.

—— 1947: *The World and Africa.* New York.

Duffy, James, 1959: *Portuguese Africa.* Cambridge (Mass.).

East Africa and Rhodesia, 1957: "Survey of the Copperbelt." Vol. 34, No. 1733, Dec. 26, p. 563.

East Africa Royal Commission, 1955: *Report* (Cmd. 9475). London.

Elias, T. Olawale, 1951: *Nigerian Land Law and Custom.* London.

Elkan, Walter, 1958: "The East African Trade in Woodcarvings." *Africa,* Vol. 28, pp. 314–23.
—— 1959: "Migrant Labor in Africa: an Economist's Approach." *American Economic Review,* Vol. 49, pp. 188–97.
—— 1960: *Migrants and Proletarians, Urban Labour in the Economic Development of Uganda.* London.
Epstein, A. L., 1959: "Linguistic Innovation and Culture on the Copperbelt, Northern Rhodesia." *Southwestern Journal of Anthropology,* Vol. 15, pp. 235–53.
Esperandieu, G., 1955: "Domestication et Élevage dans le Nord de l'Afrique au Néolithique et dans le Protohistoire d'après les figurations rupestres." *Congrès Panafricain de Préhistoire, Actes de la IIe Session, Alger, 1952* (L. Balout, ed.). pp. 551–73. Paris.
Evans-Pritchard, E. E., 1940: *The Nuer.* Oxford.
—— 1956: *Nuer Religion.* Oxford.
—— 1957: "The Royal Court of Zande." *Zaïre,* Vol. 11, pp. 361–89, 493–512, 687–713.
—— 1958: "An Historical Introduction to a Study of Zande Society." *African Studies,* Vol. 17, pp. 1–15.

Fage, J. D., 1955: *An Introduction to the History of West Africa.* Cambridge (England).
Fagg, Bernard, 1945: "A Preliminary Note on a New Series of Pottery Figures from Northern Nigeria." *Africa,* Vol. 15, pp. 21–2.
—— 1959: "The Nok Culture in Prehistory." *Journal of the Historical Society of Nigeria,* Vol. 1, pp. 288–93.
Fallers, L. A., (n. d.): *Bantu Bureaucracy.* Cambridge (England).
Federation of Rhodesia and Nyasaland, Information Department, 1959: "President Reviews University College Progress" (from Rhodesia *Herald,* Nov. 25, 1959). *Newsletter,* No. 48/59, 27 Nov., p. 6.
Fernandez, James M., 1960: "The Idea and Symbol of the Saviour in a Gabon Syncretistic Cult." Manuscript.
Field, M. J., 1960: *Search for Security; an Ethno-psychiatric Study of Rural Ghana* (Northwestern University African Studies, No. 5). Evanston and London.
Fischer, Eugen, 1913: *Die Rehobother Bastards.* Jena.
Fitzgerald, Walter, 1950: *Africa, a Social, Economic and Political Geography of its Major Regions* (7th ed. rev.). London.
Forde, Daryll, 1950: "Double Descent among the Yakö," in *African Systems of Kinship and Marriage* (A. R. Radcliffe-Brown and D. Forde, eds.), pp. 285–332. London.
—— (ed.), 1954: *African Worlds.* London.
Fortes, M., 1945: *The Dynamics of Clanship among the Tallensi.* London.
Fortes, M., and Evans-Pritchard, E. E. (eds.), 1940: *African Political Systems.* London.

Frankel, S. Herbert, 1953: *The Economic Impact on Under-Developed Societies.* Oxford.

Freyre, Gilberto, 1953: *Aventura e Rotina.* Rio de Janeiro.

Frobenius, Leo, 1926: *Die Atlantische Götterlehre* (*Atlantis, Volksmärchen und Volksdichtungen Afrikas,* Bd. X). Jena.

Fuller, Edward, 1959: "Ethnohistory in the Study of Culture Change in Southeast Africa," in *Continuity and Change in African Culture* (W. R. Bascom and M. J. Herskovits, eds.) pp. 113–29. Chicago.

Gaitskell, Arthur, 1950: "Lessons of the Gezira Scheme," in *Survey of the British Colonies, The Times* (London), pp. 7–8.

—— 1959: *Gezira, a Story of Development in the Sudan.* London.

Galletti, R., Baldwin, K. D. S., and Dina, I. O., 1956: *Nigerian Cocoa Farmers: an Economic Survey of Yoruba Cocoa Farming Families.* London.

Galloway, A., 1937: "Man in Africa in the Light of Recent Discoveries." *South African Journal of Science,* Vol. 34, pp. 89–120.

Gamble, D. P., 1955: *Economic Conditions in Two Mandinka Villages, Kerewan and Keneba* (Rev., Research Department, Colonial Office, No. RES 88/12/01, mimeographed). London.

—— 1957: *The Wolof of Senegambia* (International African Institute, Ethnographic Survey of Africa: Western Africa, Part XIV). London.

Gardiner, Robert, 1951: "Going to England," in *Other People Other Ways,* by Sir Alan Burns and Robert Gardiner, pp. 10–19. London.

George, Betty, 1960: *Education for Africans in Tanganyika.* United States Department of Health, Education and Welfare, Bulletin 1960, No. 19 (OE 14039). Washington.

Gide, André, 1947: "Avant-propos." *Présence Africaine,* No. 1, pp. 3–6.

Girard, A., 1958: "La mission des Universités d'Afrique noire." *Académie Royale des Sciences Coloniales, Bulletin des Séances* (n.s.), Vol. 4, pp. 591–614.

Gluckman, Max, 1955: *The Judicial Process among the Barotse of Northern Rhodesia.* Manchester.

Gold Coast Government, 1956: *Report of the Gold Coast Mines Board of Inquiry, 1956.* Accra.

Goldschmidt, W. (ed.), 1958: *The United States and Africa* (report of the American Assembly on Africa). New York.

Great Britain, 1903: "Congo Free State" (*Parliamentary Debates,* Fourth Series, Vol. 122, May 7–26, cols. 1289–1332).

—— Colonial Office, 1925: *Education Policy in British Tropical Africa* (report of Advisory Committee on Native Education in British Tropical Africa Dependencies, Cmd. 2374). London.

—— 1950: *Report* of the Commission of Enquiry into the Disorders in the Eastern Provinces of Nigeria, November, 1949 (Colonial No. 256). London.

Great Britain Colonial Office, 1950: Enquiry into the Disorders in the Eastern Provinces of Nigeria. *Proceedings of the Commission,* 2 vols. London.

Greaves, I. C., 1935: *Modern Production among Backward Peoples.* London.

Greenberg, Joseph H., 1946: *The Influence of Islam on a Sudanese Religion* (Monographs of the American Ethnological Society, Vol. X). New York.

—— 1955: *Studies in African Linguistic Classification.* New Haven.

Grevisse, F., 1950: "Salines et Saliniers Indigènes du Haut-Katanga." *Bulletin du Centre d'Études des Problèmes Sociaux Indigènes,* No. 11, pp. 7–85.

—— 1951: "Le Centre extra-coutumier d'Elizabethville." *Bulletin du Centre d'Études des Problèmes Sociaux Indigènes,* No. 15.

Griaule, M., 1938: *Masques Dogon* (Travaux et Mémoires de l'Institut d'Ethnologie, Vol. 33). Paris.

Groves, C. P., 1948–1958: *The Planting of Christianity in Africa* (4 vols.). London.

Guillaume, Paul and Monroe, Thomas, 1926: *Primitive Negro Sculpture.* New York.

Gulliver, P. H., 1955: *The Family Herds.* London.

Gunther, John, 1955: *Inside Africa.* New York.

Gusinde, Martin, 1955: "Pygmies and Pygmoids: Twides of Tropical Africa." *Anthropological Quarterly,* Vol. 28 (n.s., Vol. 3), pp. 3–61.

Haddon, A. C., 1919: *The Wanderings of Peoples* (rev. ed.). Cambridge (England).

—— 1925: *The Races of Man and their Distribution.* New York.

Hailey, Lord Malcolm, 1938: *An African Survey, a Study of the Problems arising in Africa South of the Sahara* (first ed.). London.

—— 1947: "British Colonial Policy," in *Colonial Administration by European Powers,* by various authors, pp. 83–97. London.

—— 1957: *An African Survey, Revised 1956.* London.

Haines, C. Grove (ed.), 1955: *Africa Today.* Baltimore.

Hamet, Ismael, 1911: *Chroniques de la Mauretanie Sénégalaise—Nacer Eddine.* Paris.

Hammond, Peter, 1959: "Economic Change and Mossi Acculturation," in *Continuity and Change in African Cultures,* (W. R. Bascom and M. J. Herskovits, eds.), pp. 238–56. Chicago.

Hance, William A., 1958: *African Economic Development.* New York.

Hanna, Marwan, 1958: "The Lebanese in West Africa." *West Africa,* Nos. 2140–2142, 2145, pp. 369, 393, 415–17, 487.

Hardy, Georges, 1930: *Vue générale de l'Histoire d'Afrique* (2nd ed.). Paris.

Harries, Lyndon P., 1954: *Islam in East Africa.* London.

Harris, Marvin, 1958: *Portugal's African "Wards"* (Africa Today Pamphlets: 2). New York.

Harris, Marvin, 1959: "Labour Emigration among the Moçambique Thonga:

Cultural and Political Factors." *Africa,* Vol. 29, pp. 50–66.
Hellmann, Ellen, 1948: *Rooiyard, a Sociological Survey of an Urban Slum Yard* (Rhodes-Livingstone Papers, No. 13). Capetown and Livingstone.
Herskovits, Jean, 1960: *Liberated Africans and the History of Lagos Colony, to 1886.* (D. Phil. thesis, University of Oxford). Manuscript.
Herskovits, M. J., 1924: "A Preliminary Consideration of the Culture Areas of Africa." *American Anthropologist,* Vol. 26, pp. 50–64.
—— 1926: "The Cattle Complex in East Africa." *American Anthropologist,* Vol. 28, pp. 230–72, 361–80, 494–528, 633–44.
—— 1936: "The Significance of West Africa for Negro Research." *Journal of Negro History,* Vol. 21, pp. 15–30.
—— 1938: *Dahomey, an Ancient West African Kingdom* (2 vols.). New York.
—— 1941: *The Myth of the Negro Past.* New York (reprinted 1958, Boston).
—— 1948: *Man and His Works.* New York.
—— 1952: *Economic Anthropology.* New York.
—— 1953–60: *Notes on African Field Research, 1953–1960.* Manuscript.
—— 1955: "Some Contemporary Developments in Subsaharan Africa," in *Africa in the Modern World* (Calvin W. Stillman, ed.), pp. 267–94. Chicago.
—— 1959: "Anthropology and Africa—a Wider Perspective." *Africa,* Vol. 29, pp. 225–238.
Herskovits, M. J. and F. S., 1933: *An Outline of Dahomean Religious Belief* (Memoirs of the American Anthropological Association, No. 41). Menasha (Wisconsin).
—— 1958: "Sibling Rivalry, the Oedipus Complex, and Myth." *Journal of American Folklore,* Vol. 71, pp. 1–15.
—— 1958: *Dahomean Narrative, a Cross-Cultural Analysis* (Northwestern University African Studies No. 1). Evanston and London.
Heyse, Th., 1951: "Notions Générales sur le Régime Foncier du Congo Belge et du Ruanda-Urundi et Legislation sur les Terres Indigènes," in *Land Tenure Symposium, Amsterdam, 1950,* organized by Afrika Instituut Leiden (P. J. Idenburg, ed.), pp. 1–30. Leiden.
Hiernaux, Jean, 1954: *Les Charactères physiques des populations du Ruanda et de l'Urundi* (Mémoires, Institut Royal des Sciences Naturelles de Belgique, 2ᵉ séries, fasc. 52). Brussels.
Hiskett, M., 1960: "*Kitāb al-farq:* a work on the Habe kingdoms attributed to 'Uthmān dan Fodio." *Bulletin of the School of Oriental and African Studies, University of London,* Vol. 23, Part 3, pp. 558–79.
Hodgkin, T., 1956: *Nationalism in Colonial Africa.* London.
Holas, B., 1957: *Les Sénoufo.* Paris.
Howe, Bruce (ed.), 1957: *COWA Survey, Current Work in Old World Archaeology,* Area 10—Northwest Africa, No. I, 1957. Cambridge (Mass.).
Huxley, Elspeth, 1939: *Red Strangers.* London.

Huxley, Elspeth, 1953: *White Man's Country; Lord Delamere and the Making of Kenya* (2 vols.). London.

Ingram, John Kells, 1895: *A History of Slavery and Serfdom.* London.

Inter-African Labour Institute, 1959: "The Housing of Workers in Urban Living Conditions in Africa." *Bulletin,* Vol. 6, No. 2, pp. 63–71.

International Bank for Reconstruction and Development, 1955: *The Economic Development of Nigeria.* Baltimore.

International Labour Office, 1953: *Report of the* ad hoc *Committee on Forced Labour* (United Nations Document No. E/2431). Geneva.

—— 1958: *African Labour Survey.* Geneva.

Johnson, James, 1958: "Education in Liberia: I." *West Africa,* No. 2153, July 19, p. 681.

Johnston, Sir Harry H., 1913: "A Survey of the ethnology of Africa and the former racial and tribal migrations in that continent." *Journal of the Royal Anthropological Institute* (n.s.), Vol. 16, pp. 375–421.

Jones, G. I., 1958: "Native and Trade Currencies in Southern Nigeria During the Eighteenth and Nineteenth Centuries." *Africa,* Vol. 28, pp. 43–54.

Jones, Thomas Jesse, 1922: *Education in Africa.* New York.

Jones, W. O., 1957: "Manioc: an Example of Innovation in African Economics." *Economic Development and Cultural Change,* Vol. 5, pp. 97–117.

—— 1959: *Manioc in Africa.* Stanford.

Jordan, A. C., 1957–8: "Towards an African Literature." *Africa South,* Vol. 1 (1956–7), No. 4, pp. 90–8; Vol. 2 (1957–8), No. 1, pp. 97–105; No. 2, pp. 101–100; No. 3, pp. 112–15; No. 4, pp. 113–18.

Joseph, Gaston, 1916: "Une Atteinte à l'Animisme chez les Populations de la Côte d'Ivoire." *Annuaire et Mémoires du Comité d'Études Historiques et Scientifiques de l'Afrique Occidentale Française,* pp. 344–8 (reprinted in G. Joseph, *Côte d'Ivoire,* Paris, 1944, pp. 97–104.

Junner, N. R., 1935: "Gold in the Gold Coast" (*Gold Coast Geological Survey,* Memoir No. 4). Accra.

Junod, Henri Philippe, 1939: "Os Indígenas de Moçambique no Século XVI e comêço do XVII." *Moçambique,* Documentario Trimestral, nos. 17–19.

Kaberry, Phyllis M., 1952: *Women of the Grasslands, a Study of the Economic Position of Women in Bamenda, British Cameroons* (Colonial Research Publication No. 14). London.

Kagame, A., 1956: "La Littérature Orale au Ruanda," in *Des Prêtres Noirs s'Interrogent,* by A. Abble, *et al.*, pp. 205–11. Paris.

Kamal, Youssef, 1926–1951: *Monumenta Cartogeographica Africae et Aegypti* (5 vols.). Cairo and Leyden.

Kenya, Colony and Protectorate of, 1957: *The Development Programme, 1957/60* (Sessional Paper No. 77 of 1956/57). Nairobi.

—— 1958: *Report on Asian and European Education in Kenya, 1958*. Nairobi.

Kenyatta, Jomo, 1938: *Facing Mount Kenya, the Tribal Life of the Gikuyu*. London.

Kimble, George H. T., 1960: *Tropical Africa* (2 vols.). New York.

Kingsley, Mary H., 1899: *West African Studies*. London.

Köbben, A. J. F., 1956: "Le Planteur Noir." *Études Eburnéennes*, Vol. 5, pp. 7–190.

Koelle, S. W., 1854: *Polyglotta Africana*. London.

Kohn, Hans, 1944: *The Idea of Nationalism*. New York.

—— 1957: article "Nationalism," in *Encyclopaedia Britannica*, Vol. 16, p. 149.

Kopytoff, Igor, 1960: *Suku Religion: A Study in Internally Induced Reinterpretation* (Ph. D. Thesis, Northwestern University). Microfilmed.

Kopytoff, Jean Herskovits, *see* Herskovits, Jean.

Krige, J. D. and E. J., 1954: "The Lovedu of the Transvaal," in *African Worlds* (D. Forde, ed.), pp. 55–82. London.

Kubbel, L. E. and Matveev, 1960: *Drevnie i Srednevekovye Istochniki po Etnografii i Istorii Narodov Afriki Iuzhnee Sakhary—Arabskie Istochniki VII–X Vekov* (*Ancient and Mediaeval Sources for the Ethnography and History of the African Peoples South of the Sahara; Arab Sources, VII–X Centuries*). Moscow and Leningrad.

Kuczynski, R. R., 1948: *Demographic Survey of the British Colonial Empire* (2 vols.). London.

Kuper, Hilda, 1947: *An African Aristocracy: Rank among the Swazi*. London.

Kuznets, Simon, 1960: "Notes on the Take-off" (Paper presented at the meeting of the International Economic Association, September, 1960). Manuscript.

Labouret, Henri, 1931: *Les Tribus du Rameau Lobi* (Travaux et Mémoires de l'Institut d'Ethnologie, Vol. XV). Paris.

Labrique, Jean, 1957: *Congo Politique*. Leopoldville.

Lalanne, Philippe, 1960: "For a United Eurafrica" (abstracted from an article in *Western World Magazine*, October, 1959). *The Belgian Congo Today*, Vol. 9, January, pp. 10–15.

La Lumière (Luluabourg, Congo), 1958: "À Monsieur Petillon, Ministre des Colonies." Vol. 2, No. 24, Aug. 1.

—— 1958–1959: "La Conférence d'Accra." Dec. 15 and Jan. 1.

Lampen, G. D., 1933: "The Baggara Tribes of Darfur." *Sudan Notes and Records*, Vol. 16, pp. 97–118.

Laye, Camara, 1953: *L'Enfant Noire* (transl. as *The Dark Child,* New York, 1954). Paris.

Leakey, L. S. B., 1952: *Mau Mau and the Kikuyu.* London.

—— 1959: "A New Fossil Skull from Olduvai." *Nature,* Vol. 184, pp. 491–3.

Lebeuf, Jean-Paul, 1938: "Les Rites Funéraires chez les Fali." *Journal de la Société des Africanistes,* Vol. 8, pp. 103–22.

—— 1956: "L'École des Peintres de Poto-Poto." *Africa,* Vol. 26, pp. 277–80.

Legum, Colin, 1961: *Congo Disaster.* London.

Lemaire, André, 1960: "L'Université Française de Dakar." *Le Monde,* No. 4659, Jan. 14, p. 3.

Leroy-Beaulieu, Paul, 1902: *De la Colonisation chez les Peuples Modernes* (2 vols.). Paris.

Libby, W. F., 1951: "Radiocarbon Dates, II." *Science,* Vol. 114, pp. 291–6.

—— 1954: "Chicago Radiocarbon Dates V." *Science,* Vol. 120, pp. 703–42.

Liberia, Republic of, 1952: *Report of the Treasury Department for the Fiscal Year 1952,* William E. Dennis, Secretary of the Treasury, Nov. 14. Monrovia.

Linton, Ralph, 1955: *The Tree of Culture.* New York.

Lipscomb, J. F., 1955: *White Africans.* London.

Little, Kenneth, 1951: *The Mende of Sierra Leone.* London.

—— 1957: "The Role of Voluntary Associations in West African Urbanization." *American Anthropologist,* Vol. 39, pp. 579–96.

Livingstone, David, 1859: *Missionary Travels and Researches in South Africa* (25th ed.). New York.

Lloyd, P. C., 1959: "The Yoruba Town Today." *Sociological Review,* Vol. 7 (n.s.), pp. 45–63.

Longmore, L., 1958: "Medicine, Magic and Witchcraft among Urban Africans on the Witwatersrand." *Central African Journal of Medicine,* Vol. 4, pp. 242–9.

Lucas, J. Olumide, 1948: *The Religion of the Yorubas.* Lagos.

Lugard, Lord Frederick D., 1922: *The Dual Mandate in British Tropical Africa.* London.

MacMichael, H. A., 1912: *The Tribes of Northern and Central Kordofán.* Cambridge (England).

Majeke, Nosipho, 1952: *The Rôle of the Missionaries in Conquest.* Johannesburg.

Maquet, Jacques J., 1954: "Le Système des Relations sociales dans le Ruanda ancien." *Annales* du Musée Royal du Congo Belge, Ethnologie, Vol. 1 Tervuren (Belgium).

—— 1954: "The Kingdom of Ruanda," in *African Worlds* (D. Forde, ed.) pp. 164–89, London.

Marquard, Leo, 1955: *The Story of South Africa.* London.

Marsh, Zoë and Kingsnorth, G. W., 1957: *An Introduction to the History of East Africa*. Cambridge (England).

Marty, Paul, 1921: *L'Islam en Guinée, Fouta-Diallon*. Paris.

Marwick, M. G., 1956: "An Experiment in Public-Opinion Polling among Preliterate People." *Africa,* Vol. 26, pp. 149–59.

Massignon, Louis, 1955: *Annuaire du Monde Musulman, Statistique, Historique, Social et Economique*. Paris.

Mathewson, J. Edw., 1957: *The Establishment of an Urban Bantu Township*. Pretoria.

Maunier, René, 1949: *The Sociology of Colonies* (2 vols., E. O. Lorimer, ed. and translator). London.

Mauny, R., 1952: "Essai sur l'Histoire des métaux en Afrique occidentale," *Bulletin* de l'Institut Français d'Afrique Noire, Vol. 14, pp. 545–95.

Mboya, Tom, 1959: *Kenya Faces the Future* (Africa Today Pamphlets, No. 3). New York.

Meeker, Odin, 1954: *Report on Africa*. New York.

Memel Foté, Harris, 1961: *Rapport sur la Civilisation Animiste* (a paper presented to the Colloquium on "The Contributions of Animism, Islam and Christianity to the Cultural Expression of the African Personality," Abidjan, Ivory Coast, April 5–12, 1961). Mimeographed.

Merriam, Alan P., 1953: "African Music Re-examined in the Light of New Materials from the Belgian Congo and Ruanda-Urundi." *Zaïre,* Vol. 7, pp. 245–53.

—— 1959: "African Music" in *Continuity and Change in African Cultures* (W. R. Bascom and M. J. Herskovits, eds.), pp. 49–86. Chicago.

—— 1959: "Characteristics of African Music." *Journal of the International Folk Music Council,* Vol. 11, pp. 13–19.

—— 1959: "The Concept of Cultural Clusters Applied to the Belgian Congo." *Southwestern Journal of Anthropology,* Vol. 15, pp. 373–95.

—— 1961: *Congo, Background of Conflict*. Evanston.

Messenger, John C., Jr., 1959: "Religious Acculturation among the Anang Ibibio" in *Continuity and Change in African Cultures* (W. R. Bascom and M. J. Herskovits, eds.) pp. 279–99. Chicago.

—— 1960: "Reinterpretations of Christian and Indigenous Belief in a Nigerian Nativist Church." *American Anthropologist,* Vol. 62, pp. 268–78.

Millin, Sarah Gertrude, 1924: *God's Stepchildren*. New York.

Minor, Horace, 1953: *The Primitive City of Timbuctoo* (Memoirs of the American Philosophical Society, No. 32). Princeton and Philadelphia.

Miracle, Marvin P., 1958: "Maize in Tropical African Agriculture." *Tropical Agriculture,* Vol. 35, pp. 1–15.

Mitchell, J. Clyde, 1956: *The Kalela Dance* (Rhodes-Livingstone Papers, No. 27). Manchester.

—— 1959: "Social Change and the New Towns of Bantu Africa" (*Working Paper No. 11,* Round-Table Conference on the Social Implications of Technological Change, 19–25 March, 1959, International Social Science Council), Paris.

Mitchell, Sir Philip, 1948: *The Agrarian Problem in Kenya.* Nairobi.

—— 1955: "Africa and the West in historical perspective," in *Africa Today* (C. Grove Haines, ed.), pp. 3–24. Baltimore.

Moffat, Robert, 1843: *Missionary Labours and Scenes in Southern Africa* (3rd edition). New York.

Moreira, A., 1956: "The 'Élites' of the Portuguese 'Tribal' Provinces (Guinea, Angola, Mozambique)." *International Social Science Bulletin,* Vol. 8, pp. 458–81.

Mphahlele, Ezekiel, 1960: "African Writing in English" (a paper presented to the International Symposium on African Culture, Ibadan, Nigeria, December, 1960). Mimeographed.

Mulago, Vincent, 1956: "Nécessité de l'Adaptation Missionaire chez les Bantu du Congo," in *Des Prêtres Noirs s'Interrogent* (A. Abble, et al.), pp. 19–40. Paris.

Mumford, W. Bryant and Orde-Browne, G. St. J., n.d.: *Africans Learn to be French, a Review of Educational Activities in the Seven Federated Colonies of French West Africa . . . in 1935.* London.

Murdock, George P., 1959: *Africa, Its Peoples and Their Culture History.* New York.

Murray, A. Victor, 1929: *The School in the Bush.* London.

McCall, D. F., 1955: "Dynamics of Urbanization in Africa." *The Annals* of the American Academy of Political and Social Science, Vol. 298, pp. 151–60.

McCulloch, Meran, 1956: "Survey of recent and current field studies on the social effects of economic development in inter-tropical Africa," in *Social Implications of Industrialization and Urbanization in Africa South of the Sahara* (D. Forde, ed.), Tensions and Technology Series, UNESCO, pp. 53–225. Paris.

Nadel, S. F., 1942: *A Black Byzantium, the Kingdom of Nupe in Nigeria.* London.

—— 1947: *The Nuba.* Oxford.

—— 1954: *Nupe Religion.* London.

Neumark, S. Daniel, 1957: *Economic Influences on the South African Frontier, 1652–1836.* Stanford (California).

Nicol, Davidson Abioseh, 1957: "The Continent that lies within us," reprinted in *An Anthology of West African Verse* (Olumbe Bassir, compiler). Ibadan (Nigeria).

—— 1960: "Some Observations on the Assimilation of Traditional African Culture in the Culture of Mass Society." *Newsletter,* American Society for African Culture, Vol. 3, No. 3, Nov. 30 (Supplement No. 17), pp. 4–6.

Niculescu, Barbu, 1958: *Colonial Planning, A Comparative Study*. London.

Nida, Eugene A., 1954: *Customs and Cultures, Anthropology for Christian Missions*. New York.

Nigeria, Department of Statistics, 1953: *Population Census of the Eastern Region of Nigeria*. Lagos.

Niles, Donald C., 1955: "Fetish Burning in the Kwango Area." *Congo Mission News*, No. 169, pp. 12–13.

Nketia, J. H., 1956: "The Gramophone and Contemporary African Music in the Gold Coast." *Proceedings of the Fourth Annual Conference of the West African Institute of Social and Economic Research*. Ibadan (Nigeria). Mimeographed.

—— 1959: Discussion of "Characteristics of African Music," by A. P. Merriam. *Journal of the International Folk Music Council*, Vol. 11, p. 19.

—— 1959: "Changing Traditions of Folk Music in Ghana." *Journal of the International Folk Music Council*, Vol. 11, pp. 31–6.

Nkrumah, Kwame, 1957: *The Autobiography of Kwame Nkrumah*. Edinburgh.

—— 1958: *News Bulletin*, All African People's *Conference*, Vol. 1, No. 1.

Northern Rhodesia Chamber of Mines, 1960: *Year Book, 1959*. Kitwe (N. Rhodesia).

Northwestern University, Program of African Studies, 1959: *Africa* (Studies of United States Foreign Policy, No. 4. Committee Print, Committee on Foreign Relations, United States Senate, 86th Congress, 1st Session, No. 4). Washington.

Norton de Matos, J. M. R., 1953: *África Nossa, o que queremos e o que não queremos nas nossas terras de Africa*. Lisbon.

Ogunsheye, Ayo, 1960: *"The African Personality: Ideology and Utopia"* (a paper presented to the International Symposium on African Culture, Ibadan, Nigeria, December, 1960). Mimeographed.

Olbrechts, F. M., 1946: *Plastiek van Kongo*. Antwerp.

Olderogge, D., 1960: *Zapadnyi Sudan v XV–XIX vv*. Trudy Instituta Etnografii, Novaia seriia, t. LIII, Akademiia Nauk SSSR. (*The Western Sudan in the XV–XIX Centuries*, Contributions of the Institute of Ethnography, n.s. vol. LIII, USSR Academy of Sciences.) Moscow and Leningrad.

Olderogge, D. A. and Potekhin, I. I., 1954: *Narodii Afriki* (*Peoples of Africa*). Moscow.

Oldham, J. H. and Gibson, B. D., 1931: *The Remaking of Man in Africa*. London.

Oliver, Roland, 1952: *The Missionary Factor in East Africa*. London.

—— 1956: *How Christian is Africa?* London.

Olivier, Lord Sidney Haldane, 1929: *White Capital and Coloured Labour*. London.

Orde Browne, G. St. J., 1933: *The African Labourer*. London.

Orde Browne, G. St. J., 1946: *Labour Conditions in East Africa.* London.

Oschinsky, Lawrence, 1954: *The Racial Affinities of the Baganda and other Bantu Tribes of British East Africa.* Cambridge (England).

Ottenberg, Simon, 1957: *The System of Authority of the Afikpo Ibo of Southeastern Nigeria.* (Ph.D. Dissertation, Northwestern University.) Microfilmed.

—— 1959: "Ibo Receptivity to Change," in *Continuity and Change in African Cultures* (W. R. Bascom and M. J. Herskovits, eds.), pp. 130–43. Chicago.

Oyono, Ferdinand, 1956: *Une Vie de Boy.* Paris.

Padmore, George, 1956: *Pan-Africanism or Communism? The Coming Struggle for Africa.* London.

Paixão, V. M. Braga, 1948: *Educação Política e Política da Educação, Tres Anos em Moçambique.* Lisbon.

Palmer, Sir Richmond, 1936: *The Bornu Sahara and Sudan.* London.

Paques, Viviana, 1954: *Les Bambara.* Paris.

Parrinder, Geoffrey, 1953: *Religion in an African City.* London.

Paulme, Denise, 1940: *Organisation Sociale des Dogon (Soudan Française)* (Études Sociologique et d'Ethnologie Juridiques, vol. XXXII). Paris.

—— 1954: *Les Gens du Riz, Kissi de Haute-Guinée Française.* Paris.

—— 1956: *Les Sculptures de l'Afrique Noire.* Paris.

Perham, Margery, 1956: *Lugard, The Years of Adventure, 1858–1898.* London.

Perham, M. and Simmons, J., 1942: *African Discovery, an Anthology of Exploration.* London.

Plaatje, Sol. T., n.d.: *Native Life in South Africa, Before and Since the European War and the Boer Rebellion* (Fifth ed.). London.

Portères, Roland, 1950: "Vieilles agricultures de l'Afrique intertropicale." *L'Agronomie Tropicale,* Nos. 9–10, Sept.–Oct., pp. 489–507.

Potekhin, I. I., 1960: "On Feudalism of the Ashanti" (paper presented to the XXV International Congress of Orientalists). Moscow.

Présence Africaine, 1958: "Le sous-équipment et les leçons du Caire." No. 17, pp. 3–8.

Price, Frank W., 1958: "World Christian and Missionary Statistics." *Occasional Bulletin,* Missionary Research Library, Vol. 9, No. 4. New York.

Radcliffe-Brown, A. R. and Daryll Forde (eds.), 1950: *African Systems of Kinship and Marriage.* London.

Raglan, Lord F. R. S., 1936: *The Hero, a Study in Tradition, Myth and Drama.* London (reprinted London, 1949 and New York, 1956).

Rattray, R. S., 1923: *Ashanti.* Oxford.

—— 1927: *Religion and Art in Ashanti.* Oxford.

—— 1929: *Ashanti Law and Constitution.* Oxford.

Ratzel, F., 1880, 1896: Völkerkunde (translated as *The History of Mankind*). Berlin and London.

Rayautra, Mamadou Traoré, 1960: *Connaissance de la République de Guinée.* Conakry.

Read, Margaret, 1950: *Education and Cultural Tradition.* (University of London, Institute of Education, Studies in Education, No. 2.) London.

—— 1951: "Cultural Contacts in Education." *Proceedings,* British Association for the Advancement of Science, Edinburgh meetings, pp. 361–8.

—— 1956: *The Ngoni of Nyasaland.* London.

Redfield, Robert, 1941: *The Folk Culture of Yucatan.* Chicago.

Redinha, José, 1953: *Paredes Pintadas da Luanda* (Museu do Dondo, Publicações Culturais, No. 18). Lisbon.

Reid, J. A., 1930: "Some Notes on the Tribes of the White Nile Province." *Sudan Notes and Records,* Vol. 13, pp. 149–211.

République Française, Ministère des Colonies, 1911: *Documents Scientifiques de la Mission Tilho* (1906–1909). Paris.

Richards, Audrey, I., 1939: *Land, Labour and Diet in Northern Rhodesia, an Economic Study of the Bemba Tribe.* London.

—— 1950: "Some Types of Family Structure amongst the Central Bantu," in *African Systems of Kinship and Marriage* (A. R. Radcliffe-Brown and D. Forde, eds.), pp. 207–51. London.

—— 1956: *Chisungu, a Girl's Initiation Ceremony among the Bemba of Northern Rhodesia.* London.

Roolvink, R. (compiler), 1957: *Historical Atlas of the Muslim Peoples.* Amsterdam.

Roome, W. J. W., 1927: *Can Africa Be Won?* London.

Rosberg, Carl G., Jr., 1958: "Political Conflict and Change in Kenya," in G. M. Carter and W. O. Brown (eds.), *Transition in Africa, Studies in Political Adaptation* (African Research Studies No. 1, Boston University, pp. 90–120). Boston.

Rouch, Jean, 1954: *Les Songhay.* Paris.

—— 1956: "Migrations au Ghana (Gold Coast) (Enquête 1953–1955)." *Journal de la Société des Africanistes,* Vol. 26, pp. 33–196 (English translation by P. E. O. and J. B. Haigham, 1954, Accra, mimeographed).

Roux, A., 1950: "Un Prophète: Harris" in *Le Monde Noir* (Th. Monod., ed.). *Présence Africaine* (Numéro special, 8–9), pp. 133–40.

Ryckmans, Pierre, 1934: *La Politique Coloniale.* Brussels.

Salazar, Antonio de Oliveira, 1957: Radio address on Portuguese policy. *Notícias de Portugal,* Supplement to No. 548, November 2.

—— 1959: "A Posição Portuguesa em face da Europa, da America e da África" (radio address delivered May 23, 1959). *Notícias de Portugal,* No. 630, May 30.

Sanson, N., 1656: *L'Afrique en Plusiers Cartes Novvelles, et Exactes; & en Traicte's de Geographie, et d'Histoire; . . .* Paris.

Schachter, Ruth, 1957: "Trade Unions Seek Autonomy" *West Africa,* No. 2075 (Jan. 19), p. 55 and No. 2076 (Jan. 26), pp. 81–82.

Schapera, I., 1930: *The Khoisan Peoples of South Africa.* London.

—— 1943: *Native Land Tenure in the Bechuanaland Protectorate.* Lovedale (C. P.), South Africa.

—— 1947: *Migrant Labour and Tribal Life, a Study of Conditions in the Bechuanaland Protectorate.* London.

—— 1956: *Government and Politics in Tribal Societies.* London.

Schlosser, Katesa, 1949: *Propheten in Afrika.* Braunschweig (Germany).

Schneider, H. K., 1957: "The Subsistence Role of Cattle among the Pakot and in East Africa." *American Anthropologist,* Vol. 59, pp. 278–300.

—— 1959: "Pakot Resistance to Change," in *Continuity and Change in African Cultures* (W. R. Bascom and M. J. Herskovits, eds.), pp. 144–67.

Schultze, L., 1928: *Zur Kenntnis des Körpers der Hottentotten und Buschmänner* (in *Zoologische und anthropologische Ergebnisse einer Forschungsreise im westlichen und zentralen Südafrika,* Vol. 5, fasc. iii, pp. 147–227) Jena.

Scotch, Norman, 1960: "A Preliminary Report on the Relation of Sociocultural Factors to Hypertension among the Zulu." *Annals of the New York Academy of Sciences,* Vol. 84, pp. 1000–9.

Seligman, C. G., 1930 (2nd. ed., 1957): *Races of Africa.* London.

Seligman, C. G. and B. Z., 1918: *The Kâbâbish, a Sudan Arab Tribe* (Harvard African Studies, Vol. II, pp. 105–185). Cambridge (Mass.).

—— 1932: *Pagan Tribes of the Nilotic Sudan:* London.

Senghor, L. and Sadji, A., 1953: *La Belle Histoire de Leuk-le-Lièvre.* Paris.

Shepperson, George and Price, Thomas, 1958: *Independent African: John Chilembwe and the Origins, Setting and Significance of the Nyasaland Native Rising of 1915.* Edinburgh.

Smith, E. A., and Dale, A. M., 1920: *The Ila-Speaking Peoples of Northern Rhodesia* (2 vols.). London.

Smith, M. G., 1954: "Introduction," to *Baba of Karo,* by Mary Smith, pp. 11–34. London.

—— 1960: *Government in Zazzau.* London.

Smith, Mary F., 1955: *Baba of Karo, a Woman of the Muslim Hausa.* New York.

Smuts, J. C., 1930: *Africa and Some World Problems.* Oxford.

Smythe, Hugh H. and Mabel M., 1960: *The New Nigerian Elite.* Stanford.

Snelgrave, Captain William, 1734: *A New Account of Some Parts of Guinea, and the Slave Trade.* London.

Society of African Culture, 1959: "The Unity and Responsibilities of Negro-African Culture" (call for The Second Conference of Negro Writers and Artists, Rome, March 25–April 1, 1959). Mimeographed.

Sofer, Cyril and Rhona, 1955: *Jinja Transformed* (East African Studies, East African Institute of Social Research, No. 4). Kampala (Uganda).

Stamp, L. D., 1953: *Africa, a Study in Tropical Development.* New York and London.

Stanley, Henry M., 1890: *In Darkest Africa, or the Quest, Rescue, and Retreat of Emin, Governor of Equatoria* (2 vols.). New York.
Stayt, H. A., 1931: *The Bavenda.* London.
Summers, R., 1957: "Archaeology in Southern Rhodesia, 1900–1955." *Third Pan-African Congress on Prehistory, Livingstone, 1955* (J. D. Clark, ed.), pp. 396–411. London.
Sundkler, Bengt G. M., 1948: *Bantu Prophets in South Africa.* London.
—— 1960: *The Christian Ministry in Africa* (Studia Missionalia Upsaliensia II). Uppsala.
Sweeney, James Johnson, 1935: *African Negro Art.* New York.

Tait, David, 1953: "The Political System of the Konkomba." *Africa,* Vol. 23, pp. 213–23.
—— 1956: "The Family, Household, and Minor Lineage of the Konkomba." *Africa,* Vol. 26, pp. 219–49, 332–42.
Talbot, P. Amaury, 1926: *The Peoples of Southern Nigeria* (3 vols.) London.
Talmadge, M., 1959: "Themes in the West African Novel." *West African Review,* Vol. 30, Nos. 383–5, pp. 657–8, 773–4, 947–8.
Tardits, Claude, 1956: "The Notion of the Elite and the Urban Social Survey in Africa." *International Social Science Bulletin,* Vol. 8, pp. 492–5.
—— 1958: *Porto-Novo, les Nouvelles Générations Africaines entre leurs Traditions et l'Occident.* Paris, The Hague.
Tauxier, Louis, 1912: *Le Noir du Soudan, Pays Mossi et Gourounsi.* Paris.
Tempels, Père Placide, 1945: *La Philosophie Bantou.* (Published in Engl. translation as *Bantu Philosophy,* Paris, 1959.) Elizabethville.
Thompson, Virginia and Adloff, Richard, 1958: *French West Africa.* London.
—— 1960: *The Emerging States of French Equatorial Africa.* Stanford.
Tobias, Phillip V., 1956: "On the Survival of the Bushmen." *Africa,* Vol. 26, pp. 174–86.
—— 1957: "Bushmen of the Kalahari." *Man,* Vol. 57, 36, pp. 33–40.
—— 1959: "Epilogue: Some Developments in South African Physical Anthropology, 1938–1958." in *The Skeletal Remains of Bambandyanalo,* by Alexander Galloway, pp. 129–54. Johannesburg.
Torday, E., and Joyce, T. A., 1911: *Notes Ethnographiques sur les peuples communément appelés Bakuba, ainsi que sur les peuplades apparentées —Les Bushongo* (Annales du Musée du Congo Belge, Ethnographie, Anthropologie—sér. III, tome II, fasc. 1). Brussels.
—— 1922: *Notes ethnographiques sur des populations habitant les bassins du Kasai et du Kwango oriental* (Annales du Musée du Congo Belge, Ethnographie, Anthropologie—sér. III, tome II, fasc. 2). Brussels.
Torres, José Condero, 1957: "Las Dependencias Españolas," in *Enquête sur l'Anticolonialisme* (Estudos de Ciências Políticas e Sociais, Centro de Estudos Políticas e Sociais, Ministério do Ultramar, Junta de Investigações do Ultramar), pp. 103–49. Lisbon.

Touré, Sékou, 1959: *La Lutte du Parti Démocratique de Guinée pour l'Émancipation Africaine* (Republique de Guinée, Vol. IV). Conakry.

—— 1960: *L'Action Politique du Parti Démocratique de Guinée; la Planification Économique* (République de Guinée, Vol. V). Conakry.

Tracey, Hugh, 1948: *Chopi Musicians, their Music, Poetry and Instruments.* London.

Trimingham, J. S., 1949: *Islam in the Sudan.* London.

—— 1959: *Islam in West Africa.* Oxford.

Tutuola, Amos, 1952: *The Palm-Wine Drinkard.* London.

Ulanov, Barry, 1952: *A History of Jazz in America.* New York.

Union of South Africa, 1959: "Promotion of Bantu Self-Government." *Bantoe,* May, No. 5, pp. 5–28.

United Nations, 1950: *Non-Self-Governing Territories,* Summaries and analyses of information transmitted to the Secretary-General during 1949. Lake Success (New York).

—— 1951: *Measures for the Economic Development of Under-Developed Countries* (No. E/1986 ST/ECA/10). New York.

—— 1956: *Demographic Yearbook,* Eighth Issue. New York.

—— 1956: *Economic and Social Council, Official Records,* 21 Session, 17 April–4 May, 1956.

—— 1957: *Yearbook of International Trade Statistics, 1956.*

—— 1957: *Non-Self-Governing Territories,* Summaries of Information Submitted to the Secretary-General during 1955 (ST/TRI/SER.A/12). New York.

—— 1959: *Economic Survey of Africa since 1950.* (No. E/CN.14/28). New York.

—— 1960: *Progress of the Non-Self-Governing Territories under the Charter,* Vol. 5, Territorial Surveys (No. ST/TRI/Ser.A/15/Vol. 5).

United Nations Educational, Social and Cultural Organization (UNESCO), 1956: "African Elites." *International Social Science Bulletin,* Vol. 8, pp. 413–98.

—— 1960: *Report on the Needs of Tropical Africa in the Matter of Primary, General Secondary and Technical Education* (General Conference, 11th Session), No. 11/C/PRG/1, Annex I.

United States Department of Commerce, 1950: "Angola (Portuguese West Africa)—Summary of Basic Economic Information." *International Reference Service,* Vol. VII, No. 129, December.

Van Bilsen, A. A. J., 1958(?): *Vers l'Independence du Congo et du Ruanda-Urundi.* Brussels.

Van der Horst, Sheila T., 1948: "Native Urban Employment (a Review Article)." *South African Journal of Economics,* Vol. 16, pp. 251–9.

Vansina, J., 1954: *Les Tribus Ba-Kuba et les Peuplades Apparentées* (Annales du Musée Royal du Congo Belge, Sciences de l'Homme, Mo-

nographies Ethnographiques, Vol. I; also published in the Ethnographic Survey of Africa, Part I, Central Africa, Belgian Congo), Tervuren (Belgium) and London.
—— 1957: "L'Etat Kuba dans le cadre des institutions politiques africaines." *Zaïre,* Vol. 11, pp. 485–92.
—— 1960: "Recording the Oral History of the Bakuba—I. Methods, II. Results." *Journal of African History,* Vol. 1, pp. 43–51, 257–70.
Verwoerd, H. F., 1954: *Bantu Education, Policy for the Immediate Future.* Pretoria.

Walton, James, 1956: *African Village.* Pretoria.
Waterman, Richard A., 1952: "African Influence on the Music of the Americas," in *Acculturation in the Americas* (Vol. II, Proceedings of the 29th International Congress of Americanists, Sol Tax, ed.), pp. 207–18. Chicago.
Watkins, M. H., 1943: "The West African 'Bush' School." *American Journal of Sociology,* Vol. 48, pp. 666–75.
Watson, W., 1958: *Tribal Cohesion in a Money Economy.* Manchester.
Westermann, Diedrich, 1937: *Africa and Christianity.* London.
Wieschhoff, H. A., 1941: *The Zimbabwe-Monomotapa Culture in Southeast Africa* (General Series in Anthropology, No. 8). Menasha (Wisconsin).
Wigny, Pierre, 1949: "Introduction" to *Plan Décennal pour le Développement Économique et Social du Congo Belge,* Vol. I, pp. xi–xxxxiii. Brussels.
Willett, Frank, 1958: "Excavations at Old Oyo and Ife." *West Africa,* No. 2153, July 19, p. 675.
Williams, Eric, 1944: *Capitalism and Slavery.* Chapel Hill (North Carolina).
Williams, Shirley, 1960: *Central Africa: the Economics of Inequality* (Research Series 215, Fabian Commonwealth Bureau). London.
Wilson, Charles, 1954: *The History of Unilever, a Study in Economic Growth and Social Change* (2 vols.). London.
Wilson, Godfrey, 1941: *An Essay on the Economics of Detribalization in Northern Rhodesia* (Rhodes-Livingstone Papers No. 5). Livingstone.
Wilson, H. S., 1960: "E. W. Blyden on Religion in Africa." *The Sierra Leone Bulletin of Religion,* Vol. 2, pp. 58–66.
Wilson, Monica, 1959: "The Early History of the Transkei and Ciskei." *African Studies,* Vol. 18, pp. 167–79.
Wingert, Paul, 1950: *The Sculpture of Negro Africa.* New York.
Wirth, Louis, 1938: "Urbanism as a Way of Life." *American Journal of Sociology,* Vol. 44, pp. 1–24.
Wolfe, A. W., 1957: *Stability and Change in Ngombe Culture* (Ph.D. Thesis, Northwestern University, microfilmed.)

Zischka, Anton, 1951: *Afrika, Europas Gemeinschaftsaufgabe Nr. 1.* Oldenberg (Germany).

Index

Index v

A NOTE ON THE TYPE

THE TEXT of this book is set in CALEDONIA, a Linotype face designed by W. A. Dwiggins (1880–1956), the man responsible for so much that is good in contemporary book design and typography. Caledonia belongs to the family of printing types called "modern face" by printers—a term used to mark the change in style of type-letters that occurred about 1800. Caledonia borders on the general design of Scotch Modern but is more freely drawn than that letter.

Composed, printed, and bound by
Kingsport Press, Inc., Kingsport, Tennessee.
Typography and binding design by
GUY FLEMING

A NOTE ABOUT THE AUTHOR

Melville J. Herskovits, Professor of Anthropology and African Affairs, and Director of the Program of African Studies at Northwestern University since 1947, was born in 1895 at Bellefontaine, Ohio. He holds the Ph.B., University of Chicago, 1920; the Ph.D., Columbia University, 1923, where he studied with Franz Boas. He has taught anthropology at Columbia, Howard, and since 1927 at Northwestern. A leading authority in his discipline, Mr. Herskovits has gone for his research in African and African-derived culture to Dutch Guinea, West Africa, Haiti, Trinidad, Brazil, and has made several extended trips over all of Subsaharan Africa. He is a member of the permanent council of the International Anthropological Congress, of the executive council of the International African Institute, and served as editor of the *American Anthropologist* (1949–52). He was the founding president of the African Studies Association, and his Professorial Chair of African Affairs is the first in the United States. His publications include *Dahomean Narrative* (with Frances S. Herskovits, 1956), *Cultural Anthropology* (1955), *Franz Boas, the Science of Man in the Making* (1953), *Economic Anthropology* (1952), *Man and His Works* (1948), *Trinidad Village* (with Frances S. Herskovits, 1947), *The Myth of the Negro Past* (1941), *The Economic Life of Primitive Peoples* (1940), *Acculturation* (1938), *Dahomey* (1938), *Life in a Haitian Valley* (1937), *Suriname Folklore* (with Frances S. Herskovits, 1936), *Rebel Destiny* (with Frances S. Herskovits, 1934), *Outline of Dahomean Religious Belief* (with Frances S. Herskovits, 1933), *Anthropometry of the American Negro* (1930), *The American Negro* (1928).

